RESEARCH TO PRACTICE IN MENTAL RETARDATION

U.S. Capitol Building, Washington, D.C.

RESEARCH TO PRACTICE IN MENTAL RETARDATION

Fourth Congress
of the International Association
for the Scientific Study of Mental Deficiency (IASSMD)

Volume I

CARE
and
INTERVENTION

Edited by

Peter Mittler, Ph.D.

Technical Editor

Jean M. de Jong

University Park Press
Baltimore • London • Tokyo

UNIVERSITY PARK PRESS
International Publishers in Science and Medicine
Chamber of Commerce Building
Baltimore, Maryland 21202

Typeset by The Composing Room of Michigan, Inc.
Manufactured in the United States of America by Universal Lithographers, Inc.,
and The Optic Bindery Incorporated.

Library of Congress Cataloging in Publication Data
International Association for the Scientific Study of
Mental Deficiency.
Research to practice in mental retardation.

Includes bibliographies and indexes.
CONTENTS: v. 1. Care and intervention.—v. 2. Education and training.—v. 3. Biomedical aspects.
1. Mental deficiency—Congresses. 2. Mentally
handicapped—Care and treatment—Congresses. 3. Mentally
handicapped—Education—Congresses. I. Mittler, Peter J.
II. Title. [DNLM: 1. Mental retardation—Congresses.
2. Education of mentally retarded—Congresses. W3 IN12U
1976r/ WS107 I61r 1976]
RC569.9.I57   1977   616.8'588   77-5455
ISBN 0-8391-1122-3 (v. 1)
ISBN 0-8391-1123-1 (v. 2)
ISBN 0-8391-1124-x (v. 3)

Contents

EPIDEMIOLOGY

EARLY INTERVENTION

WORKING WITH FAMILIES

RESIDENTIAL SERVICES

COMMUNITY SERVICES

PSYCHIATRIC SERVICES

PROCEEDINGS OF THE FOURTH CONGRESS
OF THE INTERNATIONAL ASSOCIATION
FOR THE SCIENTIFIC STUDY
OF MENTAL DEFICIENCY

Washington, D.C., U.S.A.   22–27 August, 1976
The American University

**Research to Practice
in
Mental Retardation**

Published in three volumes:
Volume   I: Care and Intervention
Volume II: Education and Training
Volume III: Biomedical Aspects

Edited by
Peter Mittler, Ph.D.
Director,
Hester Adrian Research Centre
for the Study of Learning Processes
in the Mentally Handicapped
University of Manchester,
Manchester M13 9PL, England

Contents of Volume II

Contents of Volume III

Preface

The Fourth Congress of the International Association for the Scientific Study of Mental Deficiency was held in Washington, D.C., in August, 1976, in a year celebrating not only the bicentennial of the United States but also the hundredth anniversary of the American Association on Mental Deficiency, who acted as hosts to the conference. The event was attended by 1,152 registered participants with spouses and associates representing 63 different countries; there were about 500 speakers.

The conference theme "Research to Practice" reflects the expressed needs both of research workers and of practitioners to come to a closer understanding of each others' work and skills, and to take steps to reduce what has in the past been too large a gap between them. Because the conference was attended both by full-time research workers and by practitioners working daily with mentally retarded people, ample opportunities were available both during and between sessions for them to discuss mutual problems and to realise how much they had in common.

We look forward to renewal of acquaintance and meeting newcomers in the field at the Fifth Congress of IASSMD to be held in Israel in 1979.

In bringing together the principal papers presented at the conference, we have tried to identify the main themes of the presentations and to group these under separate headings. In doing so, we have on occasion regrouped papers under one heading that were presented in different sections or symposia. Our aim in arranging the material into themes was to provide more coherence and unity to the volumes as a whole, particularly for readers who were not themselves present at the congress.

The material is presented in three volumes: *Care and Intervention, Education and Training,* and *Biomedical Aspects.* The first volume focuses on developments in service provision, and reflects a particularly strong emphasis on the theme of early intervention and multidisciplinary treatment, on the provision of community and residential services, and on questions concerned with the evaluation of such services to ensure that the needs of mentally handicapped people are met. The second volume is devoted to the theme of education and training, and is largely concerned with questions of what and how to teach, with methods of assessing the individual's abilities and needs, and with methods of determining outcome. The third volume encompasses a wide range of biomedical studies, including prevention, detection, and early treatment, as well as a consideration of the many environmental factors related to intervention, particularly those that lend themselves to treatment. The number of pages devoted to questions concerned with the effects of malnutrition was a marked feature of this congress.

Despite a generous allocation of space, we have been able to find room for only a selection of the many papers presented at the congress. We have been guided in the selection of papers by members of our editorial board, to whom the editor owes a profound debt for their immediate response to his many requests for assistance, particularly in areas outside his own competence. We also gratefully acknowledge similar valuable help from other referees, namely Professor Schneiden and Drs. G. Claridge, T. Ingram, B. H. Kirman, B. W. Richards, N. de M. Rudolph, and J. Stern.

This is the first time that the proceedings of an IASSMD congress have been printed and published commercially. We are therefore grateful for an opportunity to express our appreciation to University Park Press, whose cooperation and efficiency have been exemplary.

But the chief credit for the prompt appearance of these volumes goes to our technical editor, Mrs. Jean de Jong, who has worked tirelessly and enthusiastically to bring order out of chaos and who has brought to the task of editing these volumes her wisdom and experience gained from assisting with the proceedings of previous congresses. Readers will be in her debt to a greater extent than they can possibly realise.

P. M.

Officers of the
International Association
for the Scientific Study
of Mental Deficiency:
1973–1976

President: **Alan D. B. Clarke,** Department of Psychology, The University, Hull, Yorkshire, England.

President-Elect: **Michael J. Begab,** NIH/NICHD/MRP, Landow Building, Room C-708, 7910 Woodmont Avenue, Bethesda, Maryland 20014, United States.

Honorary Vice-President: **Harvey A. Stevens,** Waisman Center on Mental Retardation and Human Development, University of Wisconsin, 2605 Marsh Lane, Madison, Wisconsin 53706, United States.

Vice-Presidents: **Bernard E. Cohen,** Department of Pediatrics 'B', The Chaim Sheba Medical Center, Tel Hashomer, Israel.
Annalise Dupont, Demographic-Genetic Research Department, Aarhus Psychiatric Hospital, DK-8240, Risskov, Denmark.

Past Presidents: **Harvey A. Stevens, Alexander Shapiro, Stanislau Krynski.**

Secretary: **David A. A. Primrose,** The Royal Scottish National Hospital, Larbert, Stirlingshire, Scotland FK5 4EJ.

Treasurer: **Jan B. Meiresonne,** N.O.Z., Postbus 415, Utrecht, The Netherlands.

Officers of the
International Association
for the Scientific
Study of Mental Deficiency:
1976–1979

President: **Michael J. Begab,** NIH/NICHD/MRP, Landow Building, Room C-708, 7910 Woodmont Avenue, Bethesda, Maryland 20014, United States.

President-Elect: **H. O. Åkesson,** Psychiatric Department III, Lillhagen's Hospital, S-422 03 Hisings Backa 3, Sweden.

Honorary Vice-Presidents: **Harvey A. Stevens,** Waisman Center on Mental Retardation and Human Development, University of Wisconsin, 2605 Marsh Lane, Madison, Wisconsin 53706, United States.
Alan D. B. Clarke, Department of Psychology, The University, Hull, Yorkshire, England.

Vice-Presidents: **Bernard E. Cohen,** Department of Pediatrics 'B', The Chaim Sheba Medical Center, Tel Hashomer, Israel.
Ignacy Wald, Instytut Psychoneurologiczny, Al. Sobieskiego 1/9, 02-957 Warsaw, Poland.

Honorary Officers: **Stanislau Krynski, Alexander Shapiro.**

Secretary: **David A. A. Primrose,** The Royal Scottish National Hospital, Larbert, Stirlingshire, Scotland, FK5 4EJ.

Treasurer: **Jan B. Meiresonne,** N.O.Z., Postbus 415, Utrecht, The Netherlands.

Congress Organized by the
International Association
for the Scientific Study
of Mental Deficiency
in Association with the
Local Organizing Committee

Host Organization: **American Association on Mental Deficiency**

President: **Burton Blatt** (1976–1977)
*Executive
Secretariat:* **George Soloyanis**
Ellen Horn
Carolyn A. Bardwell
Susan J. Annis
John E. Loth, Jr.
Valerie Ducker

Local Organizing Committee

James D. Clements
David Rosen
George Soloyanis
Robert Erdman
Mortimer Garrison

Local Arrangements Committee

Chairperson: George 'Bud' deHaven
Ruth Adams   William McCahill
Emily Baker   James Melton
Pat Nuse Carlson Mitzi Parks
Joseph Fenton   Stan Phillips
Hilda Fishback   Muriel Rose
Iris Gordon   Stella Gore Lansing
Darryl Hagy   Raymond Terry
Elaine Hollander Bathrus Williams
Roma Kaplan   Janice Williams
                  Dennis Wyant

Scientific Program Committee

Chairperson: Michael J. Begab
Members: H. Olof Åkesson
                Joseph M. Berg
                Alan D. B. Clarke
                H. A. A. Gresnigt
                Stanislau Krynski
                Jan B. Meiresonne
                David A. Primrose
                Harvey A. Stevens
                Ignacy Wald

Proceedings Editor:
Peter Mittler

Film Review Committee

Co-Chairpersons:
Molly Gorelick
David A. Primrose

Members:
Neil Goldstein
James Magary

Acknowledgments

The International Association for the Scientific Study of Mental Deficiency gratefully acknowledges support for this publication from the President's Committee on Mental Retardation, the National Institute of Child Health and Human Development, the Bureau for the Education of the Handicapped, the Office for Handicapped Individuals, and the Rehabilitation Services Administration.

IASSMD Congress Publications

Editor and *Distributor* of the Proceedings of the *First* Congress:
  Barry W. Richards,   St. Lawrence's Hospital, Caterham, Surrey, CR3 5YA, England
  Publication date: October, 1968
  Price: $23.00 or £8.00 (inclusive)
  Pages: xliv + 982; 175 figures, 155 tables
                        (*supplies still available*)

Editor of the Proceedings of the *Second* Congress:
  David A. A. Primrose, The Royal Scottish National Hospital, Larbert, Stirlingshire FK5 4EJ, Scotland.
  Publication date: December, 1971
  Price: 115 guilders
  Pages: xxiii + 774; 136 figures, 155 tables
  Distributed by: Swets & Zeitlinger, B.V., Heereweg 347B, Lisse, The Netherlands.

Editor and *Distributor* of the Proceedings of the *Third* Congress:
  David A. A. Primrose, The Royal Scottish National Hospital, Larbert, Stirlingshire FK5 4EJ, Scotland.
  Publication date: April, 1975
  Price: $34.00 or £12.00 (inclusive) for two volumes
  Pages: Volume 1   xxv + 775; 151 figures, 208 tables
         Volume 2   x + 100; 22 figures, 25 tables

Editor of the Proceedings of the *Fourth* Congress:
  Peter Mittler,   Hester Adrian Research Centre, The University, Manchester M13 9PL, England.
  Publication date: July–September, 1977
  Prices: $24.50 per volume
  Pages: Three volumes; 1718 pages
  Published by: University Park Press, Chamber of Commerce Building, Baltimore, Maryland 21202, U.S.A.

OPENING SESSION ADDRESS
BARRIERS TO
THE APPLICATION
OF KNOWLEDGE

PRESIDENTIAL ADDRESS
FROM RESEARCH
TO PRACTICE

CLOSING SESSION ADDRESS
SOME PRIORITIES
FOR RESEARCH
IN MENTAL
RETARDATION

OPENING SESSION ADDRESS

BARRIERS TO THE APPLICATION OF KNOWLEDGE

M. J. Begab
Chairman of the Program Committee and President-Elect

It is a distinct privilege and honor to welcome you on behalf of the Program Committee to this Fourth Congress of the IASSMD. May I also extend heartiest greetings from the Local Organizing and Local Arrangements Committees, who have given extensively and graciously of their time and energies to see to your every comfort and pleasure and to otherwise ensure the success of this meeting. And we are, of course, deeply indebted to the AAMD, our host for the Congress, whose support has greatly facilitated our activities.

The Program Committee is proud of the program it has prepared for you. We have assembled most of the outstanding scientists and professional practitioners in the field. They will share with you some of the most recent findings available on every important dimension of the problem of mental retardation, and you will learn as well about many of the exciting, innovative technologies and programs designed to help the retarded live more useful, fulfilling lives. I need not belabor the point. You will agree, I am sure, that the program speaks for itself.

The theme of this Congress, "From Research to Practice" is an expression of our conviction that science must contribute not only to our knowledge of the world around us but also to the solution of human problems. There are few conditions more vexing, more complex, more costly to society, and more devastating in their impact on individuals and families than mental retardation.

The response of society to this problem, although varying in scope and orientation from one country to another, has been largely practice-directed. In the United States, for example, more than five billion dollars are spent annually on service and income maintenance programs for the retarded. Three-fourths of this sum is expended for residential care and education—general and special—while only 1.5% is for support of research. Comparable data are not available for other industrialized nations, but it seems most likely that the ratio of expenditures for services to those for research is not better, unless, of course, relatively little support for service programs is being provided.

This address was presented at the opening ceremonies of the Fourth Congress of the IASSMD, August 23, 1976.

The disproportionate emphasis on human services has always *been* the case, probably always *will* be, and undoubtedly *should* be, although the degree of imbalance clearly merits careful scrutiny. We can no longer neglect the many millions of handicapped persons and their families who need help today. It is the hallmark of all civilized and compassionate people that the dignity and freedom of *all* their citizens, even the least fortunate among them, be promoted, and that each individual be afforded equal opportunity for self-fulfillment.

Scientists and practitioners have traditionally followed parallel, rather than converging, pathways. The process begins at the point of training and career choice, and is reinforced by patterns of funding, preferential status in academia, and the conviction of many scientists that objectivity in research and program advocacy are mutually exclusive goals. This creates a communication gap between the discoverers of new knowledge and the potential users of the information. The consequences are manifold: the questions investigated are not target-oriented; laboratory findings fail to find expression in naturalistic settings; programs are implemented on a massive scale without an adequate scientific base; and competition for limited resources is generated.

In recent years, scientists have been compelled increasingly to leave their laboratories for the political arena. They have been forced to defend the value of fundamental research, without which human disease and disability cannot be effectively curbed, in order to interpret the meaningfulness of their work, to speak of their accomplishments, and, indeed, to trace the progress of research from the wellhead of knowledge to the marketplace of practice. In this process, aided and abetted by the lobbying efforts of special interest groups, there is beginning to emerge a critical mass of scientists whose primary goal is to prevent mental retardation or to ameliorate its debilitating effects. Many of them are present here today.

There is much controversy in the scientific community whether the mission-oriented approach is the shortest route to the solution of specific disease or biosocially-based problems. Some would argue—justifiably—that many of our most significant discoveries were serendipitous in nature. The breaking of the genetic code, the development of sophisticated methods of tissue culture, and the Skinnerian theory for shaping behavior are a few random examples of such research. These contributions to science, which have markedly improved our potential for preventing and treating mental retardation of genetic or biological origin, obviously apply to many other disease conditions as well, and to a basic understanding of the human organism.

However, the converse of this proposition is equally true. Antenatal diagnosis was made possible on a large scale by tissue culture and automated karyotyping procedures, but only through the progressive identification of inborn errors of metabolism and genetic disorders associated with mental retardation could these techniques be applied to human disease states. Similarly, behavior modification was only a theory until its effectiveness with severely damaged children was demonstrated by mission-oriented researchers.

In the same vein, some behavioral scientists contend that cognitive processes and behavior can be understood and possibly remedied only after normal development is fully comprehended. There is an opposing point of view—equally if not more valid in my judgment—that the study of extreme forms of behavior can provide clues to the significance of certain variables in normal function that might otherwise escape us. The contributions of psychoanalytic theory to personality development, formulated by observations of clinically abnormal patients, are a case in point.

The position being expressed here is rather simple. We cannot expect investigators in mental retardation to solve the problem alone. Whether they engage in basic, clinical, or applied studies, they will need to draw upon the findings of other scientists concerned largely with the search for new knowledge for its own sake. It is abundantly clear, however, that without the commitment of such scientists as are represented here, meaningful solutions are not likely to be found. In the last two decades we have learned more about preventing and treating retardation than in many more previous years. This came about because nations around the world decided they could no longer ignore the devastating impact of retardation and committed more of their investigative talents and resources to the search for solutions. To fully capitalize on these efforts, the findings from these separate sources must be systematically compiled and applied.

My comments thus far and the theme of this Congress imply that effective communication between scientists of various persuasions and professional practitioners can effectively transform knowledge into practice. Such conditions are necessary but not sufficient to the task. Even if we could greatly improve communication, the widely publicized goal of decreasing the incidence of mental retardation by half during the next 25 years would not be achieved unless we could successfully resolve some of the social, political, and economic issues to which the problem is so intimately bound.

The state of the economy is one of the major forces affecting mental retardation. The disadvantaged children in our countries are often subject to disease, malnutrition, inadequate health care, and poor living conditions. Often they are the products of reproductive casualty, i.e., low birth weight, prematurity, complications of pregnancy, toxemias, infectious disease processes, etc. Some have argued that the elimination of poverty, through a minimum guaranteed income, for example, could greatly reduce the incidence of damaged children and sociocultural retardation. To the extent that mild retardation is a function of undernutrition, improving the food supply for pregnant women and young children and the quality of prenatal care could have preventive impact. Unfortunately, the influence of such measures would be more keenly felt in underdeveloped countries, places where poverty is endemic and guaranteed incomes most unlikely.

The relationship of poverty to sociocultural retardation is associative, not causal. While an overwhelming majority of the retarded are poor, only a small fraction of the poor are retarded. This fraction is concentrated in families where the mothers are of low intelligence and education. The root causes of retardation in these families still need to be specified, but the evidence points more to the quality of life than to level of income.

Other factors embedded in the culture of poverty, such as family size and spacing between births, may have more direct bearing on reducing the incidence of retardation. Here we have the knowledge and the technology for birth control but less understanding of the psychological variables, societal, and religious values underlying sex behavior, procreation, and family life. Efforts to introduce massive programs of voluntary population control in nonindustrial countries have met with only marginal success.

Mental retardation is but one costly outcome, albeit a very important one, of poverty. This problem alone, however, is not likely to motivate nations to markedly improve the quality of life for their impoverished citizens. When the costs of mental retardation are added to other social costs deriving from poverty, e.g., delinquency and crime, welfare, high unemployment, drug addiction, neglect and abuse, broken homes, then the argument for social change is clearly more compelling. This suggests that if research information is to be effectively applied in preventing retardation, broader social issues need to be addressed. Advocates for the retarded may need to form coalitions with other groups to achieve these ends.

Barriers to the implementation of preventive measures apply to biological causes also. For example, we already have the means for detecting the presence or absence of abnormal conditions during pregnancy. With these methods, the incidence of Down's syndrome, the largest single cause of biologically determined retardation, can be approximately halved by providing amniocentesis to all pregnant women over 35 years of age. The logistical problems of reaching such a large group of women, performing the procedures safely, and providing expert laboratory diagnostic tests are difficult but well within the scope of technological development. Attitudinal and ethical considerations pose more complex issues. Many practicing obstetricians are reluctant to perform this procedure in the absence of confirmed genetic risk, especially with maternal age the only predisposing element of risk. Women, too, unless their pregnancies were unplanned and unwanted, are understandably hesitant to undergo such procedures on the 1 chance in 50 or more that they are carrying a defective fetus. Ethical considerations come into play when decisions regarding therapeutic abortion must be confronted. Here, advocates of the "right to life" for the unborn fetus have placed the issue squarely before the public and the courts. Even the decisions of the Supreme Court have not quelled this value-laden controversy. Whatever one's personal views on the right or wrong of the opposing positions, the implications for prevention seem clear.

Advances in the science of human genetics and the imminent development of computerized and automated health screening technologies also face barriers to implementation. Is there any value, many professionals and citizens are asking, to screening for disorders for which there is no treatment? Would interpretation to parents, for example, that their child had some chromosomol abnormality possibly associated with deviant behavior tendencies prove helpful or harmful to the child's development? Should the question of how genetics interacts with child-rearing in influencing behavior be asked at all? Issues of this kind have sparked heated debate among scientists in relation to the XYY syndrome, a chromosomal aberration sometimes associated with aggressive, criminal, or other antisocial behavior. With the expansion of screening programs and increased use of chromosome mapping techniques, it seems highly probable that scientists in mental retardation, too, will face similar controversies in the future.

Ethical concerns of this kind are obviously not confined to genetic disorders. Other conditions of biological deficit, such as low birth weight, are also subject to environmental influences. Witness the fact that such children from lower-class homes show a far higher incidence of retardation at school age than similar children from middle-class homes. Should parents be alerted to the heightened vulnerability of these children? Is the relationship likely to be adversely or positively affected?

These few examples illustrate that the application of knowledge derived from research in service programs requires more than a free flow of information between scientist and practitioner. Those among us who have committed our energies and the resources of our respective governments to an attack on the major bio-medical and social problems presented by mental retardation will be held accountable for our progress or lack of it. It is imperative, therefore, that we recognize the broad social context that may impede the implementation of scientific discovery. The notion that we already know enough to reduce the incidence of mental retardation by half by the year 2000 may or may not be valid. But if we are to achieve this goal we will need to modify our social values, improve the quality of life in deprived families, upgrade the economy, and resolve some of our moral and ethical conflicts. Only then will the fruits of science be fully harvested.

PRESIDENTIAL ADDRESS
FROM RESEARCH TO PRACTICE

A. D. B. Clarke
Department of Psychology, The University,
Hull, HU6 7RX, England

Our meeting here today was predetermined by the centenary of the American Association on Mental Deficiency, which was founded in 1876 by Edouard Seguin and five colleagues, who saw the centenary of the Declaration of Independence as an appropriate time for such a venture. We meet, then, to pay tribute to the Association, and to recognize its national and international significance. With a membership now of more than 10,000, its strength is considerable, and its influence correspondingly great; yet in this centenary year we must avoid the temptation to sentimentalize about the past.

Many of our predecessors, like ourselves, were creatures of their time, but unlike ourselves they lacked a well developed scientific methodology that enables one to discriminate between established facts and value judgments. The history of the AAMD has recently been portrayed by William Sloan and Harvey Stevens (1976). I commend it to you not only as of intrinsic interest in relation to mental retardation, but also as a social history of prime importance, reflecting the various models of man from which different attitudes were derived at different times.

In those early days, a crude social Darwinism was often apparent, and correlates were usually mistaken for causes. An over-simple genetic and eugenic theory seems to have haunted the field. And in so far as environmental factors were thought to be aetiologically relevant, parental tuberculosis and alcoholism were accorded prime importance. Yet from the 1930s onwards the impact of a developing human science began to be more obvious. From about this time the AAMD did far more than reflect the social and political attitudes of the times, but was often well in advance of general opinion. Thus the world is a better place for its existence and we must applaud the blend of scientific curiosity and humanism that prompted the founding fathers and many who followed. As in other endeavours, we stand today on the shoulders of others.

It would be inappropriate, even for an Englishman, not at the same time to recognize the Bicentenary of the United States and to offer on behalf of all of us foreigners our congratulations and good wishes. As an Englishman, too, I am bound to admit that King George III made a number of serious, and for us, expensive, errors, amounting to no less than 26, according to the Declaration of Independence signed exactly 200 years and 50 days ago.

A-7

In this address I want to offer a brief overview of some of the advances in our understanding of the nature, causes, prevention, or treatment of mental retardation, many of which have occurred since our last Congress. I want also to contrast findings that have been rapidly applied with those that have not been applied, as well as indicating examples where incorrect interpretations have led to major errors of practice. Such an approach should reveal some of our strengths and some of our weaknesses, and may serve as an hors d'oeuvres for the stronger meat of this Congress, which for the first time has a theme: from research to practice.

Clearly, preliminary accurate description must precede all scientific work into causal, preventive, or ameliorative approaches. Description may be anatomi-cal/behavioural, as in Langdon Down's classic thirty-four line delineation of the syndrome that bears his name (1866); it may be biochemical, as in Fölling's identification of phenylketonuria; it may be cytological, as in Lejeune, Gautier, and Turpin's (1959) identification of the extra chromosome in Down's syn-drome; it may be behavioural, as in Kanner's description of the autistic syndrome; or it may be experimental, as in studies seeking to identify particular assets and deficits in the retarded with a view to providing a prescription for action. Obviously, too, description may move beyond the retarded individual to a study of parental characteristics (e.g., maternal age in Down's syndrome) or to a description of the institutional, social, or ecological factors that form the context for his life. Or it may involve case-finding for epidemiological work.

Throughout this paper, and through this Congress, I hope we may continu-ally bear in mind two statements, asking ourselves whether their messages are yet justified. The first was made in 1972 by the President's Committee on Mental Retardation: *"Using present knowledge and techniques from the biomedical and behavioral sciences it is possible to reduce the occurrence of mental retardation by 50 percent before the end of the century."*

This became a major national goal. Notice the phrase *"present knowledge and techniques,"* and *"it is possible."* Whether or not the possible becomes probable may be a different matter, dependent on the resources that become available. But explicit in this passage is the argument that if research had stopped dead some four years ago, we would still have the potential for halving the in-cidence of mental retardation. There is not better justification for the theme of this Congress, because we must be forced to ask whether there is any real sign of this degree of impact by research. Is it really beginning to happen? And, if so, in what countries?

The second statement is my own, forced upon me by my awareness of research, and it complements the first. *"Using present knowledge and techniques it is possible substantially to improve the levels of functioning of most of the retarded."* Is it happening? If so, where? And, if not, why not?

In attempting to evaluate these two statements, and with the oversimplifica-tion necessary in an address of this sort, I must dichotomise the field into those conditions comprising retardation below about IQ 50, and those constituting the milder conditions. Although there are some overlapping problems, these are to a large extent separate populations differing substantially in aetiology, incidence, and prevalence, in present capabilities, and in prognosis. I propose, then, first to discuss research issues bearing upon the causes, prevention, and amelioration of the more severe grades, moving on, second, to a discussion of the same factors in relation to mild retardation.

THE SEVERER GRADES OF RETARDATION

Prevention

It cannot be urged too strongly that careful epidemiological work must be available for the evaluation of trends of decrease, increase, or stability of various conditions. An important study in England compares results of surveys in the 1920s and 1960s. The results suggest that the incidence of below 50 IQ conditions has decreased by about a third, a decrease masked in overall prevalence rates by the increased life span of the other two-thirds, particularly Down's syndrome (Tizard, 1964). Thus, ordinary social and health advances, most not specially aimed at reducing mental retardation, may have already had a considerable impact. These are likely to include the widespread use of immunization techniques against common childhood illnesses that can have neurological sequelae; early diagnosis of the rare cases in which inborn errors of metabolism can be corrected; better antenatal and natal care, in particular the increasing percentage of deliveries in hospitals rather than at home, and the more careful monitoring, therefore, of the course of labour; genetic counselling and family planning; better public health; and reducing the age at which mothers complete their families. But a word of warning here: if the social changes that reduce the age of primiparous women continue, we may well run into an increase in handicapping conditions associated with low maternal age.

Probably the single most important biomedical advance came in 1959, with the discovery of chromosomal aberrations. Since then, new findings have been frequent, and more than 100 chromosome disorders have been identified. Down's syndrome is, of course, the most common, accounting for between a quarter and a third of all cases with IQ below 50. Much rarer conditions, such as maple syrup urine disease and homocystinuria, have been discovered, and illustrate the progress being made in the differentiation of various forms of retardation by mainly biochemical techniques (Berg, 1974).

Amniocentesis for mothers at risk and the termination of pregnancies where positive results are found are likely to make an impact, and this should clearly become a routine service for all older mothers. This, together with the reducing maternal age for family completion, should reduce the incidence of Down's syndrome. As yet, except perhaps in New York City (Stein, Susser, and Guterman, 1973), there appear to be no firm figures available reflecting such a drop, which should already have started (Alberman, 1975). Two additional points should be made; first, there may well be some small risk of abortion from amniocentesis, although a recent NIH study of over 2,000 women suggests that this is not so (PCMR, 1976). Second, in Down's syndrome results are seldom clear before the eighteenth week of pregnancy, some weeks after the optimal period for termination of pregnancy (Wynne Griffith, 1973).

As Brock (1976) indicates, recent discoveries that chemical components leak into the amniotic fluid from foetuses with neural tube defects have opened a new chapter in prenatal diagnosis. In particular, the importance of alpha-fetoprotein (AFP) measurements in the early prenatal diagnosis of spina bifida and anencephaly has been established. This protein appears in foetal serum as early as the sixth week of gestation. While amniotic fluid assessment can be used to protect the mother with a history of previous abnormal pregnancies involving neural tube defects, it will not normally be applied to the vast majority of mothers for whom this is a first-time event. But AFP may be detected in very low concentrations in normal serum by radioimmunoassay, and its concentration increases in maternal blood during pregnancy. In 1974, studies established that a proportion of cases both of anencephaly and spina bifida were associated with serum AFP values at the extreme of, or outside, the normal range. Two conclusions have already emerged from a collaborative study organized by the Institute for Research into Mental and Multiple Handicap, London: first, that attempts to detect neural tube defects before the end of the first trimester are unlikely to be successful; second, that anencephaly is easier to detect than spina bifida, and that in both the efficiency is well short of 100% (Brock, 1976). Clearly, we may expect advances in these techniques, with amniocentesis following the serum screening as confirmation or otherwise of abnormal findings. Milunsky and Alpert (1976) warn, however, that "in view of the significant true false-positive rate, the greatest caution is advised in interpreting raised AFP concentrations, especially in patients not specifically at risk for having offspring with NTD."

Another major advance in the last decade has been the discovery of a method for immunizing rhesus negative mothers against Rh sensitization by rhesus positive foetuses (Clarke, 1967); another is the production of a rubella vaccine. The increasing use of surgical treatment of some forms of infantile hydrocephalus is a further example, although here its evaluation is complicated by the sometime occurrence of spontaneous arrest, and the possible selective factors determining treatment/nontreatment (Guthkelch, 1970). One is bound to add, however, that the efforts of some physicians and surgeons, using heroic methods, to keep alive grossly damaged babies for whom nature never intended survival, is giving way to a more sober appreciation of prognostic factors.

There is no shortage of potentially fertile hypotheses in the biomedical field. I will offer just two examples. The first is the well-known suggestion by Stoller and Collmann (1965) that a hepatitis virus, interacting with maternal age, plays a part in the aetiology of Down's syndrome. Currently there is evidence both for and against this hypothesis (e.g., Kucera, 1970; Baird and Miller, 1968). The second example, in a different area, is provided by C. A. Clarke et al.'s (1975) suggestion that spina bifida and anencephaly may result from the presence of residual trophoblastic material arising from a recent miscarriage. The case for and against this correlation, and the possible mechanism of interaction with the new foetus, are carefully discussed, and some potentially crucial research suggested.

Work in the field of prevention must take into account man-made agents, of which Minamata Disease was probably the most dramatic. The dangers of ionising radiations are well known, and the more extreme forms of lead poisoning are well appreciated. As a matter of fact, they were understood in the eighteenth century, when lead miners in Yorkshire, England, found it necessary to erect one-mile-long stone chimneys, built on the surface of the hillsides to the very tops, where the toxic fumes were dispersed. We also know of the dangers to young children from the internal use of lead paint in buildings. There is often legislation about the use of lead paint by professional decorators, but tenement dwellers, if they paint at all, are likely to do it themselves. In how many countries is it legally obligatory to define the dangers on tins of lead paint? There seems to be a lack of public health education on these matters. Meanwhile, as man continues recklessly to plunder his planet, lead fumes are belched into the air from automobiles. Legislation to reduce this emission is now being implemented in a few countries. Old lead water pipes are also suspect (Beattie et al., 1975) although there is controversy about the former paper (see subsequent correspondence in the *Lancet*), and Elwood et al. (1976) conclude that, if a hazard does exist, it is likely to be confined to homes in which lead water levels of over 0.8 ppm occur.

Summarising, it is evident that the potentials for decreasing the incidence of the severer grades of retardation are present, and have probably been operating for some time as a result of general social changes. Add to these the specific biomedical advances of the type I have mentioned, and the outlook looks promising. Do we really have prospects of halving the incidence of these types of retardation? Are we on target?

So far as conditions where a single cause-effect relationship is concerned, we certainly may be. For example, the decline in birth rate in some developed countries may be differentially greater among older women (S. L. B. Duncan, personal communication), and this social trend is likely to have a considerable effect. But so far as preventive services are concerned, I suspect a considerable gap between what is potentially on offer and what is taken up. It is not enough to have preventive or ameliorative services available unless they are used by all those for whom they are intended. In England, for example, there is at least one amniocentesis centre in every Hospital Region. It has been suggested (S. L. B. Duncan, personal communication) that probably less than 10% of mothers over 35 years are having this test. We suspect that here there is the usual social class gradient in the take-up of available free services. Public health education in its ordinary forms will probably fail to touch the lowest social groups, and this problem relates to most other aspects of social disadvantage.

Amelioration

Turning now to the amelioration of the severer grades of retardation, it is of interest that from about 1951 and onwards two independent streams of work in England and Holland, the one strictly experimental and the other in training centres, produced an identical finding: under certain circumstances, the moderately and severely retarded could learn well, retain that learning, and even transfer their new found skills to different tasks. Much later, the strategies that such approaches reflected were termed "normalization." As Grunewald (1969) has written "the term implies . . . a *striving* in various ways towards what is normal . . . normalization does not imply any denial of the retardate's handicap. It involves rather exploiting his other mental and physical capacities so that his handicap becomes less pronounced . . ."

It became increasingly clear in the 1950s that proper programming of learning, proper incentives, and knowledge of results could transform the skills of the moderately retarded, and sometimes of some of the severely retarded. Then behaviour modification as a formalized system developed rapidly in the following decade, again with the same general implications as the earlier work, but this time more often applied to the more profoundly handicapped. As a technology of learning, its implications are of course far wider than for retardation alone. Its very considerable efficacy for those whose learning deficits are their main problem accounts for the rapid spread of these techniques. It has also become clear that early and prolonged intervention in the home, using parents as educators, can have significant effects upon the early development of the moderately or severely retarded child. So, twenty-five years of research have totally transformed our expectancies of what can be done.

These are great achievements, but have they been translated into practice? In the main, the more severely retarded persons, except in a few centres, very rarely get the sort of help from which they can benefit. What is needed is lengthy, skilled, and hence costly, help, not unskilled caregiving. The findings to which I have referred are often either unknown to practitioners, totally misunderstood, or thought to be inappropriate. Hence, even among professionals, there tends to be a widespread underestimation of what can be done. This is serious, for low expectancies are clearly associated with poor provision and hence poor outcome. A vicious circle is then perpetuated. Moreover, Grant (1971) has shown that those staff in day training centres who are most closely in touch with these handicapped adults consistently underestimate their potential work performance, particularly if the adults are female—another example of sex discrimination, which thus permeates the IQ scale from top to bottom.

MILD RETARDATION

Assessing trends in the incidence and prevalence of mild retardation is much more difficult, because these are associated with so many complex and interacting factors. They include changes in the provision of services, the efficacy of schooling, the availability of employment, and the degree of public understanding, all in the context of increasingly demanding urban societies. It is easy, in fact, to demonstrate large increases in the numbers designated mildly retarded as a consequence of better provision. Then again, there are very large differences in prevalence rates at different ages that complicate the picture.

The role of malnutrition in damaging the young, vulnerable animal brain has received much attention in recent years (Dobbing and Smart, 1974). It is much more difficult to establish its effect on man, however, because malnutrition does not exist in isolation, being part of a generally adverse situation. Moreover, the mediating mechanisms could involve either arrest or deceleration of brain growth, relative nonresponsiveness socially of parents and children under conditions of malnourishment, or the reflection of a wider unstimulating social context, or all of these. And even an apparently more ideal investigation, such as the Dutch Famine study (Stein, Susser, Saenger, and Marolla, 1975), permits a number of alternative explanations (see subsequent correspondence in the *Lancet*; September, 1975—January 1976). Moreover, a given degree and duration of human malnutrition cannot be taken in isolation, but must be related to subsequent life history (Richardson, 1976). This important question will continue to be debated (Tizard, 1976). We do not, however, need to sit on the fence about malnutrition as a world-wide problem, for it is part and parcel of the tragic conditions under which a large proportion of our four billion fellow human beings continue to live.

Where, in the minority of mild cases, organic factors are implicated, the same general preventive principles apply as with the more severe grades. Of the remainder, a proportion owe their existence to normal genetic variation. It has recently been shown that the whole question of parent-child resemblances in intelligence is very much more complex than most writers have maintained (McAskie and Clarke, 1976). The polygenic model predicts that, without assortative mating, the single parent-child correlation is 0.5 and the mid-parent-child correlation 0.71. But there commonly is assortative mating, which should increase both of these; indeed, assortative mating for intelligence is greater than for any characteristic other than race. Genetic and environmental factors are themselves correlated, so that environment should add to genetic parent-child resemblances. Nevertheless, such resemblances are imperfect, and a number of mildly retarded are born to normal parents of average or below average intelligence, and are reared in normal environments without suspicion of organic involvement. These are the normal variants. There remains the very large group of subcultural retarded, where it is assumed that a combination of genetic and social adversity is responsible.

From the work of Skeels and onwards, it became increasingly obvious that this group can have quite a good social prognosis. But Skeels' intervention was life-long and complete, and the social outcome from average adoptive homes was very much better than that of a contrast group as well as from what might have been inferred from the social origin of the children (Skeels, 1966). The classic paper by Skodak and Skeels (1949) following up, at age 13, 100 adopted children, shows much the same thing in terms of IQ rather than in terms of social outcome. With an increasing recognition that adverse environment played a part in the aetiology of mild retardation, intervention from then onwards became an "in" concept. But with it was associated the belief that intervention would only be effective in the early years. Thus, one of the roots of the Head Start concept was an unquestioning faith in the crucial and disproportionate influence of early experience upon later development. By now there is clear evidence against this still fashionable view (Clarke and Clarke, 1976), and even in the study of animal behaviour workers such as Harlow (Novak and Harlow, 1975) have substantially rescinded their earlier pronouncements about critical periods.

Kirk's (1958) careful work, which exactly predicted the failure of Project Head Start, was brushed aside in the liberal euphoria of the mid-1960s. Jensen (1969) was correct in concluding from various reviews of Head Start that "compensatory education has been tried, and it apparently has failed," although many writers subsequently indicated that these programmes were neither compensatory nor educational, being mainly of short duration, offering free rather than cognitive activity by mostly unskilled 'teachers,' and treating the child out of the context of his home. Incidentally, the cost of Head Start between 1965 and 1970 was more than $10 billion. Here was a case of the national application of programmes against which there already existed research evidence.

Bronfenbrenner's (1974) excellent review of some 21 of the better studies selected from many hundreds of totally inadequate ones, comes near to the heart of the matter. Intervention in the home is likely to be more successful than in preschool, but those most likely to respond come from the upper crust of poor families. As has been shown repeatedly, those most in need of help fail to seek it, or if offered, to accept it or benefit from it.

While it is at last generally conceded that brief early intervention has effects that fade, it is less often appreciated that the effects of much longer early intervention that is not followed by similar stimulation will also fade. Early life is not a critical period psychosocially: although early intervention is desirable, for prevention is better than cure, later intervention may also considerably ameliorate or even overcome mild retardation. Feuerstein is one of the few researchers who are clear about this, as is evidenced in his discussion of the theoretical underpinning of his successful treatment of culturally deprived adolescents (Feuerstein and Krasilowsky, 1972).

It is, however, apparent that what has become known as cycles of disadvantage (Rutter and Madge, 1976), that is, the recurrence of social problems in succeeding generations of the same family, operate with some level of efficiency, although there are both a quite large escape rate as well as new recruitment; by definition there is always a bottom 2% arising from a range of pathologies, biological and social, together with genetic factors strengthened by assortative mating. Here we are considering one extreme of the whole issue of the correlates of social status, which appear to operate across vastly differing political systems, whether capitalist or socialist. In an important cross-cultural study, to be reported at this Congress, a comparison is made between prevalence in the United States and in an Eastern European capital (Czarkowski et al., Volume I). This report indicates that, after 30 years of greatly diminished economic and housing inequalities, occupational class in the socialist country still relates to backwardness and mild retardation. For attainment, intelligence, and a whole gamut of other mental and physical qualities, the correlates of occupational class are probably the most firmly established findings in the field of human behaviour. Yet the mechanisms by which they are mediated are far from clear.

In discussing the effects of perinatal complications, Sameroff and Chandler (1975) have shown that, except for cases of extreme damage, the social class context in which the child is reared can have a considerable effect in amplifying, modifying, or completely overcoming such handicaps. This again emphasizes the incorrectness of regarding damage as setting unalterable limits on human development, since a given degree may have a spectrum of outcomes in different individuals and in different situations. In turn, such views are entirely consistent with the findings on the effects of training or very long-term intervention with mildly mentally retarded persons.

Society needs to grasp the fact that children, unwanted and unplanned, reared by parents who are *both* intellectually limited *and* emotionally unstable, have a poor prognosis, but a normal one if they are adopted, and possibly even if adopted late (Kadushin, 1970). There is much reluctance to move children from their parents, and in the name of sanctity of the family much damage can be done. Social worker support is of little avail. In such cases, the disadvantaged need, among other things, the privileges of the advantaged in the form of voluntary family planning. The provision of clinics will have little impact, but the offer of birth control techniques taken into the home, as part of a general habilitation effort, may prevent an intolerable situation for inadequate disturbed parents and the potential victims of their union. Society needs to look less emotively and more unflinchingly at these problems, particularly in a world where the population has doubled since 1930, and continues to increase by 75 million per year.

The fact that all cross-sectional prevalence, and all longitudinal follow-up studies indicate, as age increases, a considerable diminution in mild retardation, is firmly established. These results are the most hopeful in the whole field. They probably reflect 1) camouflage after the final years of greatest intellectual demands in school or initial prop up by benefactors (Edgerton and Bercovici, 1976); 2) prolonged social learning and delayed responsiveness to society in general; and 3) delayed maturation, which appears to be a feature associated with prolonged adversity—a catch-up phenomenon also apparent for growth after mild malnutrition. They may illustrate what Sameroff and Chandler (1975) term a "self-righting tendency which appears to move children towards normality in the face of pressure towards deviation."

As Cobb (1972) has shown in an excellent review of all follow-up studies, "the most consistent and outstanding finding . . . is the high proportion of the adult retarded who achieve satisfactory adjustments, by whatever criteria are employed . . ." Cobb was in the main talking of follow-up studies of those for whom rather little had been done, the least fortunate of their peers. But one cannot entirely discount the possible effects of some sort of long-term intervention or care. Of course, there remain a proportion who contribute to problem families and other social deviancies. But we can no longer say, as did Goddard (1914) that mild retardation "underlies all our social problems" although one might add that in extreme form it mirrors some of the major problems of society.

THE GAP BETWEEN RESEARCH AND PRACTICE

After this brief overview, it is now possible to summarise, to offer a balance sheet, and to consider possible implications.

First, let us consider the prospects of halving the incidence of mental retardation within the next twenty-five years. These are potentially good in developed countries insofar as the severer grades are concerned, both for reasons of secular social trends in the age at which children are born, hopefully a reduction in family size, and improvements in public health and medical care. These changes are not specifically aimed at mental retardation, but if we add those that are, including genetic counselling, prenatal diagnosis, and the correction of rare metabolic defects, then the prospects look encouraging. However, the good outlook carries with it an implication that severe retardation will become much less common, a possibility that may affect the provision of facilities for those who survive.

So far as mild retardation is concerned, prospects of halving the incidence seem to be very, very slight, even though some follow-up studies, some adoption studies, or even later intervention indicate a potentially reasonable adult prognosis. And the knowledge gained from some expensive and careful schemes, such as those of Heber and Garber, is of inestimable value. But there seem to be no prospects of applying these nationally, and even immense social change could not at once defeat the problem, for there exists in man a perseveration of attitudes and parenting behaviour, which even when unreinforced by gross social inequalities, play a part in producing the subcultural retarded. And, as noted, there must always exist in any population a bottom 2% in regard to qualities that the population values. The question is whether society can become sufficiently humane to help develop limited assets so that the individual can function usefully and happily. Will the brotherhood of man remain an empty phrase?

Today, because the mildly retarded comprise about 75% of the whole group, and because the subcultural contribute largely to it, the prospects of reducing the overall incidence of designated mental retardation seem nowhere near as so good as those suggested by the President's Committee.[1]

The second question relates to the potentially substantial improvement in the functioning of the retarded, using present knowledge and techniques. Here the position is extremely bad. A few centres and a few institutions are doing

---

[1] Since these lines were written, this point appears to have been implicitly conceded by the President's Committee (1976) in *Mental Retardation: Century of Decision*. Washington, D.C.: Govt. Printing Office Stock No. 040-000-00343-6.

excellent work, and using to the full our new knowledge. But where substantial new resources have been offered, authorities have more often been bewitched by the need for splendid new buildings rather than by planning splendid new programmes, which are the more important. So here again is an ominous and, I fear, growing gap between our knowledge and our practice. In the main our practice is based on a model of man that research has completely overturned. Furthermore, it is still not known why some professionals appear to be very much more successful than others at releasing the social and learning potentials of the retarded.

Implications

If this analysis is correct, or even only half correct, what are the implications? I see the main ones as follows:

1) In this field, as in others, we are competing for limited resources. Hence there is a growing need for independently monitored cost-benefit analyses that clearly distinguish the benefit to the individual, to the family, and to society. A recent and exemplary analysis on the use of amniocentesis for preventing the birth of Down's syndrome children has been provided by Hagard and Carter (1976). The NIH has also funded a controlled trial involving about 2,000 pregnancies (PCMR, 1976). Laurence and Gregory (1976) urge the concentration of such services in specialist centres, where experienced staff keep the rate of abortion to a minimum and achieve a high rate of success in culturing amnion cells. We need more of these centres.

2) There is thus an increasing need for population prenatal screening for those at risk and for older mothers. Equally important, the ways in which the take-up of these services may be increased require urgent investigation. Here there is probably another large gap in application.

3) There is an urgent need for staff retraining at all levels. Pioneer demonstration projects are much more likely to be effective than the written or spoken word. Resistance to change among some staff is considerable.

4) No parent of a moderately, severely, or profoundly handicapped child should be expected to rear that child without the fullest support, from birth onwards. Where parents are unwilling or unable to provide care, the provision of small units needs extension.

5) Mild retardation poses seemingly intractable problems. It illustrates, in extreme form, the problems that beset the human condition. It is exaggerated by the gross inequalities that are obvious in most societies, but even so, general social change by itself is unlikely to cancel out these difficulties all at once. It is indeed fortunate that to some extent many of these people tend to show a shift towards normality as age increases; it seems that life experiences and the passage of time are therapeutic. But can we not do better in, first, diminishing the familial, social, and economic factors that are implicated, and, at the same time, offer better help?

6) Of many necessary omissions in my speech the gravest has been my failure to consider the developing countries. WHO has an important part to play here, and has already in 1968 produced a report on the organization of services, with the needs of developing countries, particularly, in mind. In this connection we, as an association, greatly value our formal links with WHO via the Joint Commission with the I.L.S.M.H. But we deeply regret that there is no one in WHO Headquarters at Geneva whose sole concern is mental retardation.

7) In the light of limited resources, the expansion of volunteer services is greatly to be encouraged. There are in society much latent sympathy and many latent resources.

8) Although the distinction between pure and applied research is partly overdrawn, it seems that there is currently something of an imbalance disfavouring applied research. For some the field of retardation offers a captive population upon which rather general theories may be tested. Others favour a *blitzkrieg* approach rather than a lengthier and more rewarding toil. Our journals are full of material of which the external validity is never checked. We need a much greater use of "real life" experiments. In this whole connection, I am glad to note the AAMD's interest in the ethics of human experimentation.

9) Scientists occupy a privileged position in society, but often wish for more than 24 hours in any one day. Nevertheless, more of us must be involved in seeing that our discoveries are field-tested and applied. If we do not, who will? I urge a greater involvement of us all in the corridors of power, and in the sometimes tedious dialogue with governmental agencies.

CONCLUSION

Man is becoming increasingly aware that he can be a predatory, cruel creature, and that the environment, like the bank, imposes limited credit and high rates of interest for repayment. He is belatedly coming to realise that wastage must be radically reduced. The world-wide wastage of human capabilities is no less obvious than that of material resources. In extreme form it is reflected in mental retardation. It is the task of science to reveal the ways in which our biological and social pathologies can be alleviated, and it is our task as scientists to see that these findings are widely disseminated and used with profit.

ACKNOWLEDGEMENTS

This paper was written with considerable assistance from Dr. Ann M. Clarke; the writer also benefited greatly from the advice of Drs. Sheila L. B. Duncan and F. Peter Woodford.

REFERENCES

Alberman, E. (1975) The prevention of Down's syndrome. Dev. Med. Child Neurol. 17:793.

Baird, P. A., and Miller, J. R. (1968) Some epidemiological aspects of Down's syndrome in British Columbia. Brit. J. Prev. Soc. Med. 22:81.

Beattie, A. D., Moore, M. R., Goldberg, A., Finlayson, M. J. W., Graham, J. F., Mackie, E. M., Main, J. C., McLaren, D. A., Murdoch, R. M., and Stewart, G. T. (1975) Role of chronic low-level lead exposure in the aetiology of mental retardation. Lancet 1:589.

Berg, J. (1974) Aetiological aspects of mental subnormality: pathological factors. *In* A. M. Clarke and A. D. B. Clarke (Eds.) Mental Deficiency: The Changing Outlook, 3rd Edition. London: Methuen; New York: Free Press.

Brock, D. J. H. (1976) Prenatal diagnosis—chemical methods. *In* Human Malformations. Brit. Med. Bull. 32:16.

Bronfenbrenner, U. (1974) A Report on Longitudinal Evaluations of Pre-School Programs. Vol. 2. Is Early Intervention Effective? Washington, D.C.: DHEW Publication No. (OHD) 74–25.

Clarke, A. M., and Clarke, A. D. B. (1976) (Eds.) Early Experience: Myth and Evidence. London: Open Books; New York: Free Press.

Clarke, C. A. (1967) Prevention of Rh-haemolytic disease. Brit. Med. J. 4:484.

Clarke, C. A., Hobson, D., McKendrick, O. M., Rogers, S. G., and Shephard, P. M. (1975) Spina bifida and anencephaly: miscarriage as a possible cause. Brit. Med. J. 4:743.

Cobb, H. V. (1972) The Forecast of Fulfillment. New York: Teachers' College Press, Columbia University.

Dobbing, J., and Smart, J. L. (1974) Undernutrition in the developing brain. In Development and Regeneration in the Nervous System (R. M. Gaze and M. J. Keating, Eds.) 30:2, 164. London: British Council.

Edgerton, R. B., and Bercovici, S. M. (1976) The cloak of competence: years later. Amer. J. Ment. Defic. 80:485.

Elwood, P. C., Morton, M., and St. Leger, A. S. (1976) Lead in water and mental retardation. Lancet 1:590.

Feuerstein, R., and Krasilowsky, D. (1972) Interventional strategies for the significant modification of cognitive functioning in the disadvantaged adolescent. J. Amer. Acad. Child Psychiatry 11:572.

Goddard, H. (1914). Feeble-Mindedness: its Causes and Consequences. New York: Macmillan.

Grant, G. W. B. (1971) Some management problems of providing work for the mentally disordered, with particular reference to the handicapped. Unpublished M.Sc. Thesis, University of Manchester Institute of Science and Technology.

Grunewald, K. (1969) The Mentally Retarded in Sweden. Stockholm: The Swedish Institute.

Guthkelch, A. N. (1970) Hydrocephalus and its treatment. Proc. Roy. Soc. Med. 60:1263.

Hagard, S., and Carter, F. A. (1976) Preventing the birth of infants with Down's syndrome: a cost-benefit analysis. Brit. Med. J. 1:753.

Jensen, A. (1969) How much can we boost IQ and scholastic achievement? Harv. Educ. Rev. 39:1–123.

Kadushin, A. (1970) Adopting Older Children. New York: Columbia University Press.

Kirk, S. A. (1958) Early Education of the Mentally Retarded. Urbana, Ill.: University of Illinois Press.

Kucera, T. (1970) Down's syndrome and infectious hepatitis. Lancet 1:569.

Langdon Down, J. (1866) Observations on an ethnic classification of idiots. Clin. Lect. Rep. Lond. Hosp. 3:259.

Laurence, K. M., and Gregory, P. (1976) Prenatal diagnosis of chromosome disorders. In Human Malformations. Brit. Med. Bull. 32:9.

Lejeune, J., Gautier, M., and Turpin, R. (1959) Etudes des chromosomes somatiques de neuf enfants mongoliens. C. R. Acad. Sci. (Paris) 248:1721.

McAskie, M., and Clarke, A. M. (1976) Parent-offspring resemblances in intelligence: theories and evidence. Brit. J. Psychol. 67:243.

Milunsky, A., and Alpert, E. (1976) Routine testing for Alpha-fetoprotein in amniotic fluid. Lancet 1:1015.

Novak, M. A., and Harlow, H. F. (1975) Social recovery of monkeys isolated for the first year of life: I. Rehabilitation and therapy. Developm. Psychol. 11:453.

President's Committee on Mental Retardation (1972) Entering the Era of Human Ecology. Washington, D.C.: Department of Health, Education and Welfare Publication No. (OS) 72–77.

President's Committee on Mental Retardation (1976) PCMR Message No. 42 Amniocentesis safe. February 1976. Washington, D.C.: Dept. of Health, Education and Welfare.

Richardson, S. A. (1976) The relation of severe malnutrition in infancy to the intelligence of school children with differing life histories. Pediat. Res. 10:57.

Rutter, M., and Madge, N. (1976) Cycles of Disadvantage. London: Heinemann.

Sameroff, A. J., and Chandler, M. J. (1975) Reproductive risk and the continuum of caretaking casualty. In F. D. Horowitz, M. Hetherington, S. Scarr-Salapatek, and G. Siegel (eds.), Review of Child Development Research 4:187. Chicago: University of Chicago Press.

Skeels, H. M. (1966) Adult status of children with contrasting early life experiences: follow-up study. Monogr. Soc. Res. Child Develop. 31: no. 3.

Skodak, M., and Skeels, H. M. (1949) A final follow-up study of 100 adopted children. J. Genet. Psychol. 75:85.

Sloan, W., and Stevens, H. A. (1976) A.A.M.D.–A Century of Concern. Washington, D.C.: AAMD.

Stein, Z. A., Susser, M., and Guterman, A. G. (1973) Screening programme for prevention of Down's syndrome. Lancet 1:305.

Stein, Z. A., Susser, M. W., Saenger, G., and Marolla, F. (1975) A historical cohort of the Dutch famine, 1944–45. Proc. 3rd Congr. IASSMD 44, D.A.A. Primrose (Ed.). Larbert, Scotland: IASSMD.

Stoller, A., and Collmann, R. D. (1965) Virus aetiology for Down's syndrome (mongolism). Nature 208:903.

Tizard, J. (1964) Community Services for the Mentally Handicapped. London: Oxford University Press.

Tizard, J. (1976) Nutrition, growth and development. Psychol. Med. 6:1.

World Health Organization (1968) Organization of Services for the Mentally Retarded. WHO Techn. Rep. Ser. 392. Geneva: WHO.

Wynne Griffith, G. (1973) The "prevention" of Down's syndrome (mongolism). Health Trends 5:59.

CLOSING SESSION ADDRESS
SOME PRIORITIES FOR RESEARCH IN MENTAL RETARDATION

M. J. Begab

During the past five days we have been privileged to hear reports on a remarkable array of studies on significant aspects of mental retardation. Findings from most of the major research projects on malnutrition around the world have been presented, and we have learned much about communication, biochemical and genetic disorders, screening and assessment techniques, and strategies for intervention and remediation, to name but a few. I am sure you were as impressed as I by the meaningfulness of the research, by the innovativeness of the service and training programs, and by the pervasive concern of participants with moral and ethical considerations of science and service. As this Congress draws to a close, we can take solace in the thought that we are clearly progressing on all fronts.

Yet before we return to our respective duties, it seems proper to remind us of the many dimensions of the problem still in need of definitive answers. In sober perspective, much remains to be done.

THE PROBLEM OF DEFINITION

Ironically, one of the major areas of controversy and uncertainty is in the definition of mental retardation. Even though the AAMD definition (Grossman, 1973), including both intellectual and behavioral criteria, is widely accepted in many countries throughout the world, it is not broadly applied, either in clinical settings or epidemiological research. With rare exception, prevalence studies have used a single criterion measure of IQ, and, even here, have varied on the ceiling to be imposed for inclusion in the retarded range. A variation of as little as 5 IQ points, from 70 to 75, it should be noted, would increase the overall prevalence rate of retardation approximately twofold. This lack of standardization has made cross-cultural comparisons and efforts to identify relevant social and cultural variables associated with the phenomenon exceedingly tenuous.

The failure to include adaptive behavior measures routinely for diagnostic, placement, or research purposes is probably attributable to a number of factors.

This address was presented at the closing ceremonies of the Fourth Congress of the IASSMD, August 27, 1976.

Conceptually, some authorities feel that impairments in adaptive behavior are attributable to low intelligence, and that this causal relationship distinguishes the mentally retarded from other forms of social incompetence—the mentally ill and deliquent, for example. If this concept is valid—and it certainly is for the more severely disabled—then the presence of one presumes the existence of the other, and the single criterion of IQ should suffice. At the mild level of retardation, however, the correlation between IQ and adaptive behavior is considerably less than perfect, and some individuals below 70 IQ are socially adequate while others in the borderline range are not. This suggests that standard psychometric tests may not measure daily life problem-solving ability and that personality factors in addition to intelligence are crucial to social adjustment. Some flexibility in the definition seems vital. The recent elaboration of the AAMD definition, in its emphasis on clinical judgment to supplement standard test scores of intelligence and behavior, takes cognizance of this dilemma. Measures of learning potential rather than current functioning and better assessments of adaptive skills could greatly minimize this problem.

The adaptive behavior concept has led some investigators to a consideration of environmental demands and expectations as an essential part of the assessment process. In this view, mental retardation is a relative, dynamic condition, varying as a function of particular settings. Thus, the same individual may satisfy family expectations, fail the intellectual requirements of the school, and succeed in adulthood as a wage earner, spouse, and parent. This social systems perspective (Mercer, 1973) further contends that an individual is retarded only by virtue of being labeled as such, and that the social structure in an area determines who is so designated. By contrast, the clinical perspective regards intelligence, and presumably behavior, as independent of social settings. One deemphasizes individual traits, the other the social surround. This polarity of thought has generated both heat and light in the continued pursuit of defining mental retardation.

The conflict is not merely an academic debate over classification and terminology but an issue of great social and practical import to the retarded, their families, and relevant social institutions. Many educators and rehabilitation counselors feel that the elimination of the borderline category of intelligence, as proposed by WHO and AAMD, denies service to large numbers of persons with special needs. Others view the label of mental retardation as stigmatizing and harmful and to be avoided at all costs. Members of minority groups, in whose ranks mild retardation is heavily overrepresented by virtue of socioeconomic factors, see the process as discriminatory and as having genetic overtones. The social and political sensitivities thus aroused are creating strong pressures to abolish intelligence testing and, by indirection, to limit the designation of retarded to the biologically damaged about whom all would agree. The issue is extremely delicate. Should we err on the side of including in this category some individuals who may not be retarded or should we exclude from eligibility for service others who indeed function as retarded and need help but score above some arbitrary level? Professionals and regulatory and funding agencies need more definitive answers to such questions if the interests of the mildly retarded are to be best served.

LABELING, NORMALIZATION, AND MAINSTREAMING

The concern with the adverse effects of labeling has influenced not only the definition of mental retardation, but also concepts of education and normalization as well. The growing trend toward decertifying mildly retarded children for special education is reminiscent in some respects of our earlier experience with Head Start programs. As Professor Clarke aptly pointed out in his opening address to this Congress, this nation-wide program was based upon unsubstantiated faith in "the crucial and disproportionate influence of early experience upon later development." Evidence from both human and animal studies has cast doubt on the critical period theory and the value of compensatory education, at least as applied in that program in the early 1960s.

The rationale for mainstreaming stems in part from dissatisfaction with special education programs, but perhaps primarily from the allegedly detrimental effects of labeling. Comparisons of children from special versus regular classes offer no conclusive evidence regarding the relative merits of each setting (MacMillan, 1974). Efficacy studies for the most part show no significant differences between the groups on measures of academic achievement, although the special class children are better in social adjustment. In a study of Aberdeen children, special class graduates in their late teens and early adulthood had fewer incidents of antisocial or delinquent behavior and demonstrated more positive adaptation to work and in social relationships than similar IQ children from regular classes (Richardson, personal communication).

The equivocal nature of data bearing on the "mainstreaming" issue derives largely from methodological problems. Special classes differ from regular classes in significant ways: curricular materials, teacher/pupil ratios, teacher training, segregation, and labeling. Any one or combination of these factors may influence outcome.

Furthermore, the children in the two types of classroom settings are not the same. The majority of youngsters in special classes are identified and referred for placement by the teachers because of substantial behavioral and learning problems. Their subsequent labeling, through intelligence testing, only confirms what the teacher suspected from other behavioral indices. Given the fact that special class children pose more overt problems than their regular class, low IQ counterparts at the time of placement, yet are better adjusted at a later point in time, the notion that labeling is necessarily detrimental is difficult to sustain.

Even should labeling prove damaging to the child's concept of himself and to his intellectual and social performance, there are many unanswered questions about who does the labeling, how broadly the label is applied, and what prompts the label in the first place. There is good reason to believe from various studies that the retarded child labels himself and that his self-concept is the mirror image of how he is perceived by others (Gottlieb, in press). Perceptions of a retarded child by his peers or teachers are a function of his communication skills, behavior patterns, physical appearance, cognitive deficits, and personality disposition, rather than an externally imposed label. Placement in a regular class, therefore, where his deviance is more apparent, may prove a disservice to the "special" child.

We cannot say with scientific certitude at this time that the move to mainstream retarded children will be more harmful or beneficial. It is clear, however, that we need more empirical data than is currently available before committing ourselves on a national scale to the abandonment of the special education system.

Normalization and deinstitutionalization are other areas in which further research is urgently needed. Here, too, past investigations, plagued by methodological weaknesses, offer little direction to patterns of care and training. As in the studies mentioned earlier, sampling biases are a major problem. To compare institutional residents with others in different settings who differ on important physical and behavioral attributes and to make judgments on the import of extremely complex administrative and program components is a very dubious practice.

There is, of course, no debate on the need to remove retarded persons from the inhumane living conditions and stultifying atmosphere that characterizes some institutions. Not all such facilities are bad, however, nor are all community-based care programs good. Even a child's own family, if neglectful and abusive or merely rejecting, is less desirable than a child-oriented institution. This is why some children improve, rather than decline, in performance after placement.

Thus far, the scientific community, with a few notable exceptions (Tizard, Grad, Raynes), has shown little interest in the study of institutions from a social organization perspective. Neither have we looked in any systematic way at the concept of congregate group care and its impact on socialization and development. The often expressed criticism that institutions foster and prolong dependency because of their regimentation and constraints on behavior may have some validity. Limited opportunity for self-determination and decision-making can inhibit growth, but this outcome has also been noted in a recent study of board and care facilities (Edgerton, 1975). Even a child's own home is not exempt, for dependency is also a consequence of overprotectiveness by parents.

The current emphasis on community-based services is not a new development. However, despite the establishment of half-way houses, group care homes, and an increased use of foster family care, there has been no systematic effort to determine what factors within these various settings are most contributory to successful placement. In this area, as in the others mentioned earlier, philosophical dictates and grave concern with the quality of *existing* forms of care have precipitated massive programs to relocate retarded persons. We must be mindful, however, that social isolation is possible in the heart of town, and there is always the danger that the alternatives may prove little better than current practice. Previous studies of foster home care, for example, indicate that retarded children are the least successfully placed, being shifted frequently from home to home (Maas, 1959). Such experiences are damaging. We clearly need reliable data on which children can profit from family living, what personal qualities and knowledge foster parents should possess, and the community support systems required to supplement the parental role. Evaluation of recently initiated programs and experimentation with new models of care are essential if we are to avoid mistakes similar to those of the past in the institutional field.

COMMUNICATION DISORDERS

The move toward community-based services highlights, more than ever before, the need for more research into communication disorders. Of the various attributes shared by retarded persons of differing degrees of handicap, perhaps none are more common than deficiencies in language acquisition, speech articulation, and communication skills in general. It goes without saying that children who cannot communicate have no chance for independent survival in the community.

Deaf or hearing impaired children are susceptible to functional retardation. It is critical that they be identified early in life if the consequences of sensory deprivation are to be avoided. The use of operant techniques for audiometric testing of infants as young as one year of age and for previously untestable severely handicapped persons has proven effective and needs to be more widely applied and further refined.

More recent research efforts have demonstrated that the severely and profoundly retarded can acquire nonverbal communication skills (Carrier, 1976). Using plastic symbols in a matching to sample and sequencing paradigm, these individuals, formerly totally isolated from any meaningful interaction with their human environment, can now put words and simple sentences together. Even these rudimentary skills have significant value for adaptation. Belatedly, we are beginning to learn that in language and communication, as in other areas of behavior, we have underestimated the potential of the severely disabled. The problem is not always in the inability of the individual to learn, but in the practitioner's inability to teach.

Further insights into the mechanisms and processes underlying communication, both verbal and nonverbal, are indispensable to prevention and treatment of retardation and related disorders.

PREMATURITY, LOW BIRTH WEIGHT, AND MALNUTRITION

Among unresolved problems in biomedical causes of mental retardation, those deserving highest priority relate to prematurity (small-for-date babies), low birth weight (under 2500 g), and malnutrition. Moderate to severe handicaps are a common sequelae to shortened gestational age. Roughly two of three infants delivered at 28 weeks of age are handicapped; whereas only one in three at 32–34 weeks is affected. A similar gradient applies to birth weight. Eighty-five percent of children weighing 950 g or less are seriously damaged. Among those weighing 1350–1500 g, the incidence is 35% (Lubchenko, 1972). Clearly, these obstetrical problems must be overcome if these causes of retardation are to be prevented.

Low birth weight, like sociocultural retardation, resists simple solutions because it is not the result of a single etiological agent. Many factors are associated with the phenomenon: inadequate prenatal care, maternal diet, maternal diabetes, dysfunction in the initiation of labor, the age of the mother, her prepregnancy weight, smoking, race, the previous birth of prematures, the number of previous children, and teenaged unwed motherhood are some examples. Some of these, you will recognize, are confounded by low socioeconomic status.

Biomedical science and practice have made some meaningful advances with this problem. Infant mortality rates have steadily declined over the past 25 years in all or most developed countries. Infant morbidity, which relates to many of the same etiological agents of prenatal origin, has followed a similar pattern. In some instances, obstetric practice has enabled some infants to survive who otherwise would have perished, although the survivors are sometimes neurologically damaged.

At Stanford's Premature Infants Research Center, mechanical ventilation to keep the airways open in infants suffering from respiratory distress syndrome has saved over 85% of these babies without damaging effects on the lungs and eyes. Various assaults on the low birth weight phenomenon are encouraging. Nutritional supplementation of women during pregnancy is another example. In the Guatemala study reported at this Congress (Klein, 1976), caloric supplementation during pregnancy reduced the incidence of low birth weight in babies and dramatically decreased infant mortality. The continuity of improved nutrition during childhood resulted in better motor and manipulative skills. A controlled field trial experiment on a United States urban population found that a daily protein-calorie supplementation during pregnancy had a favorable effect on birth weight of infants born to women at high risk by virtue of their low prepregnant weight (under 110 pounds) and smoking (Susser, 1976). According to epidemiological data, the small mean differences in birth weight of 125 g achieved in most programs of supplementation account for about half of the variance in low birth weight and perinatal mortality between treated and untreated groups.

The data presented at this Congress on nutritional studies in both animals and humans highlight the important role of this factor in mental development, but at the same time demonstrate the complexity of the issues. There is more to the problem than feeding the hungry, although an effective international program would certainly have a meaningful impact. It seems, however, that *what* is eaten may be just as critical as *how much* is eaten. Thus, wheat, unfortified by protein, may have limited value for populations in underdeveloped countries deficient in this essential food property. Other nutritional deficiencies in pregnant women vary with income and race, suggesting that differences in food patterns and eating habits frequently have strong psychological and cultural roots and need to be addressed. Efforts to supplement migrant farm women in Colorado, for instance, did not fully succeed because such factors were not fully appreciated. It should be recognized, too, that even when the pregnant woman is neither malnourished nor undernourished, her fetus may, by virtue of dysfunctions in the transport of nutrients across the placenta, be in trouble. How often this occurs is uncertain, but it denotes another important area of needed inquiry.

Whereas low birth weight and prematurity are primarily biological in origin, the sequelae that follow this condition, except in cases of obvious neurological damage, have strong social determinants. Epidemiological data indicate that whatever the cause, children in the range of 1500–2500 g are more likely to function as retarded or demonstrate learning disabilities if they are members of the lower social class than if they are middle class (Douglas, 1956; Drillien, 1964). The role of other social forces also applies to *postnatal* malnutrition. In a study of Jamaican children who had suffered an acute episode of malnutrition requiring hospitalization, it was found that the largest contributor to the variance in IQ was the social background and mental stimulation of the child, and the smallest contributor was the severe malnutrition (Richardson, 1976). Such studies suggest that the consequences of malnutrition, before or after birth, cannot be studied in isolation from deprived social circumstances in which they generally occur. Furthermore, birth weight as a dependent variable, except for very small babies, may by itself have little predictive value for later development. In this mental retardation-related phenomenon, we have an excellent example of biosocial interactive processes requiring collaborative, multidisciplinary research for full understanding.

These are only a few of the areas in need of study to understand the causes of prematurity. We need more fundamental research in intrauterine contractions and the onset of labor and the forces that trigger this process prematurely. The physiology of the placenta and transport mechanisms are still incompletely understood, and the role of hormonal dysfunction, prenatal infection, and maternal diabetes are other important areas for investigation.

GENETIC DISORDERS

Genetic disorders, of which Down's syndrome is the prime example and most common occurrence, represent another priority area for future research. It has been estimated that one child in every 150 to 200 live births in the United States has a major chromosomal anomaly and a larger number have minor anomalies. Also, about one-third of children in pediatric wards are hospitalized for genetic and genetic-related disorders. The relationship of these anomalies to mental retardation is not completely understood.

Considering the extensive nature of research in genetics in general and Down's syndrome in particular, it may seem strange to designate it a priority area. We have, indeed, learned much about its chromosomal properties, incidence and prevalence, and physical and behavioral characteristics. Despite these efforts, we have not yet been able to document the cause of nondysjunction. We have many opinions, but few hard facts. Investigators in Australia have proposed that a hepatitis virus interacting with maternal age plays an etiological role (Stoller and Collmann, 1965). Others suggest that the egg cells in the mother, which are present at her birth, are increasingly susceptible to damage through exposure to physical and chemical agents. Still others hypothesize preovulation exposure to radiation, repeated abortions, and poor spacing of pregnancies as possible causes.

It could be argued that with antenatal diagnosis and therapeutic abortion we now have the technology to prevent Down's syndrome without having to know its causes. The value of this procedure, while considerable, should not be overestimated, however. Some of the barriers to the application of this technology were expressed in my remarks at the opening of this Congress. Amniocentesis, despite its clearly demonstrated safety, is nevertheless an invasive procedure. It is regarded as surgery and requires experience and skill to perform. Relatively few laboratories are set up to conduct, without error, the diagnostic assays required. Conceivably, in less skilled hands—a possibility in any significant extension of resources—safety and accuracy might be sacrificed. In today's malpractice-oriented societies, the reluctance of obstetricians to perform antenatal diagnostic procedures under less than highly compelling circumstances, such as a previously defective birth or a carrier for Tay-Sachs disease, is readily understood. Women share similar concerns about the procedure and there are the additional barriers posed by religious, moral, and social values. Cost, too, is a factor. These factors, singly or in combination, may explain why less than 5% of the women whose pregnancies are sufficiently suspect to warrant amniocentesis actually have it done.

It seems to me that research on genetic disorders, particularly of the nondysjunctive type, must proceed on many fronts. If we can isolate the cause or causes, preventive measures short of abortion may be developed. In this way, older women who earnestly desire to be mothers could do so with impunity and avoid the social and psychological trauma and guilt feelings that often accompany abortion. With the trend toward careers and delayed marriage for women, pregnancies after 40 years of age are likely to increase.

Since the etiology of Down's has escaped us thus far and may still be years away, alternative, noninvasive technologies for antenatal diagnosis should also be investigated. It is difficult to forecast how biochemical tests, fetoscopy, amniography, and other technologies can be applied to this objective, but progress in these areas has been rapid and promising.

SOCIOENVIRONMENTAL RETARDATION

In any list of priorities for research in mental retardation, the search for solutions to socioenvironmentally induced retardation must clearly rank very high. The disproportionate prevalence of this form of retardation merits this attention. But there are many other compelling reasons as well, because these individuals, who are concentrated exclusively in the most disadvantaged segments of the population, exhibit many of the other social ailments associated with poverty. The role of low intelligence in crime, delinquency, emotional disorders, drug addiction, alcoholism, etc. is still unclear and may be indirect, but it is meaningful nevertheless. Logic would suggest that individuals subject to stress are vulnerable to these forms of behavior, and few would argue that the failure, frustration, and feelings of inferiority the retarded experience are sources of stress. The social costs attendant upon these problems are burdens communities are obliged to deal with.

Fortunately, the mildly retarded also have the best potential for adult adjustment, and many succeed even without special help. Better understanding of their cognitive processes, improved methods for assessing their learning potential, and the development of technologies for training academic, social, and work skills could markedly heighten their productivity. Some gains have already been made in these areas, but more work is clearly needed (Feuerstein, 1976).

The etiological basis for mild retardation is still obscure. Most authorities, however, believe that genetics and socioenvironmental forces are the primary agents, and that their interaction determines intellectual function. Whatever the contribution of each to the human equation, there is ample evidence that phenotypic expression of an individual's genotype can be influenced by environmental factors. The degree of plasticity of intelligence is still debatable, but experiments in different parts of the world support the view that the magnitude of potential change is sufficient to move significant numbers of children outside of the retarded range of intellectual performance. This is even more true for adaptive behavior, which may be more amenable to change than intelligence. Head Start, for example, may have failed to increase the intelligence of children, but it did affect socialization and skills in interpersonal relationships. Perhaps, in our preoccupation with IQ scores, we have overlooked an equally, if not more, important facet underlying adult social behavior.

Over the years, a number of intervention-type studies—some dating back nearly 40 years—have demonstrated the impact of changing environments on intellectual performance (Skeels, 1939; 1966). These studies indicated that maternal nurture and a favorable family and social environment over the total period of childhood could reverse mental retardation.

More recently, intervention strategies have taken on a predominantly child-focused flavor. Most of these ventures accelerated mental growth initially but could not sustain these gains as the child left the enriched atmosphere of the preschool setting for the stultifying regimen of the ghetto schoolroom and unaltered family environment. These short-term successes, but long-range failures, were interpreted by geneticists as support for their position. Others felt the fault lay in the form of intervention starting too late in life, stopping too soon, and lacking educational focus.

Most of the criticisms were incorporated in the now well-known Milwaukee intervention project (Garber, 1975). In addition, the mothers of the children were also helped through vocational training and placement and given guidance in homemaking and child-rearing. The experimental and control groups of children have maintained a differential of about 30 IQ points throughout the course of study. Both groups have declined in measured intelligence since entering regular school, although the experimental group is still within the average range. The control group is approaching retarded performance.

Other intervention strategies have adopted family-focused tactics and techniques. Goals have varied. Some are directed toward improving child care and homemaking skills (Parsons, 1960). Others try to involve the parents as teachers to stimulate the language and mental development of their children (Levenstein, 1975). These, and many other home intervention projects, view the mother as the primary socializing agent and are directed toward helping her discharge these responsibilities more effectively. Here, too, successes have been noted, but the targets of such intervention for the most part have been poor, but generally motivated families.

At this point in time, our knowledge of effective modes of intervention is rather crude. Child-focused strategies that start from the cradle and continue well into the school years are very costly, and their impact, while promising, needs further verification. The notion that we must intervene in infancy—the critical period theory—is not fully substantiated, and is in fact challenged by the success achieved with adolescents, as is reported in this Congress (Feuerstein, 1976). This issue warrants further investigation.

Intervention in the home has both theoretical and practical appeal. If families are the source of deprivation, changes in parent-child interactions are essential to provide continuity of reinforcement between the preschool and home. The practical appeal is in its economy. Home visitation and group meetings are far less costly than preschool programs. Unfortunately, the mothers who need help have limited education and low intelligence, may lack motivation for change, and distrust "intruders." We still have to learn how to reach these families, sustain their cooperation over time, and improve their parenting and teaching skills. Such knowledge would have implications for a wide range of social problems.

CONCLUSION

In this outline of priority areas for research, I have been guided by my personal perceptions of urgent needs of the field, by my selective biases as a social scientist, and by the potential for early pay-off in prevention and improved services. There is no intent to downplay areas of research not mentioned here, nor to deny the continuing and indispensable contributions of fundamental research in the biomedical and behavioral sciences.

Yet, if we are to achieve the goals of prevention and treatment, we must marshal our scientific talents and resources in a concerted attack on these major dimensions of the problem.

REFERENCES

Carrier, J. (1976) Design and application of a data system for development of a set of language programs. Presented at Lake Wilderness, Washington Conference, June, 1976. *In* E. Sackett (ed.), Observing Behavior, University Park Press, Baltimore. In press.

Douglas, J. W. B. (1956) Mental ability and school achievement of premature children at eight years of age. Brit. Med. J. 1:1210.

Drillien, C. M. (1964). The Growth and Development of the Prematurely Born Infant. Baltimore: The Williams & Wilkins Company.

Edgerton, R. (1975) Issues relating to the quality of life in mentally retarded persons. *In* The Mentally Retarded and Society: A Social Science Perspective (Eds. Begab, M. J., and Richardson, S. A.) Baltimore: University Park Press.

Feuerstein, R. (1976) Mediated learning experience: A theoretical basis for cognitive modifiability during adolescence. Proc. 4th Congr. IASSMD, Vol. 2. In press.

Garber, H. L. (1975) Intervention in infancy: A developmental approach. *In* The Mentally Retarded and Society: A Social Science Perspective (Eds. Begab, M. J., and Richardson, S. A.) Baltimore: University Park Press.

Gottlieb, J. (1976) Observational studies of social adaptation: An educatonal perspective. Presented at Lake Wilderness, Washington Conference, June, 1976. *In* E. Sackett (ed.), Observing Behavior. University Park Press, Baltimore. In press.

Grossman, H. J. (Ed.) (1973) Manual on Terminology and Classification in Mental Retardation. Spec. Publ. No. 2. Washington, D.C.: AAMD.

Klein, R. E., Irwin, M., Engle, P. L., Townsend, J., Lechtig, A., Martorell, R., and Delgado, H. (1976) Malnutrition, child health and behavioral development: Data from an intervention study. Proc. 4th Congr. IASSMD, Vol. 3. In press.

Levenstein, P. (1975) Message from home: Findings from a program for nonretarded, low income preschoolers. *In* The Mentally Retarded and Society: A Social Science Perspective (Eds. Begab, M. J., and Richardson, S. A.) Baltimore: University Park Press.

Lubchenko, L. O., Delivaria-Papadopolous, M., and Searls, D. (1972) Long-term follow up of premature infants, II. J. Pediat. 80:509.

Maas, H. S., and Engler, R. (1959) Children in Need of Parents. New York, N.Y.: Columbia University Press.

MacMillan, D. L., Jones, R. L., and Aloia, G. F. (1974) The mentally retarded label: A theoretical analysis and review of research. Amer. J. Ment. Defic. 79:241.

Mercer, J. R. (1973) Labeling the Mentally Retarded. Berkeley, California: University of California Press.

Parsons, M. H. (1960) A home economist on services to families with mental retardation. Children, September–October.

Richardson, S. A. (1976) Personal communication.

Richardson, S. A. (1976) The relation of severe malnutrition in infancy to the intelligence of school children with differing life histories. Pediat. Res. 10:57.

Skeels, H. M., and Dye, H. B. (1939) A study of the effects of differential stimulation on mentally retarded children. Proc. AAMD 44:114.

Skeels, H. M. (1966) Adult status of children from contrasting early life experiences. Monogr. Soc. Res. Child Dev. 31: No. 105.

Stoller, A., and Collmann, R. D. (1965) incidence of infective hepatitis followed by Down's syndrome nine months later. Lancet 2:1221.

Susser, M., Stein, Z. A., and Rush, D. (1976) Prenatal nutrition and subsequent development. Proc. 4th Congr. IASSMD, Vol. 3. In press.

RESEARCH
AND
POLICY

RESEARCH TO PRACTICE IN MENTAL RETARDATION
Care and Intervention, Volume I
Edited by Peter Mittler
Copyright 1977 I.A.S.S.M.D.

INTERNATIONAL MODELS FOR RESEARCH UTILIZATION
National Institutes on Mental Retardation

G. A. Roeher
*National Institute on Mental Retardation, York University
Campus,Toronto, Canada*

BACKGROUND

Mental retardation ranks among the world's most complex and challenging problems. In spite of recent encouraging service and research program developments, the basic problem remains, and compared to general progress in human services, the status of those affected has improved only minimally. What accounts for the limited *real* progress? One reason is the underutilization of existing knowledge. This paper discusses an organizational model designed to accelerate efforts toward bridging the gap between research and practice.

In recent decades change-agent or catalytic vehicles have been created to realize seemingly unattainable goals, e.g., the Manhattan Project, which developed the atomic bomb, and the National Aeronautics and Space Administration (NASA), created for the Apollo project to land man on the moon—entities capable of programming infinite scientific knowledge and complex engineering components into a coordinated single thrust.

Similar systemic organizational methodology can be applied to the social behavioral field (a necessity for major progress in the field of mental retardation). The conditions for success include: a) A clear objective of the goal and the motivation and determination to do what is required for success. b) An appreciation of the potential contribution of the basic and applied sciences and an

This paper is a condensation of the one presented to the Fourth International Congress of the International Association for the Scientific Study of Mental Deficiency, Washington, D.C., August 25, 1976, and incorporates the central statements made by two other speakers—Dr. M.J. Thorburn of Jamaica, and Donald Crawford of Australia.

understanding of the diverse elements that need to be coordinated and focussed. c) A (catalytic) vehicle capable of mobilizing and integrating the technical resources with the sociopolitical (decision-making) forces. An attempt to develop such a vehicle has been made in Canada and has since received attention in other countries.

In Canada, as elsewhere, the early efforts of parents and friends of mentally retarded persons developed into a strong nation-wide citizen-action movement known as the Canadian Association for the Mentally Retarded (CAMR). It consists of over 370 local community service agencies, ten provincial federations, and one national federation. Anticipating the problem, the CAMR decided, in 1963, to develop a national entity modelled on the aforementioned concepts. This took the form of a National Institute on Mental Retardation (NIMR).

BASIC ASSUMPTIONS

The rationale for the development of an Institute, in addition to the above, was quite specific, namely: a) The practitioner and scientist lacked adequate means for effective communication with each other—a tangible entity was necessary that could represent and merge both. b) That changes in attitude toward research, training, and service program activities, and toward retarded people themselves, continue only as long as there are dynamic, well-informed and organized citizen-action groups. c) The flexible characteristics of dynamic radical volunteer movements tend to give way to the more typical rigidity and defensiveness associated with any body that develops vested interests once initial goals have been achieved. (The intent was that an Institute would provide the necessary leadership and technical-professional guidance to counter such developments. d) It was believed that in order for a citizen movement to remain an effective leader and catalyst for change, it needed to develop a technical-professional sophistication of its own in parallel with governments, institutions of higher learning, professional groups, and other agencies.

STRUCTURE

The NIMR is, therefore, designed as a problem-solving entity to provide a balance between stimulating research and translating existing knowledge into action programs. Translating these requirements into a workable action plan required an innovative organizational approach whereby the technical or non-technical interests could and would need to share decision making, and be mutually participating yet provide reasonable degrees of freedom for program staff.

Structurally, the NIMR consists of a building located on York University campus, but owned and operated by the CAMR, and serves as the nation's technical and professional resource for governments, institutions of learning, and other agencies serving the disadvantaged. It contains extensive training and research facilities. It also accommodates the national office of the CAMR, thus blending the technical with the citizen-action operations.

Programatically, the underlying criteria are that problems undertaken be national in scope, long-range, and involve collaboration, where possible, with other existing organizations and institutions throughout the country. Since there is no precedent for this sort of operation and since it is, itself, an experimental-demonstration project, the Institute tends to reflect a blend of both traditional and innovative attitudes and approaches.

PROGRESS IN PROGRAM ACTIVITY

Though the concept was developed in 1963, the Institute opened formally in 1970. It is still very much in the developmental phase, yet it has achieved some significant goals.

The central national information service (general and technical) is one of the most complete and effective in the world (in fact, it serves as an international reference for the International League of Societies for the Mentally Handicapped). The Institute has also launched study-action programs in such areas as manpower and training, research and evaluation, program development, legislation, consumer organization and revitalization, and international developments.

PROGRESS AS A CHANGE-AGENT

Activities undertaken to date illustrate that an entity of this kind can be a major catalyst for influencing and accelerating major change on a national scale and realizing greater utilization of existing resources. One such example is a project undertaken, known as "The Plan for the 70s." In 1970, in response to a request from the citizen body (the CAMR) for a long-range program development plan that could narrow the knowledge-practice gap, the NIMR recommended the implementation of a nation-wide Series of Experimental Comprehensive Community Services projects (known as ComServ), designed to demonstrate that total comprehensiveness and continuity can be achieved in nonsegregated community service systems—and thus eliminate the need for institutions.

Realization of such a series requires a monumental, complex plan of action, involving extensive research into modern organizational systems and the development of: plans and guidelines; large numbers of specially trained personnel (staff and volunteers); evaluation systems; new governance models; strategies to change attitudes towards newer program philosophies; innovative service program delivery approaches; and methods to overcome resistance to change from workers in the field, governments, the public and the voluntary movement itself.

In just over six years of formal operation, the CAMR, by blending its citizen-action resources with those of the technical Institute, has created a quiet revolution in Canada that is now changing the attitudinal and program climate from the approaches developed in past decades, to modern ones stressing normalization, integration with generic programs, and truly comprehensive community services delivery systems. In order to create this nation-wide change, the Institute, at the instruction of the CAMR, is guiding the above-mentioned series of experimental and demonstration projects. Each project strives to develop an ideal test model under specified conditions. The extent to which this ideal can be achieved will be demonstrated in the latter phases of each of the projects. Each experimental project is phased on a seven-year time frame.

The demonstration in turn serves to create "ripple" or a multiplying effect on the country as a whole. The Plan for the 70s is intended to stimulate implementation of comprehensive community services, along modern concepts, in all communities within the country. The series is based on rigid experimental methodology, and an hypothesis that the problem of institutionalization, or segregation of services, will only be eliminated when better alternatives have been developed and demonstrated.

It is essential to stress that the success of this series, or any similar plan, requires the support and participation in a highly coordinated fashion of provincial and federal governments, the private sector (special and generic agencies), industry, and institutions of learning. Such vast resources could not be mobilized and coordinated without a technical entity sophisticated in organizational systems knowledge and technique and the support and involvement of an effective citizen-action movement.

The Institute is viewed by the volunteers (CAMR) as having a special status, unlike a conventional national office, which is looked upon as an operation designed to respond to membership needs. It acquires a significant degree of influence and strength of its own by virtue of its competence and performance record. It also gains potential for effectiveness by being able to relate directly to governments and other agencies, who more readily accept such advice from a technical institute than from a national office of a citizen-action movement. It blends the strength of the two.

Other activities undertaken include the development of nation-wide manpower standards and criteria for curriculum development, recognition and certification of workers, career development opportunities, and integrated training and preparation schemes. Here the Institute serves as the technical entity through which national and provincial manpower councils (public and voluntary) can function and achieve consensus towards nation-wide objectives.

The Institute also experiments with and conducts short-term training to update and upgrade training in the field, or to introduce new topic areas.

PROBLEMS, RISKS, AND POTENTIAL

New and unconventional approaches to problem solving generally encounter mixed reactions, and may be viewed as idealistic, threatening, or attempts at control. The reaction to the Institute concept was no exception. Such reactions need to be anticipated and should be viewed as positive, natural, and desirable because they serve to maintain a balance between idealism, theory, and reality. Provided the initial momentum and support is sufficient to launch an entity of this kind through its developmental phase, long-range support can be expected to grow with the increasing recognition that it is an effective medium through which *all* interested parties in the field are able to communicate cooperatively, express leadership, and implement large-scale, complex and long-term developments—and that each benefits from such efforts. The limited, but significant, interest in research in the early stages of the MR citizen movement (with a resultant considerable investment in public and private funds) waned, in part because of the focus on service program development, but also because of a growing disenchantment with the technical-professional effort. In Canada this interest is being revitalized because the citizen body perceives itself as an integral part of the technical-professional field via its sponsorship of the Institute. The CAMR already anticipates that its "Plan for the 80s" will emphasize prevention and research—recognizing that if the current experimental and demonstration ComServ project series achieve their goals, the basic service goal will have been realized and the next major thrust, therefore, is reduction of the problem itself. The Institute is expected to then play an even greater role in bridging the knowledge-practice gulf.

FRENCH LANGUAGE INSTITUTE

In 1971 the CAMR established a similar French language institute located at the University of Quebec in Montreal, Institut National Canadien-Francais pour la Deficience Mentale (INCF). Like the NIMR, it is sponsored and directed by the CAMR and integrated with the NIMR.

INTERNATIONAL DEVELOPMENTS

In recent years other countries have studied this model. The National Association for Retarded Citizens (U.S.A.) has launched the NARC Research and Demonstration Institute, with objectives similar to those of the Canadian model.

Many countries of the world have not enjoyed the extensive support and interest generated in some of the economically wealthier nations. Yet they, too, have a need for a catalytic vehicle to cope with the situation. The Caribbean Association on Mental Retardation (a federation of societies from some 20 Caribbean nations) launched the Caribbean Institute on Mental Retardation and Developmental Disabilities, again with similar objectives but also with some problems peculiar to that region. It has already demonstrated superior ability in the mobilization and channeling of national and international resources into the region.

The Australian Association for Mental Retardation is working in concert with the Australian Group for the Scientific Study on Mental Deficiency to launch an Australian Institute on Mental Retardation. Its success depends on a realization of basic financial support. The New Zealand Society for the Intellectually Handicapped also has announced plans to launch an institute.

In February, 1976, the program working group of the Pan American Congress on Mental Retardation recommended that similar models be established for groups of neighboring countries in South America.

PREDICTION

Since the evidence to date suggests that technical institute operations under the direction of citizen movements accelerate and reinforce the voluntary organization itself, this could become a significant pattern in the coming decade. If so, it would create the potential to realize a network of national and regional (internation) institutes for world-wide interchange of technical and service data, techniques, and personnel—a critically important need in overcoming the barriers to the application of knowledge.

RESEARCH TO PRACTICE IN MENTAL RETARDATION
Care and Intervention, Volume I
Edited by Peter Mittler
Copyright 1977   I.A.S.S.M.D.

THE PRESIDENT'S COMMITTEE ON MENTAL RETARDATION LOOKS AHEAD TWENTY-FIVE YEARS

F. J. Krause
President's Committee on Mental Retardation,
Washington, D.C. 20201,
United States

SUMMARY OF A MAJOR SESSION

This session presented highlights of a report to the President of the United States by the President's Committee on Mental Retardation (PCMR), titled *Mental Retardation: Century of Decision.* The author is executive director of the Committee, and the panelists Henry V. Cobb, Cecil B. Jacobson, Beth Stephens, and Phillip U. Martinez and Mrs. Margaret Ulle are members.

The report to the President is the core of a multi-volume series on the past, present, and future of mental retardation. It is the result of 18 months of concentrated effort by Committee members, consultants, staff, and a broad cross-section of experts in the mental retardation profession and other fields. Panelist Cobb was coordinator and senior writer.

Mental Retardation: The Known and the Unknown was the first to be published in the series. It presents current knowledge and gaps in knowledge of the many aspects of the subject.

The core volume discussed in this session examines the issues in mental retardation and sets national guidelines for the next quarter century, stating them in the form of goals, objectives, and recommendations.

A companion publication in preparation is an historical perspective of the mental retardation field and a related assessment of the current situation, with a review of shifting trends in the treatment of retarded persons.

Rounding out the series is a report on trends in state services. An update of an earlier PCMR report on Federal programs is also being considered.

The entire series is designed to be not an end in itself, but a starting point to stimulate discussion and action that will lead toward a better life for those who are retarded, and to lower the risk of retardation for those yet unborn.

The goals and recommendations in the main volume relate to all levels of the public and private sector. The report will be of significance to federal, state, and local governments; to program planners and providers of services; legislators; educators; the medical and legal professions; news media; and relevant professional and volunteer organizations.

Central throughout the series are the major goals of the President's Committee on Mental Retardation:

1. to reduce the occurrence of disability from mental retardation;
2. to promote humane services that will enable retarded persons to achieve their potential in the most normal, least restrictive setting possible;
3. to help retarded persons achieve the rights of full citizenship and public acceptance.

The Committee worked with a group of "futurists" in making an educated estimate of what the future holds for society, and the mentally retarded population in particular. In a series of brainstorming sessions and resultant papers, the futurists tackled questions such as the social and economic future of society as a whole, and how a changed economy and social climate will affect retarded persons. They discerned trends—some of them conflicting—in labor, leisure time, attitudes, individual rights versus the rights of society, and so on. In general, their outlook was optimistic.

While there were no firm conclusions on the shape of things to come, provocative questions were explored: Will a future society place more emphasis on the values of achievement, or on the acceptance of each human being? How will retarded people be affected by changes in the "work ethic"? Food production? Housing? Transportation? Technology?

The PCMR regional forums, conducted over the past several years across the country, were a major source of information on current strengths and weaknesses in the mental retardation field. From them came the voices of those on the front lines in the battle against mental retardation.

Equally potent, but with a different perspective, were the ideas that the Committee sought from leaders of national organizations active in mental retardation.

The *Century of Decision* series attempts to distill the information gleaned from every quarter. The resultant goals, objectives, and recommendations represent the concerted thinking of several thousands of people—including retarded persons themselves. It is the Committee's hope that these proposals will act as a call to action and will form the basis of policy for the coming decades.

The major subjects covered in the report that have stated goals are: Full Citizenship and Legal Rights; Prevention: The Right to Be Well Born (biomedical); Prevention: The Right to a Good Start in Life (environmental); Humane Service Systems; Mental Retardation as an International Problem; The Role of Government; and Public Attitudes.

The goal for Full Citizenship and Legal Rights is: The attainment of full citizenship status, in law and in fact, for all mentally retarded individuals in the United States, exercised to the fullest degree possible under the conditions of disability.

Objective[1] I of that goal is: The assurance of maximum freedom to exercise legal and constitutional rights and responsibilities.

Objective II calls for the assurance of maximum access to a free and open community.

Among the numerous recommendations[1] are a review and revision of all states statutes relating to mentally retarded and other handicapped persons; prevention and corrective programs for retarded offenders; and state laws and local ordinances to protect the rights of handicapped persons to appropriate housing, free of discriminatory zoning regulations, and inappropriate licensing standards and codes.

The goal for Prevention: The Right to Be Well Born is: Reduction of the incidence of mental retardation from biomedical causes by no less than 50% by the year 2000.

The four objectives dealing with biomedical prevention are: 1) Full commitment of the people of the United States to the prevention of mental retardation that develops in the prenatal period; 2) A health delivery system that assures equal access to quality care at reasonable cost; 3) Continued advancement of knowledge through research; and 4) A total campaign of public education on the known means of preventing mental retardation.

Recommendations call in part for family planning, genetic diagnostic and counseling services for high-risk parents, comprehensive maternal and child health care; early screening and immunization, and continued and improved research in reproductive biology, nutrition, and the effects of toxic agents.

The goal for Prevention: The Right to a Good Start in Life is: To reduce the incidence and prevalence of mental retardation associated with social disadvantage to the lowest level possible by the end of this century.

Objectives include: 1) Elimination of prejudice and discrimination based on race, ethnic membership or social class; 2) Improvement of environment and living experience through attacking conditions that impede or distort full development among poor and minority groups; 3) Equal educational opportunity for all; 4) Adequate controls on allocation and use of public funds in order to safeguard the interests of disadvantaged populations.

Included in the recommendations are: A national program to assist low-income parents in the early developmental training of their children; improvement

---

[1] Excerpted and paraphrased in some cases.

of the total home and community environment for minority, poor, and otherwise deprived people; better access to child development centers; culturally sensitive assessment rather than inappropriate standardized tests for placement of children in special classes; research and development on individualized education for all children; and retraining of teachers and school personnel to sensitize them to the needs of disadvantaged children.

The goal for Humane Service Systems is: Adequate and humane service systems for all retarded persons in need of them.

Under this heading there are six objectives: 1) A comprehensive array of service resources to meet the needs of retarded persons in all sections of the U.S.; 2) Free choice and decisions by every retarded person or his personal representative regarding residence, services and choice of representative: 3) A personal representative for every retarded person who wishes or needs one; 4) Maximum opportunity for every retarded person to live in a local community setting of his choice; 5) Maintenance by all serving agencies of standards of quality and accountability acceptable to the community and to the retarded person served; and 6) Adequate research maintenance and utilization and manpower development to implement the most effective service delivery possible.

Among the recommendations are: Federal action in collaboration with states to guarantee essential developmental, supportive, and protective services; coordinated, simplified, and unified procedures to ease the way for applying for services and to determine eligibility; recognition by Federal and State agencies of the right of a retarded person to choose services needed; statutory and financial support for recruitment and training of service brokers for retarded clients; appropriate and adequate community services to help retarded persons remain in homes of their choice.

The goal for Mental Retardation as an International Problem is: The attainment of international cooperation to prevent and ameliorate mental retardation.

Objectives are: 1) Full participation of U.S. governmental and nongovernmental agencies and organizations in international bodies concerned with mental retardation; 2) International assistance programs to utilize any country's resources in the mental retardation field; and 3) International information exchange on all aspects of mental retardation, as a United States policy.

Recommendations encompass: Use of United Nation agencies, AID, Partners of the America's PREP program, and other similar agencies as channels for international exchange; attendance at relevant international scientific meetings; support for exchange of visiting groups to this and other countries.

The goal for Public Attitudes is: To achieve a firm and deep public acceptance of mentally retarded persons as members-in-common of the social community and as citizens in their own right.

Objectives that follow the goal are: 1) Emphasis on the individual worth of every human being, and recognition of the right to be different; 2) Confidence in solution of economic and energy problems that will allow a shift toward human values; and 3) Use of new communications techniques to promote greater understanding of handicapped persons as individuals, and to spread the knowledge of prevention of handicapping conditions.

Among the many recommendations are: education of teachers and students to include a deeper awareness of the feelings of all children who are in any manner handicapped; expansion of education for parenthood; encouragement of voluntary action; and a continuing public education program, including a built-in community relations component in every relevant agency.

The goal for The Role of Government is: Equitable, coordinated, efficient, and effective use of public resources in mental retardation programs.

Objectives include: 1) Establishment of planning systems for mental retardation on federal, state, and local levels; 2) Development of means within each agency to execute such plans; and 3) Federal and State accountability for effective services to mentally retarded consumers.

The recommendations include: An advocate for retarded clients in each major relevant department; a case-finding and access program to find and guide retarded persons to services to which they are entitled; and periodic monitoring of program achievements in terms of client improvement.

The concluding chapter of the report deals with costs and results. It points out that the major portion of America's retarded people are mildly or moderately retarded. With support and encouragement they can become producers rather than users of community resources.

Public and private money invested in developmental programs for these mildly and moderately handicapped people can produce returns both in economic and human terms.

Returns on investment in prevention yield even higher dividends. *For every dollar spent on preventive health care, public education, and research, $100 can be saved.*

The estimated 300,000 severely and profoundly retarded persons require total care at an annual average cost approaching $18,000 each.

"If by the year 2000, prevention could cut their number in half," according to the report, "the annual savings would be $2.7 billion." The savings in emotional distress, family disruption and quality of life would be incalculable.

The presenters urged that political, professional, and public attention be focused on mental retardation—as a problem that *can* and *will* be solved. They said that while all the goals in this major PCMR report may not be reached by the year 2000, in the next 25 years we can make dramatic progress.

SOME RECENT PCMR PUBLICATIONS

Available (Free) from PCMR, Single Copies Only

Mental Retardation and the Law A quarterly compilation of legal actions affecting the rights of retarded persons. Reports new cases and status of actions previously brought. DHEW Publication No. (OHD) 76-21012.

MR 74: A Friend in Washington Eighth Annual Report of PCMR, reviewing one year in the life of the Committee, as it works to prevent and ameliorate mental retardation. DHEW Publication No. (OHD) 75-21010.

Naive Offender, The   Findings of a Conference on dealing with retarded persons who get into difficulties with the law.

Available from U.S. Government Printing Office, Washington, D.C. 20402 (Remittances to be made payable to: *Superintendent of Documents*)

Changing Patterns in Residential Services (1976)   Report on residential facilities for mentally retarded persons. Originally published in 1969, it includes some new and some revised chapters by 14 authors discussing models in the U.S. and abroad, stressing the normalization principle.

Mental Retardation: Century of Decision (1976)   A report to the President making recommendations for the next 25 years on prevention, humane services, and full citizenship for retarded persons. 156 pp. Price: $3.15—Stock No. 040-000-00343-6.

Mental Retardation: Past and Present (1976)   Reviews the historical shifts in our treatment of retarded persons, and assesses where we stand today.

Mental Retardation: The Known and the Unknown (1976)   This publication compiles for the first time existing statistical and factual information about the extent, the causes, and the treatment program for mentally retarded citizens. Price: $2.45—Stock No. 017-090-00021-6.

Mental Retardation: Trends in State Services (1976)   Identifies trends in State and local services for mentally retarded persons, and the impact of Federal assistance. Based on a telephone survey. Price: $1.20—Stock No. 040-000-00345-2.

New Environments for Retarded People (1975)   An album of facility designs from many countries. Price $1.15—Stock No. PR 36.8:M52/EN8.

People Live in Houses (1975)   Describes representative group homes, foster homes, and other types of residential settings for children and adults. Price $1.70—Stock No. PR 36.8:M52/H81.

Residential Services for the Mentally Retarded: An Action Policy Proposal (1970)   A proposed policy on residential services for public and professional review: Promotes improvement in standards and development of a national policy on living conditions in public and private residential facilities for mentally retarded persons. Price 75¢—Stock No. PR 36.8: M52/R31/3.

Screening and Assessment of Young Children at Developmental Risk (1973)   Price: $2.65—Stock No. PR 36.8:M52/SCR 2/2.

What Are We Waiting For? (1975)   Report of a conference on early intervention with high-risk infants and young children, focusing on the needs for mother/child/professional interaction. Price: 80¢—Stock No. 040-000-00336-3.

ATTITUDES

RESEARCH TO PRACTICE IN MENTAL RETARDATION
Care and Intervention, Volume I
Edited by Peter Mittler
Copyright 1977   I.A.S.S.M.D.

TOWARD INTERNATIONAL COMPARATIVE STUDY OF SOCIETAL CONCERN FOR MENTALLY HANDICAPPED PERSONS

L. Lippman
New York University Medical Center,
550 First Avenue, New York, N. Y. 10016, United States

In my presentation to the Third Congress of the IASSMD, "What the United States Can Learn from Europe" (Lippman, 1975), I summarized my observations, made during two earlier visits to several European countries, on the relationships between attitudes of "the public" and patterns of service programs for mentally retarded persons. I suggested that some of us in the United States had learned a good deal, but that we had only begun to apply the insights in our treatment of retarded persons in our own country.

My original goal was to discover whether or not there are indeed differences in the modes of treatment between the United States and some other cultures; if there are, what are the underlying forces that bring them about; and is it possible to modify attitudes (or other factors) in the United States in order to evoke more appropriate treatment of retarded persons in our society.

When I tried to put my conclusions to practical use, I discovered that even though many other persons, from various perspectives, had reached the same conclusions that I had regarding the superiority of programs in Sweden, Denmark, and elsewhere, social scientists wanted harder evidence than my impressionistic observations. What was needed, they suggested, was objective information amenable to quantification. So I have, in the past two years, developed a measuring instrument that should lead to a way of scoring that is verifiable and reliable. I call it a *Set of Indicators of Societal Concern for Mentally Retarded Persons.*

The objective was to develop a series of items on which factual information could be obtained, which could be tabulated, and which would lead to a series of scores. The scores, then, would allow comparison of one society with another,

17

and also the observation of trends over time. In order to be meaningful, however, the items must measure, in some relevant way, aspects of a society's concern for its mentally retarded members. This was the task to which I addressed myself, and of which I have now completed the first phase.

To begin with, I defined the unit of measurement as the individual state within the United States. (Ultimately, I plan to modify the set of indicators to obtain national scores, and then to utilize the results for cross-national comparisons, but I have not yet reached that stage of development of the instrument.) I then developed, on the basis of my own experience, reading, and observations, a series of major subject areas under which I expected the significant elements for measurement would fall. I interviewed a number of national and international leaders in the field, and I solicited formal statements of goals from three major national organizations in the field: the American Association on Mental Deficiency, the National Association for Retarded Citizens, and the President's Committee on Mental Retardation. From the interviews and the organizational statements I obtained additional perspectives that enriched, but did not substantially change, the preliminary conceptualization I had developed.

The next step was to formulate a questionnaire, by means of which I proposed to validate the concept. In its final form, it consisted of 153 items, under nine subject-area headings. I then sent the questionnaire to some 330 persons, asking each one to indicate his or her judgment as to whether each item was Highly Important, Important, Not Important, or Undesirable. I also invited suggestions for additional items, or any other comment, under each subject and also at the end. The questionnaire was sent to professional workers in the field of mental retardation; to parents of retarded persons and other actively interested citizens; to official spokespersons for the citizen advocacy movement; and to public officials responsible, in the 50 states, for planning, implementing, and coordinating programs of service to mentally retarded individuals. (I drew the names and addresses from three sources: the membership of the American Association on Mental Deficiency; state presidents, state executives, and national board members of the National Association for Retarded Citizens; and the roster of the National Association of Coordinators of State Programs for the Mentally Retarded.)

There were 212 usable replies. Allowing for deaths and otherwise undeliverable mail, this represented better than a 70 percent response rate. To interpret the responses, I required that more than half of those responding to an item should call it Highly Important for it to be included among the items validated. Most of my own preliminary judgments were indeed supported by the pattern of responses (although I must admit there were a few surprises). The resulting instrument (the *Set of Indicators* that was my objective for this project) consists of 105 items under eight subject-area headings: *Living Arrangements, Economic Security, Health Services, Education, Social Services, Work, Legal Rights and Liberties,* and *Government Services and Funding.*

Let me pause to note that there have of course been other efforts at the development of social indicators. In fact, the concept of indicators originated in economics, and the Gross National Product is perhaps the most familiar example. In the United States, the major effort has been *Social Indicators, 1973* (U.S. Office of Management and Budget, 1974), and the principal categories were: Health, Public Safety, Education, Employment, Income, Housing, Leisure and Recreation, and Population. There have been similar efforts in several other countries, and some are more elaborate. Among the best known are those of Great Britain (1970-1973), France (1973), Germany (1973), Sweden (cited in Ramsøy, 1974), Norway (cited ibid.), and Japan (1973). The Organisation for Economic Co-operation and Development (1973) has published an international comparison of such social reports; and the United States effort was critically reviewed, soon after its publication, at a conference of international authorities in social science and statistics (Van Dusen, 1974). There is, thus, an evolving effort among social scientists to develop widely applicable measures to determine the quality of life of the peoples of the world. Until now, however, there has been no effort to apply such measures specifically to the treatment of mentally retarded persons. (The closest approach was the evaluative method known as PASS (Wolfensberger and Glenn, 1973), but this is designed to assess individual facilities or programs, rather than a whole society.) More important still, the social indicators are utilized to measure, and to compare over time, the level of consumption or comfort or happiness of a population, whereas the indicators I have undertaken to develop would provide a measure of the *level of concern of a society* for its mentally retarded persons.

The eight broad subject-area headings that evolved in the project I am describing, then, were consistent, if not identical, with those that are being developed as social indicators for somewhat different purposes in several countries. The component items, however, are substantially different—for the very reason that they have been selected to measure a different variable.

Perhaps you will be interested in some of the specific outcomes of the questionnaire. As might be expected by anyone familiar with the United States, the most emphatic responses came to the questions dealing with residential services and with education. On residential care (which for purposes of the instrument meant state institutions unless otherwise specified), feelings were so strong that some of the questions were misinterpreted. The consensus was unmistakably in favor of the smallest possible bed-capacity. In response to a series of items proposing that residential facilities for retarded persons "should be under 5,000 beds in total capacity . . . under 2,000 beds . . ." and so on down to "under 50 beds," not only did overwhelming majorities reject the higher ceilings as Undesirable, but quite a few thought even 50 was too large (Table 1). It is perhaps ironic that in Sweden, which many consider a model for the United States to emulate, there is a more temperate official attitude, which recognizes some circumstances in which public residential care is indeed preferable to the

Table 1. Response pattern on size of institution

Item	Judgment[a] of largest number of respondents (by percent)
Residential facilities for mentally retarded persons	
60. should be under 5,000 beds in total capacity	Undesirable, 61.1
61. should be under 2,000 beds	Undesirable, 58.9
62. should be under 1,000 beds	Undesirable, 54.2
63. should be under 500 beds	Undesirable, 38.0
64. should be under 100 beds	Highly Important, 31.4[b]
65. should be under 50 beds	Highly Important, 57.2

[a]Alternatives offered were Highly Important, Important, Not Important, Undesirable.
[b]Subgroup analysis showed that male and female respondents, professionals and laymen, generally agreed with the larger consensus. On Item 64 ("under 100 beds"), however, males split equally (31.6 percent each) between Highly Important and Undesirable, and on the same item professionals split equally (27.6 percent each) between Highly Important and Important, while laymen gave the largest number of their check marks (41.7 percent) to Undesirable.

alternatives. (Grunewald, 1974, pp. 25-26; *cf.* President's Committee on Mental Retardation, 1974.)

There was also a series of items regarding the appropriateness of state residential services by age and by degree of handicap. The response pattern showed a strong resistance to residential services for the mildly retarded and for young children, a resistance that declined with rising age and increasing severity of handicap (Table 2).

On education, in answer to questions asked in a variety of ways, the respondents consistently indicated their views that every child, no matter how retarded, is entitled to education in the public school system, and for at least as many years as other children. Of the entire series, the only item on which the

Table 2. Responses on appropriateness of state residential services (by percent of total respondent group)

(Items 67-75) State facilities should provide residential care services for	Under age 6	Age 6 to 18	Adults
mildly retarded	Undesirable 61.1	Undesirable, 52.6	Undesirable 50.5
moderately retarded	Undesirable, 55.0	Important, 36.8	Undesirable, 35.3
severely and profoundly retarded	Highly Important, 40.5 Important, 40.5	Highly Important, 48.5	Highly Important, 55.8

response pattern was unexpected was the one that stated, "The school day should be as long for retarded children as for other children." Although the largest number of respondents called this Highly Important, they did so by only 36.2 percent, and the item therefore failed of inclusion in the validated set of indicators. A number of respondents chose to write in comments on this item, and their individual observations showed that their reactions were thoughtful rather than stereotyped. This kind of differential response encouraged me to have confidence in the results.

Of all the 153 items, the response pattern that most astonished me came on the item: "Every family with a retarded child should receive a regular cash grant from the government." Child allowances are so commonplace in European countries—and not only for retarded children—that I anticipated substantial support from this respondent group, in view of the fact that many were parents and others were paid advocates. Instead, the item was unmistakably rejected, with 52.4 percent calling it Undesirable. I interpret this to mean that the American value system, whatever it may represent, prevails over personal self-interest or professional commitment.

Where the instrument stands today, then, is that it has been conceptualized, for a specific purpose, and it has been consensually validated as indeed measuring that which we wish to measure. The next step is to test it in the field; that is, to determine whether the data called for by the instrument are in fact available, and, if available, whether they are amenable to quantification, to scoring, and to tabulation. This is an empirical test, and I propose to undertake it by sampling states (of the United States) to discover whether, as I believe, the instrument is usable.

As a result of the field testing, I expect that it will be necessary to make refinements in the instrument, but then it should quickly be possible to apply it to all the states, thereby obtaining baseline date for future comparisons. It will also be possible to aggregate the individual state findings to obtain a national score, which will likewise lead to the detection of trends over time.

Even this, however, is merely preliminary to my long-range objective, which is to adapt the instrument for cross-national use. The international implications are thus clear: With the instrument, appropriately modified, it will be possible to undertake objective, quantified measurement of societal concern for mentally retarded persons, allowing cross-national (as well as longitudinal) comparisons. The findings, in turn, should lead to review, reassessment, replanning, and restructuring of program and service patterns, toward the more appropriate and more effective treatment of mentally retarded persons in all our societies.

SUMMARY

To compare how different societies provide for the mentally retarded persons in their populations, it is desirable to have an objective, quantifiable measuring standard. Such an instrument has been developed, initially for use at the level of the individual state within the United States. Ultimately, it will be adapted for cross-national evaluation and comparison.

REFERENCES

France, Institut National de la Statistique et des Etudes Economiques (1973) Données Sociales. Paris: Imprimerie National.

Germany (Federal Republic), Bundesministerium für Arbeit und Sozialordnung (1973) Gessellschaftliche Daten 1973. Bonn: Presse- und Informationsamt der Bundesregierung.

Great Britain, Central Statistical Office (1970–1973) Social Trends, Nos. 1-4. London: H.M.S.O.

Grunewald, K. (1974) The Mentally Retarded in Sweden. Stockholm: Swedish Institute.

Japan, Economic Planning Agency (1973) Whitepaper on National Life 1973: The Life and its Quality in Japan. Tokyo: Overseas Data Service Company.

Lippman, L. (1975) What the United States can learn from Europe: A comparison of attitudinal patterns and their effects on programs for the mentally handicapped. Proc. 3rd Congr. IASSMD 1:127. (Ed. Primrose, D. A. A.) Larbert, Scotland: IASSMD.

Organisation for Economic Co-operation and Development (1973) List of Social Concerns Common to Most OECD Countries. Paris: OECD.

President's Committee on Mental Retardation (1974) Residential Programming: Position Statements by the National Association of Superintendents of Public Residential Facilities for the Mentally Retarded, Washington, D.C.

Ramsøy, N. R. (1974) Social indicators in the United States and Europe: Comments on five country reports. *In* Social Indicators, 1973: A Review Symposium (Ed. Van Dusen, R.A.) Washington, D.C.: Social Science Research Council.

United States Office of Management and Budget (1974) Social Indicators, 1973. Washington, D.C.

Van Dusen, R. A. (Ed.) (1974) Social Indicators, 1973: A Review Symposium. Washington, D.C.: Social Science Research Council.

Wolfensberger, W., and Glenn, L. (1973) PASS: A Method for the Quantitative Evaluation of Human Services. Toronto: National Institute on Mental Retardation.

RESEARCH TO PRACTICE IN MENTAL RETARDATION
Care and Intervention, Volume I
Edited by Peter Mittler
Copyright 1977 I.A.S.S.M.D.

PARADIGMS FOR RESEARCH ON ATTITUDES TOWARD THE MENTALLY RETARDED

S. L. Guskin

Department of Special Education, Indiana University,
2805 E. 10th St., Bloomington, Indiana 47401, United States

Among professionals in the field of mental retardation, there is probably general agreement that attitudes toward the retarded are of significance because of their potential influence on the provision of services for the retarded, on the implementation of programs, on the behavioral reactions of others to the retarded, and on the self-esteem of retarded individuals. These widely held beliefs about the importance of attitudes toward the retarded have led to numerous studies, many of which have been excellently reviewed by Gottlieb (1975a). He pointed out the lack of consistency of findings and a number of serious methodological problems with such research. One of his major criticisms is that studies of attitude towards the retarded utilize different terms to refer to the retarded and use different definitions or even no definition of mental retardation. This critical review stimulated me to ask further questions about this research literature. I was particularly interested in unraveling the underlying thinking and strategies common to most research on attitudes towards the retarded in the hope that this might suggest more promising directions for future research.

The theoretical frameworks underlying most attitude research, whether within or outside the field of mental retardation, may be categorized for convenience into four broad classes: psychodynamic, sociological, cognitive, and behavioral. One of the most well-known psychodynamic formulations in the field of attitude study is that of the "authoritarian personality" (Adorno et al, 1950), which searched for the roots of negative reactions to minority groups in a rigidly controlled, autocratic family life that allowed no expression of hostility within the family. Repressed hostilities could only be expressed towards outsiders: foreigners, minority groups, etc. Many positive relationships between authoritarian personality measures and negative attitudes towards minority groups were obtained. Although many methodological criticisms have been raised regarding this research effort, it has been a source of stimulation to many investigations, including at least one study of attitudes towards the disabled.

Another psychodynamic construct that has often been related to attitudes is "anxiety." Groups that appear strange or different are said to arouse anxiety, which may lead to unfavorable attitudes. This seems to be the assumption underlying the hypothesis that greater contact with the retarded should lead to more favorable attitudes.

Sociological formulations frequently appearing in the attitude literature include deviance and labeling theory and social power and status constructs. Among the hypotheses to be drawn from a sociological approach are that attitudes towards the retarded are a function of a perceived threat to the social order, that they are related to persons having been formally labeled retarded, and that such labeling will lead the retarded to behavior consistent with others' role expectations.

The most widely disseminated cognitive approaches to attitude study are cognitive dissonance and balance theory, both emphasizing consistency of beliefs. Dissonance theory has focused on the influence of one's behavior on one's beliefs. It proposes that if you have carried out an action you will change your beliefs to be consistent with it. Thus, if you have committed yourself to become a teacher of the retarded you are likely to become more favorably disposed to the retarded. Consistency theories are concerned about the balance among attitudes. One would propose that if I like Mr. Jones and I know he believes strongly in mainstreaming retarded children, I am likely either to become more favorable to mainstreaming or less friendly with Mr. Jones.

The final theoretical category I suggest is behavioral, and this appears to involve at least two contradictions. Behaviorists tend to be atheoretical and avoid "subjective" topics such as attitudes. Nevertheless, one can define attitude in behavioral terms such as approach and avoidance behaviors. If so, then the behaviorist might be interested in the modification of approach behaviors by others toward the retarded and would anticipate that general reinforcement and shaping principles would be applicable.

For brevity I have omitted a number of formulations, including Hovland, Janis, and Kelley's work *Communication and Persuasion* (1953) and the promising work on attribution theory by Heider (1958) and others. However, even this brief overview suggests that there are a number of formulations that could be fruitfully applied to attitude research in mental retardation. Unfortunately, they have been only rarely utilized in systematically formulating research in this area.

Although research on attitudes towards the retarded has not been guided by theory, it has been derived from a number of research traditions or general research strategies that may be termed research paradigms. One such paradigm is the public opinion survey. Gottwald's (1970) survey of public beliefs about mental retardation and a study by Connaughton (1974) of physicians' beliefs about the retarded are examples of this approach. Such studies generally are aimed at determining the appropriateness of knowledge held about the retarded as well as favorability of attitudes. Thus, Connaughton reports that while almost all pediatricians and a majority of general practitioners are well informed about certain aspects of mental retardation, a substantial minority of general practitioners have very negative attitudes and serious misunderstandings in this area and have been giving inappropriate advice to parents of retarded children. Such findings have significant practical implications for the education of physicians.

A somewhat related type of study investigates stereotypes or commonly held beliefs about categories of persons such as the retarded. Thus, an opinion survey such as Gottwald's (1970) can determine whether or not there is a consensus on the traits assigned to the retarded. However, unlike most survey research, investigations of stereotypes of the retarded have not been carried out with large, representative samples (Gottwald is an exception). The concern has generally been not to get very accurate estimates of the proportion of people who believe this or that, as it is in the sample survey, but to compare the beliefs held about different groups. Thus, Willey and McCandless (1973) find that the traits commonly assigned to special class educable mentally retarded (EMR) children by regular class children in the same school are far more negative than their descriptions of children in other regular classes.

In contrast with opinion surveys and studies of stereotypes, which heavily emphasize the content of beliefs commonly held, most attitude studies emphasize individual differences among respondents in the favorability of overall attitude. Thus, rather than reporting the proportion of respondents who answer this way or that on each item, most attitude studies attempt to obtain a single, reliable score for each respondent summarizing his attitude. These scores are obtained by attitude-scaling procedures, such as those of Guttman, Likert, or Thurstone. Groups of respondents, such as regular and special education teachers, may then be compared on mean attitude score, or individual differences in overall attitude may be correlated with other characteristics of individual respondents, such as age, education, or amount of contact with the retarded. Recent advances in applying this strategy have included the use of new, highly sophisticated item-writing and scaling procedures, such as Jordan's (1971) application of Guttman's facet analysis to the development of an instrument for comparing attitudes toward the retarded across cultures. The application of factor analytic techniques to existing sets of items, as in Gottlieb and Corman (1975), has also helped in the interpretation of attitudinal data.

In the general field of social psychology, the individual differences, or correlational, approach has become relatively unpopular, having been replaced by an interest in experimental attitude change studies. Yet, in the area of mental retardation, very few studies of attitude change exist and most of these are studies of the effects of institutional tours on the attitudes of students, with very mixed findings resulting. There are more exceptions to this underemphasis on attitude change if one broadens the definition of attitude to include socio-metric and expectancy studies.

While all of the approaches previously described involve asking persons to describe whole social categories, e.g., "the mentally retarded," sociometric research asks respondents to characterize their willingness to interact with individuals they know. Rather than the respondent obtaining a score, the child he has responded to gets the score. These scores are correlated with other individual difference measures on the rated children. The most common finding has been that the less intelligent a child is, the less often he is chosen as a friend. Happily, in sociometric research a number of studies have investigated the possibility of changing negative attitudes. Thus special education researchers (Chennault, 1967; Lilly, 1971; Rucker and Vincenzo, 1970) have been able to demonstrate favorable changes in peer acceptance as a result of experimentally introduced treatments, although there appears to be no maintenance of gains after the intervention has been ended.

Finally, we come to what has been one of the most widely known educational research paradigms in recent years, the expectancy study, first popularized by Rosenthal and Jacobson (1968) and most recently excellently reviewed by Brophy and Good (1974), Dusek (1975), and Braun (1976). The expectancy study differs from other attitudinal studies in that the attitude or expectancy is typically established by the experimenter in a teacher by labeling the child, and the consequences for teacher and pupil *behavior* are examined. Since most recent investigations have failed to support the initial dramatic report by Rosenthal and Jacobson (1968), this paradigm is beginning to lose favor. In the field of mental retardation, findings have generally been negative. Those studies that have demonstrated an influence of the label "mentally retarded" have shown the label to influence how an observer *perceives* a child rather than changing how persons interact or teach or how the "retarded" child learns. Even when merely examining influence on judgment of the observer, results are not consistently obtained if the observer has information other than the label to rely on. Thus, when Yoshida and Meyers (1975) and Gottlieb (1974) provided observational data on academic competence, the label was ineffective. In another labeling investigation by Gottlieb (1975b), children were observed showing either aggressive or nonaggressive behavior. Only when aggressive behavior was observed did the retarded label influence judgments of the child.

Having briefly reviewed the most common research paradigms employed in the study of attitudes towards the retarded, it is time to ask if these approaches are sufficiently promising to serve as models for further inquiry or if they have such serious limitations that alternatives must be sought. Certainly, there is little theoretical underpinning for most attitude research in mental retardation. Where hypotheses exist, they are rarely more than empirical predictions based on common sense assumptions, e.g., that experience with the retarded will result in more favorable attitudes. The closest to a theoretical framework is the expectancy formulation, and even this has generally been reduced to the simple hypothesis of the self-fulfilling prophecy that labels will result in outcomes consistent with the label.

One of the results of having only inadequate theoretical formulations to guide research is that empirical findings tend to be inconsistent. Without a theory you are left with accumulated knowledge: e.g., sometimes retarded labels have effects and sometimes they don't; and, institutional tours can change attitudes, sometimes in a favorable direction, at other times in an unfavorable direction. A talented reviewer (such as Jay Gottlieb, 1975a) can make some sense of the findings by comparing results from a number of studies using different samples and instruments. Similarly, a clever investigator can demonstrate the vulnerability of naive hypotheses and a weak methodology by carefully designed research. However, these are poor substitutes for beginning with a theoretical framework. In short, without a solid framework generalizability is likely to be nil, findings varying with the accidental choice of a sample, a measuring instrument, or a particular wording of instructions. The lack of generalizability means that such research findings can have little utility for practitioners, which is the purpose of most research in a field such as ours.

If current approaches are inadequate, what alternatives do we have? One possibility would be to try to apply some of the broad theoretical frameworks (psychodynamic, sociological, etc.) described earlier. The problem with that strategy is that it is derivative of problems and issues important in other fields and may contribute to those academic disciplines but provide little improvement in understanding of our particular area. I think it is more promising to develop conceptual frameworks deriving from a careful analysis and understanding of the content in which we are interested. We must, however, get away from simple correlational, one variable at a time, linear predictions such as "labeling a child retarded results in his being responded to less favorably" or "attitude towards the retarded improves with experience with retarded persons."

One valuable strategy is to develop causal or sequential models to guide hypotheses and research. I will illustrate this approach utilizing the phenomenon of teacher expectancy effects since I am most familiar with this area. Figure 1 is an attempt to summarize graphically what I believe to be the most common sequential-causal formulations underlying teacher expectancy studies. Figure 1b is the oversimplified "self-fulfilling prophecy": "expectancy leads to achievement," i.e., if you expect a child to perform poorly, he will achieve poorly. Figure 1a provides one explanation of how the self-fulfilling prophecy might operate. If a child is labeled mentally retarded, others expect him to perform poorly in academic areas, so they teach him less new material, as a result he only has the opportunity to learn a lesser amount of material and this results in poorer academic performance, which in turn confirms the initial retarded label. This, of course, is an oversimplification, too, and is by no means the only causal formulation possible. Thus, Figure 1c is a graphic presentation of the expectancy

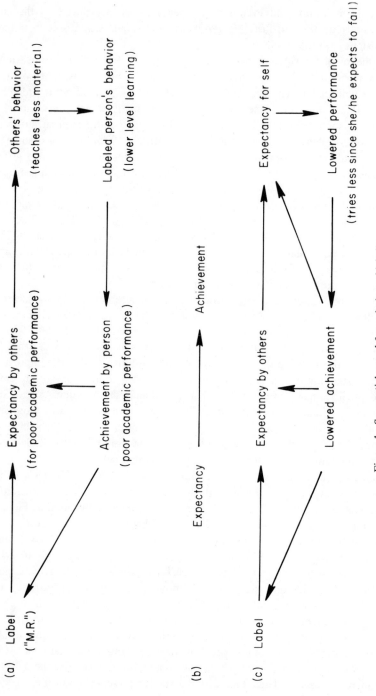

Figure 1. Sequential causal formulation of labeling.

formulation that Rosenthal seems to favor. Note that it differs from Figure 1a on the right side. Expectancy effects are seen as being mediated by changes in self-evaluation or "self-expectancy." The lowered expectancies of others lead to the child's feeling less adequate, which leads to reduced motivation and reduced effort in learning situations, which then result in lowered achievement, which in turn reduces both the child's and teacher's expectancies for future performance, and so on.

Other causal models for expectancy effects have been spelled out in detail by Brophy and Good (1974) and Braun (1976). I am not arguing for any particular formulation here, only that some attempt be made by an investigator to explicate the expectancy model utilized and follow its dictates when engaging in further research on this topic. This requires far more detailing than is present in the figure shown here. Each arrow in the diagram implies some further causal processes or assumptions. Thus, in Figure 1a there is an arrow indicating that lowered expectancy leads to teaching less material. It may seem perfectly obvious how this happens but in fact this phenomenon has only rarely been convincingly established and even these findings have not been replicated when minor procedural changes have been made in experiments. It appears that somehow the label and task must be framed in a way that leads a teacher to expect that teaching less material is more appropriate. Similarly, the arrows from "teaches less" to "lower level learning" to "poor academic performance" can be shown to be invalid for certain achievement criteria with retarded children. In research on long-term memory of retarded children, it has been shown that repetition or overlearning results in recall at normal levels but that performance suffers when the material has not been overtaught. The model in Figure 1a encourages covering new material rather than repeating old material. Thus, the model should work only when the child can learn as much when the material is presented briefly as he can when it is repeated often.

The general principle to be applied to studying attitudes toward the retarded is that investigators should indicate how they believe the attitudes have been formed or can be changed and/or how these attitudes are to influence outcomes, spelling out as many of the steps in the sequence as possible. Not only would this facilitate communication and theory building; it would lead investigators to much more promising methods of operationalizing their hypotheses. Right now, the outcomes of studies seem to be largely a result of the extent to which investigators have an intuitive understanding of the underlying influence processes involved, or the patience they have in piloting varying operational definitions of their constructs until they hit on the right one, i.e., the one that supports their hypotheses.

The suggestion that we explicate as many steps as possible in the process we wish to study is a very general one. The sequential model shown here also alludes to, but does not emphasize, another important feature that should be incorporated in conceptualizing attitude research with the retarded—a temporal framework. While this sequence occurs over time, the time involved may be anything from a few minutes (less than 20 minutes in Beez, 1968) to a year or more (as in Rosenthal and Jacobson, 1968), and the model shown does not consider the importance of such differences.

There are a number of ways in which time may enter into investigations significantly: How long does one hold attitudes towards an individual who has been labeled retarded? How have attitudes towards the retarded as a group changed over the years? One intriguing temporal concept deriving from sociology is the concept of "career," which has become more well known in the field of mental retardation as a result of the work of Jane Mercer (1973). Just as one can have an occupational career, one can have a career in the role of "retarded person," with one's status changing over one's life history. Figure 2 is one way of graphically illustrating the career of the child labeled retarded. Notice that the dependent variable (shown along the left margin) is the perceived competence of the retarded individual. We might even substitute "favorability of attitude towards the retarded individual." Curve *a* represents changes in parents' perceptions or attitudes during the life of their mildly retarded child. This curve hypothesizes that at birth the child is seen as normal, and that this perception shows only a minor decrement before school age, at which point parental perceptions of competence begin to drop until they finally hit bottom at "fairly incompetent" when he enters a special class. Attitudes towards the child's competence then remain at that level until he is mainstreamed, when they show a brief, sharp, but moderate recovery, followed by a hypothesized fall off again when he begins to fail in regular classes, hitting bottom once more when he drops out of school. His perceived competence then begins to increase until he is seen as normal again by his parents ten years after leaving school. Notice how this graphic conceptualization allows one to summarize efficiently a number of hypotheses about events that occur over an extended period of time. It also suggests that if the model holds, it is ludicrous to generalize from examining labeling effects at one point in time or to assume that results follow simple linear patterns. It is rare to find studies that actually follow a phenomenon over time. Edgerton, however, has recently reported dramatic changes over a ten-year period in retarded adults' concerns about labeling. In the earlier study (Edgerton, 1967), although the adults had been living in the community for some time, there was a great deal of anxiety about the retarded label and a feeling of degradation associated with. In contrast, ten years later these issues had little salience for them (Edgerton, 1975).

In addition to temporal variables, it is important that a number of other classes of variables be systematically incorporated into attitude research. Certainly the level of mental retardation is one. Notice the difference in predictions one might make for the career of the severely retarded individual. Figure 2b hypothesizes a rapid drop in perceived competence between birth and age three, the gradual but modest increase upon entering day school, the drop again upon

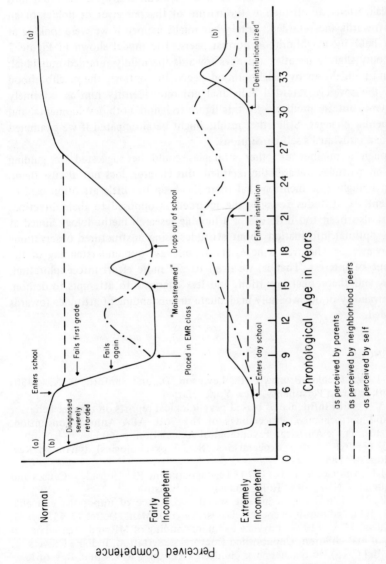

Figure 2. The "career" of the labeled child: perceptions of child competence as a function of child age, child characteristics, labeling events, and perceiver. *Curve a* represents a mildly retarded individual. *Curve b* represents a severely retarded individual.

31

being institutionalized, the sharp recovery upon deinstitutionalization, followed by a small fall off, which might be anticipated as a result of realistic appraisal of limitations.

Another class of variables that must be systematically incorporated into conceptualizations of attitude is the nature of the perceiver or holder of an attitude towards the retarded. Note what might happen if we were looking at attitudes held by neighborhood normal peers. The model shown in Figure 2 predicts only slightly negative attitudes towards the mildly retarded individual; he is almost unlabeled by neighborhood peers. In contrast, the neighborhood peers of the severely retarded individual not only identify him as extremely incompetent, but are predicted by this figure to ignore both developmental and environmental changes. Still other results might be anticipated if we examined the retarded individual's self-perceptions.

Although a number of other strategies could be suggested for guiding research on attitudes towards the retarded, this chapter does not discuss them. However, I might just mention that there has been too little attention paid to the content of attitudes towards the retarded as opposed to their direction. There has also been too little use of a flexible research methodology aimed at obtaining optimal information about attitudes using unstructured observations and interviews or whatever is necessary to increase our understanding of the phenomena of interest. That is, we need to put more effort into exploration, discovery, and theoretical invention, and less energy into attempts to demonstrate the validity of our woefully inadequate understanding of attitudes towards the retarded.

REFERENCES

Adorno, T. W., Frenkel-Brunswik, E., Levinson, D., and Sanford, R. N. (1950) The Authoritarian Personality. New York: Harper.

Beez, W. V. (1968) Influence of biased psychological reports on teacher behavior and pupil performance. Proceedings of the 76th APA Annual Convention. Washington, D.C.: American Psychological Association, p. 605.

Braun, C. (1976) Teacher expectations: Social psychological dynamics. Rev. Educ. Res. 46:185.

Brophy, J.E., and Good, T. L. (1974) Teacher-student Relationships: Causes and Consequences. New York: Holt, Rinehart and Winston.

Chennault, M. (1967) Improving the social acceptance of unpopular educable mentally retarded pupils in special classes. Amer. J. Ment. Defic. 72:455.

Connaughton, M. C. (1974) Physician's understanding of MR and their advice to parents of MR children. Unpublished Doctoral dissertation, Indiana University.

Dusek, J. B. (1975) Do teachers bias children's learning? Rev. Educ. Res. 661.

Edgerton, R. B. (1967) The Cloak of Competence. Berkeley: University of California Press.

Edgerton, R. B. (1975) Issues relating to the quality of life among mentally retarded persons. In The Mentally Retarded and Society: A Social Science

Perspective (Eds. Begab, M. J. and Richardson, S. A.) Baltimore: University Park Press, p. 127.

Gottlieb, J. (1974) Attitudes toward retarded children: Effects of labeling and academic performance. Amer. J. Ment. Defic. 79:268.

Gottlieb, J. (1975a) Public, peer, and professional attitudes toward mentally retarded persons. *In* The Mentally Retarded and Society: A Social Science Perspective (Eds. Begab, M. J. and Richardson, S. A.) Baltimore: University Park Press, p. 99.

Gottlieb, J. (1975b) Attitudes toward retarded children: Effects of labeling and behavioral aggressiveness. J. Educ. Psychol. 67:581.

Gottlieb, J., and Corman, L. (1975) Public attitudes toward mentally retarded children. Amer. J. Ment. Defic. 80:72.

Gottwald, H. (1970) Public awareness about mental retardation. Research Monograph, Council for Exceptional Children.

Heider, F. (1958) The Psychology of Interpersonal Relations. New York: Wiley.

Hovland, C.I., Janis, I. and Kelley, H. (1953) Communication and Persuasion. New Haven: Yale University Press.

Jordan, J. E. (1971) Construction of a Guttman facet designed cross-cultural attitude-behavior scale toward mental retardation. Amer. J. Ment. Defic. 76:201.

Lilly, M. S. (1971) Improving social acceptance of low sociometric status, low achieving students. Except. Child. 37:341.

Mercer, J. R. (1973) Labeling the Mentally Retarded. Berkeley: University of California Press.

Rosenthal, R., and Jacobson, L. (1968) Pygmalion in the Classroom: Teacher Expectation and Pupils' Intellectual Development. New York: Holt, Rinehart and Winston.

Rucker, C. N., and Vincenzo, F. M. (1970) Maintaining social acceptance gains made by mentally retarded children. Except. Child. 36:679.

Willey, N. R., and McCandless, B. R. (1973) Social stereotypes for normal, educable mentally retarded, and orthopedically handicapped children. J. Spec. Educ. 283.

Yoshida, R., and Meyers, C. E. (1975) Effects of labeling as educable mentally retarded on teachers' expectancies for change in a student's performance. J. Educ. Psychol. 67:521.

RESEARCH TO PRACTICE IN MENTAL RETARDATION
Care and Intervention, Volume I
Edited by Peter Mittler
Copyright 1977 I.A.S.S.M.D.

ATTITUDES TOWARD MAINSTREAMING RETARDED CHILDREN AND SOME POSSIBLE EFFECTS ON EDUCATIONAL PRACTICES

J. Gottlieb
Nero & Associates, Inc., RCA Building, 1901 North Moore Street, Arlington, Virginia 22209, United States

A recent report issued by the President's Committee on Mental Retardation (PCMR) stated that public attitudes have always played a critical role in determining the fate of mentally retarded people. Although the PCMR report paid most attention to the importance of public attitudes, it also acknowledged the importance of professionals' attitudes by recommending that course work in mental retardation be included in curricula for all professional students preparing to work with retarded people. To illustrate the effects that public and professionals' attitudes could have on the lives of mentally retarded people, we need only consider the fact that the long-held view of mentally retarded people as being dangerous to society was largely instigated by professional caregivers who needed justification to expand the institutional movement during the latter part of the nineteenth century (Lazerson, 1975). Similarly, the initial growth of special classes for mentally retarded children was the result of teachers' perceptions that slow-learning children were troublesome and had to be educated in special schools (Esten, 1900).

Gradually, the perception of retarded people as being dangerous was replaced by the perception of the "eternal child" who had to be protected but who could also benefit from appropriate intervention strategies. The perception of retarded people as poor unfortunates still lingers on, as is suggested by recent data that indicate that retarded adults were perceived as honest and kind but also as sick, ignorant, and inferior (Gottwald, 1970). Similar attitudes were also reported for mentally retarded children, who were perceived by nonretarded peers to be kind and honest while at the same time as sick and dumb (Gottlieb and Gottlieb, 1976).

Given the importance of people's attitudes in shaping the lives of mentally retarded people, we must also know how these attitudes will affect and be affected by the recent movement to have the mentally retarded participate in the mainstream of community and school life. It is especially important to know the impact of people's attitudes on retarded school children now that the Congress has enacted legislation requiring all handicapped children to be educated with nonhandicapped children to the maximum extent feasible. The presence of retarded children in regular classrooms for substantial portions of the day is likely to affect the various parties involved in mainstreaming: the community-at-large, including the parents of nonretarded children; the regular classroom teachers, who, historically, have been told that retarded children are different and require separate educational facilities; and the peers, who will be required to interact with retarded children on a daily basis. What do we know about the attitudes of these groups of people whose attitudes could either facilitate or impede the educational performance of mainstreamed retarded children?

ATTITUDES OF COMMUNITY RESIDENTS

Community residents represent a potent force in shaping school policies. They exert control over the school budget, elect school administrators, and generally approve any major change in educational practices. The focal role of the community residents would suggest their attitudes toward mainstreaming would play a major role in deciding on the way that it becomes implemented in the schools. Unfortunately, very little data are available regarding the community residents' attitudes toward mainstreaming of retarded children and it does not appear that their views were represented in decisions on how to mainstream children. One study that was concerned with public attitudes toward school integration found that parents of school-age children expressed less favorable attitudes toward integration than adults who did not have school-age children (Gottlieb and Corman, 1975). These data suggest that as parents become personally affected by mainstreaming practices they may be likely to express their opposition, at least until they are assured that the presence of retarded pupils in their children's classes will not adversely affect the latter. Unfortunately, few data are available to attest to the effect of retarded children on the academic performance of nonretarded children. The very meager data that do exist suggest that during the first year of mainstreaming, nonretarded children having retarded classmates perform more poorly in certain subject areas than nonretarded children who do not have retarded classmates (Bradfield, Brown, Kaplan, Rickert, and Stannard, 1973).

One limitation of the investigation conducted by Gottlieb and Corman was their failure to specify the severity of mental retardation to which their subjects responded. Consequently, the investigators could not determine whether their subjects' attitudes vis-a-vis attitudes toward school integration were directed toward the presence of mildly retarded pupils in their children's classes or whether their attitudes reflected feelings about a moderately or severely retarded child who was to be mainstreamed.

Siperstein and Gottlieb (1976) extended the findings of Gottlieb and Corman by examining adults' attitudes toward mainstreaming mildly and severely retarded pupils. Siperstein and Gottlieb found that adults were significantly more receptive to the idea of mainstreaming mildly retarded children than severely retarded pupils. More specifically, these investigators reported that adults believed that: a) special classes were less justified for mildly retarded pupils than for severely retarded pupils, b) the transfer of a mildly retarded child to a regular class would be less likely to cause problems than the transfer of a severely retarded youngster, c) integration would foster more social acceptance of mildly retarded than severely retarded pupils, d) mildly retarded children would be less likely to be discipline problems, and e) integration would be of greater benefit to mildly retarded children than to severely retarded children. In sum, the data reported by Siperstein and Gottlieb generally indicated that adults did not express favorable attitudes toward mainstreaming severely retarded pupils. On the other hand, subjects were generally receptive to mainstreaming mildly retarded pupils.

Although the data reported by Siperstein and Gottlieb suggest that community residents are not receptive to the idea of mainstreaming severely retarded pupils, a provocative question that must be raised was suggested by Sigelman (1976) in a different but related context. Sigelman questioned whether public attitudes should even be considered when developing community residence programs for mentally retarded adults. More specifically, Sigelman stated that the method of *fait accompli,* that is, placing community residences in neighborhoods without first consulting the residents of the community, may prove no less effective in the long run than the approach in which neighbors' attitudes are explored in advance. The parallels to the implementation of mainstreaming programs in the public schools are obvious. The question that should be addressed empirically is whether or not it is any more effective to apprise parents of nonretarded children in advance that their children are likely to be enrolled in classes with retarded children than it is not to apprise them in advance. Very little research has addressed the attitudes of community residents in general and parents in particular vis-a-vis school programming, and especially mainstreaming. The above question would represent an auspicious first step in a research program designed to improve our understanding of community and parent attitudes.

ATTITUDES OF TEACHERS AND SCHOOL ADMINISTRATORS

Few would disagree that the ultimate success of mainstreaming programs rests largely in the hands of professional school personnel, including regular classroom teachers and school administrators. To the extent that school professionals are inimical to the philosophy of mainstreaming, they could adversely affect the mentally retarded child's educational experiences. Despite the critical role played by school professionals, and especially the teacher, few studies have addressed the issue of school professionals' attitudes. Those that have studied the problems have generally reported inconclusive results.

Shotel, Iano, and McGettigan (1972) studied teachers' attitudes toward the integration of educable retarded children in regular classes and found that attitudes became significantly more negative as the regular class teachers gained one year's experience with the retarded children. Guerin and Szatlocky (1974) reported that 62% of the teachers they interviewed expressed positive attitudes toward integration, 19% expressed neutral attitudes, and 19% expressed unfavorable attitudes. These investigators did not indicate the criteria they employed to determine attitude favorability and as a result the data are difficult to interpret. Finally, Gickling and Theobald (1975) assessed special and regular class teachers' attitudes by means of a 46-item questionnaire and concluded that there was no overwhelming support on the part of regular or special class teachers to do away with self-contained classes for mildly handicapped children. Sixty percent of the sample (N = 326) felt that self-contained classes had proven to be more effective than regular classes for mildly handicapped pupils. The authors found that only 40% of the teachers could be considered as strongly favoring a mainstreaming approach for educating mildly handicapped children.

Research pertaining to school administrators' attitudes are almost as inconclusive as they are for teachers' attitudes. Payne and Murray (1974) found that 59.3% of the suburban principals they questioned accepted the integration of mildly handicapped children, while only 46.4% of the urban principals accepted integration of the mildly handicapped. The picture was considerably different for the acceptance of trainable retarded children, with less than 10% of the suburban and less than 5% of the urban principals accepting the philosophy. On the other hand, Guerin and Szatlocky (1974) reported that all administrators whom they interviewed, except for one, favored the philosophy of integrating handicapped children.

If one accepts the proposition that school professionals' attitudes are critical to the success of mainstreaming practices, then a number of questions arise. With respect to teachers' attitudes a major question that requires clarification is why they generally harbor negative attitudes, or at least do not express favorable attitudes. One possibility for these patterns of expressed attitudes is that regular class teachers feel inadequate to deal with the problems of mentally retarded children. Gickling and Theobald's (1975) data lend support to this proposition. Those investigators reported that less than 15% of the elementary and secondary teachers felt that they had the necessary skills to help exceptional children. If teachers feel threatened by the fear of not being able to help retarded children, we would expect a negative pattern of attitudes to emerge. In order to improve teachers' attitudes toward retarded children and toward mainstreaming, as the PCMR report states is a necessary goal, we must first acquire some understanding of why their attitudes are negative and require change. It is an inordinately difficult task to improve attitudes before we know precisely what has to be changed.

PEER ATTITUDES

One of the primary forces behind the movement to mainstream retarded children was the belief that self-contained classes stigmatize children and that they would be less stigmatized if they were placed in regular classes (e.g., Dunn, 1968). Unfortunately, the available data to date do not support this assumption. Most of the research suggests that mainstreamed retarded children are less well accepted by peers than are segregated retarded children (Goodman, Gottlieb, and Harrison, 1972; Gottlieb and Budoff, 1973; Iano, Ayers, Heller, McGettigan, and Walker, 1974), although some data do exist that indicate that mainstreamed retarded adolescents are better accepted than segregated children (Sheare, 1974). Gottlieb (1976) suggested that the reason why integrated retarded children continue to be rejected by their nonretarded peers is that their (EMRs') behavior does not conform to the standards of the nonretarded classmates. Because they are no longer labeled and are expected to behave as normal children do, EMR children become socially ostracized when exhibiting behavior that violates group norms. If the assumption regarding the rejection of mainstreamed retarded children is correct—and further research is required to affirm its validity—then it suggests that retarded children require training in acceptable modes of behavior in regular classes before their placement in them. It may be too late to train EMR children's behavior once they are integrated into regular classes, because considerable research data suggests that first impressions form easily and are durable.

POSSIBLE EFFECTS OF ATTITUDES ON EDUCATIONAL PRACTICES

Although very little information is available regarding the attitudes of people toward retarded children or toward mainstreaming, the evidence that does exist does not present an overly favorable picture.

There are a number of ways that people's attitudes could affect educational practice. Despite the potential importance of community residents, especially parents, in shaping school policies, whatever influence they may exert would have to be executed by school personnel, the people who have the most direct control over ongoing school practices. Consequently, it is most fruitful to examine the options available to school personnel in programming for main-streaming.

If we operate under the premise that school people are not especially supportive of mainstreaming retarded children, as some of the evidence reviewed indicated, they could decide to integrate retarded children with nonhandicapped peers for the minimum amount of time that the law allows. Even though the recent Congressional act (Public Law 94-142) mandates integration to the maximum extent feasible, there are few guidelines offered to suggest what the maximum extent is, or how it is to be determined. Thus, principals, teachers, and psychologists can structure a program for retarded children in which they spend much of the day in resource rooms or self-contained classes with handicapped peers.

Another possibility is that regular class teachers who harbor negative attitudes will not develop the individualized curriculum activities that the retarded child is likely to require. If the mainstreamed retarded child is simply provided the same level of academic demand as his nonretarded peers, he is not likely to achieve as much as he otherwise could.

Yet another possibility is that the regular and support teachers will shirk the major responsibility for planning the retarded child's educational program.

Also, principals and teachers could bring pressure on parents to accept an educational program that the parents do not believe is in the best interests of their child. Although the law provides for due process hearing, not many poor parents can afford the services of an attorney to represent them at these hearings. Without some form of representation, it is hardly probable that the parents will be able to refute successfully the arguments of professionals.

Professionals' attitudes are not the only source of concern. The attitudes of peers are especially important to retarded children. Mainstreamed EMR pupils who are constantly taunted by their peers, who are often referred to as dummies, retards, and other epithets, are not going to enjoy their school experiences. As the mainstreaming of handicapped children becomes an accepted aspect of school programming, one of the critical needs will be the development of curriculum units that emphasize the individuality of people, that people are different in ability and appearance, and that they should be valued for what they are. Mainstreaming does not involve retarded children exclusively. Just as the curriculum for retarded children will have to be modified, so, too, will the curriculum for the nonhandicapped children.

SUMMARY

Educating retarded children in the least restrictive environment is now the law. However, there is a critical need to determine the extent of public and school personnel support if mainstreaming is to be fully effective in improving education for retarded children. To date, the available evidence fails to uncover such support.

REFERENCES

Bradfield, R. H., Brown, J., Kaplan, P., Rickert, E., and Stannard, R. (1973) The special child in the regular classroom. Except. Child. 39:384.

Dunn, L. M. (1968) Special education for the mildly retarded—Is much of it justifiable? Except. Child. 35:5.

Esten, R. A. (1900) Backward children in the public schools. J. Psycho-Asth. 5:10.

Gickling, E. E., and Theobald, J. T. (1975) Mainstreaming: affect or effect. J. Spec. Educ. 9:317.

Goodman, H., Gottlieb, J., and Harrison, R. H. (1972) Social acceptance of EMRs integrated into a nongraded elementary school. Amer. J. Ment. Defic. 76:412.

Gottlieb, J. (1976) Observational studies of social adaptation: An educational perspective. Paper presented at conference, Application of Observational-ethological Methods to the Study of Mental Retardation, Lake Wilderness, Washington.

Gottlieb, J., and Budoff, M. (1973) Social acceptability of retarded children in nongraded schools differing in architecture. Amer. J. Ment. Defic. 78:15.

Gottlieb, J., and Corman, L. (1975) Public attitudes toward mentally retarded children. Amer. J. Ment. Defic. 80:72.

Gottlieb, J., and Gottlieb, B. W. (1976) Stereotypes and behavioral intentions toward mentally retarded and crippled children. Unpublished manuscript.

Gottwald, H. (1970) Public Awareness about Mental Retardation. Reston, Virginia: Council for Exceptional Children.

Guerin, G. R., and Szatlocky, K. (1974) Integration programs for the mildly retarded. Except. Child. 41:173.

Iano, R. P., Ayers, D., Heller, H. B., McGettigan, J. F., and Walker, V. S. (1974) Sociometric status of retarded children in an integrative program. Except. Child. 40:267.

Lazerson, M. (1975) Educational institutions and mental subnormality: notes on writing a history. In The Mentally Retarded and Society: A Social Science Perspective (Eds. Begab, M. J. and Richardson, S. A.) Baltimore: University Park Press.

Payne, R., and Murray, C. (1974) Principals' attitudes toward integration of the handicapped. Except. Child. 41:123.

President's Committee on Mental Retardation (1976) Mental Retardation: Century of Decision. Washington, D.C.: Department of Health, Education and Welfare.

Sheare, J. B. (1974) Social acceptance of EMR adolescents in integrated programs. Amer. J. Ment. Defic. 78:678.

Shotel, J. R., Iano, R. P., and McGettigan, J. F. (1972) Teacher attitudes associated with the integration of handicapped children. Except. Child. 38:677.

Sigelman, C. K. (1976) A Machiavelli for planners: community attitudes and selection of a group home site. Ment. Retard. 14:26.

Siperstein, G. N., and Gottlieb, J. (1976) Parents' and teachers' attitudes toward mildly and severely retarded children. Unpublished manuscript.

ETHICAL
AND RELATED ISSUES

RESEARCH TO PRACTICE IN MENTAL RETARDATION
Care and Intervention, Volume I
Edited by Peter Mittler
Copyright 1977 I.A.S.S.M.D.

THE MENTALLY RETARDED
Valuable Individuals or Superfluous Population

B. Farber and E. Royce
Department of Sociology, Arizona State University,
Tempe, Arizona 85281, United States

The aim of research on mental retardation is the eventual elimination of those biological and social conditions that lead to social incompetence and intellectual disablement. It would seem that cognitive and social inadequacies often block the mentally retarded from filling useful social positions and from fully integrating themselves into society. Along with several ethnic minorities, the aged poor, and the severely physically handicapped, the retarded are superfluous insofar as the major institutions of the society are concerned (Farber, 1968). But, bit by bit, the genetic components of mental retardation are being uncovered, prenatal diagnosis perfected, and medical techniques of remediation discovered. Simultaneously, household attributes detrimental to child development are being discerned, distortions in early mother-child interaction detected, and the cultural influences on maladaptive behavior located. Presumably, in some distant future, we will be able to apply these findings and to engineer lives so that "mental retardation" will be wiped out.

It is possible, however, that many problems that we associate with mental retardation have little to do with personal defects or with remedial pathologies in the social system. They may instead inhere in the very conditions of social order, or at least in the social order as it is presently established. In order to gain insight into the nature of these problems, I would like to present the results of a mental experiment, a technique applied by sociologists in order to undertake functional analysis (Merton, 1957; Johnson, 1960). I shall describe a world in which all biological and social conditions leading to intellectual impairment have been identified and are capable of control. What then follows from this ability to control intelligence? I shall present the results of my analysis to you as if I were speaking to a scientific assembly five hundred years from now. Suppose that the year is 2476, and I am addressing members of the Congress of Human Engineering.

> Fellow human engineers: This year, we are celebrating the 400th anniversary of the invention of the Savant computer implant, which has revolutionized modern society. In pre-Savant days, five centuries ago, history records that people actually had to congregate in schools to relearn each generation even such simple mechanics as reading and number manipulation. The cultivation of talent through time-consuming, expensive, and often unsatisfactory education was the only way to equip personnel for highly technical tasks. Today, however, with basic knowledge—in languages and mathematics—being phased into the implantee directly, and with the capability of transplanting Savants from one generation to the next, society is assured of an abundance of highly trained and proficient personnel and of progress through successive memory gains from generation to generation.[1] Compared with the intellectual capacity made possible by the Savant, "natural" brains are, to use those ancient terms, feebleminded or even imbecilic. Certainly, the Savant has been a source of tremendous benefit. At the same time, this glorious demon continues to precipitate crises in the social order. Perhaps the most effective way to illuminate our present predicament is to review the history of the Savant.
>
> The Savant was made possible by a series of engineering feats beginning with the development of microscopic computer components and sophisticated surgical techniques.[2] By the twenty-second century, engineers had already produced highly complex brain supplements for skull implantation. But in these early experimental stages, research was still oriented toward overcoming and/or supplementing cognitive deficiencies in an effort to eliminate mental retardation. The first Savant computer implants were crude, and the early implantees could only slightly improve upon their previous intellectual capacities. With improvements in memory activation, feedback mechanisms, and brain-computer interface, further experimentation produced highly promising results: chimpanzees who were chess wizards and children with Down's syndrome solving differential equations.[3] It was at this point that scientists, now clearly perceiving the potentialities of the Savant, directed their research toward augmenting normal intellectual functioning.

---

[1] Because the Savant makes possible successive memory gains over generations, early myths about the genetic inheritance of acquired characteristics and the existence of group memories—the racial unconscious—have become a scientific reality. (See Lisa Watson and Jacqueline Crick, *Savantism and Lamarckianism* (New York, 2402).)

[2] A definitive history of the origins of the Savant is of course Michael Richard Toynbee's *The Savant Transformation* (Cambridge, 2353).

[3] The immediate impact of these experiments on society was for industry to demand mass production of chimpanzee Savants (CHIMSAV) and for organized labor to call for an end to Savant experimentation and the destruction of all existing Savants. In the end, the government invoked the principle of creative scarcity and restricted Savant implanting to humans.

History records the competition among nations over the development of Savant components and the subsequent race for brain-power supremacy. The international scene was calmed somewhat when the Savant-producing nations agreed to share their technology with other countries. Global strife, however, soon gave way to the domestic unrest that persists to this day. Regretfully, technological improvement often brings forth more moral and legal issues than it solves. Technically, it was possible three centuries ago for virtually all members of society to have full Savant capabilities, which at that time was a Cattell ratio of 24,000, using the old Stanford-Binet norm of 100 as a base. With a complete distribution of full-capacity Savants, though, it was feared that the social order would break down.

To avoid chaos, the Congress of Political Processes, utilizing the concept of creative scarcity, devised our present-day system of social stratification based upon a differential distribution of Savant implants. The status A class, comprising leaders in scientific, humanistic, political, and industrial fields, receives full-power Savant implants in all areas of intellectual functioning. The status B class, consisting of industrial and governmental specialists and middle-range intellectuals, receives Savant implants with full-capacity Cattell ratios for only those particular abilities needed for occupational and cultural specialties.[4] The status C class, technicians and skilled workers, receives Savants commensurate with their job requirements. Status D class, which holds the unskilled laborers and the consumers of popular culture, provides the basic pool of people and their children who are eligible for Savant implants. Finally, there is the Status E class, the ineligibles who for one reason or another have lost their right to a Savant implant.

A major step in the stabilization of the social order came in 2154 when the Congress of Justice ruled that the individual implantee is the legal owner of his or her implant, and Savant inheritance laws were passed to enable parents to transmit their implants to their children.[5] The inheritance of Savants staved off many problems during the past three centuries. But now we are facing a difficulty that has haunted societies through the ages: A demand for the reallocation of personal property, and of course the Savant is our most treasured possession.

Major demographic shifts and social developments, begun as early as the twentieth century, may provide us with an insight into our current problems concerning the Savant and its distribution. The twentieth century laid the groundwork for intensive-energy technologies—nuclear and solar—and brought profound changes in occupational and social structure in our society. Particularly in the United States, the great migrations at the end of the nineteenth century helped to create an urban society. These surges in urban population accompanied vast industrial expansion. As the twentieth century wore on, the core institutions—the economy, government, and

---

[4] At this time, however, the spillover effects of specialized Savants upon general mental functioning are still not fully understood. (See Benjamin Axelrod, "How Specialized Are Status B Savants?" *International Journal of Experimental Savant Psychology,* 2475, 327, pp. 596–602.)

[5] This landmark decision was enunciated in a brilliant opinion by Justice Daniel Alan Brandeis and has been reprinted in *The Savant and the Law* (New York, 2178), edited by Tanya B. Rashi and Julia Mae Rambam.

education—increased in complexity manyfold and required much more technical training and social sophistication for effective operation than ever before. To meet this need, the proportion of the work force in professional, administrative, and technical occupations rose enormously.

This modification in occupational structure was accompanied by dramatic demographic shifts. One was the drastic decline in foreign immigration—since industry's need for unskilled workers languished. Another was the decline of the agricultural population. Advances in agricultural technology and the virtual extinction of the small farmer made possible the influx of rural and small-town populations to the cities. Then, when these resources were virtually exhausted, there came an increased reliance upon women and other persons who traditionally had been marginal to highly-trained segments of the labor force. It became acceptable (and even desirable) to be highly mobile, to reduce the impediments of having children, and to subordinate domestic loyalties to work commitment.

These demographic transformations produced transformations in socialization. The participation of new groups in a set of institutions requires their learning appropriate social norms. Just as in the United States the theme of the nineteenth century had been the Americanization of immigrants, the major movements of the twentieth century focused upon the normalization of groups formerly considered to be superfluous or marginal to the core of the public culture—the educational, political, and economic institutions (Farber, 1968). Normalization took various forms—Civil Rights movement in the case of ethnic minorities, the Women's Liberation Movement, the Mainstreaming Movement among the handicapped, the Advocacy Movement, and so on. These movements were based on the assumption that social inequality is rooted in factors over which individuals have no control, most of all ascribed status; that is, the idea that one's birth is a major determinant of personal destiny. Normalization was intended to eliminate ascribed status and personal misfortune as elements in governing schooling, occupation, marital choice—all summed up by the concept "life chances."

What was the result of these twentieth century movements? First, of course, they did bring many people who previously had been marginal or superfluous into the economy, and in doing so, they inflated the educated labor pool. Yet, declining birthrates, declining immigration, and declining foreign markets, together with other complex factors, capped off industrial expansion and created a surplus of potential bureaucratic, technical, and professional workers. With this surplus, unemployment rates increased, and wages and salaries were depressed.

This situation occurred, we must remember, as the general educational level of the population rose. The intended elimination of ascribed status as a basis for personal destiny meant that people had rising expectations of economic and occupational achievement because of their higher educational qualifications. But as early as the twentieth century, social scientists had found that as educational levels in a society rose, they rose for people at all levels. Consequently, those groups previously at the bottom in education remained at the bottom. Overall, education as a resource merely underwent inflation (Boudon, 1973).

But problems occurred not merely for those who remained in their previous position of relative deprivation; with the expansion of the educated work force, they occurred also at higher educational levels. The twentieth century is not unique in generating problems of unmet rising expectations because of a general rise in educational level. Historians tell us that even around 1820:

Just because France had created an excellent educational system, the educated youth . . . , whose supply exceeded the demand, faced what they considered a bleak future. The France of the Restoration abounded with doctors without patients, lawyers without clients, and young men spending their time in waiting rooms of the high and mighty. Not really being in demand, these young men suffered not only from material discontent but also from a deep seated spiritual malaise (Coser, 1971).

In the twentieth century, marginal groups—ethnic minorities, the poor, the physically handicapped, the mentally retarded—were treated in ways that led to exaggerated hopes for upward social mobility on the principle of equality of opportunity. As one disillusioned, retarded man told an interviewer in a research project, "I have had a hard life. I tell you. If I had to live it over, I wouldn't do it" (Henshel, 1971). Objectively, this young man's living conditions were on the whole better than most of his retarded contemporaries. But the idea that literally all ascribed attributes should be wiped away in determining social rewards produced disappointment—disappointment resulting from the discrepancy between, on the one hand, generated hopes and expectations and, on the other hand, actual conditions and realizable goals.[6] At the same time, this idea of equality of opportunity engendered fear in a majority of the population that their lot in life was insecure; they were faced with a threat of status loss—a decline in their hold on resources. Their reaction to this threat, as has occurred in other times and other places, was to ensure the inoperativeness of the principle of equality of opportunity (Hofstadter, 1963).

Realizing the potential destructiveness wrought by unmet heightened expectations, present-day Savant society has had to make certain assumptions about social life. First, it has had to accept the axiom that "some envy appears for any degree of inequality, and that envy is proportional to inequality" (Boudon, 1976). Second, it has introduced the assumption that upward social mobility—the heightening of expectations and meeting those heightened expectations—should be determined by the principle of randomized opportunity.

Let me explain the principle of randomized opportunity. It is opposed both to the principle of equal opportunity and to the principle of allocating careers according to talent. The principle of equal opportunity involves the neutralization of effects of ascribed status and personal misfortune in fostering upward mobility. It is the equivalent of giving everyone a Savant and thereby raising everyone's expectations for preferential treatment in occupation and allocation of resources—just as educational inflation had done earlier in history. Given the scarcity of preferred occupations and resources, this principle would inevitably create disappointment and resentment for large segments of the population. Consequently, Savant society has had to abandon the principle of equal opportunity as unworkable.

The principle of allocating careers according to talent has other deficiencies. If upward social mobility is based only on talent, then the person

---

[6] Compare with Komarovsky (1964) for the effects of disappointment over the failure to be upwardly socially mobile on self-esteem and marital relationships in working class families.

who lacks talent (or fails to pursue a career consonant with his or her talent) feels much guilt, frustration, and envy, while the person with talent is in constant anxiety over the stability of his position—his continued access to resources. Twentieth-century studies show that this principle, too, is highly destructive to personal integrity and social order.[7] Besides, as a matter of practical concern, with Savant implantation the exact degree of "natural" competence is of little interest.

This leaves us with the principle of randomized opportunity. According to this principle, all Status D persons (as well as those who have served their punishment time in Status E) have an equal opportunity to move into a Savant status by random selection. Social science findings from the twentieth century have indicated that the poor and working class of that time regarded social mobility as a matter of "fate" or "luck" (Cohen and Hodges, 1963); what Savant society has done is to formalize this conception into a method for actually determining upward social mobility. The number of implantations at any time is sufficient to maintain hope of receiving one. This hope of social mobility has somewhat mitigated the amount of envy generated by inequality. True, the envy is there and is often expressed openly. But it is this fine balance between envy and hope that motivates Status D and E people to live within the Savant scheme of things.

And now to our present danger! There is a growing black market in Status A Savant implants. This black market is so widespread that it is bringing unrealistically high expectations to buyers, expectations that cannot be met by our social order; and corresponding fears of possible status loss are emerging among those who now occupy Status A positions. Fellow human engineers, what should be done? We could salve our guilt by arbitrarily deciding that we can indeed have a whole society of Savants and then try to work out difficulties afterwards. But I am fearful that the problems generated by the mass distribution of intellectual competence are inherent in our social structure: While we recognize the right of each individual to be intellectually competent in principle, we must maintain individual differences—indeed, even group differences—to sustain our social order and to ensure the continued fulfillment of expectations for each Savant class. In fact, the only times we were able to establish a goal of a Status A Savant for everyone were in the early years when this was impossible. At this time, we must end the black market sales of Savants and to eliminate its illegal possession: We must destroy illegal intelligence before the Savant inflation destroys our social order!

This ends the mental experiment. What are my conclusions? To begin with, no matter what controls I placed on the allocation of Savants, the end result was similar: The successful remediation of mental retardation led eventually to a general inflation of intelligence in the society, with the least intelligent persons still in a position of relative deprivation. What began as a strategy for remediation, ironically, ended as the very means for sustaining the condition it was intended to correct. But the possibility of a constantly escalating level of intelligence leads to still another question: Is there an upper limit to the intellectual resources that a society can manage? But this question requires my

---

[7] See the mental experiment by Michael Young (1958) describing the events of 2033.

return to Savant society for yet another mental experiment. At any rate, the study of social conditions relevant to mental retardation should lead ultimately to more general questions about social order and its contradictions.

SUMMARY

A futurist mental experiment is performed that assumes that contemporary social and biological bases of intellectual disability have been eradicated. The results suggest that social order requires the persistence of mental retardation and eventually tends to turn remedial strategies into means for perpetuating those very phenomena they were designed to eliminate.

ACKNOWLEDGMENT

We are grateful to Rosanna Farber for her valuable suggestions and comments—no superfluous person is she!

REFERENCES

Boudon, R. (1973) Education, Opportunity, and Social Inequality. New York: Wiley-Interscience.

Boudon, R. (1976) Review essay of John Rawls, A Theory of Justice. Contemp. Sociol. 5:104.

Cohen, A. K., and Hodges, H. M. (1963) Characteristics of the lower-blue-collar class. Soc. Probl. 10:303.

Coser, L. A. (1971) Masters of Sociological Thought. New York: Harcourt Brace & Co. p. 32.

Farber, B. (1968) Mental Retardation: Its Social Context and Social Consequences. Boston: Houghton Mifflin, pp. 3–22 and 103–118.

Henshel, A. (1971) The Forgotten Ones: Case Studies of Chicano and Anglo Retardates. Austin: Rehabilitation Research and Training Center in Mental Retardation, University of Texas, p. 153.

Hofstadter, R. (1963) The pseudo-conservative revolt. In The Radical Right (Ed. Bell, D.) New York: Anchor Books, pp. 75–95.

Johnson, H. M. (1960) Sociology, A Systematic Introduction. New York: Harcourt Brace & Co., p. 75.

Komarovsky, M. (1964) Blue Collar Marriage. New York: Random House, pp. 285–293.

Merton, R. K. (1957) Social Theory and Social Structure. New York: Free Press, pp. 56–60.

Young, M. D. (1958) The Rise of the Meritocracy, 1870–2033. New York: Random House.

RESEARCH TO PRACTICE IN MENTAL RETARDATION
Care and Intervention, Volume I
Edited by Peter Mittler
Copyright 1977 I.A.S.S.M.D.

A THEORY OF THE NEW LEISURE CLASS
Some Philosophical Reflections on Residential Life for the Multiply Handicapped Adult

F. P. Woodford
Institute for Research into Mental and Multiple Handicap,
16 Fitzroy Square, London, W1, England

At the end of the nineteenth century Thorstein Veblen published his sociologica
classic, *The Theory of the Leisure Class*. He showed that leisure was not so mucl
the reward as the inescapable obligation of a certain class. In this paper I shall
attempt to show that handicapped adults are also confined to a kind of leisure
class whose activities are extremely limited. I believe that if we study the way of
life of the traditional leisure class we can learn how to serve the severely
handicapped adult who is in residential care in a much better way.

Members of the leisure class in the nineteenth century were in general envied
by the common mass of people, whose usual fate was unremitting toil. However,
we know from novels of the period that the life of the landed gentry was not all
a bed of roses. Women, in particular, were trapped in an uneventful way of life
that was for many of them irksome—and for some, a cause of desperation: shut
up for most of the year in a draughty country house set in the sodden fields,
with little company except for their servants and an infrequent glimpse of the
villagers and the vicar, relieved only occasionally by a few weeks' holiday in Bath,
London, or Baden-Baden. Their lives were often a burden to them; their mortal
enemy, boredom.

They, like the heavily handicapped, were born into a life of obligatory
leisure that could easily develop into a torment but that could, by careful

management, be moulded into a thing of purpose and pleasure. This is why I think we can usefully study the points of similarity between this fate and that of the mentally and physically handicapped.

There may be many objections to my analogy between these two classes of people. Let me first meet the objections of those who maintain that the handicapped should never be in isolated country-house residences in the first place, but mixing with nonhandicapped persons in the community. I should clarify that I am talking about the extremely heavily handicapped adults who simply could not manage a semi-independent life in the community, and furthermore *do not want to try to do so*—a point sometimes overlooked by the overzealous reformer. In my view, these residents can achieve a highly satisfying life in their artificial environment—which, as I hope to show, is no more artificial than the country-house environments described by Jane Austen and Thackeray—*provided* that we regard the handicapped not as a feeble work force but as members of a new leisure class.

When I first visited and studied certain residential centres run by the Spastics Society in England I was struck by a paradox. There, according to a common pattern in such centres, the residents spent most of their days in a work centre doing dull, repetitive contract work, whereas they filled their evenings and weekends very happily writing letters, love stories, pornography, and even poetry, as well as playing chess, making music, or listening to it. The idea of a work centre stemmed, of course, from the concept—not in itself a bad one—of *industrial therapy,* in which the satisfaction of making something both tangible and saleable, especially in groups, is supposed to exceed the actual drudgery involved. This concept has recently been reinforced by the ideal of 'normalization,' in which attempts are made to encourage and enable the handicapped to live as normal a life as possible. The argument goes that in normal life, most nonhandicapped people work; the large majority work in factories; hence, factory-type work brings the handicapped closer to normal life. This simplistic view overlooks the fact that people have all sorts of jobs in normal life, and mechanical assembly work is only one of them. In my view, normalization should attempt to encompass more of the variety we encounter in everyday life.

Work centres are also intended to overcome the problems of boredom. Now, boredom was a dreaded evil for the leisure class depicted by Tolstoy, Dickens, and Flaubert, especially for those obliged to stay at home, namely the women and the less robust of the men. How did they combat it, and construct a life that had purpose and meaning? Let us think through a typical day in a country house, say as pictured in Jane Austen's Mansfield Park.

The ladies began their day by being woken by a servant, dressed by a maid, and served breakfast—as the handicapped are. After breakfast, the ladies retired to the morning-room, there to read over and discuss the letters of the day and to reply to them. This apparently simple activity can be a source of immense pleasure, and we should do more to help the handicapped derive that pleasure.

After correspondence, the ladies would turn to household management: ordering meals, doing or examining household accounts, choosing materials for wallpaper or curtains—all activities that, as we now know, are accessible even to the quite severely handicapped, at least in some measure.

With household organization disposed of, an hour might then be spend in sketching or painting in watercolour, the younger ladies probably being under the guidance of a drawing master. Late in the morning would come the time for receiving calls from neighbours; if nobody called, there was always the need to practise the harpsichord or piano or some newly published ballads. In fine weather, a turn in the shrubbery would fill out the morning, or else a walk to the village to match a ribbon, purchase embroidery silks, or visit the dressmaker. (Substantial local shopping would, of course, be all arranged between the cook or housekeeper and the local tradesmen, who delivered provisions to the Hall in bulk.) I need not labour the points of similarity to the organization of a residential centre for the handicapped. Let us just bear in mind the activities filling the time of the lady of leisure: reading, writing, organizing, making music, painting, visiting, light shopping, and arranging for her personal adornment. Enlightened, well-run centres enable their handicapped residents to engage in all these activities—but such centres are, in my opinion, far too few . . . at least in Britain.

Let us return to our Jane Austen ladies. Their luncheon was followed by rather more strenuous outdoor activities: visiting families of similar means and status at rather long distances, for which the carriage would be requisitioned; and, in addition, other expeditions to local points of interest or beauty, often devised in order to entertain the houseguests—themselves another source of entertainment (and responsibility). Here is where I think we could do wonders by pressing the analogy. My Institute's research has shown that day visits to another residential centre are extremely popular with residents, and there is no reason that I can see against exchanging groups of residents between centres for country-house visits of 3-4 weeks or even longer. Every centre has its transport facilities, so that the *cost* of such short or longer visits would be minimal—yet they are an enormously rich source of new ideas, something for the residents to talk about and think about on their return, as well as being a basis on which they can press for improvements in their own centre when they get back home.

Dinner in the eighteenth or nineteenth century country house might be either a purely family affair, or an occasion for yet more entertaining, with the chance to see new faces and embark on new relationships. After dinner there would be music-making, conversation, cards, perhaps charades, and, when there were enough young people present, dancing. Overt or covert flirting—or, more seriously, matchmaking—would give zest to these simple entertainments; or failing that, gossip. Professional entertainers (usually musicians) were only occasionally employed; much reliance was placed on bringing in new acquaintances, or ringing the changes in combining the old ones, as a source of entertainment. Again, I believe, we should press the analogy: I think the handicapped would derive vastly greater enjoyment from making their own entertainment than from the endless watching of professional entertainers on the television screen.

The practical usefulness of this analysis is as follows: We do in fact know a good deal about the activities of the leisure class Veblen was talking about because we can study them in detail in nineteenth century literature, where they are described with great psychological insight. Their activities were not mere transitory fads: they had been evolved over the course of centuries by hundreds of leisured people in many countries as solutions to the problems of enforced leisure, boredom, and feelings of uselessness and purposelessness. Many can be adopted without change, as practical alternatives to the deadliness of sorting plastic cutlery into cellophane packets.

Other activities need some degree of modification or adaptation. For instance, painting in watercolours may need head-probes or other devices to enable a resident to hold the brush. Although these may seem formidably cumbersome to the able-bodied, painting has proved a popular occupation in the centres where a drawing teacher has been introduced. Listening to music is simple to arrange in these days of transistor radios and tape recorders, but listening with some degree of understanding, discrimination, and historical sense needs guidance and cultivation; some variant of the music master is needed. Writing letters, poems, and essays, even with the aid of an electric typewriter, may require superhuman efforts for a handicapped person and seemingly endless, patient teaching—but what an extraordinary spiritual triumph when the difficulties are surmounted and the resident breaks through, perhaps for the first time if he has no speech, into the world of communication with friends and relatives. Games are also important for communication, and electronic and other gadgets are increasingly being developed to enable the handicapped to participate in indoor games, including educational ones (Anon. 1976). The handicapped can learn to play a variety of instruments—not particularly well, but I suspect that Jane Austen's Emma was no Rubinstein either. We in our Institute have recently taught groups of residents to make video recordings from their wheelchairs and to edit the tapes into a satisfying film. This group use of a modern medium is to my knowledge something entirely new, although it has of course been known for years that many sports, including riding and dancing, can be enjoyed by the handicapped.

My belief is that all these activities would make life richer and fuller than filling the day with a kind of work that is merely the means of making money. I would far rather see the residents put together a monthly or quarterly magazine than assemble cardboard display boxes of hideous cutlery for Woolworths. What is more important, so would a good many of the residents—as the research by our Institute's team has shown. Let me hasten to add that about half the residents in the centres we have investigated do enjoy repetitive manual tasks and find the more intellectual leisure activities provided in some centres a strain; they should by no means be forced away from what they prefer, but offered alternatives. I believe, with the social philosopher Sir Karl Popper, that the highest societal good is maximum freedom of choice.

The provision of leisure activities as alternatives to factory-type work would, of course, involve some changes in staff roles. It is not coincidental that most of the activities I have named (other than visiting) require a leader or teacher, and it may be that houseparents will have to acquire such roles or be replaced by teachers. Few handicapped adults have been *educated* for a life of leisure, as the landed gentry were. However, there are no insuperable practical difficulties in this: handicapped adults are as much entitled to Further Education as anybody else—some would say, more so. To those who object that adults do not take kindly to being put back in school I submit (a) that this has not been the reaction in centres where subject teachers have been introduced, and (b) that everything hinges on the teacher's attitude. If the instruction is provided not in a spirit of benevolence to the unfortunate but in the service of enhancing the life style of a leisure class, all will be well.

Finally, let us not confuse leisure, which demands application and cultivation, with idleness—as I fear the sturdy man in the street may do. Already I hear him objecting "Why should I pay to support these people in idleness? The handicapped should work for their living like everybody else." *Should* they? I think not. The amount of work needed by a severely handicapped person to get through a day of rising, washing, dressing, eating, drinking, excreting, moving about and going to bed, which the rest of us take for granted, seems to me work enough. It is surely Society's obligation—*our* obligation—to help the handicapped achieve those mundane things and then over and above that to educate them for, and enable them to lead, a life of intellectual and spiritual grace as members of a recognized, new leisure class.

I realize that such recognition will not come easily. As Stanley Parker remarks, in a recent paper on the sociology of leisure (Parker, 1975), "Cultural norms, inherited from the past, socialize us into the belief that work is good and idleness reprehensible. So the long-term unemployed and the retired, who ought to be able to adjust to a life of total leisure, in fact mostly find this extremely difficult." It is up to us to make it less difficult for the handicapped.

SUMMARY

An analogy is drawn between multiply handicapped adults housed in isolated residential centres and the women and menfolk of the former landed gentry. It is suggested that consideration of the pastimes and activities devised by the latter to counteract boredom and isolation could lead to the provision of a more satisfying and dignified way of life for the handicapped than the present factory work—oriented approach.

ACKNOWLEDGMENTS

The ideas in this article are not necessarily shared by my colleagues, but the data, where given, were provided by my colleagues Mr. Paul Cherrett and Miss Karen Boston, to whom I am also indebted for critical comment. Financial support by the Spastics Society is gratefully acknowledged.

REFERENCES

Anonymous (1976) Noughts and crosses for spastics. New Scientist 20:133.
Parker, S. (1975) The sociology of leisure: progress and problems. Brit. J. Sociol. 26:91.

RESEARCH TO PRACTICE IN MENTAL RETARDATION
Care and Intervention, Volume I
Edited by Peter Mittler
Copyright 1977 I.A.S.S.M.D.

CONCERNS OF THE COMMUNITY ABOUT EXPERIMENTATION ON HUMAN SUBJECTS

J. F. Childress
Center for Bioethics, Kennedy Institute, Georgetown University, Washington, D.C. 20057, United States

Since the revelations of the terrible Nazi experiments there have been numerous individual and collective expressions of concern about research involving human subjects. Various medical and legal codes (such as the Nuremberg Code of Ethics in Medical Research, Katz, 1972) now embody that concern about what may legitimately be done on behalf of scientific progress. Yet concern about this issue has fluctuated in the United States. In 1966, *The New England Journal of Medicine* published Beecher's important article on "Ethics and Clinical Research," which documented many cases of unethical and questionably ethical experimental procedures. In the early 1970s, disclosure of the Tuskegee Study (in which many black men suffering from syphilis were not being treated) provoked outrage. Indeed, the Tuskegee Study and the availability of fetuses for research after the Supreme Court in *Roe* v. *Wade* and *Doe* v. *Bolton* overturned restrictive abortion laws were two of the main reasons for Congressional action to create the National Commission for the Protection of Human Subjects of Biomedical and Behavioral Research, whose mandate, in part, is to "conduct a comprehensive investigation and study to identify the basic ethical principles which should underlie the conduct of biomedical and behavioral research involving human subjects. . . ." (Public Law 93-348). This commission, appointed in December, 1974, recommended fetal research guidelines in 1975 and will probably finish its other tasks early in 1977.

While I could examine these and other examples of individual and community concern about experimentation, it would also be in accord with my assigned topic and more useful to construct a framework of ethical justification of research involving human subjects. This framework builds on recent and current debates about experimentation; indeed, it is an attempt to present the major ethical concerns in a coherent, systematic way.

Justification involves giving reasons to show that an act or policy is right, all things considered, when there is some reason for thinking that it might be wrong. *Nontherapeutic* experimentation—experimentation designed to obtain knowledge not for the subject's own benefit—stands in need of justification. There is a moral presumption against nontherapeutic experimentation because it exposes persons to risks or at least interferes with them even when it does not impose serious risks. Imposition of risks and interference require justification. The burden of proof is on those who propose the research. Nevertheless, there are conditions under which the presumption against nontherapeutic experimentation can be rebutted or overridden. Most of the recent ethical and legal discussion of experimentation has focused on the consent requirement, perhaps because of the conviction that if there is consent, there is no injury. However, because consent is only one of several indispensable elements in the justification of experimentation, to concentrate on it to the exclusion of other concerns is a mistake. A complete ethical analysis and justification of experimentation includes ends and consequences as well as means, teleological as well as deontological concerns. I propose to present the main ethical considerations in a systematic way, indicating the order in which they experientially and logically arise in the justification of research involving human subjects.

1. There must be a morally important reason, a *just cause,* for undertaking the research. To draw the issues in terms of a dichotomy between "moral values" and "scientific progress" may be misleading, for often science serves moral ends. The hard question is how much weight we should give to the moral values that are invoked to justify research including the use of human subjects. Some ends are "moral" in that their pursuit is not "immoral," others are "moral" in that their pursuit is "morally required." Saving society might fall under the latter, while some forms of improving the human condition might fall under the former and might even be considered ideal or supererogatory actions that merit praise. Nevertheless, given the contributions of medical science to human well-being, we can at least hold that the aims of some research are morally justified and perhaps even mandatory.

2. The use of human subjects in such research should be a matter of *last resort*; their use must be *necessary.* An ethically justified use of human subjects must be preceded by other studies and research, including animal experimentation. After these other studies and research, we must still need to know how human beings respond before it is justified to use them. The Nuremberg Code of Ethics in Medical Research holds that "the experiment should be such as to yield fruitful results for the good of society, *unprocurable by other methods or means of study....*"

3. The third criterion more explicitly raises the matter of scientific hypotheses and research designs that are implicit in the second criterion: there must be a *reasonable prospect* that the protocol will result in the knowledge that is sought. Again, animal experimentation is a precondition. As the Nuremberg

Code indicates, "the experiment should be so designed and based on the results of animal experimentation and a knowledge of the natural history of the disease or other problem under study that the anticipated results will justify the performance of the experiment."

4. The research involving human subjects must also meet the principle of *proportionality;* there must be a proper ratio between benefits and risks. As the Department of Health, Education, and Welfare's guidelines of May 30, 1974, indicate, a review must determine whether "the risks to the subject are so outweighed by the sum of the benefit to the subject and the importance of the knowledge to be gained as to warrant a decision to allow the subject to accept these risks. . . ." According to our first criterion, it is necessary to determine the value of the end that is sought; this fourth criterion adds the consideration of risks and their comparison with the benefits—an indispensable but difficult task. "The degree of risk to be taken should never exceed that determined by the humanitarian importance of the problem to be solved by the experiment" (Nuremberg Code).

5. In the fifth place, the research must have the subject's *voluntary and informed consent.* This requirement of consent is based on fairness and respect for the autonomy of persons. Without this requirement, the subject would be only a tool in the hands of the investigator. Consent is different from approval, for we may approve all sorts of actions by others without consenting to them. Consent is a right-creating action; it creates rights in others (see Plamenatz, 1968). But it creates rights only when it is informed and voluntary, and difficulties abound in determining the degree of voluntariness and the amount and quality of information that are sufficient. Since full and complete information is impossible, is "reasonably informed" consent sufficient? Can prisoners and military personnel be said to give "voluntary" consent to participation in experimentation? Is proxy consent for the mentally incompetent and for children adequate? These and similar questions need the most careful attention.

One additional point needs to be made. Much of the information that the researchers must convey to prospective subjects really concerns the first four criteria for ethically justified experimentation, for example, the benefits, risks, and their ratio. A prospective subject may agree that the research is justified according to the first four criteria, but refuse to participate for various reasons. Whether we would say that normal adults have a duty to participate in research is, I think, unclear. In the case of an emergency, such as a plague that threatens the country, we would affirm such an obligation. In normal circumstances, we might argue that there is an obligation based on fairness to participate as research subjects because we have derived benefits from medical advances that were in part made possible by the sacrifices of others (see Childress, 1971; McCormick, 1976). (It would be instructive also to consider when we would be willing to override the requirement of informed consent. A state of emergency or necessity of an extreme sort could conceivably justify a draft, which would, of course, have to meet standards of fairness.) Others, however, contend that participation is only an act of charity or supererogation.

I suggest that these five criteria establish necessary conditions for ethically justified research involving human subjects. Each of them must be met for nontherapeutic experimentation to proceed. Furthermore, these criteria should be considered in roughly the order that I presented them. This is not, I think, an arbitrary or idiosyncratic point but rather one that reflects something about the structure of moral deliberation and reasoning. These criteria are arranged in a serial order so that, at the very least, the question of benefits should be addressed first. Without an affirmative answer to that question, there is no need to consider the other criteria, including informed consent. Likewise, even if there is dispute about the order of criteria 2 to 4, the requirement of informed consent should be the final one. Despite the temptation to refer to consent first (as in the Nuremberg Code), it should come last because it should not be raised unless the other criteria are met. To concentrate on informed consent may lead to a distortion of the other ethical requirements for experimentation. One reason for its prominence in the discussions may well stem from its logical position in this serial arrangement. Even when the other conditions are met, there may be difficulty in getting voluntary and informed consent. If so, the use of human subjects is unjustified. In this serial arrangement, we consider each criterion in turn, but each one must be met, for each one establishes a necessary condition. If informed consent cannot be obtained (at least from a proxy), the research does not satisfy the full set of moral standards.

In addition to these five criteria, there are two others that merit attention, although I do not think that failure to meet them renders any particular experiment unjustified.

6. The sixth standard is an ideal of justice to which we should aspire in our society: the selection of subjects for participation in research should be fair and just. Are the risks and benefits of research distributed within the population in a manner that will "withstand scrutiny"? (Gray, 1975). In these remarks I am especially concerned about the risks of participating in research. Hans Jonas has proposed the principle of "identification" for recruitment of subjects: selection of participants who can "identify" with the goals and purposes of scientific research. Obviously, this principle suggests initial recruitment from within the scientific community. But then "one should look for additional subjects where a maximum of identification, understanding, and spontaneity can be expected—that is, among the most highly motivated, the most highly educated, and the least 'captive' members of the community." Then there is an order of preference: "The poorer in knowledge, motivation, and freedom of decision (and that, alas, means the more readily available in terms of numbers and possible manipulation), the more sparingly and indeed reluctantly should the reservoir be used, and the more compelling must therefore become the countervailing justification"

(Jonas, 1969). In practice, we tend to take advantage of the weak and powerless, the poor and uneducated, the imprisoned and institutionalized mentally infirm, the sick on the wards, etc. This selection is made mainly in terms of convenience, not necessity, and it is hardly warranted by the principles of justice that we affirm in the distribution of risks.

7. Violation of the seventh principle also does not render an experiment unjustified. This principle is that justice calls for compensation of subjects for research-related injuries. (I have not dealt in this paper with compensation for participation in research. Such compensation should probably be for time and inconvenience, rather than participation, and it should not constitute an "undue incentive.") Currently, reparative justice covers some of the injuries sustained by research subjects when the investigators are negligent (i.e., impose undue risks or are careless) or when they fail to get informed consent. An injured subject may sue for reparative justice under the tort of battery or negligence. Although we need this tort approach, particularly as a method of control, we need to supplement it with a policy of compensatory justice for injuries that do not result from an investigator's fault. Injured research subjects have a claim not merely to our humanitarianism or beneficence, but to our justice. We owe research subjects compensation for injuries because they assume a position of risk for society. Scientific progress is of value to the community that encourages, sponsors, and even mandates some research. Thus, the community ought to accept responsibility for those who assume a position of risk on behalf of and often at the behest of the community. The subject's consent should not be construed as a waiver of a claim to compensation. An analogy may make this point: in military service, we have both volunteers and draftees, but we do not discriminate between them in compensating for injuries. Consent is an expression of a willingness to participate in research for the social welfare (regardless of the individual subject's particular motives), and it should not excuse society from its duty of compensatory justice.

Although there are other ethical issues in experimentation, particularly in the matter of control of research and researchers, these seven are among the most important; the first five are necessary conditions of ethically justified research, while six and seven indicate policies that we ought to implement in accord with principles of justice. All of them, however, point to a model of experimentation in which the research subjects are not mere subjects but collaborators, partners, and "co-adventurers" with researchers for the sake of scientific knowledge (see Ramsey, 1970).

SUMMARY

This paper deals with the justification for research involving human subjects, risk-benefit analysis, the requirement of informed consent, and the appropriateness of using certain classes of subjects, such as fetuses, children, prisoners, and mentally retarded persons in institutions, as well as other criteria.

REFERENCES

Beecher, H. K. (1966) Ethics and clinical research. New Engl. J. Med. 274:1354.

Childress, J. F. (1971) Civil Disobedience and Political Obligation. New Haven, Connecticut: Yale University Press.

Gray, B. (1975) Human Subjects in Medical Experimentation. New York: Wiley, p. 253.

Jonas, H. (1969) Philosophical reflections on experimenting with human subjects. Daedalus 98:235, 237.

Katz, J. (1972) Experimentation with Human Beings. New York: Russell Sage Foundation, pp. 305—306.

McCormick, R. A. (1976) Experimental subjects: Who should they be? JAMA 235:2197.

Plamenatz, J. (1968) Consent, Freedom and Political Obligation. 2nd Edition. London: Oxford University Press.

Ramsey, P. (1970) The Patient as Person. New Haven, Connecticut: Yale University Press.

RESEARCH TO PRACTICE IN MENTAL RETARDATION
Care and Intervention, Volume I
Edited by Peter Mittler
Copyright 1977 I.A.S.S.M.D.

CONSENT PROCEDURES
A Conceptual Approach to Protection Without Overprotection

H. R. Turnbull, III
*Institute of Government, University of
North Carolina, Chapel Hill,
North Carolina 27514, United States*

THE FUNCTION OF LAW

As a general rule, the law usually reflects the ethical values of a society. Sometimes, of course, it clings to those values in the face of challenges to them, and at other times it accedes to those challenges and enables us to adopt other new and more highly cherished values. This, however, is not the proper forum to discuss the function of law, except to note that, in the context of a seminar on biomedical and behavioral research on humans, it is clear that the law presently mirrors the values that we of the Western world hold dear. In brief, it reflects the ethical considerations involved in that kind of research.

The Ethical Value of Self-Determination

I believe that, in the context of research on humans, the ultimate ethical value is self-determination. Whether we characterize it as self-determination, individual autonomy, or fate control, we are speaking about a person's interest in having the maximum control over what happens to him, consistent with the rights of others.

I also believe that this ultimate value is summed up in the principle that experimentation on a human should not be conducted, as a general rule, without the person's prior consent.

The relationship between the value of self-determination and the principle of consent is perfectly clear. Consent is the device or the mechanism whereby we put into effect the value of self-determination. If experimentation may not, as a general rule, be undertaken without consent, then the individual's power to grant or withhold his consent to be experimented upon is the means by which he controls his fate, expresses his individuality, and determines what happens to him. Without the legal right to consent or withhold consent, a person has no legal power to activate the value of self-determination. Thus, the law that states that consent is required before a person may be made the subject of an experiment mirrors our ethical values.

Legal Procedures and Consent Procedures

One way that the law operates is to devise procedures that enable us to put the power of law behind the ethical values mirrored in substantive law.

In the context of human experimentation, the law does this by devising procedures that are, it is hoped, essentially fair to all persons who have an interest in experimentation on humans. Before I discuss those procedures in detail, I believe it is useful for us to pay attention to the reason that the law is so concerned with procedures as a means by which we put our ethical values into operation.

The reason is simple: lawyers and lawmakers tend to believe that fair procedures will produce fair and acceptable results.

If a procedure is fair in the sense that it permits all persons who have a stake or an interest in a matter to be heard by an impartial and independent person, it is more likely, we believe, that the results of the procedure will reflect the interests, claims, and rights of each of those persons. Perhaps the result will not always strike an acceptable balance between those interests, claims, and rights, but the chances are greater that it will than they would be if the procedure did not permit all of the interests, claims, and rights to be heard.

We also believe that because the results are arrived at fairly, they will be more acceptable. When all people having an interest in a matter have had a chance to be heard, they are often more willing to abide by the result than when they have not had such a chance. In addition, the innumerable people not having a direct interest in the matter and not having an opportunity to be heard are likely to accept the result because they know that those who are directly affected have had a fair chance to be heard.

Finally, all of us—whether we are directly affected or not—are concerned that we deal fairly with each other. We want the government to deal fairly with us, and we want our fellow citizens to deal fairly with us. Our interest in fair play as a broad governmental and social value is reflected in our concern with fair procedures.

For these many reasons, then, the law has combined the ethical value of self-determination with the mechanism of consent and the legal requirement of a fair procedure in order to assure that research on humans is not likely to abuse the human subject.

The Three Elements of Consent

As a matter of general law, consent consists of three elements, each of which must be present in order for consent to be effective. These are capacity, information, and voluntariness.

Briefly stated, capacity refers to a person's mental process or the faculty by which he acquires and acts upon knowledge. The element of information—informed consent—focuses on "what" information is given and "how" it is given; the basic test is whether the disclosure is full and effective, whether it is designed to be fully understood, and is in fact understood. Finally, voluntariness refers to the absence of force, fraud, deceit, duress, overreaching, or other ulterior form of constraint or coercion.

When applying these three elements of consent to the mentally retarded, there are difficult threshold problems. In the first place, a person may be retarded but still not lack capacity; the fact that he is retarded is, however, evidence that he lacks full capacity.

In the second place, when a person's mental capacity is in question because of his retardation, one is concerned that the explanation of information is at an appropriate level of comprehension, that the disclosure is designed to be fully understood, and that it is in fact understood. Mental impairment does not prevent adequate disclosure, but it does suggest that the fullness and effectiveness of disclosure should be carefully scrutinized.

Finally, the test of voluntariness is compounded by questions related to whether or not the retarded person is more likely to give his consent because, among other reasons, he is in an institution or in custody, he is involuntarily detained or committed, he is overly eager to please and do as others ask him to do, he lacks experience in similar situations, he is more susceptible to inducements or threats because of his mental capacity, or he is unable to obtain independent advice and consultation.

Peer and Ethical Review Bodies

In order to safeguard the retarded subject and to take into account these threshold questions of whether the retarded subject can satisfy all three elements of consent, HEW regulations and recent court decisions have created a new form of safeguard, commonly known as the peer or ethical review body, sometimes called a consent committee. This body has two purposes: first, to review the proposed research and pass upon its scientific methodology; and second, to ensure that consent is adequate and effective.

In discharging the latter function, the ethical review or consent committee will inquire into whether or not the retarded subject has capacity to consent; if it determines he does not, it will determine whether a legally valid substitute consent is obtained, i.e., consent from a person legally empowered to give or withhold consent on behalf of the subject himself. It also may exercise a veto over the proposed investigation by withholding its approval on the grounds that the investigation is too risky, intrusive, or irreversible for any consent to be ethically tolerated.

It is interesting that the safeguard of the ethical review committee also is known as the consent committee, interesting because it tells us something significant about consent and procedures.

The "Impartial" Committee

The membership of the committee typically consists not only of scientists trained in the methodology of research, but also of laymen untrained in the scientific method.

Why does a committee typically consist of both types of members? It is because a fair procedure cannot exist where the interests, rights, and claims of all persons having a stake in the research are not heard or cannot be represented.

Our notions of fair play are violated if the "judge" who rules on proposed experimentation with humans is likely to be a committee overloaded with members from the scientific community who, arguably, are inclined to favor research but not to inquire closely into the issue of whether effective consent has been obtained and whether the research should go forward notwithstanding the securing of effective consent.

Just as we do not trust a person with a stake in a dispute to be the judge of who wins the dispute, so we do not entrust the review procedure to persons arguably inclined to favor research. We suspect that the interests of people opposing the research will not be given due consideration by those who are inclined to favor research. I hesitate to say that our suspicions are well founded, only that they exist. Indeed, it is my impression that the instances in which a researcher has placed a higher value on his investigation than on his subject and may have abused his subject are less frequent than those in which he has refrained from putting his subject to unacceptable risk in spite of the effect it might have on research. Nevertheless, those instances of abuse have a substantial effect on consent procedures and give rise to the requirement of peer and ethical review.

An adequate consent procedure, then, requires impartiality on the part of the persons judging whether consent is effective.

However, more than impartiality is involved. Ethical considerations are very much involved, which is why a review committee is characterized as an ethical review committee. The ethical considerations address not simply the matter of whether or not consent is effective, but also whether or not the research should be undertaken even if effective consent has been obtained.

Ethics, Research, and Ethical Review Committees

It is an unfortunate fact that some research on humans, even when it has been consented to, has been viewed as intolerable because of the nature of the research itself. Some research is shocking to our collective conscience by today's standards, and some will be shocking by tomorrow's. What causes us to be morally outraged—to feel that our own society's standards of decency and humaneness have been violated—may be the view, argued by some, that research that is fully and effectively consented to should proceed forthwith, that consent alone justifies any research.

None of us would condone a view that consent alone justifies any research, however shocking the research may be. Some innate and frequently poorly articulated standards of decency, ethics, and humaneness should cause us to withhold our approval of some research, even when consent has been obtained.

It is because some research has the potential for shocking our individual and collective consciences and for violating our sense of decency and humaneness and our ethics and values, that we have insisted, in our laws shaping the consent committees, that the views of laymen be represented and heard.

We place our trust in the common man, in laymen, and in our peers, to feel the same outrage as we might feel and to express the same opposition to ethically intolerable research that we would express.

By requiring that laymen—our peers—serve on consent committees and that consent committees review more than the scientific methodology and the adequacy of consent, we have created a device for infusing research with ethics. We have resorted to the power of the law—agency regulations or court orders—to secure an ethical objective, which is to prevent research that is shocking to our consciences. Beyond that objective, of course, is the goal of ensuring, to the extent we can, that our notions of decency and humaneness are taken into account in biomedical and behavioral research and are preserved, to the extent the law can preserve them, for our present and future benefit.

After all, research is only one of many ways in which we relate to each other. How it is conducted, the procedures under which it is conducted, and the nature of the research itself reveal much about how we value each other and hence how we value ourselves. To the extent that it can, the law—through the separate requirements that consent be obtained and ethical review be given—seeks to ensure that ethical considerations permeate research and are not slighted in the pursuit of knowledge. By the same token, the law seeks to enable us to hold a mirror up to ourselves in which we may look without being repelled by the reflection we see. We do not wish to see a reflection that tells us that we are less decent and less humane because we have permitted indecency and inhumaneness to occur in the conduct of research on humans. It is a function of law to enable us to see ourselves in a more acceptable light.

SUMMARY

Ethical considerations in human experimentation and research are mirrored in law. The law's approach to the concerns is to devise procedures that are fair—that prevent abuse without simultaneously preventing research. Underlying the procedural safeguards, however, are concepts about research and ourselves and our ethics.

RESEARCH TO PRACTICE IN MENTAL RETARDATION
Care and Intervention, Volume I
Edited by Peter Mittler
Copyright 1977 I.A.S.S.M.D.

ETHICAL USE OF BEHAVIOR MODIFICATION TECHNIQUES

P. Roos
National Association for Retarded Citizens, 2709
Avenue E East, Arlington, Texas 76011, United States

Although man has yearned to control his own destiny since antiquity, realistic progress toward this goal has been made only in recent years. Advances in the biological and behavioral sciences now hold the promise of prolonging life, combatting disease, and altering individual behavior. Indeed, our expanding technology may soon allow us to shape individual futures and, ultimately, to exercise control over the destiny of humanity.

As we gain increasing control over our individual and collective destinies through the application of scientific technology, we are being faced with serious ethical, moral, and legal issues. The potential ethical liability of the scientist seems directly proportional to the effectiveness of his technology. Hence, because behavior modification is proving to be relatively successful in achieving specific objectives, it has become an increasingly frequent target for legal and ethical criticism.

VALUE OF BEHAVIOR MODIFICATION

Behavior modification refers to procedures derived from learning theory that are employed to alter behavior that is considered to be undesirable (Gardner, 1970). It has already proven to be immensely useful in developing specific skills in retarded individuals, as well as in eliminating undesirable behavior, and impressive evidence has been accumulated documenting its value. Advantages of behavior modification include the following:

> The techniques have been successfully applied to a wide range of individuals, including nonverbal, severely handicapped and "seriously disturbed" persons. A broad spectrum of behaviors has been successfully altered using behavior modification, including hallucinations, self-destructive actions, vomiting and anorexia, so-called sexual "perversions," and classical psycho-

neurotic symptoms. Procedures have also proven highly successful in developing a wide variety of skills, ranging from the simplest self-help skills to complex language and social behavior. The techniques can be applied by relatively unsophisticated persons, including direct care staff, teachers, and parents. In general, results are achieved relatively quickly when compared with other procedures.

Procedures have been developed that are suitable for group application, thereby maximizing their efficiency. Results are usually highly specific, predictable, objective, and quantifiable.

ETHICAL AND LEGAL ISSUES

Ethical and legal issues relate primarily to two aspects of behavior modification; namely, the use of aversive conditioning and the selection of goals. Each of these aspects raises important questions.

Aversive Conditioning

Manipulations of the environment that weaken antecedent behavior are referred to as negative reinforcement. The procedures vary in degree of intrusiveness from simple withholding of positive reinforcement (extinction) to administration of highly painful stimuli, such as electric shock (aversive conditioning). Since certain forms of aversive conditioning can be traumatic and intrusive, special safeguards are warranted to ensure that ethical and legal principles are not being violated. The following guidelines have been proposed with regard to the use of aversive conditioning (Roos, 1974, 1976):

Aversive conditioning should be used only when alternative procedures have proven to be ineffective and/or when their use is clearly advantageous over alternatives.

When used, aversive consequences need to be clearly defined and differentiated from procedures that are likely to meet with social condemnation. For example, "time out" should be differentiated from "seclusion"; the latter is often interpreted as a dehumanizing practice devised for staff convenience.

Care must be taken that the ends warrant the means, so that the probable discomfort of the aversive procedure is outweighed by weakening or eliminating more traumatic behavior (e.g., self-mutilation). Special care must be exercised that benefit to the client rather than benefit to his advocate or to the staff entrusted with his care remains the basis for deciding whether or not to use aversive conditioning.

The client or his advocate should be fully informed of the specific aversive conditions that are to be used, and he should agree to their use before their initiation. Rachman and Teasdale (1969, p. 174) have made a similar point: "Aversive therapy should only be offered if other treatment methods are inapplicable or unsuccessful and if the patient gives his permission after a consideration of all the information which his therapist can honestly supply."

Aversive conditioning should not be used with institutionalized mentally retarded persons unless approved by independent monitoring groups representing professional review and ethical-legal review.

Goals

The altering of complex behaviors effecting change in what might be described as "attitudes" or "personality" has been viewed with alarm by those who advocate the concept of individual "freedom" and interpret motivation as a product of "autonomous man" (Skinner, 1972). The behavior modifier is open to the criticism that he is curtailing the "freedom of choice of other human beings" by manipulating their "personality."

Even when the assumption is made that the shaping of behavior is desirable under some conditions, questions can be raised regarding the basis on which goals or "target behaviors" are selected, and by whom. Situations in which the client is unable to set goals or in which he selects goals that clearly conflict with cultural standards or his own welfare raise the issue of determining the conditions under which the behavior modifier's goals should supersede those of his clients.

The following specific guidelines have been proposed for the selection of goals of behavior modification procedures (Roos, 1976):

> The specific goals of each procedure should be clearly described to the client or—in the event he is incompetent—to his parent, guardian, or legal advocate.
>
> The client, or—in the event he is incompetent—his parent, guardian, or legal advocate, should approve all specific goals of each procedure used.
>
> Goals should be adopted only to the extent that they foster the development of the client. Care must be exercised that the convenience of staff, parents, or guardians not be the principal basis for adopting any program goals. Criteria of developmental programming have been described (Roos, McCann, and Patterson, 1971) as consisting of 1) increasing the complexity of the client's adaptive behavior (e.g., locomotion skills), 2) improving his competence in coping with the environment (e.g., opening doors, using tools), and/or 3) enhancing his human qualities, as culturally defined (e.g., speech, social manners).
>
> In the case of institutionalized mentally retarded persons, goals should be reviewed and approved by two independent review bodies with regard to professional and ethical-legal considerations. Some goals, because of their general desirability and almost universal applicability, can be given blanket approval as being suitable for all clients. These include strengthening behaviors involved in self-help skills, mobility, and language, and weakening self-mutilation and inappropriate self-stimulation. Other goals should be specifically reviewed and approved by the appropriate review bodies.

Minimizing Criticisms

Other approaches that should help to minimize criticism of behavior modification include the following:

Results need to be systematically monitored on a continuing basis, with particular attention to the long-range implications of the procedures, generalization and extinction phenomena, the occurrence of "spontaneous recovery," and the appearance of "symptom substitution."

The possible impact of procedures on the behavior modifier deserves special attention. Procedures that lead to rapid and dramatic changes in clients are likely to be highly rewarding to the behavior modifier, who is therefore more likely to repeat such procedures. Hence care must be exercised to ensure that the selection of procedures is not a function of their reinforcing effect on the behavior modifier.

Results should be continually subjected to scientific evaluation in order to foster empirical objectivity and to guard against dogmatism, fanaticism, or reliance on authority for justification of programs.

Means must be carefully differentiated from ends. Behavior modification refers to means or methodologies that have the potential for achieving desirable or undesirable results. As Skinner (1972, p. 150) has stated: "Such a technology is ethically neutral. It can be used by villain or saint. There is nothing in a methodology which determines the values governing its use."

Review Bodies

As previously noted, independent monitoring of behavior modification programs is highly desirable. The functions and composition of two separate review bodies have been detailed in connection with assuring adequate legal and ethical safeguards of behavior modification programs (May, Risley, Twardosz, Friedman, Bijou, and Wexler, 1975; Roos, 1974, 1976). These committees include: 1) a professional review committee composed of persons with recognized expertise in behavior modification, and 2) a committee on legal and ethical practices (or human rights committee), including consumer representatives (and, if practical, consumers) and one or more attorneys. The primary responsibility of the former committee is to evaluate the professional validity of procedures and goals and the qualifications of those directing and implementing programs. The latter committee is primarily responsible for evaluating the ethical and legal aspects of procedures and objectives, assuring that individual rights are protected, and monitoring consent procedures. Specific guidelines have been proposed for the operation of these review bodies (May et al., 1975).

BEHAVIOR MODIFICATION AND OTHER APPROACHES

The ethical and legal issues raised by behavior modification are equally applicable to other forms of psychotechnology. Indeed, procedures such as psychosurgery, electroconvulsive therapy, and chemotherapy are very probably more intrusive, less reversible, and carry higher risk. Consequently, guidelines designed to safeguard the rights of clients undergoing these procedures are more desperately needed than in the case of behavior modification.

Other procedures not usually considered to be forms of psychotechnology also involve aversive practices and/or the selection of goals and should, therefore, likewise receive ethical scrutiny. However, they differ from behavior modification in a number of important dimensions that render them less vulnerable to potential criticism:

> Behavior modification's success rate opens it to the criticism of "controlling" human beings. Since the relationship between means and ends is usually explicitly stated, the effectiveness of the procedures is readily ascertained. Techniques that do not have a high success rate in achieving predictable outcomes, on the other hand, are not likely to be perceived as "controlling."
>
> Behavior modification's insistence on specifying concrete objectives likewise emphasizes the "controlling" aspects of the procedures, whereas approaches that strive to accomplish ephemeral objectives such as "fostering self-actualization," "fulfilling human potentials," or "increasing self-awareness" are much less vulnerable to this criticism.
>
> Reliance on highly specific and objective procedures has earned behavior modification the criticisms of being "mechanistic" and "dehumanizing." In contrast, approaches based on esoteric and ambiguous procedures (often couched in humanistic and idiosyncratic verbiage) foster the impression of "art rather than science."
>
> Emphasis on clearly stipulated, immediate consequences likewise fosters the impression of a manipulative and controlling procedure. Other approaches tend to rely on subtle and delayed consequences, particularly when they are aversive, such as "manipulation of the transference," use of "direct interpretation," and transferring clients from less to more restrictive institutional settings.
>
> Finally, frank manipulation of the physical and interpersonal environment renders the behavior modifier more vulnerable to attack as a controlling agent than his colleagues who operate in the relative isolation of the "therapeutic hour."

Aversive consequences are used widely to influence behavior in many approaches other than behavior modification. Frequently these approaches do not explicitly acknowledge the use of aversive consequences, and as a result they have generally been less vulnerable to criticism. Nonetheless the same ethical and legal issues are involved and the procedures should receive the same scrutiny. Examples include parental punishment of their children, law enforcement, and such "therapeutic practices" as the use of Antabuse in the treatment of alcoholism and institutionalization.

Likewise, all efforts designed to alter human behavior in a specific direction are based on goals that, in contrast to the highly specific goals of behavior modification, are usually implicit and often vague. Hence parents usually strive to have their children adopt the parental standards; advertising campaigns are designed to foster the purchase of specific products; political campaigns aim to elect specific politicians; and religious missionaries seek to convert persons to a specific religion. Likewise, most forms of psychotherapy are typically based on (often implicit) value judgments of the therapist. The following list illustrates typical judgments likely to underlie therapeutic efforts (Roos, 1974):

Heterosexuality ("genital primacy") is preferable to homo- or auto-sexuality (Freud, 1957).

Interpersonal intimacy is preferable to isolation (Sullivan, 1953).

Insight is preferable to low self-awareness (Rogers, 1951).

Rationality is preferable to irrationality (Ellis, 1973).

Economic productiveness is preferable to economic dependency (an idea basic to vocational rehabilitation).

CONCLUSION

Behavior modification is by no means unique in raising serious ethical and legal questions. Its vulnerability to criticism is in part a function of its highly explicit and specific methods and in part a function of its success. Other approaches may use techniques that are highly intrusive and that aim at achieving behavioral change of equal or greater import (e.g., "changing personality" or "altering basic values"), but vagueness and a relative lack of objective success have tended to minimize the types of criticisms that have been leveled at behavior modification.

Nonetheless, *any* procedure that uses aversive consequences raises ethical and legal issues, as does any procedure designed to change human behavior. It is most appropriate for behavior modifiers to recognize these issues and to adopt practices designed to protect the rights of their clients. It is to be hoped that those using other approaches to change human beings will follow suit.

SUMMARY

While behavior modification has proven to be of immense value, important ethical and legal issues are being raised regarding the use of aversive conditioning and the selection of behavioral objectives. Specific guidelines are proposed to minimize potential criticisms. Similar ethical and legal issues apply to the other forms of psychotechnology.

REFERENCES

Ellis, A. (1973) The no cop-out theory. Psychology Today 7:56.

Freud, S. (1957) Collected Papers. London: The Hogarth Press.

Gardener, W. I. (1970) Use of behavior therapy with the mentally retarded. *In* Psychiatric Approaches to Mental Retardation (Ed. Menolascino, F. J.) New York and London: Basic Books.

May, J. G., Risley, T. R., Twardosz, S., Friedman, P., Bijou, S. W., and Wexler, D. (1975) Guidelines for the Use of Behavioral Procedures in State Programs for Retarded Persons. Arlington, Texas: National Association for Retarded Citizens.

Rachman, S., and Teasdale, J. (1969) Aversion Therapy and Behavior Disorders: An Analysis. Coral Gables, Florida: University of Miami Press.

Rogers, C. R. (1951) Client-centered Therapy. Boston: Houghton Mifflin.

Roos, P. (1974) Human rights and behavior modification. Ment. Retard. 12:3.

Roos, P. (1976) Safeguards for experimental procedures in residential facilities for mentally retarded persons. Testimony presented before the National Commission on the Protection of Human Subjects in Washington, D.C., on April 10.

Roos, P., McCann, B., and Patterson, E. G. (1971) A Developmental Model of Mental Retardation. Arlington, Texas: National Association for Retarded Citizens.

Skinner, B. F. (1972) Beyond Freedom and Dignity. New York: Alfred A. Knopf.

Sullivan, H. S. (1953) The Interpersonal Theory of Psychiatry. New York: W. W. Norton.

EPIDEMIOLOGY

RESEARCH TO PRACTICE IN MENTAL RETARDATION
Care and Intervention, Volume I
Edited by Peter Mittler
Copyright 1977 I.A.S.S.M.D.

SEVERE MENTAL RETARDATION AMONG CHILDREN IN A DANISH URBAN AREA
Prevalence and Provision of Services

A. H. Bernsen
Demographic Institute, DK 8240 Risskov, Denmark

Denmark has a well-established tradition for both medical registration, including mental retardation, and general population registration, both of which are facilitated by the attitude of the citizens and the size of the country, thus providing an optimal field for epidemiological research. However, community surveys concerning severe mental retardation have not been carried out in Denmark during the past thirty years.

At the second WHO consultation on mental retardation service in November, 1970, in Copenhagen, it was decided to carry out parallel studies on prevalence, handicaps, and services provided for severely retarded children in Camberwell, London, and Aarhus, Denmark.

This chapter describes case-finding procedures in Aarhus, the results of the prevalence study, including services provided for the children and comparisons with results from Camberwell in 1967, as well as with a survey undertaken in 1962 in the same area as the present study.

A one-day census carried out on July 1, 1970, was designed to ascertain all children aged 0-14 years who were severely intellectually retarded (IQ < 50) and whose parents were living in the community of Aarhus on census day.

Aarhus is situated on the mid-east coast of Jutland and is the second largest town in Denmark, covering 468 square kilometers. The total population on census day was 233,162 persons, of which children under 15 years constituted 21.7%, or 50,667 persons. As a center of trading, industry, and education,

Aarhus resembles urban areas in general and provides extensive medical and social services to its population.

The Danish National Mental Retardation Service (DNMRS) takes care of all mentally retarded persons referred to and accepted by the service, independent of the degree of their retardation. A legislative duty is placed on "persons or authorities on whom, according to the circumstances, the responsibility rests to attend to the affairs of the persons in question" to give notice to the service. However, except for rare cases, i.e., about 1%, the practice has for many years been not to refer a person unless the near relatives, commonly parents, have accepted referral.

Since April, 1970, the registration office of the DNMRS has operated by means of electronic data processing. The system is further described in Dr. Annalise Dupont's publication (1975).

CASE-FINDING PROCEDURES

The line of action for case-finding procedures must naturally be confined to local characteristics, and this presentation does not intend to be a generalized guideline. It only reflects what we thought would be the most effective in our area and what was done, leaving a small hope that it might give ideas to others interested in this field.

The case-finding procedures were planned as follows: 1) collection of basic information on possible probands from the DNMRS' registration office, 2) collection of material from an index of other sources in which children are under observation, or, if the handicapped are treated, health visitors' agency, paediatric department, child psychiatric hospital, state institute for speech defectives, child guidance clinic, orthopaedic hospital, and the hearing centre.

This positive search, based upon nearly 43,000 records, was very intensive. Whenever the child's history, diagnosis, or other conditions could have any possible relationship to mental retardation, the child was regarded as a proband until the opposite was proved.

Because the catchment area for many of the institutions involved exceeded the community of Aarhus, the next step was to exclude children whose parents' residence on census day was outside the chosen area. This was done by means of a list from the social welfare authorities that covered all inhabitants in the community on September 1, 1970. Further exclusion took place after record evaluation, i.e., if the record contained information about normal development, placement in normal school, or if the child had died before census day. If there was any doubt about the child's level of functioning, information was obtained from the school psychologist, family doctor, or kindergarten. The last step before final inclusion was a psychological examination or re-examination. The period of field work lasted from September, 1972 to December, 1975.

The majority of probands were naturally obtained from the DNMRS, the number being 145 children. A few examples will illustrate how new children were included in the study. The health visitors' agency receives information about all live-born children in the community of Aarhus. The service is utilized in 99.5% of the referrals. The referral form contains basic information about the family, the mother's general health, complications during pregnancy and delivery, congenital malformations of the child, and his condition 24 hours postnatally. The index revealed 1,441 records indicating special conditions that could be attributed to mental retardation and they were read systematically. The children had been followed for one to three years. Special attention was paid to failure to thrive, illness, and developmental milestones. The search revealed 28 new children who could possibly be severely retarded, but after collection of further information from general practitioners, hospital departments, kindergartens, and school psychologists, only two children fulfilled the criteria and were included in the study.

The diagnostic files of the paediatric department contained 3,313 record numbers under diagnoses or diagnostic groups related to mental retardation from January 1st, 1955 to March 31st, 1973. About one-third of these were reduplications, i.e., the same number was found for instance under the diagnoses of mental retardation and cerebral palsy, hemiplegia, or epilepsy. The remaining 2,320 records were all scrutinized and 1,448 of these could be excluded, either because the record contained information about normal development or death of the child before census day. In 872 cases, information concerning the child's name, birthday, diagnosis, special examination results, and parents' names, birthdays, and addresses were collected, but 659 of these cases could be excluded on account of the criteria of residence. Of the 213 children remaining, 102 were known already, and possible new probands were to be found among the residual 111 children. After having checked on supplied information, as was mentioned previously, 23 children fulfilled the criteria of severe mental retardation and entered the study as new probands. Table 1 shows the number of children found as new cases according to the source of finding.

RESULTS

A total of 171 children under the age of 15 were found to be severely mentally retarded in the community of Aarhus on July 1st, 1970. The sex distribution shows 96 males and 75 females, a male:female ratio of 1.28:1. The male preponderance is in agreement with results of most other investigations in this field. However, it is impossible to answer the question of whether or not there is a real excess of males among severely retarded children from the results of the present study because the difference in rates for males and females of the respective populations is within the nonsignificant limits ($p > 0.05$).

Table 1. The number of children found as new cases according to source of finding

Source	Number of children
Mental Retardation Service EDP Registration	133
Files of MRS regional centre + new referrals to this centre	12
Health visitors agency	2
Paediatric department	23
Child psychiatric hospital	0
State Institute for Speech Defectives	1
Child guidance clinic	0
Orthopaedic hospital	0
Hearing centre	0
Total	171

Table 2 shows how the 171 children are distributed by sex and five-year age groups in absolute numbers and in rates per 1,000 of the specific population. The prevalence rate is 3.38 per 1,000 for the age group 0–14 years. There is a steady increase in the prevalence rates from the youngest to the oldest age group and the difference is significant ($p < 0.01$). Such a difference might be explained partly by variable intensity in the case-finding procedures in the different age groups. This cannot be the explanation in the present study, because the whole search procedure according to Danish conditions will secure a reliable intensity even in the youngest age group, and, furthermore, scrutinizing of records was undertaken by one person only. The most obvious reason for the increasing rates must be the diagnostic difficulties, both medical and psychological, in very young children or the process of retardation, for instance in certain diseases.

If we turn to the service provided for the 171 children, Table 3 illustrates that about two-thirds of the children are living at home. These children are equally represented in the age groups 0–4 years, 5–9 years, and 10–14 years— while representatives of the children in residential care increase from the youngest to the oldest age group.

Table 2. Severely mentally retarded children in Aarhus on July 1, 1970, by sex and five-year age groups[a]

Age group	Absolute number			Rates per 1,000		
	Male	Female	Male and female	Male	Female	Male and female
0–4	27	20	47	2.75	2.12	2.45
5–9	31	27	58	3.67	3.23	3.45
10–14	38	28	66	5.12	3.87	4.50
0–14	96	75	171	3.74	3.00	3.38

[a]Absolute number and rates per 1,000.

Table 3. Accommodation for severely mentally retarded children in Aarhus on July 1, 1970, by five-year age groups, absolute number, and percentages

Accommodation	Age group 0–4		Age group 5–9		Age group 10–14		Age group 0–14	
	Number	%	Number	%	Number	%	Number	%
Living at home	37	(21.6)	38	(22.2)	34	(19.9)	109	(63.7)
Residential care	10	(5.9)	20	(11.7)	32	(18.7)	62	(36.3)
Total	47	(27.5)	58	(33.9)	66	(38.6)	171	(100)

Table 4. Service provided for home-living severely retarded children in Aarhus on July 1, 1970, by five-year age groups[a]

Service	Age group			
	0–4	5–9	10–14	0–14
Home with no provision	18.1	2.3	0.6	21.1
Normal kindergarten	1.8	1.8	–	3.5
MRS kindergarten	0.6	7.6	1.8	9.9
MRS special care unit	1.2	2.9	2.3	6.4
Junior training center	–	3.5	9.9	13.5
Green school	–	4.1	5.3	9.4
Total	21.6	22.2	19.9	63.7

[a]Expressed as percentages of total number (171) in the community.

A more detailed picture of the service provided for the home-living children is presented in Table 4. The figures represent the percentages of the 171 children by age group and the kind of service received. Most striking is that more than one-fifth of the children and their families, mainly in the youngest age group, 0–4 years, receive no provision except maybe a visit by a social worker. Some of the children in residential care also attend day institutions like kindergartens, training schools, and green schools run by the DNMRS. Altogether, 54% of the children in the present study receive some training.

The design of the present study creates possibilities for making comparisons with the results of the 1967 Camberwell study (Wing, 1971), and with a 1962 Danish study covering the Aarhus area (Brask, 1972).

Table 5 shows the age-specific prevalence rate per 1,000 in these two studies and the present one. The Camberwell study is remarkable in that there is very little difference between the prevalence rates in the three age groups. Especially noteworthy is the high rate in the youngest age group. This is probably explained

Table 5. Prevalence of severe mental retardation among children 0–14 years in three investigations[a]

	Investigation		
Age group	Århus 1962	Camberwell 1967	Aarhus 1970
0–4	1.13	3.12	2.45
5–9	2.81	3.69	3.45
10–14	3.69	3.57	4.50
0–14	2.55	3.43	3.38

[a]Expressed as rates per 1,000.

by a well-organized handicap observation system and good provision of services even for very young severely retarded children. However, recently Wing has disclosed that the figures for the under-fives are not reliable because children "at high risk" are included who may not be regarded as severely retarded at the time of school entry, while, on the other hand, some severely retarded children are not picked up until that time (Wing, 1976). Interestingly, no significant difference could be found by means of the chi-square test ($p > 0.05$) in any of the age groups if the results from Camberwell and those of the present study are compared.

On the other hand, comparisons between the 1962 Aarhus study and the present study show a significant difference in the 0–4 year age group ($p < 0.01$), and for the total group 0–14 years the difference proves to be significant at the 0.02 level. Neither the 5–9 year age group, nor the 10–14 year age group reach a significant level of 0.05. These facts can easily be explained. The 1962 Aarhus study included only severely retarded children registered in the DNMRS. The total prevalence rate of 2.55 per 1,000 therefore represents the registration prevalence. If the registration prevalence is calculated for the present study, it is found to be 2.72 per 1,000, and no significant difference can be demonstrated in the registration prevalence in the two surveys.

CONCLUSION

The conclusions that can be drawn from these results are: Even in a country with a very well-developed medical registration and care system, as in Denmark, it is possible to demonstrate discrepancies between the registration prevalence of severe mental retardation among children and the prevalence of this condition in the community. Consequently, future planning of services for the severely retarded children and adults can be more efficient if based on results obtained from intensive community surveys.

SUMMARY

Some results concerning prevalence and provision of services from a 1970 census investigation on severely mentally retarded children are presented. Special attention is paid to case finding procedures. Comparisons are made with results from the Camberwell census, 1967, and with a 1962 survey undertaken in the same area as the present study.

REFERENCES

Brask, B. H. (1972) Prevalence of mental retardation among children in the County of Aarhus, Denmark. Acta Psychiatr. Scand. 48:480.
Dupont, A. (1975) Mentally retarded in Denmark. An epidemiological study of

21,000 registered cases. Some results of a census, May, 1974. Dan. Med. Bull. 22:243.

Wing, L. (1971) Severely retarded children in a London area: prevalence and provision of services. Psychol. Med. 1:405.

Wing, L. (1976) Severely retarded children in Camberwell. *In* Psychiatric Services in Camberwell and Salford, Statistics from the Camberwell and Salford Psychiatric Registeres 1965-1974, Appendix C, p. 111.

NOTE ADDED IN PROOF:

This chapter is an abbreviation of a much longer article first published in 1976 in *Acta Psychiatrica Scandinavica* (Volume 54, pp. 43—66). The author is grateful to the editor of *Acta Psychiatrica Scandinavica* for permission to publish this version.

RESEARCH TO PRACTICE IN MENTAL RETARDATION
Care and Intervention, Volume I
Edited by Peter Mittler
Copyright 1977 I.A.S.S.M.D.

SOME ECOLOGICAL, SCHOOL, AND FAMILY FACTORS IN THE INTELLECTUAL PERFORMANCE OF CHILDREN
The Warsaw Study— Preliminary Results

M. Czarkowski, A. Firkowska-Mankiewicz,
A. Ostrowska, M. Sokotowska,
Z. Stein, M. Susser, and I. Wald
Division of Epidemiology, School of Public Health,
Faculty of Medicine, Columbia University,
600 West 168th Street, New York, N.Y. 10032, United States

From an epidemiological study conducted in Warsaw, we evaluate the influence of specified family-mediated factors on cognitive development and mild mental retardation among 11-year-old children.

Numerous studies in Western societies have shown the extent to which various environmental factors external to the family may contribute to the association of parental occupation and education and mental retardation. Children from families of manual and unskilled laborers, in comparison with their peers from families of nonmanual and better educated workers, have generally been poorly housed and poorly schooled, have had inferior health care and have often suffered from discrimination in social and public life. Other studies have emphasized the importance of factors mediated through the family in the etiology of mild mental retardation. Although family-mediated factors are clearly influental in cognitive performance, the precise nature of these factors has still to be specified.

With rare exceptions, typical environmental factors that are external to the family and those that are mediated by the family tend to coincide in Western societies, making it difficult if not impossible to ascertain the relative contribution of each factor to cognitive performance. The situation in Warsaw provides an experimental opportunity, in that factors external to the family can be separated from those mediated by the family with less chance of confounding than in any other society to which we have access. Here housing conditions and residential districts particularly have lost their significance as indicators of class affiliation. Almost completely destroyed during World War II, Warsaw was rebuilt on the basis of new principles and with an altered architectural system. The pre-war slum districts have disappeared. They lost their character by being dispersed among enclaves of the intelligentsia. A far-reaching equalisation of housing and social standards was effected at the same time in large sections of the city rebuilt after the war and particularly in the entirely new districts. Many thousands of people live in almost identical apartments, shop in identically built and provisioned stores, and use similar catering and cultural centers. Warsaw inhabitants, legally at least, also benefit in common from equally accessible and similarly equipped networks of schools and health facilities.

It is thus quite natural for Warsaw children of varied social strata (based on parents' occupation), to live in the same districts, in buildings and homes of similar standards, to attend the same schools, and to use similar medical facilities. All these circumstances in the established urban environment of Warsaw should permit a clear separation of factors mediated by the family from factors external to the family. For the past three years we have therefore been studying the effects of family influences on intellectual performance in Warsaw schoolchildren.

In this first presentation of our results, we confine ourselves to the consideration of the influence of parents' education and income, family size (representing factors that are mediated by the family), and the characteristics of schools and districts (representing factors that are external to the family). Cognitive performance is measured by score on the Raven's Progressive Matrices test, a group test of nonverbal intelligence.

DATA SOURCES AND METHOD

The study required the definition of ecological, school, and family factors, and a survey of intellectual performance.

Ecological Factors

Warsaw comprises 79 districts (equivalent to census tracts). For each district information was sought on seven dimensions: demographic characteristics of the population, housing, schools, cultural facilities, services (including health services), crime, and employment and income. From official sources we abstracted 31 items relating to these dimensions for each district.

Factor analysis (principal component) was used to obtain two factors that differentiated between districts. One factor we termed "metropolitanism," and the second factor "social marginality." Districts characterised by these factors were not highly differentiated from other districts. However, districts highly loaded on "metropolitanism" were downtown districts, and those lowly loaded were more distant. The districts highly loaded on "marginality" tended to be the districts that before World War II were inhabited by so-called *lumpenproletariat:* homes in these districts had in the main survived the wartime destruction of the city.

School and Family Factors

Descriptive statistics for all Warsaw schools were collected, covering the physical environment, facilities, quality of teachers, number and type of pupils, and achievement of pupils. In this paper we rely on three measures: 1) the average number of pupils per class, 2) the percentage of teachers in the schools who have university degrees, and 3) the average percentage of pupils repeating grades.

Information on parental education and occupation was obtained in the survey and used in the analysis that follows.

Intellectual Performance

A population measure of intellectual performance was obtained by administering a nonverbal group test (Raven's Progressive Matrices Test) to all Warsaw children who had been born in 1963 (i.e., children who were ten to eleven years old at the time of testing). A vocabulary test and an arithmetic test were administered at the same time, but the results will not be reported here. Psychologists carried out all the testing in the regular school situation.

We identified a population of 14,238 children in the birth cohort, of whom 13,625 (95.7%) were tested. A number were excluded because they had left Warsaw (2.2%); the remaining 2.1% could not be reached.

RESULTS

The preliminary findings are set out in the three tables below.

In Table 1 we show that the mean score on the Raven intelligence test falls consistently with the occupational status of the father and of the mother, and that there is a corresponding rise in the proportion of low scores. The risk of being a low scorer is increased sixfold for children of parents in the lowest occupational categories.

In Table 2 a comparable table is constructed, showing mean scores and the proportion of low scores according to the education of parents. The gradient for

Table 1. Raven's Progressive Matrices in Warsaw children: Mean scores and percentage of low scores (<70), by selected occupational categories of parents[a]

Occupational category	Fathers				Mothers			
	Mean	(S.D.)	% Low	N	Mean	(S.D.)	% Low	N
Upper professional	106.23	(12.75)	2.8%	3,429	106.93	(12.70)	2.4%	2,019
Lower professional	101.69	(13.83)	4.9%	3,470	103.49	(13.35)	3.5%	5,121
Skilled manual	96.21	(15.01)	8.7%	5,360	97.14	(14.85)	8.3%	3,518
Unskilled manual	91.97	(16.67)	16.6%	593	91.95	(15.71)	13.8%	1,604
				12,852				12,262

[a]S.D. = Standard deviation. N = Number of children tested.

Table 2. Raven's Progressive Matrices: Mean scores and percentage of low scorers (<70), by educational index of parents[a]

Educational index of parents	Mean	(S.D.)	% Low	N
Highest 1—both parents at university	107.43	(12.34)	2.3%	1,956
2—1 parent at university, 1 parent at secondary	104.70	(13.16)	3.2%	2,012
3—both parents at secondary, or 1 parent at primary + 1 parent at university	102.00	(13.50)	4.2%	2,615
4—1 parent at secondary, 1 parent at primary	98.88	(14.72)	6.5%	2,535
5—both parents at primary	95.07	(15.20)	10.1%	3,489
Lowest 6—1 primary, 1 less than primary	92.64	(15.85)	14.9%	768
				13,375

[a]S.D. = Standard deviation. N = Number of children.

the means, and the increase in risk of being a low scorer are similar to those shown in Table 1.

In Table 3, a correlation matrix between parental, ecological, and school variables is set out. It seems that there may well be some residential clustering in Warsaw, because the "metropolitanism" factor correlates 0.19 to 0.32 with parental variables, and −0.32 with one of the school variables. In spite of this, the correlations of ecological and school variables with the Raven test range only from 0.03 to 0.09, while the correlations of parental variables with the Raven test range from 0.29 to 0.32.

DISCUSSION AND CONCLUSIONS

The city of Warsaw has special characteristics in addition to those we assumed would distinguish it from others, and which led us to choose it for study. Before we discuss the significance of the results of this study, we should note that Warsaw is a capital city with an unusually high concentration of parents (both mothers and fathers) with higher education, in professional occupations, working full time, and with small families. All these factors together can be expected to skew the distribution of cognitive performance and raise the mean. However, as a result of using locally standardized scores for the Raven's Progressive Matrices Test, 6% of children have scores that fall more than two standard deviations below the Warsovian mean.

We may now turn to our initial assumptions about the special characteristics of Warsaw. The history of the city, razed to the ground and rebuilt under a socialist regime committed to a set of political and economic priorities different from those that prevail in capitalist societies, led us to expect that changes at the institutional and societal level would have altered the ecological structure of the

Table 3. Correlation matrix to show interrelationships of parental factors, ecological factors, and school factors in Warsaw

	Parental factors[a]				Ecological factors		School factors			Raven
	F's ed	M's ed	F's occup	M's occup	Metro	Margin	No. pupils	Teacher's degree	% Repeaters	Raven
F's ed	1.0									
M's ed	.73									
F's occup	.88	.65								
M's occup	.68	.85	.62							
Metropolitanism	.22	.22	.20	.19						
Margin	.02	-.01	.03	.01	-.33					
No. pupils	.10	.09	.08	.08	-.05	.34				
Teacher's degrees	.13	.12	.12	.11	-.32	-.02	-.13			
% Repeaters	-.17	-.17	-.15	-.15	-.21	-.02	-.15	-.1	1.0	
Raven	.32	.30	.29	.30	.10	-.03	.07	.07	.09	1.0

[a] F = Father; M = Mother; ed = education; occup = occupation.

city. Our data in the main support this assumption. Thus the composite variables that describe "metropolitanism" and "social marginality," and the variables that describe schools, bear but slight relation to the distribution of educational and occupational levels of parents.

The dissociation of these variables that describe the environment external to the family from variables that describe family environment and position thus effectively cancels out these external factors in our analysis. In these data, the contribution of the ecological and school variables to cognitive performance is a very small one. One cannot say from our study, however, that they are not salient factors in cognitive performance (although one might say so from other studies), but only that societal changes have removed whatever effects these factors might have from the reach of measurement. (An alternative but less likely explanation for these results, which we intend to explore further, is that our measures of ecological and school factors are insufficiently sensitive to detect their effects.)

These results allow us to use the situation in Warsaw to address a crucial question, which is, the extent to which the relations of cognitive performance to the family-mediated factors of occupation and education persist in the form characteristic of more traditional societies. The relations of parental occupation and education with cognitive performance that we have had in our results leave no doubt about their strong association.

Since parental occupation and education, as indicators of family status and culture, are so clearly separated from the external environment of families, we believe that they can be interpreted as indicators of familial effects. On the basis of our studies so far, we are not in a position to apportion these effects among social and genetic factors. It is evident that societal changes over a generation, however, and the equalization of ecological advantages and exposures, have failed to override the forces within families that determine their intellectual characteristics. These results suggest to us that for the further elucidation of the determinants of cognitive abilities, we need to turn our attention to family factors.

EARLY INTERVENTION

RESEARCH TO PRACTICE IN MENTAL RETARDATION
Care and Intervention, Volume I
Edited by Peter Mittler
Copyright 1977 I.A.S.S.M.D.

IMPORTANT CONSIDERATIONS IN THE REVIEW AND EVALUATION OF EDUCATIONAL INTERVENTION PROGRAMS

D. J. Stedman
Frank Porter Graham Child Development Center,
University of North Carolina, Chapel Hill,
North Carolina 27514, United States

In 1972, the Secretary of Health, Education, and Welfare, Elliott Richardson, commissioned the author and four educational scholars (Dr. Ira Gordon, University of Florida, Dr. Ron Parker, Random House, Dr. Paul Dokecki, George Peabody College, and Dr. Nicholas Anastasiow, University of Indiana, under contract HEW-OS-72-205) to review the effectiveness of "early education intervention" programs. A principal concern was the apparent difficulty of moving small, successful, research programs into more widespread practice, a typical problem in American education. Special focus was placed on projects addressing high risk, preschool-aged children.

The review included a close examination of the research literature, on-site visits to highly recommended projects, and extensive interviews with fourteen competent and respected researchers in the field.

MAJOR FINDINGS OF REVIEW

The results of a close examination of more than forty longitudinal intervention research programs for high risk children included the following major findings:

1. It has been demonstrated without much doubt that how a child is raised and the environment into which he is born have a major impact on what he will become.
2. Factors such as race and sex do not appear to be related to the child's ability to profit from intervention programs.
3. The family's methods of establishing social rules leave little doubt that early family environment (parental language styles, attitudes toward

achievement, parental involvement and concern for the child) have a significant impact on the child's development before he reaches his second birthday.

4. In situations where families are so disorganized that they cannot supply a supportive environment, an intensive external supportive environment may contribute to the child's development.

5. The effects of a stimulating or depriving environment appear to be most powerful in the early years of childhood, when the most rapid growth and development take place. The primary locus of the child during these early years is the home. Therefore, home-based intervention programs or one-to-one teacher-child ratio stimulation activities appear to be the most appropriate and effective during this period.

6. There is evidence that the effects of early intervention programs for children are strengthened by the involvement of the child's parents.

7. Description of the training conditions that handicap a child or lead to a child's success is possible only in general terms.

8. The socioeconomic status and entry IQ level of the child bear an uncertain relationship to the child's ability to profit from intervention. Design problems and the current state of the art in measurement render the effect of these factors difficult to determine.

9. Where access to children can be gained in the early years, preferably during the language-emergent years (1 to 2 years of age), intervention programs will be more effective than those begun at later ages.

10. Between the ages of 4 and 6 years, a systematic organized program can contribute significantly to a child's social and intellectual development.

11. The effects of intervention programs appear to last only so long as the child remains in the intervention program. They appear to last longer in home training studies and "wash out" sooner in school programs.

12. Follow-up studies of children in intervention programs usually show that initial gains are no longer measurable. This is partially attributable to the fact that we cannot determine at this point whether it is because of program failure, problems of measurement, inadequate criterion measures, or the later interfering effects of other competing environments such as the home and school.

13. The quality and motivation of the staff are directly related to the success of the program and therefore are prime factors in determining the extent to which a program is exportable or replicable.

Seldom Answered Questions

Some findings are worthy of special note because they address frequently asked but seldom answered questions of importance to researchers and educational practitioners:

1. In Successful Programs, Gains Occur Regardless of Age of Entry The start age of children placed in intervention programs has varied across projects from those starting at a few months of age to a beginning age of 5 or 6 years. Results reported by at least one study have shown that children who enter learning-to-learn programs at age 4 make gains of nearly 20 IQ points, which are maintained during the following 2 years. Children who enter at age 5 make smaller gains for each of the 2 years (9 points the first year and 7 points the second year). Although these results suggest differential gains as a function of age of entry, it does not answer the correlated question of whether gains would be sustained after the first year in the absence of such a program.

However, data from another project indicate that children who made gains in the project when they entered did not lose those gains as long as they remained in the program. The data do not strongly support any one year as the more preferred year to realize gains in intellectual growth.

Hence, the general conclusion must be that programs have been effective with all ages and one cannot specifically support the advantages for work at any one year versus another.

None of the studies reviewed gives support to a well-defined critical period as a preferred time for preschool or early childhood intervention. Essentially, programs can be designed that will work effectively with a wide age range.

A comprehensive review of intervention programs in 1970 suggested that vulnerability to adverse influences at certain ages does not necessarily imply a correlated time when children are especially sensitive to treatment. This study supported the contention that, based on our current level of knowledge, intervention can be justified throughout the period of early development and possibly beyond.

2. In Successful Programs Gains Occur Regardless of Sex Studies have reported that girls have higher initial IQs than boys, while also observing that the sex of child was not related to gain scores. These findings are supported in general by other investigators, many of whom do not separate IQ scores by sex when reporting gains because of the lack of differences.

3. In Successful Programs Gains Occur Regardless of Race Studies again report that although Whites enter with higher initial IQ scores, race is not a significant variable in considering gain scores.

4. Differential Gains in IQ Scores Occur as a Function of the Entering or Initial IQ Score, the Program Intensity, and the Duration or Length of Time a Child is in the Program In general, the lower the initial IQ the greater the gain in IQ in the intervention program. Again, the more intense the program, the greater the gain. In addition, the longer a child is in a program, the more likely he is to have a higher IQ gain. Finally, the interaction between intensity of program and duration in program contributes to differential gains. Some researchers, for example Bronfenbrenner, attribute the high initial gains to the phenomenon of regression to the mean and characterize them as being inflated for that reason.

5. In Successful Programs Gains Occur Regardless of Program Approach but Some Programs Appear to be Better than Others Although almost all kinds of programs have shown gains in IQ scores, when specific comparisons are made among programs, some differences do occur. In general it should be stated that some programs work, while others do not. In those that are successful, it is apparent that it is due to a higher degree of *structure* of program. In general, the more structure, the greater the gain in IQ of participating children. A large-scale comparison among programs has been conducted using four groups (regular nursery school; children from low-income families in middle-class nursery groups; Montessori or perceptual motor skill groups; and an experimental group with a highly structured format). When gain scores on the Stanford-Binet were compared, the experimental group (the structured program) was seen to have the largest gains. It should be mentioned that the experimental group emphasized verbal behavior that would tend to influence test scores. Although the remaining three groups may have excelled on other measures, the program of the experimental group resulted in the largest gain on intelligence test scores (IQs).

Cautions

There are a number of serious cautions that emerge from the review and consideration of the research and development activity in this area.

Insufficient Sample Size Most projects have an insufficient sample size either for us to base the extent of trust and credibility in their outcomes that we do or for us to be led to massive intervention service programs based on these outcomes.

Insufficient Research There is insufficient research in the area to date. After 10 years the number of well-designed and well-executed studies still number less than 40.

Insufficient Time in Program The majority of studies do not involve the subjects in the intervention program for a sufficient amount of time to allow for long-term change or an adequate test of the intervention program.

Insufficient Attention to Effects of Mixing Insufficient attention is being paid to the effects of mixing varieties of children, handicapped and nonhandicapped, in order to improve the learning environment in which the intervention program is taking place.

Inadequate Measures The current measures available to assess change in children as a result of intervention program effects are inadequate in number and quality.

Low Utility and Low Reliability of Pretest Scores The low utility and low reliability of pretest scores from high risk children, due to their meager amount of experience with testing or the evaluation approach, may lead us to infer greater gains from posttest scores than should be inferred as resulting from intervention activities.

Doubt about Critical Periods   There is increasing doubt about the value of certain critical periods; therefore, the extent to which we can continue to emphasize only one period when we can expect positive outcomes of early intervention activities to occur is questionable.

Failure to Individualize Programs   There is a typical failure to individualize programs. That is, there is a homogeneity of treatment across heterogeneous groups whether it be social class, IQ level, sex, minority group, or other critical feature.

Cultural and Value Differences   There are often significant cultural differences among minority and ethnic groups leading to differential reactions to intervention programs. This may lead to exaggerated responses from the children in either direction. Also, there are in many cases extreme value differences between subjects, their families, and the project staff that may lead to inadequate or inappropriate intervention program components and results.

Narrow Goals   Program goals are often too narrow and constricted. There is more to development than IQ.

Parental Support Factor   There are certain gains or responses to the intervention activities that are related to the motivation of the parents to encourage and assist their child to participate in the program. This parental support factor is not often considered as a part of what accounts for the success of intervention programs.

Logistical Problems   There are severe logistical problems in connection with both the conduct of longitudinal studies and the development of exportable intervention program components.

Insufficient Number of Replications   There is an insufficient number of replications of special studies showing positive or hopeful results.

Cost   The cost of longitudinal studies has resulted in too few comprehensive studies, including health, education, social, and parent program components.

In general, the group concluded that preschool educational intervention programs *do* have important and positive effects on the *IQ* of children. The results are often uneven and transient. There has not yet been sufficient research to warrant the selection of one specific set of program components as being contributive to cognitive and social gains.

Obstacles and Problems in Conducting Studies

A number of obstacles and special problems in conducting studies appear to be adding to the difficulty of making definitive statements, based on research, about determinants of effectiveness and credibility of outcomes.

Inadequate Control Groups   Given the problem of adequately describing the population, it rarely becomes possible to determine the adequacy of the control group. Rarely are children selected from the same population pool and randomly assigned to treatment groups.

Treatment Drift Once an evaluation model is adopted, decisions are made to change the program according to information gathered. This is a highly acceptable practice in the remediation of children's deficiencies. However, as this occurs, the intervention program is no longer being conducted as originally described. As a longitudinal study refines its procedures, new strategies are invented, thus markedly changing the original procedures. Frequently the change is not described in the write-up.

Press to do Well Most innovators are funded to demonstrate the effectiveness of a given idea or program. They are expected to succeed. Given the press to succeed, the program is constantly revised and modified based on pupil responses. Similar to the problem of treatment drift above, the program in operation often bears little resemblance to the written proposal.

Teacher Effect Evidence indicates that the teacher, not the program, may be the crucial variable in creating change. It has been indicated that the method or program adopted interacts with the stylistic treatment of the teacher. The teacher factors that are relative to the change are highly idiosyncratic and difficult to control. One research has identified four major clusters of teacher variables based on control and expressions of warmth. Another researcher has pursued other sets of personality factors of the teacher that influence pupil change. Yet another has identified planning and supervision as more important to the program than the curriculum components themselves. How you do something may be more important than what you do.

Teachers Reach Criterion Performance Frequently a program is developed by an innovator who then hires a staff to conduct the program. In the experience of the authors, it frequently takes as long as two to three years before the staff can conduct the program as originally conceived. Massive in-service efforts are needed in all intervention programs in order to effect frequent supervision and evaluation of teacher performance. Some personnel will not be able to reach criterion performance and will need to be replaced.

Ethics with Human Subjects The innovator, in dealing with human subjects, cannot manipulate the research environment unless he is sure he will not damage the child in any way. This ethical "restriction" is necessary in working with human subjects and limits the degree of manipulation the innovator can apply. For example, does one take children away from their mothers in order to work intensively with them?

Continuity of Staffing As with life-span research projects, it is difficult for a principal investigator to commit himself over his own life span. If the principal investigator leaves the project, there may be a shift in focus or interest when a new principal investigator takes over. There is also staff turnover and change in staff training or staff development activities, especially in university-based programs where graduate students are used extensively.

Testing Procedures Again, as with life-span research projects, testing schedules, instrument revision, and discontinuity and low correlation between tests brought into the long-term testing activity contribute problems in the conduct of the project as well as difficulties in data interpretation.

Data Processing Masses of data can accumulate in longitudinal studies that can present both problems of data processing and difficulties in decision-making about which data to process. This is especially problematic for the new researcher in the intervention field.

Environmental Changes Children in longitudinal studies are often influenced by major shifts in the community or neighborhood environment, which may then have a direct effect on the outcome of the intervention activities. Shifts in cultural mores, social attitudes, and values may have similar effects.

Attrition The mobility of the American family is well known. While techniques are available to adjust to subject attrition, it is an expensive process and often requires resources not provided in the intervention programs. It is essential that large subject samples be acquired and maintained over a long period of time in order to circumvent the problems caused by subject attrition.

Interpretation Problems

Often, the intepretation of the results of well-designed and well-conducted studies constitutes a major task. The group attempted to examine the nature of interpretation problems and suggested the following:

Nature of the Population In working with high risk youngsters, the set of variables associated is multiple and often incomparable. For example, the construct "culturally deprived," as it is used by different research workers, includes: income level, racial differences, inadequate diet, protein deficiency, punitive child-rearing practices, low language stimulation, isolation, oppression, high disease rates, alcoholism, and so on. It often is assumed that all of these factors contribute the same influence. Clearly, the state of the art of knowing how to deal effectively with high risk populations is not developed to the point at which the population of children can be described with the precision needed to replicate a study. In addition, children who live in poverty are still found in markedly different environments—for example, compare the immigrant worker's child to the child of the inner-city dweller or the sharecropper. The life experiences are markedly different.

Problems of Program Description One of the major problems in interpreting intervention programs is that often the program descriptions are not sufficiently detailed for us to understand what it was the innovator did. Global terms are frequently used that make it difficult either to replicate or to isolate the variables that were related to the treatment. For example, a study of adopted versus nonadopted children may not adequately define the nature of the treatment; i.e., what happened in the homes that did not happen in the orphanages? Longitudinal intervention studies rarely describe all of the procedures by which they undertook their program. On the other hand, it is frequently impossible to describe exactly what was done. A major intervention program may have components that deal with classroom experiences, parent training, improved nutrition, medical screening, and vision and hearing tests. Ascribing treatment success to any one variable is a tenuous procedure.

Failure to Develop Appropriate Instruments   One of the major difficulties in conducting studies with children is specifying exactly what evaluation the innovator will be able to perform following the intervention. Many programs specify IQ scores as their end objective. However, IQ scores are unreliable and invalid for most minority group children, and, in addition, IQ refers more to traits related to school performance than to cognitive functioning. The appeal of the behavioral-oriented programs is their tendency to limit their goals to observable behaviors. However, the weakness of this approach is that one is still left with the problem of defining the "internal processes" of the child and frequently minor and sometimes irrelevant behaviors.

Global measures of intelligence and achievement are inappropriate measures for program impact. Intelligence measures assume common cultural experiences, equal opportunity to learn, and equal motivation to do well on the tests. For most minority group children these assumptions cannot be met.

Achievement tests contain many items aimed at reasoning ability rather than at the skill under treatment. For example, as much as 50% of the items on elementary school reading tests are inference problems rather than reading problems. Reading is learning a set of abstract arbitrary symbols and relating them to another set of symbols that are spoken, that is, speech. Children can relate words to print and learn that the printed word stands for the spoken word or for objects, but unless long trials of memorization, drill, and practice techniques are used, children do not understand the abstraction of graphemics until ten to twelve years of age. Thus, many "reading" tests are misnamed; they would be more appropriately titled "reasoning from reading" tests.

Intuitive Appeal of Gains Scores   In spite of the work of Cronbach, Thorndike, and others, who demonstrated that gain scores are unreliable, statistically indefensible, and subject to great misinterpretation for individuals or groups, there still exists great pressure for programs to demonstrate effectiveness by measuring gains on the same instrument.

Measurement should not concern itself with change as measured by gain scores but by performance of the desired behavior that defines the criterion performance. Criterion-referenced tests are difficult to construct unless the behaviors are readily observable. For example, it is easier to specify that as a result of the program children will be able to count to ten or identify six primary colors than to specify that they will develop a positive self-concept and attitude towards others.

Inadequate or Naive Theory of Human Behavior   Many longitudinal studies fail to conceptualize the nature of how humans learn and the processes of development. The results of these studies can easily be misinterpreted, and dubious reasoning is often employed in interpreting their results. Recent findings in developmental theory and learning have been massive. The human organism is an impressive information processor from the moment of birth. However, many still fail to recognize the infant's capacity to process information and continue to perceive the child as a passive receptor of information—thereby attributing to their training procedures more power than is likely to be present. Equally, the innovator who works with the handicapped child frequently views all the child's lacks in terms of and as a function of his handicap without taking into account his age and the normal stages of growth and development.

Retrospective Data, Time, and Cost   Most retrospective data collected from teachers and parents bear little resemblance to the child's actual functioning. The unreliability of these data makes longitudinal studies all the more necessary. However, longitudinal studies take time and careful record keeping. It may be twenty years before the effects of the intervention program can be fully measured. Longitudinal studies are costly ventures, although they may be the only means by which some questions can be answered.

Delayed Effects   Rarely do longitudinal studies measure delayed effects of their treatment. For example, does the program introduced in kindergarten have any measurable effects on adolescent behavior? Rarely do school programs measure adult attitudes, voting habits, reading habits, or other goals that were part of the school curriculum.

Narrow Focus of the Program   Some longitudinal studies become so specialized and deal with such a narrow population that they cannot be replicated. For example, a program that provides a one-to-one teacher/pupil ratio for six hours a day, six days a week, with supporting psychological, medical, and speech staff would be difficult to find in a regular school.

Sample Problems   The size of the sample and the representativeness of the sample must be more seriously taken into account. Samples have generally been too small to allow for much generalization. The results of a program that also limits itself to a unique population have little generalizability to other populations of high risk children. Further, shrinkage of already small samples occurs over time and contributes to the lack of follow-up results or effects.

The Effect of Continued Assessment or Observation   The effects of continuous testing in long-term studies, including observer effects, can have an equal or perhaps greater effect on performance than some or all of the program components. In many programs the continuous assessment and the intervention curriculum are confounded in such a way that attribution of which contributed to change is prevented. In some cases continuous assessment of control groups may contribute to equal change as compared with the experimental group, therefore leading to an inability to measure the effect of the intervention program itself. In some cases, researchers suggest that continuous assessment is equivalent to minimal intervention. Intervention studies are no less immune to the Hawthorne effect than any other study.

In the final analysis, even given the cautions, design problems, and difficulties with data interpretation, it was felt that we already know a great deal about the effectiveness of educational intervention. In general, there are positive effects. A host of factors operate to make education more or less effective for the individual child, including child variables, setting variables, and the characteristics of the intervention program and the people delivering it.

More research in the field is required, along with carefully described curriculum components and the best child variable control possible within the bounds of natural groupings of children. If there is a prime obstacle it is lack of measurement tools for social, affective, and interpersonal change as well as academic gain. Methods for coding and analyzing observational data lag far behind other methods in the social sciences.

Finally, the expensive, long-term, longitudinal study of development in children is still the best strategy for discovering environmental effects. The major difficulty here is getting public or private resources to support these operations.

It was Will Rogers who said "Plans get you into things but you got to work your way out." He could have been talking about this aspect of our work.

SUMMARY

A comprehensive review of major longitudinal intervention research was undertaken in order to examine effectiveness. Results include major findings, such as cautions in designing such research, interpreting data from such studies, and implementing methods from intervention studies.

RESEARCH TO PRACTICE IN MENTAL RETARDATION
Care and Intervention, Volume I
Edited by Peter Mittler
Copyright 1977 I.A.S.S.M.D.

EARLY INTERVENTION, EDUCATION, AND TRAINING OF PRESCHOOL CHILDREN

M. E. de Lorenzo
*Mental Retardation Section, Inter-American Children's
Institute (OEA), Montevideo, Uruguay*

Children are ready to learn from the time they are born. When one works with infants, one is very impressed by the ordered morphology that gives structure to early behavior.

By the same token we must ask how functions operate in the economy of the infant, especially in the development of cognitive activity. We may infer from our studies and those in the literature that cognition is immanent in behavior; for example, we can see that sucking, which at first is mainly a reflex activity, soon patterns itself to the contingencies of the environment in a way that plainly reflects a massive amount of information processing.

There is now good evidence that "the structure and functional organization of parts of the central nervous system may be modified by changes in the internal and external environment." The chemical capacity to "connect between neurons" appears to be altered by experience and represents, in a sense, "a type of learning" (Bronfenbrenner, 1968).

However, in order to learn the computer-like brain requires a programmer; in most cases this programmer is the mother. There are now indications that the mother-infant (or caregiver-infant) interaction in the earliest days shapes not only the initial behavior pattern, but also the electrochemical circuits of the thinking process in the brain.

The infant's capacities both for processing stimulation coming from the environment and for developing new behavioral responses to it, should be shaped and enriched from birth. Empirical observations amply support the belief that, from the point of view of further mental growth, early infancy is a very sensitive period of development.

We think it is the early environment plus the continuing environment that influences the child. There is, however, a great lack of experimental data that could reveal what are the critically important kinds and amounts of stimulation, probably inherent in mothering, that are necessary for cognitive, affective, and social development.

Parents are ready to teach their children if we make them aware of such a role. Some teaching tools are available. Professionals know how to use these tools to help parents help their children. But here the links of the chain often fail to connect. The time lag between a child's readiness to learn and the start of appropriate mental stimulation can often determine the extent of ability or disability for life.

We assume that it is better to prevent damage than to try to repair it: better to begin treatment of a damaged infant than of an older child. To prevent impairments and secondary involvements, it is better to begin in the preschool years than later on, and to adapt teaching to children's special needs. In every step of our planning, amelioration blends with prevention. The services we plan today have to serve tomorrow's needs.

Different sorts of risk call for different avenues of action. This does not imply that early intervention can do the job alone. Follow-through in the long-term and a continuum of services are needed.

Different types of risks require different avenues of action. Just as too much stimulation is damaging, so is too little. The timing and nature of stimuli and the pacing of actions must be carefully known before attempting to expose an infant to them. One group of children includes those at risk for central nervous system disorders because of causes independent of wealth, race, and social status—it may happen in all segments of society. The other group, a much larger one, especially in the underdeveloped countries, includes children at risk for sub-optimal psychosocial conditions on the basis of poverty, emotional deprivation, and segregation. These children pay the ultimate price of social injustice.

THE ECOLOGY OF EARLY INTERVENTION

Children's Rights

What are the priorities where children are concerned? Indeed, what rights do children have anyway? The United Nations General Assembly in November, 1959, adopted the Declaration of the Rights of the Child, in recognition of the need for special safeguards for children, including legal protection, by reason of their physical and mental immaturity. The Declaration proclaims, among other things, the child's right to healthy growth and development, supported by special care and protection. It further includes adequate prenatal and postnatal care, as well as adequate nutrition, housing, recreation and medical services, with special treatment, education, and care for the child who is physically, mentally, or socially handicapped. The child should also be protected against neglect, cruelty, and exploitation. All children in less developed countries fall into the category of those requiring "special treatment": the parameters of suffering in the underdeveloped countries are underlined by disease syndromes that are climate- and environment-related and by problems of transport, water quality and supply, and sanitation in the rural areas.

In this context the plight of the child has a key significance. The increasing efficiency, in commercial and technological terms, of conventional curative medicine masks the inhumanity of infant neglect and child mortality. We must ask ourselves whether the underdeveloped countries, or "the South" in contrast to the industrialized countries in "the North," are to become a vast sickness pool of starving children deprived of life in its richest sense and menaced by the threat of premature death; and this question may be particularly relevant in the case of Latin America, where very little education and health care is available to the rural and suburban poor, whose true problems and their solutions lie in the continent's need for economic independence and self-reliance.

If we are to find an appropriate strategy of intervention for the child of a family living in the depths of poverty, we must first understand the nature of the problems the parents face in bringing up their children.

If a program is to be effective it has to effect a major transformation of the environment of the child and the persons in his milieu. The essence of the strategy is a primary focus neither on the child nor on his parent, nor even on the dyad or the family as a system; the aim is to effect changes in the "context" in which the family lives. These changes in turn enable the parents, siblings, family and community as a whole to exercise the functions necessary for the child's development.

Ecological intervention must be the first step in any sequential strategy for prevention and amelioration that is to provide the family with adequate health care, nutrition, housing, and employment. In Latin America the majority of the early intervention programs in existence vary inversely with the degree of deprivation that affects the families. The neediest families are not even reached. Public-supported programs are very few. Again we may ask ourselves, what is happening, what prevents society from making use of its knowledge? Ecological intervention almost invariably requires not just changes having a direct impact on children and family, but also institutional changes, such as housing, health, nutrition, schools, transportation, churches, work, work schedules, and a host of other conditions determining when and how a family can spend time with its children.

We would like to include here a proposal we made during two different meetings held in Latin America, one in July, 1976 in Montevideo, Uruguay, and the other in Brazil, in August, 1976, at a seminar related to a Multinational Project on Special Education. The global approach presented represents one practical effort to break through the conservative models of isolated, fragmentary programs of intervention.

THE PACKAGE PROGRAM

The purpose of this model was to try to elaborate the optimal package program for child care with limited resources. The chain of reasoning that led to this target begins with the recognition of poverty, of the lack of resources to adequately fund a nation-wide general health and education service, and of the need to make the best use of those resources that are available. The term "package" embodies the recognition of the multiplier effect: that the impact of concerted delivery of all the inputs is greater than would be the mere total of benefits conferred by individual inputs added together, by consecutive rather than simultaneous implementation.

The package concept is therefore more than a fashionable phrase: it is a key idea in the context of resource limitations. The package resolved itself into the following five groups, with all the social inputs entered into the first group—including, somewhat artificially, the socialization process, which in fact represents a dimension with which the other inputs correlate, rather than an element in itself (Figure 1).

PROGRAMS OF EARLY INTERVENTION AND EDUCATION

Assumptions

The following quote is from Nancy Robinson (1976): "One of our problems until now is that to a large extent we have acquiesced to a dichotomy between programs for the poor and programs targeted toward *the handicapped*." For political reasons, it has not usually been acceptable to acknowledge that the War on Poverty was a War on Borderline and Mild Mental Retardation—but it was, and it was the most direct and meaningful way we could have acknowledged that a mental handicap of even mild degree is a distinct detriment to a productive life in a highly technological society. A perfect society has never existed, but incremental reduction of poverty and injustice, year by year, is a real possibility. Poverty breeds mental handicap; racial discrimination breeds mental handicap; unemployment breeds mental handicap; crowded housing breeds mental handicap; discouragement breeds mental handicap; isolation and indifference breed mental handicap.

It is generally argued that preventive and ameliorative efforts will best succeed when parents see themselves as absolutely central to the process. Urie Bronfenbrenner's (1974) analysis of the initial efforts of center-based and home-based compensatory programs demonstrates pretty convincingly that it is largely when the parents see themselves in an absolutely central role as the educators of their children that programs are likely to be effective. The patterning of our early intervention program, begun many years ago (1964) in Escuela de Recuperación Psíquica No. 1, Montevideo, Uruguay (de Lorenzo, 1967),

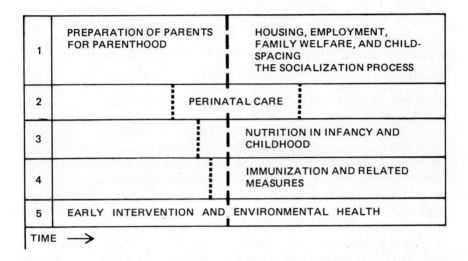

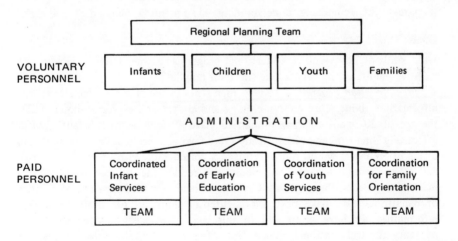

Figure 1. Diagrammatic representation of the optimal package program for child care. *Top:* Time scheme for preventive and ameliorative efforts. *Bottom:* Implementation of programs. (Adapted from *Action for Children*, Uppsala, Sweden: Dag Hammerskjold Foundation.)

rested in large part on this assumption, approaching parents gently and respectfully, helping them to recognize their importance and power as their children's skillful teachers. Yet, it is also clear that this works with some parents, while with others it does not, and that in some obvious cases it is foolish and/or cruel to depend only on this avenue to help the child.

Priorities

We would do well to set legitimate priorities for educational intervention, to define goals in a way that we can measure, and to pursue those goals as efficiently as possible. Depending on the needs of the situation, the goals will be quite diverse. With respect to disadvantaged populations, goals involve opening social, intellectual, and economic doors, through effective services and through enhancement of the learning and coping skills of children. With respect to children whose biological integrity has been more specifically compromised, our goals might include more focused targets, e.g., 1) occasionally, the possibility of remediating an early emotional, perceptual, or even biologically based learning problem in order to avert mental handicap; 2) remediation of a specific handicap or lag, such as a sensory deficit, spasticity, or a language delay; 3) achieving a greater degree of competency in self-help skills to free others from basic caregiving and to enhance self-respect and independence; 4) increasing social competence, even if this entails only looking at a person who is talking and responding to him with a smile; and 5) supporting families who are dealing with the stresses of recognizing, understanding, and nurturing the handicapped child.

Goals

What kinds of behavioral or educational programs can one design to change and improve the life of the very young and their families?

Preconception Programs   Today's high school student has available excellent information about reproductive biology and contraception. Yet, women under the age of 20, many of them unmarried, have planned births substantially less effectively than women in biologically more favorable age brackets. Reduction in births to teenagers would not only make a considerable impact on prematurity and other prenatal hazards, but would also reduce the number of children of premature parents, that is youngsters not yet ready for the heavy responsibilities of parenthood. We have been shortsighted, I think, in the limited range of information we have given and in our lack of evangelical vigor about the necessity for truly rational choice. How often have we told highschoolers that appealing little babies will grow into demanding, independent, saucy preschoolers who will need consistent, patient, and astute parenting every day of the year—and eventually will grow into complicated adolescents like themselves? Have we talked about the implications of having a handicapped child? Have we reminded them often enough of their solemn responsibilities in taking on the life of a dependent and malleable human being, of the implications of their choice not only for themselves and the child but for society as a whole?

What holds for teenagers holds as well for other high risk groups, either high risk for producing children with congenital problems or high risk for failure or ineptitude as parents. Included here are parents who are mentally retarded, psychotic, alcoholic, or psychopathic, as well as others whose risks are primarily medical in nature. Many of these adults are lonely and hopeful that a child will be a companion, someone to be loved, and to love in return. While these feelings are understandable—indeed, one feels very sympathetic towards such persons— they are not sufficient qualifications for parenthood.

It will be many years, if ever, I suspect, before we as a society begin to decide who may have children or under what circumstances, but meanwhile it is our responsibility to educate people vigorously about the total picture. Prevention of mental retardation, then, begins with rational choices based on knowledge and perspective (Robinson, 1976).

Parents' Rights versus Children's Rights   Parents, having lost or relinquished a child, can usually bear another, but children have no choices. Controversial as it is, the conflict between the rights of irresponsible parents and unprotected children is, I hope, far from settled. Our society accepts an unbelievable degree of irresponsibility from parents before freeing the children to be adopted by others, meanwhile subjecting too many children to subtle forms of abuse and neglect, to instability and disorganization, and frequently to marked degrees of understimulation. The proportion of such children who actually become retarded is unknown, but it is likely that because of these early experiences, a great many of them fail to ever reach their optimal achievement in school or any other aspect of life. Even those who are placed in foster homes and eventually adopted have borne a heavy cost. Many more continue to reside, off and on, in families where their most basic needs for attention, stimulation, and encouragement are unmet. Prevention of such a drama should be a responsibility of a caring society, a society dedicated to children and their healthy growth.

Home Visitors for All!   In our society we need to reinforce parental roles. Home visitors serve as mediators, helping parents to be more effective, to receive the newborn, to interpret the behavior of siblings, and to serve the family as a whole over a long period of time. We do not need specialists or costly delivery of services. The role of the "home visitors" may be a preventive, primary one.

Infant Intervention and Stimulation Programs   The fastest-growing special education enterprise at the moment consists of programs targeted at the infant known to have sustained damage or to be at a high degree of risk. Most of these programs help parents acquire caregiving skills designed to enhance development. Some rely on home visits; some bring mother and child to a clinic; a few consist of group programs. Some of the infants are usually given physical therapy and language stimulation. Any program targeted toward infants is going to be expensive, and true efficiency is difficult to achieve. Consequently, these programs are unlikely to ever be available for large numbers of infants. However, they offer a unique opportunity to support families during a particularly critical time, when they are coming to terms with the fact of handicap and are beginning to cope, and it is our responsibility to devise ways of making those services available and less costly through innovative approaches.

Preschool Intervention Programs   Intervention programs with both damaged and high risk preschool-age children have been developed for the last decade and should be established as a responsibility of every educational system. While again our evidence about the actual benefits of such programs to handicapped or potentially handicapped youngsters is meager, what evidence there is tends to point in the right direction.

We do have some interesting indirect evidence that we are probably doing the right thing with respect to a wide range of children, evidence like the marked improvement in the responses of preschool children to the 1972 standardization of the Stanford-Binet. In any event, I think most of us agree that early education for children showing any kind of developmental disability is usually a good idea, and the more structured the program, by and large, the better. Retarded children seem to need more step-by-step teaching, with carefully modulated tasks and directed teaching. They seem to require much more than the ordinary degree of consistency in teaching and control of the consequences of their behavior.

Modifications of Existing Personnel Categories   To staff these intervention programs, especially those that deal with handicapped children whose needs are multiple, we probably need some new categories of workers specifically trained in an interdisciplinary fashion.

The home visitors I referred to previously, for example, might be paraprofessionals or they might be an entirely new kind of specialist whose training is designed from the beginning for that role.

For work with handicapped infants, toddlers, and their parents, we might look to a new professional category, one that might be called a *developmental specialist*. A greater degree of cross-disciplinary collaboration is called for in intervention models. The relative failure so far demonstrates the need for integrated programs, structured around careful cost-effective evaluations, approaching the problem from the direction of the needs of the community as a whole rather than from the point of view of specialists in isolation. It exposes the extent to which our present medico-educational channels produce "professionals" whose own élite status and privilege is conducive to class defensiveness and a reluctance to cross the barriers set up by their own specialties. A number of apparently effective home-visitation programs have demonstrated that personnel with a high degree of technical knowledge are not crucial when the primary goal is orienting the parent's skills, interest, and dedication to their educational role especially in the rural and deprived areas.

We admit to shortage of finance and of human and physical resources in programs to combat the afflictions of children and to promote their welfare. I am persuaded that there is a lessening of enthusiasm to save lives of both children and adults when consideration must be given to financial implications involved in resources and facilities.

Parent preparation and education are associated considerations that represent a relatively new synthesis in health work; they are not so much a single medical input as a battery of concerns that lie at the edge of, if not outside, the range of activity of the ordinary doctor and educator.

Because intervention programs require the collaboration of social workers or cross-cultural experts, sociologists and educational psychologists are invited to participate in devising them. The successful program as a whole can only be created through the mediation of these social considerations, since the overall direction must be determined by the broadest criteria and this is the area of widest social implication. In-depth work is now under way in this field, for example by the Human Ecology Research Station (HERS) at Cali in Colombia, which is seeking to test the hypothesis that "many of the problems of under-nutrition, poor health and underdevelopment of human biological resources (are) interrelated and . . . require more than simple medical solutions" (McKay et al., 1973). The HERS programs, including combinations of nutritional supplementation, health care, and behavior stimulation, will result in the child's increased capacity to profit from formal education later in life by reducing the intelligence gap, and the earlier the program commences in the life of the infant, the more permanent the reduction will be.

SUMMARY

More than a decade ago early intervention programs began to be applied as a strategy for counteracting the destructive effects of poverty or central nervous system injuries on human development. This approach has appeared in different well-designed experimental programs in Latin America. The results shown in the data may shed some light on some questions of scientific and social value. Follow-up data are available and may be found in two types of early intervention projects: 1) intervention in mother and child centers, and 2) home visiting and teaching and work with the child's parents and siblings.

REFERENCES

Bronfenbrenner, U. (1968) When is infant stimulation effective? *In* Environmental Influences (Ed. Glass, D. C.) New York: Rockefeller University Press, p. 251.
Bronfenbrenner, U. (1974) Is Early Intervention Effective? Volume II. Cornell University: Children's Bureau.

de Lorenzo, E. (1964) Early intervention with high risk infants. Montevideo, Uruguay: Instituto Interamericano del Nino.

de Lorenzo, E. (1967) Investigation on spontaneous development and development in a group of subjects studied from birth. Proc. 1st Congr. IASSMD, Montpellier, p. 323.

McKay, H., McKay, A., and Sinisterra, L. (1973) Behavior intervention with malnourished children: A review of experiences. *In* Nutrition Development and Social Behavior (Ed. Kallen, D.) Washington: US DHEW. Publ. No. 13-242, p. 121.

Robinson, N. M. (1976) Prevention: The future society. The future of very early intervention and education. Presented at a meeting of the AAMD, June, 1976.

RESEARCH TO PRACTICE IN MENTAL RETARDATION
Care and Intervention, Volume I
Edited by Peter Mittler
Copyright 1977 I.A.S.S.M.D.

THE MILWAUKEE PROJECT
Indications of the Effectiveness of Early Intervention in Preventing Mental Retardation

H. Garber and F. R. Heber
*Waisman Center, University of Wisconsin, Madison,
Wisconsin 53706, United States*

The Milwaukee Project is a study of the efficacy of early, direct, intensive family rehabilitative therapy as a means of preventing mental retardation in families at high risk. The study was actually begun more than ten years ago, when, under the direction of Professor Heber, the Rehabilitation Research and Training Center in Mental Retardation at the University of Wisconsin began a comprehensive study of the problem of mild mental retardation. This category of retardation has suffered both from little and poor research—although it comprises the largest number of the mentally retarded—and from the traditional view that genetics was the prime determinant of a moveable but essentially unalterable developing intellect.

The data from our preliminary study have been reported at these meetings previously, but I would like to review two major findings upon which our subsequent research was based. The prime concern of our preliminary survey was to find clues that would lead to the early ascertainment of high risk factors related to mild mental retardation. The mildness of this form of retardation has interfered with the early detection that would permit planning an experimental manipulation of a high risk sample.

This research is supported in part by grant 16-P-56811/5-11, from the Social and Rehabilitation Service of the Department of Health, Education and Welfare.

We found two major clues: first, that although there is higher incidence of mentally retarded persons among the low socio-economic populations, certain specifiable families among the most disadvantaged were disproportionately responsible for the number of mentally retarded children. From our high risk survey area in Milwaukee, which had only two and a half percent of the city's population but one third of the educable mentally retarded children for the entire city, we found in one sample that 45% of the mothers were responsible for nearly 80% of the children with IQs below 80. (See Heber, Dever, and Conry (1968) for a more extensive discussion of the epidemiological data.)

Our second major finding was that these families at high risk could be identified by low maternal IQ, i.e., an IQ of 80 or below. Mothers whose IQ level was below 80 produced offspring who showed an intellectual growth curve distinctly different from that of offspring of mothers who were of similar socio-cultural background but of higher IQ. The offspring of seriously disadvantaged mothers with IQs below 80 decline markedly in IQ level from normal to retarded between infancy and maturity.

It was the hypothesis of the Milwaukee study that high risk families could be identified early, before the offspring's IQ declined, and that a direct intensive comprehensive family rehabilitation program could mitigate depressing environmental circumstances and thereby allow normal intellectual development. (See Heber and Garber (1973 and 1975) for details of the experimental design.)

Forty families, each with a child between three and six months of age and a mother with a WAIS IQ below 75, were accumulated over an extended period of time from an economically depressed census tract in the inner city of Milwaukee. There were no significant birth anomalies in any of the children, who were therefore normal but at up to 16 times greater risk for retardation. The forty families were assigned to either an experimental or a control group. There were no significant differences in early birth measures between the two groups of children.

The experimental group of families began a six-year program. The program consisted of a vocational and social education program for the mothers and an educational program for the children. Part of the program for the mothers consisted of a job training program together with a remedial education program. Later efforts included parent counseling and family crisis intervention.

The educational program for the children began shortly after they reached three months of age. The children were brought daily, year round, to a special neighborhood center that we prepared and staffed with teachers specially trained to work with infants. The children were placed in an elaborate educational program that was both extensive and somewhat innovative, involving close cooperation between the curriculum supervisors Hoffman and Harrington and a staff of paraprofessional and certified teachers.

The control families—the mothers and their babies—were placed on the same assessment schedule as the experimental families. We began to test the children from both groups at six months of age with the Gesell Developmental Schedules and then continued at 18 months with language assessment, and at 24 months with Cattell and Stanford-Binet tests and psychological learning tasks. When the children reached the age of 30 months we began our mother-child interaction assessment. A series of more sophisticated tests of language development began when the children were 36 months old.

Our assessment of the vocational and social status of the mothers has included personal interviews, home inventories, observations during mother-child interactions, attitude surveys, and reports on job and earning status, as well as IQ and literacy tests.

Let me briefly describe the results of the maternal rehabilitation program. Initially, we concentrated on developing job skills in the mothers, and then on developing their reading skills and home management skills. The data from the maternal program showed that although initially the job success rate varied considerably both within and between groups, our most recent survey showed there were more mothers from the experimental than from the control group who were employed, especially if we include as working those who remain at home because of a preschool-age child. Furthermore, in those cases where the mothers are working, there is a difference of nearly $40 in average weekly salary in favor of the experimental mothers. A significantly greater proportion of experimental mothers are literate when compared to the control group; however, in neither group is the literacy level especially high.

The most significant positive changes for the experimental mothers as compared to the control mothers occurred in three areas. These mothers changed their self-concept and self-confidence to be more positive. They also changed the manner in which they interacted with their children: they became not only more responsive but more verbal. This change in behavior can probably be interpreted as a reflection of their changed attitude about their importance as parents. The control mothers, on the other hand, continued to have a low level of confidence; they viewed their children as just one more problem in life, and were relatively nonresponsive in interaction with them.

The differences between the experimental and control children are even greater. The transformed measures of the many different assessments made on the children indicate that the differential across all the measures throughout the program remains very strongly in favor of the experimental children.

In experimental problem-solving tasks, the experimental children's performance was faster and more successful. They were enthusiastic and conscientious about the tasks, tending to use strategy behavior where appropriate. In marked contrast, the control children were unenthusiastic and relatively passive, tending to be uninterested and/or unable to develop appropriate problem-solving skills.

In our experimental assessment of language development, the earliest divergence in performance was on the language schedules of the Gesell between 14 and 18 months. The language differential between the two groups has continued and shows perhaps the most dramatic differences between the two groups. In Table 1 there is illustrated a partial summary of some of the more sophisticated measures of language development, such as tests of grammatical comprehension, sentence repetition, and morphology, and the Illinois Test of Psycholinguistic Abilities. I have tried to show, by some of the diagonal lines drawn, that differences in language development are on the order of nearly two years. The implications for school of this differential in language performance before school should be obvious.

It is these same skills in language that we observed powerfully demonstrated in the mother-child interactions. It was the experimental child in the dyad who was responsible mainly for the strength of the interaction. In other words, the elicitation of the appropriate events for problem-solving was by the child; the prodding and shaping of the mother's verbal responses was done by the child. In effect, the child supplanted the mother in the dyad as the educational engineer. No such changes occurred in the control mother-child dyads.

Thus by the time the children entered the first year of school there were substantial differences in their performance on IQ tests. Across the six-year school program, on the Stanford-Binet, the mean IQ of the experimental group was about 123, compared to 94 for the control group. At 72 months the experimental group was at 121 and the control group at 87 on the Stanford-Binet.

We should now discuss briefly our preliminary findings and where they lead us. Of course these findings are based on our primary conclusion that it is possible to prevent this form of mental retardation.

First, let me discuss the high risk detection technique. The use of the high risk criteria—severe disadvantagement and low maternal IQ—did provide the heretofore essentially unavailable opportunity to identify children at high risk and prevent retardation. When we compare the data from our original high risk survey group for offspring of below-80 IQ mothers with the intellectual growth pattern of the siblings of the actual target children and the data from our control children, they follow the same downward trend. Thus the phenomenon of declining intellectual growth in children selected from families according to our high risk criteria is reliable.

However, a note of caution is in order here: the use of a statistical definition in order to transcend the usual required expression of pathology as a criterion in mental retardation may well encompass several kinds of children, including some who do not need help and some who cannot be helped (Garber, 1975). This technique needs to be further improved in order to increase its selectivity and in order to avoid the possibility of stigmatizing individuals with the label "at risk for retardation," which is perhaps as serious as actually being labelled retarded.

Secondly, the mothers in our study were not the same. We have noted significant positive changes in the experimental mothers' attitudes and in their behavior in general. We have suggested previously that as a result of direct,

Table 1. Language tests[a]

| Age | Grammatical comprehension test | | | | Sentence repetition test I | | | | Picture morph | | Berko morph | | ITPA PLQ | |
| | % Subtests correct | | Features acquired | | % Exact repetitions | | % Structures preserved | | % Items correct | | % Items correct | | | |
	E	C	E	C	E	C	E	C	E	C	E	C	E	C
3	21	4	5	0	26	12	61	39	27	12				
3.5	40	9	12	1	47	18	80	55	35	22				
4	41	11	15	1	56	24	89	63	37	24	21	17		
4.5	60	15	18	4	61	28	92	73	43	28	27	17		
5	71	30	19	8	62	36	95	81[b]	46	29	27	19[c]	114.0	84.7
5.5	76	40	19	10	43	22	77	47	54	44	29	19		
6					47	27	84	64	65	49	39	21	107.8	87.3
6.5					53	38	94	77			36	19		

[a] E = Experimental group; C = Control group.
[b] Sentence repetition test II given at age 5 and after.
[c] Revised tests given after age 5.

intensive, and, in effect, a personal contact with these families, they became more responsive and more receptive to suggestions from responsible outsiders, whom they had previously regarded with hostility and suspicion.

Through the early part of the study we regarded the mothers and the families as generally the same. Now, some ten years down the road, we find that is not true. Though the selection criteria for all the families and mothers were the same, there are differences between them in terms of family process (Garber, 1976). Poverty and low IQ are poor indicators of family process. Some of our mothers and their families have gained considerably from the intervention effort and have demonstrated this strength by the way the family now operates. Other families still need help, at least occasionally, while some families will need perhaps constant, but certainly extended, help through time.

In other words, it is a mistake to treat all families alike. A rehabilitation intervention effort for severely disadvantaged families that disregards this fact will find its efforts less efficient and less effective. Some of our mothers can now understand how to effectively mediate the everyday experiences of life for their families, while others probably will never learn. To the extent, then, that we can differentiate between such families, we can develop more efficient and more effective approaches to the rehabilitation of severely disadvantaged families.

Thirdly, this same concern for individual differences must be demonstrated for children. Our educational program was very successful, in major part, I think, because we related to the individual child and his individual needs. There is no cookbook that can provide some one educational recipe for all children. In Figure 1 I have illustrated the Wechsler IQ data for the experimental and control children, beginning at four years of age and continued as part of intervention follow-up assessment. The average age of the sample, which is incomplete, is about nine years—with some children three years or more out of the early education program. As you can see, there has been some decline for both groups after the intervention ceased and after the repeated frequent testings ended. However, most important is that performance for the experimental group is normal and a differential of 20 or more points has been maintained between groups on the WISC performance. Our extensive data on language and learning support this differential in performance and make it difficult to conceive that the experimental group's performance will ever be the same as the control group's.

There is, though, a need to be concerned. Not all our children were the same and it is unlikely that the intense early educational intervention is sufficient to maintain all these children through life. They have yet to experience the influence of poor schools, distractions from peers, the continuation of an oppressive environment, and parents who are still mentally retarded (Garber, 1975). The distributions of IQ performance scores of the two groups are quite disparate, with little overlap. There are children in both groups whose abilities are quite different. At 96 months (where our scores are complete) one-third of

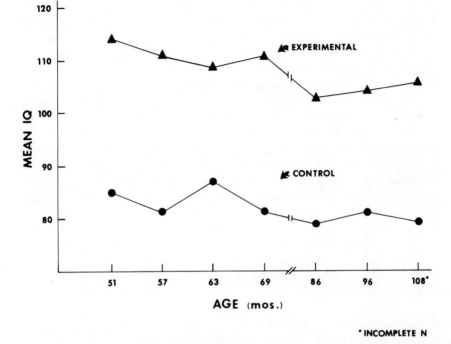

Figure 1. Experimental and control group mean IQ (WPPSI, WISC).

the controls had IQs below 75 (WISC), a traditional test score criterion for placement in special classes for the mentally retarded. By contrast, the lowest IQ scores for experimental children are two at 88.

The experimental children are now undergoing the most difficult part of their lives—public school. Reports from school indicate that the experimental children are having behavior problems. These are usually the result of their high level of verbal behavior, which sharply contrasts with their peers and gives them the ability to confront the teacher. Above all, the Milwaukee Project children were given confidence, skill, and practice in the use of language as an effective tool for interacting with the adults in their lives. It has been difficult for the schools to cope with these children. In part the problem is complicated not only by the schools' inability to deal with these problems appropriately, but also by the parents' inability to understand the nature and seriousness of school problems. They trust that the school knows best—a great mistake. The schools, on the other hand, think the parents are not interested.

Thus, even while we were successful in preparing the mothers in the experimental group for employment and in changing attitudes positively, we have been less effective in changing each mother's social patterns and her ability to remain free of the conflicts that we had previously been able to assist in resolving. There are again reports of children going to school hungry and inappropriately dressed, and of physical beatings by parents to solve minor school adjustment problems.

It is our interpretation that early intervention into the lives of seriously disadvantaged families at risk for retardation with a direct, intensive, and comprehensive rehabilitation effort can effectively prevent retardation. But it is important to note that neither are all such families doomed to failure nor can all such families be successfully helped.

A more thorough understanding of the differences between disadvantaged families is necessary so that we know to what extent certain families can mediate and extend the educational process of school, i.e., once given help to do so, and which families cannot, and so must have extended family support from outside.

From our own research and that of others, it appears that many families, although having in common many key indicator variables, are quite different in family process. Further, although children from these families respond favorably in a fairly similar fashion to preschool programs, there is a difference in how the benefits from such programs are sustained. Cases range from total family disruption to situations in which the family process approximates our stereotype of the middle-class family.

We continue to be cautious in interpreting our data because we are mindful that it is only a small portion of time and a small portion of the experiences in the lives of these families that we have influenced. Many years came before we entered their lives and many years are yet to come—especially for the youngest. It must be continually kept in mind that there is yet considerable room for all members of these families both to learn and to unlearn appropriate and inappropriate behaviors. However, the responsiveness to our program demonstrated by these families indicates that with direct, intensive rehabilitative programming mental retardation can be prevented in the high risk seriously disadvantaged.

SUMMARY

The efficacy of early intervention with a family rehabilitation program to prevent mental retardation from occurring in families at high risk was studied. This summary report includes family, preschool, and early follow-up data from the study. Particular attention was paid to experimental measures of learning and language performance, in addition to standardized assessment data.

REFERENCES

Garber, H. (1975) Intervention in infancy: A developmental approach. *In* The Mentally Retarded and Society: A Social Science Perspective (Eds. Begab, M. J., and Richardson, S. A.) Baltimore, Maryland: University Park Press.

Garber, H. L. (1976) Compensatory post-natal intervention. Paper presented at the meeting of the American Association on Mental Deficiency, Chicago.

Heber, R., Dever, R., and Conry, J. (1968) The influence of environmental and genetic variables on intellectual development. Behavioral Research in Mental Retardation. Eugene, Oregon: University of Oregon.

Heber, R. and Garber, H. (1973) Progress Report II: An experiment in the prevention of cultural-familial retardation. Proc. 3rd Congr. IASSMD, The Hague.

Heber, R., and Garber, H. (1975) The Milwaukee Project: A study of the use of family intervention to prevent cultural-familial mental retardation. *In* Exceptional Infant, Vol. 3: Assessment and Intervention. New York: Brunner/Mazel.

RESEARCH TO PRACTICE IN MENTAL RETARDATION
Care and Intervention, Volume I
Edited by Peter Mittler
Copyright 1977 I.A.S.S.M.D.

THE ACCELERATION AND MAINTENANCE OF DEVELOPMENTAL GAINS IN DOWN'S SYNDROME SCHOOL-AGE CHILDREN

A. H. Hayden and N. G. Haring
Experimental Education Unit, Child Development and Mental Retardation Center, University of Washington, Seattle, Washington 98195, United States

BACKGROUND INFORMATION

In 1969 the Model Preschool Center for Handicapped Children was funded by the Bureau of Education for the Handicapped as one of the first projects in the Handicapped Children's Early Education Program. In January of 1971 a special service and demonstration program was initiated by the Model Preschool to serve eleven Down's syndrome children between 18 months and 3 years old. Since then, the program has been expanded to the point where it currently serves over 50 home-reared Down's children between birth and 6½ years of age. By the fall of 1974, several of these children had completed the preschool curriculum and were ready for placement in primary classes. In order to provide a reasonable continuation of service for those children, a collaborative arrangement was undertaken with the Special Education Department of the Seattle Public School System to form special, primary-level Down's syndrome classes in a public school, patterned after the behaviorally based program provided at the Model Preschool.

Generally, the Model Preschool Center has been quite successful in generating and maintaining high rates of developmental progress in Down's syndrome children. While children between the ages of birth and 12 months are only able to perform about 62% of the tasks expected of their normal peers, children who have been in the program for several years and fall between the ages of 60 and 72 months are typically performing 95% of the tasks expected of normal children (Figure 1). This pattern of continued and accelerating developmental gains is quite different from those noted by other investigators. A cross-sectional study of Down's children between the ages of 4 and 18 years

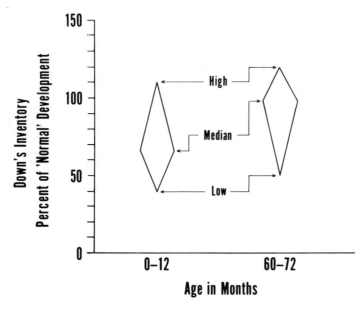

Figure 1. The high, median, and low scores for children in the Model Preschool Down's Infant Program (0–12 months) and the Model Preschool Down's Kindergarten Program (60–72 months).

usually shows a pattern of continuously *decreasing* levels of relative performance (Figure 2). Whether the pattern observed in the Model Preschool is different because of superior programming or because the children are generally younger than those previously studied was a matter of concern.

The new primary classes offered an opportunity to test the hypothesis of eventual declines in relative performance, but lacked the resources to document relevant variables and to undertake the complex analyses for resolving the question satisfactorily. Therefore, special funding for a research program was sought and obtained from the Research Division of the Bureau of Education for the Handicapped. This paper briefly describes the nature and preliminary results of that research.

SPECIFIC RESEARCH QUESTIONS

1. Is it possible to replicate and apply the basic behavioral approach of the Model Preschool Center in a public school setting, and, if so, what specific adaptations in curriculum and procedures are necessary to serve school-aged Down's syndrome children?

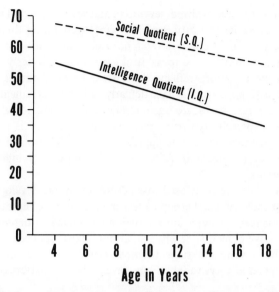

Figure 2. Decreasing relative level of performance on intelligence and social performance testing with age in Down's syndrome, as compared to normal children (adapted from Cornwell and Birch, 1969, by Smith and Wilson, 1973).

2. Will the Model Preschool Program, or some adaptation thereof, be sufficient to maintain or accelerate the developmental gains of these children throughout their involvement in the program?
3. Are there any observable relationships between the developmental gains of these children and their personal characteristics, family backgrounds, or program histories?

BASIC RESEARCH DESIGN

The basic research design does not dictate any program or changes in program for any child. Rather, the research is designed to carefully *monitor* the developmental patterns of Down's syndrome children over a period of three years and to *precisely document* each child's personal characteristics, family background, current program, and program history.

Developmental Progress Assessments

Several different types of performance assessments are being conducted on a regular basis with each experimental subject. Intelligence tests (usually the Peabody Picture Vocabulary Test or the Stanford-Binet) are administered semi-annually or annually. Standardized developmental scales (Denver Developmental Scale or Vineland Social Maturity Scale) are employed during alternate quarters throughout the year and a criterion-referenced objective checklist developed by the Model Preschool staff is used to monitor each child's quarterly progress. This Down's Syndrome Inventory reflects the basic curriculum through which each child is expected to progress; it is a particularly valuable instrument for assessing teaching effectiveness. Items are age-referenced according to when a normal child might be expected to master them, so the inventory is also useful for assessing the degree to which a child approximates normal levels of development. Finally, information concerning early major developmental milestones is obtained from parents.

Performance data are being used to establish the overall developmental levels and patterns of each child and group to test the prediction of eventual decline in relative performances. Analyses are also being conducted to determine if major differences in developmental levels or patterns exist between easily defined subgroups of the experimental subject sample. Detailed analyses of the impact of child and program-history variables on developmental patterns will be conducted.

Case History Data

Information on more than 130 separate history variables is collected via a parent reporting process. Where possible, technical information is independently verified through contacts with other persons associated with the child's case history. In general, variables relate to the socio-economic status of the child's natural and (if different) present parents, medical history, and program history.

Basic descriptive analyses have been conducted on case history data. Discriminate analyses will be conducted to determine which, if any, aspects of the case history appear to have a predictive relationship with preschool and/or school-age developmental gains.

Present Program Observations

Observations are conducted regularly in the primary classrooms to determine the extent to which Model Preschool procedures are being employed and to document any necessary adaptations of those procedures. The results of classroom observations and interactions between research staff and regular classroom personnel are being used to document the replicability and applicability of the Model Preschool program in a public school setting.

SUBJECTS

Two groups of children associated with the Model Preschool Down's Syndrome Program are the primary targets of the investigation: children who are presently enrolled in the Model Preschool and who will eventually transfer to the public school program, and children who formerly attended the Model Preschool and are presently enrolled in the public school program. By analyzing the progress of these children, we can assess the impact of one approach to education, consistently applied throughout the preschool and early school-age programs.

Two additional groups of children are studied for comparison and contrast: children who never attended the Model Preschool Center but who are enrolled in the public school primary level program; and children who are neither graduates of the Model Preschool nor enrolled in our primary level program, but who are served by other programs throughout Washington State. Both contrast groups provide diverse backgrounds that will help in explicating the role of early experiences in determining later gains.

Case history data are collected on all groups, but current child progress information is collected only on the two groups associated with the Model Preschool and the first contrast group. In analyzing developmental patterns, therefore, emphasis is placed on data concerning children presently enrolled at either the Model Preschool Center or in the Seattle Public Schools Down's syndrome program: these are the *experimental subjects*. Children who are neither at the Model Preschool Center nor enrolled in the Seattle program are considered *nonexperimental subjects* and serve primarily to estimate the degree to which the experimental samples represent the total population of Down's syndrome children in the state. Basic analyses concerning the developmental patterns of this last group can still be completed through the case history form.

Complete files have been compiled for 94 experimental subjects: 13 Model Preschool graduates presently enrolled in the Seattle program, 53 children currently enrolled in the Model Preschool, and 28 school-age children enrolled in the Seattle program who did *not* previously attend the Model Preschool. Case histories have also been compiled for an additional 50 nonexperimental subjects throughout Washington. By the end of the study, data should be available on 110 experimental subjects and 100 nonexperimental subjects.

Demographically, all groups are comparable. In each, there are approximately the same number of males as females; karyotypes show that 95% of the total sample are standard trisomy 21, 3% are mosaics, and 2% are translocations; and the age range of mothers at the time of the Down's birth was 17 to 45 years, with a mean age of 33 for both fathers and mothers. Initial investigations suggested that 47% of the sample have other associated handicapping conditions, but audiological tests indicate that the number of children with hearing losses is likely to be much larger than originally estimated. Age ranges of the three experimental groups differ: 20 to 78 months for the Model Preschool children (median = 42 months), 72 to 118 months for the Model Preschool graduates (median = 96 months), and 70 to 162 months for the non–Model Preschool graduates (median = 118 months). These age differences could explain many of the observed differences in developmental gains; however, fortunately, there are several nonexperimental and experimental subjects who can be satisfactorily matched for age for analyses where age alone might make a significant difference.

PRELIMINARY RESULTS

To date, only analyses of major group differences have been completed. Analyses concerning the relationships between child characteristics, personal histories, and developmental gains will be conducted. Since the Down's Syndrome Performance Inventory is the most frequently employed performance measure, data from that instrument have been used as the primary dependent variable. The relationship between scores on the Down's Inventory and scores on the standardized instruments is quite high, however, usually varying by less than three or four percentage points in any case.

The biggest question addressed concerns the prediction that Down's children will decline in relative ability with advancing age. Analyses of Model Preschool children indicated that, at least up to 72 months, performances *improved* (Figure 1); but other research has suggested that older children tend to score lower (Figure 2). After one full year, the relationship between developmental level and age was analyzed for all Model and Contrast children to see which pattern of development would prevail.

Results of the first comparisons are in Figures 3 and 4. The Model Preschool children and graduates continue to demonstrate a positive relationship between age and developmental level (i.e., older children tend to score higher), whereas the Contrast group displays exactly the opposite relationship. The Contrast group appears to be following the prediction one might make on the basis of previous studies (e.g., Cornwell's results are indicated by the dotted line). Based on these data alone, one might conclude that the Model Preschool program is affecting an overall change in the developmental patterns of Down's syndrome children: older children score higher. The children in the Model group are generally younger than those in the contrast group, however, and the comparison might not be entirely reasonable. A separate analysis was conducted, therefore, using only those children in each group who could be reasonably matched for age (Figure 4).

It would appear that *both* groups are accelerating. The Model group is improving at slightly higher rates, and is considerably higher overall, but both groups demonstrate the same basic relationship between age and developmental level. This suggests the possibility that the Model Preschool program is *not* changing the basic developmental *patterns* of its children, but simply maintains the same developmental pattern at a higher overall *level*.

This hypothesis was supported by analyses conducted on the results of second-year assessments. Model Preschool children and graduates are still performing well above the Contrast group, but are now similar to the Contrast

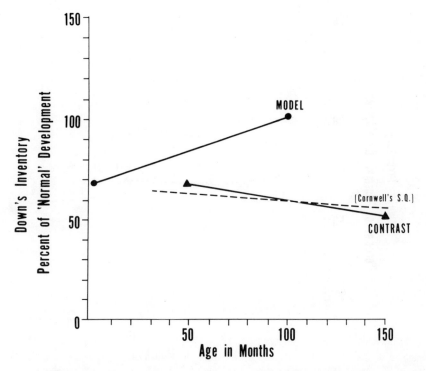

Figure 3. The relationship between age and developmental level for all children in each group assessed during the school year 1974–75.

group in the relationship between age and developmental level for both the overall analysis and the age-matched analysis (Figures 5 and 6).

The analyses described have been "cross-sectional": taking only one score from each child and examining the relationship between age and developmental level across children of different ages. From these analyses, one must conclude that older Down's children do score lower than younger Down's children. However, there are at least two reasons why that picture might emerge. First, as is commonly assumed, present programs may simply be incapable of maintaining high rates of developmental gains in Down's children. On the other hand, the older Down's children studied in this and other investigations had less refined preschool experiences than their younger counterparts. As a result, they may have *started* lower and have not yet overcome that initial disadvantage. The apparent downward pattern may not result from a *decrease* in the scores of older children, but rather, from an *increase* in the relative scores of younger children. To test this hypothesis, it is necessary to look at the developmental rate of each child.

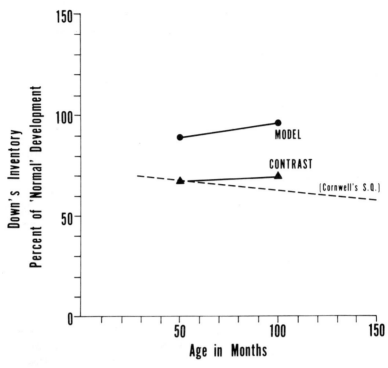

Figure 4. The relationship between age and developmental level for *age-matched* children in each group assessed during the school year 1974–75.

Figures 7 and 8 illustrate the relationships that were discovered between age and the *rates* of developmental gain achieved by the children in each of the two groups. When reading the charts, a gain per month of "zero" indicates that the child is maintaining his developmental score and progressing at the same rate as a normal child in acquisition of new skills. A positive gain score indicates that the child is growing faster than a normal child, and a negative score indicates that the child is growing more slowly than a normal child. The first notable feature of these two charts is that both groups appear to be growing at rates very near or *above* the rate of development expected for normal children. While these children may be performing below normal *levels,* therefore, most of them are "catching up." Older Model Preschool graduates tend to be progressing more slowly than present Model Preschool pupils, however, while exactly the opposite relationship is demonstrated in the Contrast group. Again, that might be a function of improved preschool programs for the younger children, but it is less comforting, nevertheless. In the analysis of age-matched children, both groups appear to be very similar, with a slight upward pattern in the Model group and a slight downward pattern in the Contrast group. This picture is a little more encouraging, suggesting that as the basic behavioral approach of the Model Preschool Program is applied to older children, essentially normal rates of progress can be achieved—even if those children did not have the advantage of such a program during the preschool years per se.

The apparent decline in rate of progress for older Model Preschool graduates could be a function of their general performance level. When they entered the Model Preschool program as infants or very young children, their deficits were frequently quite large—there was a lot of room to grow. Exposure to the program produced rapid progress (in excess of that expected for a normal child); by the end of preschool, many were performing very near the levels of normal peers. Upon approaching normal *levels* of performance, however, it apparently became more difficult to maintain *higher* than normal *rates of progress,* and they "tapered off"—keeping up with their normal peers, but not surpassing them. This hypothesis is supported somewhat by the fact that the older Contrast children (i.e., those with the greatest deficits, in Figures 3 and 5) are apparently

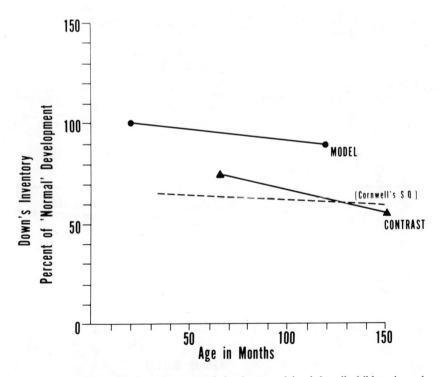

Figure 5. The relationship between age and developmental level for all children in each group assessed during the school year 1975–76.

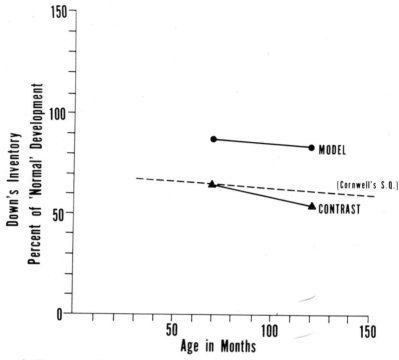

Figure 6. The relationship between age and developmental level for *age-matched* children in each group assessed during the school year 1975–76.

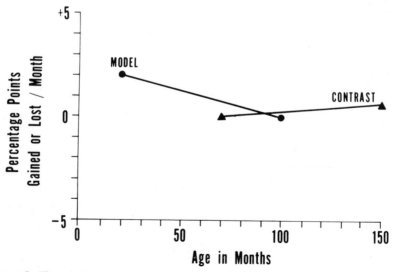

Figure 7. The relationship between gain or loss in developmental level and age for all children in each group during the assessments conducted in both school years 1974–75 and 1975–76.

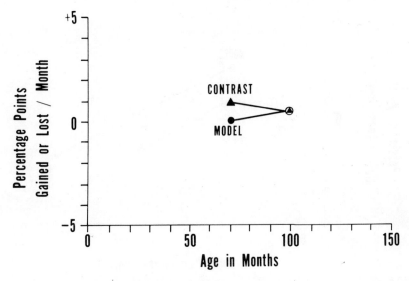

Figure 8. The relationship between gain or loss in developmental level and age in *age-matched* children assessed during school years 1974–75 and 1975–76.

making better progress than their younger counterparts (Figure 7). To test the hypothesis more explicitly, an analysis was conducted in order to reveal the relationship between performance level (i.e., relative deficit) and rates of progress (Figure 9).

It appears that Model group children tend to grow at *faster* than normal rates if their performances are below the 95% level of their normal peers, and *slower* than their normal peers if their relative developmental level exceeds 95%. The dividing line is not really that precise; and in a separate analysis it was determined that all Model group children with a developmental level of less than 78% were growing faster than their normal peers, and all children with scores above 100% (i.e., "normal") were progressing at a rate slightly below their normal peers. Between the developmental levels of 78 and 100%, children in the Model group did not have a common developmental pattern: some were progressing at higher than normal rates, others at slightly lower than normal rates.

The same pattern is found in the Contrast group. The whole Contrast group is lower than the Model group, however, crossing the "normal rate of progress" line at a score of 61% instead of 95%. Indeed, while the children in the Model group did not begin to decelerate in developmental progress as a group until they achieved a developmental level of 100%, children in the Contrast group above a developmental level of 74% were all decelerating.

Here at last is some indication that early preschool experiences, at least of the type provided by the Model Preschool Program, are valuable in assuring greater successes later in life. The Contrast group appears to be "seeking" a

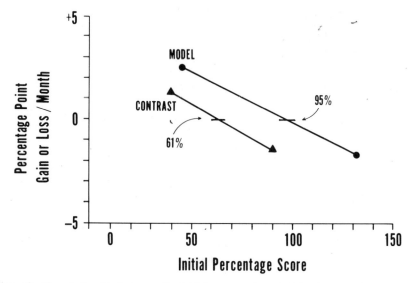

Figure 9. The relationship between the initial scores and rates of developmental progress in all children tested both in school year 1974–75 and in school year 1975–76.

developmental level of about 61% of normal functioning, while the Model group appears to be seeking a level closer to 95% of normal functioning—well within normal "tolerances." Whether or not these patterns will continue and be confirmed by the coming year's data remains to be seen, but the outlook is encouraging.

SUMMARY

In studying 94 children over two years, it would appear that there *is* an inverse relationship between age and developmental level: older Down's syndrome children tend to score lower, relatively speaking, than younger Down's children. These results tend to confirm previous investigations (e.g., Cornwell et al., 1969). There is reason to believe, however, that the developmental patterns one sees by analyzing a *cross-section* of children at different ages does *not* represent what will happen to the *individual* children. Several other relationships must be considered.

First, during the preschool years, at least in a program like that of the Model Preschool Center, children *increase* in developmental level and progress rates as they grow older and have had longer exposure to the program.

Second, most children continue to grow at normal or above normal rates of development beyond the preschool years, even if they were not involved in an exemplary preschool program.

However, children who did not attend the Model Preschool program appear to be leveling off at 61% of normal development, while Model Preschool graduates appear to be leveling off at approximately 95% of normal development. While a behavioral program seems to be of value with *any* Down's child, therefore, it is apparently of greater value if begun during the early preschool years.

The results of these investigations are still *quite* tentative; many of the conclusions drawn to date must remain in question. If nothing else, however, at least there is now reason to believe that the conclusions drawn from *previous* studies were in themselves quite pessimistic.

ACKNOWLEDGMENT

The authors are grateful to the appropriate Editors of the American Association on Mental Deficiency and the W. B. Saunders Company for permission to reproduce Figure 2 both from the original and from its adaptation (see References).

REFERENCES

Cornwell, A. C., and Birch, H. G. (1969) Psychological and social development in home-reared children with Down's Syndrome. Amer. J. Ment. Def. 74:341.
Smith, D. W., and Wilson, A. A. (1973) The Child with Down's Syndrome. W. B. Saunders Co., Philadelphia.

RESEARCH TO PRACTICE IN MENTAL RETARDATION
Care and Intervention, Volume I
Edited by Peter Mittler
Copyright 1977 I.A.S.S.M.D.

HOME-BASED PROGRAMS FOR MOTHERS OF YOUNG CHILDREN

S. W. Gray
*The John F. Kennedy Center for Research on
Education and Human Development and
George Peabody College for Teachers,
Nashville, Tennessee 37203, United States*

My topic is that of home-based programs for parents and children from low-income families, those often called culturally disadvantaged, but whom we might more simply call the poor.

These programs differ somewhat in emphasis but share a basic concern with low-income families. I should like to use my work and that of my colleagues over the past 15 years as illustrations of what such programs are like, the kinds of help offered to parents, chiefly mothers, and the kinds of measurable changes that may be expected to occur in parents and children. Our work is also illustrative of how programs develop over time as one learns, often slowly and painfully, new and more effective ways of approaching problems. Solutions appropriate to the early 60s may be less so in the mid-70s.

Our program starts with the assumption that the mother is literally the child's first teacher, the controller and programmer of his learning experiences. In doing this she occupies two vital roles. She serves as controller of stimulus events; that is, she is the one who determines which events in the home impinge upon the infant and child. She is the controller of the reward system as she responds to the behavior of the child either positively, negatively, or neutrally.

The studies I shall report have for the most part been in low-income homes—small urban and rural, with black and with white families.

We have been struck by two great strengths in most of the homes we have visited. These families have a deep concern for their children; they have the same goals and aspirations as more affluent parents. And they have a deep underlying reservoir of potential for improving their lives, although it is sometimes difficult to tap. These two strengths provide the opportunity for an intervention program focused on helping parents of young children come closer to realizing their hopes for their children.

Low-income families are highly variable, but there are some things in common. A lack of economic resources over years and over generations engenders other limitations. Our emphasis has been on the educational implications of the situation. The goals of our parents are similar to those of middle-income parents, yet there is usually a lack of knowledge of the instrumental steps. The parents want their children to do well in school but do not know what to do to help a child towards this goal. They see themselves as being controlled by events rather than being able to assert any measure of control upon events, including the behavior of their young children. They are overburdened. They need a concrete approach specific to their own life situation. They need help in being able to cope with their own particular situations, each different from the other.

With these strengths and limitations in mind, we have for over a decade explored ways of working in the home. We have found that it is possible to make the mother a more effective teacher, or educational change agent, by an extended series of weekly home visits, eight months or longer. When we have worked with the focus upon a given child in the home, the effect has spilled over to the other children in the family, a phenomenon we have termed vertical diffusion. Also, other parents living in proximity to our homes become interested in our research program, and often try to reproduce within their own homes such aspects of the intervention programs as they have been able to see or learn about—a situation we have called horizontal diffusion (Klaus and Gray, 1968).

Our first entry into the field of home visiting was rather casual in inception. In the Early Training Project (Gray and Klaus, 1970), which Rupert Klaus and I began in 1961, a group intervention program for the children was planned for three summers. In the months between, weekly home visits were made, originally as a bridge from one summer to the next. In this endeavor, a skilled individual, with preschool and social work background, met in the home with each mother for an hour a week. She brought materials, and showed the mother how to use them effectively with the child. There was one interesting and unexpected finding. We tested the younger siblings of the children with whom we had been working, and compared them to younger siblings in the local and distal control groups. The younger siblings of the experimental groups showed Binet IQs approximately 13 points higher than those in the two control groups (Klaus and Gray, 1968).

Our next study under the direction of James O. Miller and Barbara Gilmer (Gilmer, Miller, and Gray, 1970) was one in which we tried systematically to separate possible effects of a home visiting program from those of an assembled program. Our earlier study had confounded the two. This second study involved three differential treatments for the children. In one group, there was a special group program for the children for 2½ years before entrance in the first grade. In the second group, the children came to a preschool that duplicated the first. In addition, the mothers were involved once a week in a sequence of training experiences, designed to enable them to work more effectively with their young children. In a third group no child came to an assembled program, but there were weekly home visits. The study was a massive one and findings complex. There are three interesting findings, however, I shall mention briefly.

With the so-called target-age children, the age group in the assembled preschool, the additional involvement of the mother did not increase the children's performance on tests of intellectual ability or language as measured at the end of the intervention. Both groups, however, were superior to the home visitor group and to a comparison group.

With the younger siblings, however, superiority was shown in the performance of the children in the two groups in which there was mother involvement. Both these groups were superior to the group in which there was involvement of the child but not the parent and to the comparison group. Results two years after intervention had ceased suggest that children whose mothers were involved in the program had maintained their early gain. In the groups in which the mothers were not involved there had been a slight decline.

Since we were increasingly impressed by the need to begin when children were very young, our next endeavor under the leadership of Bettye J. Forrester was with the mothers of infants aged 8 to 18 months (Forrester et al., 1970). This turn to mothers of infants was largely the result of the pervasive emphasis of our programs that they should be *developmental* rather than *remedial*. This study showed remarkable gains for the experimental group, as much as an average of 18 points on the Bayley Mental Scale, and similar gains on two other measures. A follow-up six months later, however, indicated that these infants were no longer significantly different from the control group. This finding disturbed us. One of our conclusions was that perhaps the program was too specifically directed at infancy and served the mothers less well as their infants became toddlers, with the problems of behavior management associated with that age.

The study we are just completing is based upon our earlier findings, our successes and our failures. We have called it the Family-Oriented Home Visiting Program, since the emphasis is on helping the mother with all her young children and in enlisting the father where feasible. It has as its central goal, as do all our programs, that of helping the parent to become a more effective teacher and a more effective programmer of the educational potential of the home.

There are two major reasons why we embarked upon this study. Gains in early intervention programs typically show decline in the follow-up periods. If a program focused on giving the parents sustaining skills and procedures that work over a variety of ages, perhaps it would have a more lasting effect over time. The competence the mother develops in dealing with her toddler will stand her in good stead when her infant reaches that stage; work with the preschooler will serve later for the toddler.

There is also the reality of the mother's situation. She must be concerned with all her children. Also, it seems reasonable, rather than simply looking for spillover effects as we did in earlier studies to capitalize on this spread of effect from the beginning.

This study has a rather complicated design involving nine months of weekly visits to mothers (and sometimes the fathers as well) in homes in which there are two or three children under five years old, and, for half the mothers, monthly contact in the year following. There is a control group randomized from the original list of eligible and interested families.

The program has nine specific objectives. Here are a few: improving the mother's teaching style, helping her with behavior management, helping her organize her day and her home situation to provide more educational opportunities for her children, and encouraging more reciprocal language behavior between mothers and children. Each visit is tailor-made for a specific family because of the wide variability in families. The home visitor works with the mother rather than the children as her major focus, although naturally the children are involved for most of the time. The one-hour visit centers on the use of educational materials, wherever possible materials that can be used effectively across different ages, although with somewhat different purposes in mind. These materials are easily obtained—inexpensive toys, or, more often, materials that the mother can construct from household discards such as coffee cans, old magazines, and scraps of fabric.

Both the mothers and the children of the families were pretested, and in June of this year finished their third posttest, two years after the major intervention. A third posttest has been completed, but is not yet analyzed.

Our results are modest, but they are positive. We have found that mothers have improved the stimulus potential of the home, as measured by a test devised by Bettye M. Caldwell (Bradley and Caldwell, 1976). This effect was more marked on the second posttest than the first, suggesting a sustaining effect for the mothers. A measure of maternal teaching style, locally developed (Sandler et al., 1973), was also used. Here again the experimental mothers were superior to the control mothers. Again the effect was slightly more marked at the end of the second posttest.

The families were selected so that each had a toddler 16 to 24 months old at the time of the pretest. These children proved superior on a locally devised test of receptive language (Atyas, 1974) immediately after the intervention. Because of the youth of the children, on intelligence tests our most stable results are from the second posttest. Here the experimental group was slightly but significantly superior to the control group on the Binet.

What have we learned over the years?

First of all, we have been able to make positive changes in mothers as effective educational change agents, both as better teachers and as better programmers of the environment for their young children, and the children have improved in intellectual competence. I should like to emphasize that these effects, although statistically significant, have been modest. One cannot hope, with weekly home visits, to offset to any marked degree the effects of poverty over years and generations. Such an approach is only one of many steps needed to avoid that diminution of potential so common in poor and deprived homes, for social problems are massive and complex. But at least it is a step in what we hope is the right direction.

SUMMARY

This report describes the author's research over the years with special home-based programs for low-income parents of young children who may be considered potentially at risk. Special emphasis is placed on a recently completed study with mothers initiated in 1972, and now in the follow-up phase.

REFERENCES

Atyas, J. (1974) Assessing Language Ability in Children 18 to 36 Months of Age. Nashville, Tennessee: Demonstration and Research Center for Early Education, George Peabody College.

Bradley, R. H., and Caldwell, B. M. (1976) Early home environment and changes in mental test performance in children from 6 to 36 months. Dev. Psychol. 12:93.

Forrester, B. J., Hardge, B. M., Brooks, J. P., Outlaw, D., and Boismier, J. (1970) Home Visiting with Mothers and Infants. Nashville, Tennessee: Demonstration and Research Center for Early Education, George Peabody College.

Gilmer, B., Miller, J. O., and Gray, S. W. (1970) Intervention with Mothers and Young Children: A Study of Intra-family Effects. Nashville, Tennessee: Demonstration and Research Center for Early Education, George Peabody College.

Gray, S. W., and Klaus, R. A. (1970) The early training project: A seventh year report. Child Dev. 41:909.

Klaus, R. A., and Gray, S. W. (1968) The early training project for disadvantaged children: A report after five years. Mongr. Soc. Res. Child Dev. 33 (No. 4).

Sandler, H. M., Dokecki, P. R., Stewart, L. T., Britton, V., and Horton, D. M. (1973) The evaluation of a home-based educational intervention with preschoolers and their mothers. J. Commun. Psychol. 1:372.

RESEARCH TO PRACTICE IN MENTAL RETARDATION
Care and Intervention, Volume I
Edited by Peter Mittler
Copyright 1977 I.A.S.S.M.D.

EARLY EDUCATION OF THE HANDICAPPED
Program Variables and Components of an Exemplary Program

M. B. Karnes and R. R. Zehrbach
*Institute for Child Behavior and Development, University
of Illinois, Champaign, Illinois 61820, United States*

HISTORICAL BACKGROUND

Although numerous kindergartens and nursery schools were initiated both in Europe and this country in the late nineteenth and early twentieth centuries, the major milestone in the United States seems to be the work of Skeels and Dye (1939, 1966), who demonstrated in the early 1930s the effects of stimulation on the development of children under three who had been diagnosed as mentally handicapped and moved from an orphanage to an institution for the mentally retarded. A one-to-one interaction with older individuals classified as mentally retarded provided intensive stimulation for these young children. In an average span of one and a half years, these thirteen subjects gained an average of 27.5 IQ points in contrast to the mean loss of 26 points for the comparison group who remained in an orphanage with limited stimulation. A follow-up study revealed that all experimental subjects had become self-supporting and were functioning as middle-class individuals, while four of the contrast subjects remained institutionalized and seven worked at low-level jobs. Further, their histories revealed poor social adjustment, frequent unemployment and mental illness. The median scholastic attainment of the experimental subjects was twelfth grade, while that of the contrast group was less than third grade.

In 1948, Samuel A. Kirk (1958) initiated a five-year pioneer research program with young, mentally retarded children aged three to six years. The findings were compatible with those of Skeels and Dye.

This speech is a condensation of a chapter, Early education of the handicapped: Issues and alternatives. *In* Bernard Spodek and Herbert Walberg (eds.), Early Childhood in Education. Chicago, Ill.: The National Society for the Study of Education, 1976.

In the mid-sixties, federal funds triggered a wave of preschool innovations that concentrated on the young disadvantaged child and his family. Although the earliest interest concentrated largely on center-based programs with children aged three to five years, the importance of involving younger populations in an educational program emerged quickly. It soon became apparent that there was more than one way to deliver services, that a number of educational approaches were viable, and that parents would and could become better teachers of their children. In addition, the overriding hypothesis regarding the importance of early education had been reinforced: the development of young, disadvantaged children could be accelerated if appropriate services were made available. Further, such intervention was highly successful with age groups younger than had first been considered.

Concurrent with this research thrust was the initiation of Head Start in the summer of 1965, a program that represents the most extensive national endeavor to educated preschool children to date. The Head Start experience made it evident that the early years are the critical years, especially in the lives of low-income and handicapped children. This awareness led leaders in the field to seek legislation that would fund the development and dissemination of viable preschool models for young, handicapped children. Thus, the Handicapped Children's Early Education Assistance Act (PL 90-538) was enacted in 1968. The large majority of the first programs concentrated on three- to five-year-old children; more recently the Bureau of Education of the Handicapped (BEH) has encouraged the development of model programs for handicapped infants. Interest in the development of model programs for handicapped children who are gifted is also emerging.

COMPONENTS OF AN EXEMPLARY PROGRAM

A review of a number of early education programs for the handicapped and of the findings of research-based programs for the disadvantaged reveal certain characteristics that set exemplary programs apart from others (Karnes, 1975). All components are not necessarily present in all programs; however, exemplary programs tend to exhibit a number of these.

Early Identification

The importance of early identification of the handicapped cannot be too highly stressed if the program is to be an exemplary one. Obviously screening and identification are essential first steps before prescriptive programming is possible. It is relatively easy to identify a low-incidence handicapped child or, at an early age, the blind, deaf, severely orthopedically handicapped, seriously emotionally disturbed, or markedly mentally retarded child. The identification of the mild and moderately handicapped young child presents a quite different and more complex problem.

It seems imperative, then, to develop, validate, and implement mass manda-tory screening programs to locate both moderately and severely handicapped children. Important aspects of such an effort appear to be: 1) further develop-ment and refinement of effective screening instruments, 2) legislation requiring screening at early ages, 3) mandatory registration of handicapped children by physicians, 4) information programs to enlighten the general public regarding the identification of and programming for handicapped children, 5) alternative programs with strong parent components, and 6) a delineation of the rights and responsibilities of parents and agencies.

Effective Means of Delivering Services

Selection of an appropriate delivery system is another important component of an exemplary program. Screening and identification procedures are of little value without an effective means of delivering services that meet the special needs of handicapped children. Four major systems for delivering services to young handi-capped children seem to have emerged: 1) home-based, 2) home-based followed by center-based, 3) home- and center-based, and 4) center-based. Although common goals and objectives often cut across these categories, there are certain rather clear distinctions that make categorical discussion useful and enlightening.

Instructional Model

A well-defined instructional model for structuring the program seems to be characteristic of exemplary programs. The complexities of comprehensive pro-gramming require a framework that helps to organize the program. In fact, as a general rule, one model is not sufficient to complete the broad spectrum of program goals. The most effective programs seem to be those with the most clearly delineated models.

Positive Approach

A positive approach characterizes exemplary programs, and this approach is extended not only to the handicapped child but to everyone involved in the program, including parents. To help maintain positive attitudes, plans and procedures must be based on positively-stated goals that are realistic, concrete, and understandable to professionals and parents alike.

Strong Emphasis on Language Development

A large portion of handicapped children have lags in language; thus, most programs for handicapped children place a strong emphasis on language devel-opment.

Attending to Total Development

Since a handicapping condition eventually affects all aspects of development, effective programs attend to the total development of the child.

High Child-Adult Ratio

Since handicapped children have complex needs, a high adult-child ratio is essential. One adult to every four children is considered minimal, and severely handicapped children may require a one-to-two or one-to-one ratio.

Careful Planning

Careful planning is another characteristic of an exemplary program. Careful planning includes the establishment of long-range goals as well as the statement of specific objectives to meet these goals for each handicapped child in the program.

Flexible Time Use

Another characteristic worth mentioning is the flexible use of time. Initial work with a child may require a heavy investment of time, for social relationships must often be established before classroom participation is feasible. When appropriate social behavior has been developed, staff and child time must be redirected toward other objectives. Similarly, the development of self-help skills at one stage of a child's development may be given primary emphasis, but as he acquires these skills, the emphasis should be directed to cognitive or social development.

Appropriate Instructional Materials

To accomplish the goals and objectives of a program, attention must be given to the selection of appropriate instructional materials. Materials must be interesting to the child, hold his attention, and motivate him to engage in activities.

Humanistic Approach

Above all, an exemplary program demonstrates a humanistic approach to children, parents, and staff. Each individual is viewed as a human being who deserves respect, consideration, and an opportunity to develop and use his abilities.

Interdisciplinary Approach

The complexity of the problems of young handicapped children requires multi-faceted expertise that is only available through an interdisciplinary approach. Each specialist must have an opportunity to gather, interpret, and present data to members of an intervention team. Only through sharing can information be synthesized and integrated to formulate a total understanding of the child and his family and to develop a viable plan.

Preservice Training

Preservice training of staff with a heavy emphasis on practical experiences is important when launching a new program. Although an exemplary program can be accomplished with a strong inservice training component, as a rule excellence is more quickly attained with personnel who have had high quality preservice training.

Ongoing Inservice Training

Thus, an ongoing inservice training program using a variety of methods and techniques must be an integral part of an outstanding program for young handicapped children. Time must be allotted in the daily schedule for such activities.

Strong Parent Involvement

A strong parent involvement component is found in almost all programs of merit. A flexible, many-faceted approach to involving parents is essential.

Ongoing Internal and External Evaluation

Ongoing evaluation, both internal and external, distinguishes exemplary programs from those of lesser merit. The continuous gathering of data, its analysis, and the application of this information to the improvement of the program is essential in quality programs.

Comprehensive and Efficient Record Keeping

Any program of merit must have a comprehensive and efficient record keeping system. Complex problems require the careful collection and recording of data so that both gross and subtle interactions that interfere with the child's learning can be identified and alternate plans devised.

Effective Feedback

An effective feedback system to children, parents, and staff is essential in accomplishing goals. Each person involved needs to know in positive terms how he is functioning and he needs this information as quickly as possible and in terms that are meaningful to him. A feedback system enhances motivation, fosters enthusiasm, and decreases anxiety and useless effort.

Strong Leadership

Strong leadership is essential in an exemplary program. Programs require honest advocates, and leaders must be able to inspire others to contribute fully to the accomplishment of program goals.

Effective Communication Systems

Programs of excellence develop effective systems of communication. Program staff must be aware of the needs of each child and his family members, and of the contribution that each member of the team can make.

Full Use of Community Resources

Programs for young handicapped children require the full utilization of all community resources that can contribute to the development of the handicapped child and his family.

Compatible Physical Facilities

While no set blueprint for housing an exemplary program for the handicapped has been developed, physical facilities must be compatible with program goals. Programs that serve orthopedically handicapped children typically have modifications to accommodate wheelchairs and require special furniture and equipment for physical therapy. Programs with other goals have physical facilities to reflect these goals, such as the equipment for the deaf or blind.

Appropriate and/or Innovative Transportation

Appropriate and sometimes innovative ways for transporting children, parents, and even staff are developed in exemplary programs. Buses with special lifts are essential for the orthopedically handicapped, and drivers and bus supervisors trained to handle young handicapped children are also found in quality programs.

Placement and Follow-up

Placement and follow-up of children into other programs is an essential part of a program of excellence. Established procedures help to make the transition from one level to another and to ensure that needed services are provided. In addition, organized follow-up provides feedback that helps to improve the existing preschool program for the handicapped.

Good Public Relations

Effective programs work toward developing and maintaining good public relations. All types of media are used to develop an understanding of the program—personal presentations before community groups, television and press releases, brochures, visitation days, the use of volunteers—all of these contribute to the support of the program by the community at large.

Administrative Support

Administrative support is crucial in promoting and maintaining a high level of operation. This support includes not only reinforcement from immediate supervisors but also from higher levels of administration. Personnel working in a program for young handicapped children need to be aware that the administration endorses the program and appreciates the efforts of everyone involved. In the last analysis, the administration is largely responsible for ensuring that all components of an exemplary program are present. When this is the case, high staff morale is almost invariably found.

REFERENCES

Karnes, M. B. (1975) Education of pre-school age handicapped children. *In* Special Education—Needs—Costs—Methods of Financing. Report of a Study (Eds. McClure, W. P., Burnham, R. A., and Henderson, R. A.). Urbana, Illinois: Bureau of Educational Research, College of Education, University of Illinois.

Kirk, S. A. (1958) Early Education of the Mentally Retarded. Urbana, Illinois: University of Illinois Press.

Skeels, H. M. (1966) Adult status of children with contrasting early life experiences. Monogr. Soc. Res. Child Dev. 31:(No. 3).

Skeels, H. M., and Dye, H. B. (1939) A study of the effects of differential stimulation of children. Proceedings of the Annual Convention of AAMD. 44:114.

RESEARCH TO PRACTICE IN MENTAL RETARDATION
Care and Intervention, Volume I
Edited by Peter Mittler
Copyright 1977 I.A.S.S.M.D.

PREVENTION OF DEVELOPMENTAL RETARDATION IN HIGH RISK CHILDREN

C. T. Ramey and F. A. Campbell
*Frank Porter Graham Child Development Center, University
of North Carolina at Chapel Hill, North Carolina 27514, United States*

To be born poor should not subject an individual to a lifetime of intellectual retardation, substandard achievement, and ill health, yet all too often it does.

Children who live in poverty disproportionately show developmental retardation. Such deficits may have organic causes, but frequently no organic basis can be found for the developmental retardation.

Hunt (1961) and Bloom (1964) have suggested that the low quality of environmental inputs to the poverty level child may be an important factor in the etiology of retardation. Specifically, children from homes of extreme poverty may be deprived of various early learning experiences in comparison to children who are economically more privileged.

The complex and interlocking problems of economic deprivation, increased illness, and intellectual stifling in deprived environments present an enormous challenge to those who seek to intervene and to improve the opportunities and accomplishments of the disadvantaged child.

During the 1960s investigators of child development joined together to press for early intervention programs that had remediation of developmental retardation as their target. Enthusiasm for such endeavors was dampened somewhat by published findings that indicated that Project Head Start had achieved far less spectacular results than had been anticipated (Westinghouse Learning Corporation, 1969).

One explanation for the early Head Start results may lie in the timing and intensity of the early Head Start programs. Perhaps too little program was being applied too late in the child's live to offset fully the cumulative and pervasive effects of his environment.

One response to the preliminary Head Start data was the creation of developmental day care programs such as those conducted by Weikart in Ypsilanti, Michigan and Heber and Garber in Milwaukee, Wisconsin.

Although social, emotional, and physical development are included among the targeted areas for intervention in most programs for disadvantaged children, it is cognitive development that has received the most systematic evaluation. Indeed, in several cases cognitive development appears to be the only area receiving systematic evaluation. This concentration on cognitive development is due, in part, to the fact that procedures for assessing cognitive or intellectual processes are more advanced at present than are assessment procedures for social and emotional development.

Our chapter focuses on the intelligence test results from an early intervention project designed to prevent developmental retardation.

THE CAROLINA ABECEDARIAN PROJECT

In the fall of 1972, the Carolina Abecedarian Project was begun as an attempt to bring together a multidisciplinary team of researchers who would address themselves both to demonstrating that developmental retardation could be prevented and to examining how various psychological and biological processes were affected by such preventive attempts.

To accomplish this objective target children are randomly assigned either to a day care group (experimental group) or to a home group (control group). All children enter the program at birth and the experimental group children begin attending the day care facility when they are between six weeks and three months of age. The day care curriculum is designed to provide supportive experiences in the areas of physical and motor development, perceptual and cognitive development, language development, and social development.

Both the experimental and the control subjects receive the following services:

1. Family support social work services: On a request basis from the parents and from routine visits to all families, the Abecedarian Project seeks to provide all families with goods, services, or guidance . . . in such areas as obtaining legal aid, family planning, food, clothing, or housing . . . that will help to keep the families intact.
2. Nutritional supplements: Each child in the experimental group receives the bulk of his nutrition at the day care center. Breakfast, lunch, and an afternoon snack are served each day. To help control for the effects of nutrition upon development, the control group receives an unlimited supply of free formula for the first fifteen months of life.
3. Medical care: The pediatric staff at the Frank Porter Graham center provides care for the children attending the center. An arrangement with a local primary care clinic is used to provide care for the control group.
4. Transportation: Transportation to and from the center is provided for all subjects participating in the project.

5. Payment for participation: All mothers are paid for participating in any nonmedical evaluations.

After target children are born, qualifying families are pair-matched on maternal IQ, number of siblings, and total high risk scores, and are randomly assigned to either the experimental or the control group. To date, 87 families have been offered membership in either the experimental or control group and 86 have accepted. All families remain in the program except four, three of whose infants died in the first year of life, and one family whose child was withdrawn because the parents moved to another state.

To assess the program's impact, a variety of experimental procedures and standardized tests of development are used. This chapter focuses on the results to date from standardized tests of intelligence.

We use standardized tests of development in our program for two reasons. First, we consider that the children's tested developmental level provides an excellent evaluation of the program's overall effectiveness. Second, the use of standardized tests allows us to make direct comparisons of our program with other programs of its kind.

The testing schedule is heaviest during the first year, when behavioral change is most rapid. The Bayley Scales of Infant Development are administered every three months beginning at three months of age up to 12 months, then finally at 18 months. Thereafter we give the Stanford-Binet, Form L-M, each year beginning at 24 months, going up to 48 months. The Binet data that will be presented are based upon the 1972 norms, because we chose to compare our infants with today's population. Bear in mind, however, that the means we report are accordingly depressed an average of 10 points relative to other such means derived from other projects that may have been reported in the 1960s and early 1970s.

Finally, data will be reported from administration of the verbal section of the McCarthy Scales of Children's Abilities given at 30 months of age.

This chapter addresses two major questions. First, what are the test results of the Frank Porter Graham project to date? Second, do the Center and Control children show differential rates of passing certain types of test items?

RESULTS

Figure 1 contains a histogram depicting the Bayley and Binet test results up to age 36 months. For purposes of simplicity, we will include only the Bayley scores at 6, 12, and 18 months and the Binet scores at 24 and 36 months. We have complete data on 55 children up to age 24 months; to date only 28 children have attained the 36-month assessment age so the latter results must be considered preliminary. Two things are immediately apparent: First, consistent with previous findings by Nancy Bayley and others, our group of infants,

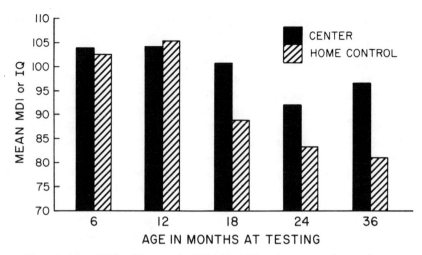

Figure 1. Mean MDI or IQ scores for high risk children in center and control groups.

despite their background of poverty, show no disadvantage on standardized infants tests during the first twelve months, but there is some decline in tested developmental level thereafter. Second, this decline exists for the control group but not for the center group.

The Bayley test scores were analyzed using a multivariate analysis of variance (MANOVA), which takes into account the nonindependence of the repeated test scores on the same infant. A group (center or control) X age (6, 12, 18 month) MANOVA was performed. The Bayley and Binet scores are treated separately because it was not considered desirable to include scores on different tests in the same analysis. The MANOVA results for the Bayley are summarized in Table 1. As can be seen, for the Bayley MDI scores there is a significant group X age interaction and a significant main effect for age at testing. Further, analyzing the age-at-testing results for each group separately, it can be seen that there is no effect for age or time within the center group; but there is a highly significant age effect in the control group.

We have used t-tests of the significance of the differences between means to find where the actual time changes occur. You will note that the t-tests show no significant changes over time for MDI scores in the center group. The control group is in marked contrast, however. For this group, while there is no significant change in the MDI from the 6- to 12-month tests, there is a highly significant change from 12 to 18 months—a drop of 16 points.

Tests of significance levels of the mean differences in MDI for the center and control groups at each age show that the only point at which they differ is at 18 months, with the center group showing an eleven-point advantage. The center group has remained stable over time, but there is a drop in the control group.

Table 1. Summary of MANOVA of Bayley MDI of 6, 12, 18 months in center and control groups

A. *Test of Bayley MDI*

Source	df	f	p
Group	2,51	2.03	
Group X age	2,51	5.25	0.008
Time	2,51	12.37	0.001
MDI linear	1,52	13.14	0.001
MDI quadratic	1,52	14.11	0.001
Age–Center group	2,51	0.89	
Age–Control group	2,51	0.73	0.001

B. *Test of Bayley PDI*

Source	df	f	p
Group X age	2,51	1.09	
Age	2,51	8.82	0.001
PDI linear	1,52	7.64	0.008
PDI quadratic	1,52	9.12	0.004

We find that the PDI scores do change over time but that this change is the same for both groups. There is a significant decline of seven points from 12 to 18 months, or a drop from a mean of 103 to 96. Both scores are within normal limits, and it is our clinical impression that the drop actually represents the non-cooperation of toddlers rather than a real decline in motor development.

Because others have found significant sex differences in performance on infant tests, we did all these analyses initially classifying the children by both sex and by group. There were absolutely no sex differences found on either type of the Bayley scores or on the Binet IQ scores at any age level, so the factor of sex differences can be discounted in our infant test findings to date. This is made very clear in the results of the Stanford-Binet tests given at 24 and 36 months. These findings are summarized in Table 2, Parts A and B. Analysis of variance shows that there is a significant difference in the 24-month Stanford-Binet IQ scores obtained by the center and control groups. The center group's mean is 93, the control group's mean is 82, and *t*-tests of the differences between mean scores confirms a significant advantage for the center group over the control group.

The 36-month results are based on only one cohort of children and are thus preliminary. We are presenting them as information but with the definite precaution that they are representative of only half the number of children considered up to this point. The preliminary results in Part B of Table 2 suggest that the trend seen in the 24-month data is continued a year later. There is a significant difference between the groups; the center group's mean score is 97, the control group's mean is 81, a 16-point advantage for the center group over the control group.

To understand more fully the nature of the differences in test performance that exist between the center and control children, we have examined the test items themselves. Mindful of the drawbacks associated with factor analytic techniques applied to age-scale data, we have followed the prevailing trend set by Ronald Wilson, Jerome Kagan, and others and have classified the Bayley items a priori into logical groups according to the function being tested. We grouped the 77 items administered at 18 months into four categories labeled: language,

Table 2. Results of analysis of variance and *t*-tests of mean differences on Stanford-Binet scores at 24 and 36 months

Part A. *24 Months*

1. Summary of ANOVA

Source	df	f	p
Sex	1	0.10	
Group	1	5.19	0.03
Sex X group	1	0.15	

2. *t*-Test of means

Group	$\overline{X}$	S.D.	N	t	df	p
Center	92.34	14.06	29	2.69	47	0.010
Control	83.96	8.57	25			

Part B. *36 Months*

1. Summary of ANOVA

Source	df	f	p
Sex	1	0.01	
Group	1	5.70	0.02
Sex X Group	1	0.00	

2. *t*-Test of means

Group	$\overline{X}$	S.D.	N	t	df	p
Center	96.79	16.25	14	2.48	26	0.020
Control	81.14	17.06	14			

perceptual-motor, problem-solving and imitation. We then computed the percentage of children passing each item separately for center and control groups. Arbitrarily, we required a 20% minimum difference in percentage passing each item to regard the item as discriminating between groups. With this criterion we found eleven Bayley items on which the center children surpassed the control children. Five of the items were language items; the other six were perceptual-motor items. There were no items in either the problem-solving or imitation categories that reached the criterion of difference we had set. On no item at all did the control group reach the criterion to exceed the center group.

Similarly, the Binet items were examined for group differences. For this comparison we used the item classification by Valett (1965). Valett used six classes, with a few items being double classified. Our groups of children again show clear-cut center and control differences. Of the 42 items considered, there was a 20% or greater difference favoring the center children on 17 items. One item had a reversal from 24 to 36 months. This item, repeating two digits, was passed by more center than control children at 24 months, with the opposite being true at 36 months. This reversal constituted the only instance in which the control group reached our arbitrary criterion of a 20% differential advantage over the other group.

The largest group of Binet items differentiating the center and control children was visual-motor, which had five items; general comprehension had four, and memory and concentration and judgment and reasoning each had three; two items were vocabulary. If we were to apply our same system of classification to the Binet items that we used for Bayley items, the overwhelming majority would be labeled language, with the remaining mostly falling into the perceptual-motor category. Of the 17 items differentiating the two groups, ten would be language and seven would be perceptual-motor.

We feel that two points are suggested by this brief item inspection. First, high risk children traditionally begin to show a decline in tested developmental level between 12 and 18 months, the age at which language is beginning to develop. Our center children appear to have a language advantage over the control children, and this may be one reason why their tested developmental level is more stable over time.

This possibility is reinforced by results from the Verbal Scale of the McCarthy Scales of Children's Abilities, administered to 25 experimental children and 23 control children when they were 30 months of age. The verbal scale at 30 months has a normative mean of 50.0 and a standard deviation of 10. The tests constituting the Verbal Scale assess the child's ability to express himself verbally, and also assess the maturity of his verbal concepts. At 30 months the experimental group obtained a mean score of 48.68 (S.D. = 9.45) and the control group received a mean score of 43.83 (S.D. = 9.14). This difference in favor of the experimental group was significant by t-test comparison ($t=1.81, df=46, p <$ 0.05 one-tailed).

Second, and somewhat less expected, the center children also show a distinct advantage on nonlanguage items on the Binet involving visual-motor skill and concentration. Perhaps the day care experience is enhancing their ability to work with their hands and to see relationships.

SUMMARY

We think that this research makes two major points. First, because the children in the control group are actually showing a decline in tested intelligence whereas the experimental group is not, the evidence indicates that our early intervention is preventing early and progressive developmental retardation. Second, the results from the item analyses of the Bayleys and the Binets suggest that language differences between the two groups is a plausible major factor in accounting for group difference.

REFERENCES

Bloom, B. S. (1964) Stability and Change in Human Characteristics. New York: Wiley.

Hunt, J. M. (1961) Intelligence and Experience. New York: Ronald Press.

Westinghouse Learning Corporation (1969) The Impact of Head Start. Athens: Ohio University.

Valett, R. (1965) A Profile for the Stanford-Binet (L-M). Palo Alto, California: Consulting Psychologists Press.

RESEARCH TO PRACTICE IN MENTAL RETARDATION
Care and Intervention, Volume I
Edited by Peter Mittler
Copyright 1977 I.A.S.S.M.D.

EARLY CHILDHOOD INTERVENTION
Nonhandicapped Peers as Educational and Therapeutic Resources

M. J. Guralnick
*National Children's Center, 6200 Second Street, N.W.,
Washington, D.C. 20011, United States*

The principles of normalization and mainstreaming have provided a conceptual framework for the integration and reintegration of handicapped people into schools and society in general. This process has also set the occasion for renewed interest in the roles that peers can play in fostering the development of handicapped children. Interestingly, much of the research regarding the developmental aspects of peer interactions has occurred at the preschool level. In part, this reflects the fact, as Wolfensberger (1972) indicated, that integration in early childhood programs would be relatively easy because these programs typically tend to be flexible and individualized, as well as consisting of children of various ages and sizes. He further noted that "particularly at this age level, normal peers seem to constitute nonthreatening models from which the handicapped (especially the retarded) children learn much more than they typically do from their impaired 'peers' " (p. 51).

The importance of peer influence in the normal course of events, especially as a socializing agent, has certainly not gone unrecognized (Hartup, 1970). Nevertheless, the recognition that peers can act systematically as agents of change in conjunction with therapists, teachers, experimenters, and the like, particularly with regard to their less advanced peers, has been a more recent phenomenon. Perhaps the most critical point to have emerged from an analysis of this process is that in order for nonhandicapped peers to effectively function as educational and therapeutic resources for those who are handicapped, carefully planned interactions are essential (Guralnick, 1976).

The purpose of this chapter is to review some of the underlying concepts and major findings in this area. Primary concerns will be: 1) the development of social interactions of handicapped children as a result of assistance by nonhandicapped children, and 2) an examination of the nature of linguistic interactions among children at various developmental levels and the potential for facilitating language development in less advanced children.

SOCIAL INTERACTION

Reciprocal social interactions among young children as well as the quality of their interactions with play materials is closely linked to a variety of personality, cognitive, and affective factors. Teacher demonstrations, reinforcement procedures, and a variety of environmental manipulations have all met with some success in promoting social development in handicapped children, but clear limitations have also been evident. In this regard, Bricker and Bricker (1971) have suggested that nonhandicapped children may well function more adequately than teachers as models for delayed children in the area of social play.

Empirical support for this notion was obtained in a study by Devoney, Guralnick, and Rubin (1974) that demonstrated that the introduction of nonhandicapped peers into a play situation resulted in a marked positive change in the frequency and quality of play among handicapped children. Of importance, however, is that this only occurred when the teacher systematically structured a variety of activities. Moreover, it was noted that, probably as a direct result of the integration experience, the handicapped children engaged in a much more sophisticated and organized type of play than had ever previously been observed. In fact, this play often seemed to be an abbreviated form of the complex interactions displayed by the nonhandicapped children.

A systematic follow-up of this work by Guralnick (1976) demonstrated quite clearly the potential value of nonhandicapped children as a resource. Focusing on specific handicapped children whose play and social interaction skills were poorly developed as measured by the Parten (1932) scale, the aid of two nonhandicapped peers was enlisted in an attempt to promote more productive play. Following the lead of Wahler (1967), training sessions were provided for the nonhandicapped children using role playing and verbal descriptions in an attempt to teach them to model appropriate play and to selectively attend to the handicapped child's appropriate behavior. This technique produced a substantial effect. After a few sessions with all three children playing in one area (systematically replicated across materials and children), the handicapped child's solitary and resistant play had been replaced by play mostly of an associative and cooperative nature. In addition, the frequency of positive verbalizations to peers greatly increased and corresponded to the increase in higher level play.

A detailed analysis of the interactions here revealed that two mechanisms appeared to be operating. On the one hand, the more advanced peers provided models for appropriate behavior. The second mechanism consisted of the systematic use of social and activity consequences for appropriate behavior by peers. This technique, in conjunction with modeling, has proved to be an extremely powerful treatment in positively affecting the social play behavior of handicapped children. It is important to note, however, that modeling alone appears to be insufficient in producing change in children in this situation, especially those with relatively severe deficits (Guralnick, 1976).

Accordingly, available evidence indicates that whether one achieves success here or not appears to depend on the systematic way in which grouping and instruction take place. We know from other work that these interactions among children at different developmental levels do not occur spontaneously (Ray, 1974), with the consequence that careful planning and arranging of events are prerequisites for success.

LANGUAGE INTERACTIONS AND
THE LINGUISTIC ENVIRONMENT IN INTEGRATED SETTINGS

As noted above, an increase in social play interaction among children at different developmental levels produced a corresponding increase in positive verbalizations. In addition, it has been demonstrated (Guralnick, 1976) that nonhandicapped peers' speech can influence certain characteristics of the speech of handicapped children. In particular, for handicapped children whose linguistic competence exceeds their usage, the salient reinforcement by teachers of a nonhandicapped child's extended and grammatically complete speech can result in more advanced speech by the handicapped child. Although there are many possible explanations for this, Kazdin's (1973) suggestion that reinforcement in these circumstances serves as a discriminative stimulus identifying those behaviors that will be reinforced seems most plausible. In addition, this concept may provide important implications for modeling and vicarious reinforcement effects among children at various developmental levels.

Observational data have revealed that the social and linguistic environments of handicapped children are quite different in settings consisting of children at various developmental levels, especially those including nonhandicapped peers, than in settings consisting entirely of a more homogeneous group of handicapped children. A recent investigation by Guralnick and Paul-Brown (1976) was carried out to examine more carefully the nature of the linguistic interactions that exist among handicapped and nonhandicapped preschool children. This study was prompted by the recognition of the importance of the linguistic environment in the development of the language-learning child. More particularly, it was designed to examine the way in which nonhandicapped children address handicapped children and to evaluate those interactions in terms of their potential for facilitating or adversely affecting the linguistic development of the handicapped child.

The literature regarding the nature of maternal-child speech interactions provided a useful framework for this work and has clearly suggested that mothers adjust virtually all aspects of their speech in accordance with the linguistic and cognitive capacity of their children, and that these adjustments have the effect of making language learning easier (Broen, 1972; Snow, 1972). In fact, Rondal (1976) has recently shown that the language environment provided by mothers of handicapped and nonhandicapped children is virtually identical when children are matched in terms of mean length of utterance (MLU), and suggested that mothers of handicapped children are making language adjustments that are as appropriate (and as facilitating) as do mothers with normally developing children.

Accordingly, looking at the child-child linguistic environment, we asked if nonhandicapped preschool children make similar adjustments in their verbal communications when addressing children at various developmental levels. Specifically, nonhandicapped peers were asked to instruct children who were classified as manifesting mild, moderate, severe, or no handicaps. Classification was based on IQ scores in accordance with the American Association on Mental Deficiency categories and MLU. Speech to the four groupings of children by nonhandicapped peers was recorded and analyzed in terms of a wide range of linguistic parameters designed to reflect measures of verbal productivity and grammatical complexity. The results indicated that, indeed, nonhandicapped peers did alter their speech in accordance with the developmental level of the child they were addressing. In general, consistent with the mother-child findings, speech tended to be more frequent, more complex, and more diverse when addressing children at higher developmental levels. A similar pattern was observed for measures obtained during free-play periods.

These data suggest that the linguistic interactions that exist among handicapped and nonhandicapped children may well be appropriate and provide input that has developmental significance for the handicapped children. Should further research confirm this contention, additional empirical support for the notion that nonhandicapped peers can function as educational and therapeutic resources in integrated settings will have been obtained.

From a methodological perspective, further analyses should focus on following sequences of verbal and nonverbal interactions. It would be useful here to note correspondences among the semantic, syntactic, and pragmatic aspects of communication. Consequently, we should seek to determine the kinds of adjustments made by the speaker, for example, in direct response to the verbal and nonverbal behavior of the listener. That is, if noncompliance to a direct request occurs, does the next utterance include a reduction in the length of the utterance and, if so, what syntactic, semantic, or other behavior changes occur? A detailed analysis along these lines should provide specific answers to questions that none of the previous studies without this methodology has been able to offer.

CONCLUSIONS

Certainly, at this point in our knowledge, considerably more research on the dynamics, structure, and limitations of peer influence are in order. A number of parameters appear most worthy of study, and they include, among others, the chronological age of the peer group, the developmental level and level of observational skill of the handicapped children, the type of behavior focused upon, the degree of classroom structure and available resources, grouping characteristics, and the characteristics of the nonhandicapped children. In any case, evidence is accumulating that more advanced preschool children can indeed be considered resources and assist in the growth and development of their handicapped peers.

SUMMARY

A review of recent experiments conducted in settings integrating handicapped and nonhandicapped preschool children is presented. Studies involving social and play interactions as well as a detailed analysis of the linguistic environment provided by nonhandicapped peers suggest the importance of peers as resources in these settings. A number of conceptual issues are raised as well.

REFERENCES

Bricker, D., and Bricker, W. (1971) Toddler research and intervention project report: Year I. IMRID Behavioral Science Mongraph No. 20, Nashville, Tennessee: Institute on Mental Retardation and Intellectual Development, George Peabody College.

Broen, P. A. (1972) The verbal environment of the language-learning child. American Speech and Hearing Association Monograph, No. 17.

Devoney, R., Guralnick, M. and Rubin, H. (1974) Integrating handicapped and nonhandicapped preschool children: Effects on social play. Child. Educ. 50:360.

Guralnick, M. J. (1976) The value of integrating handicapped and nonhandicapped preschool children. Amer. J. Orthopsychiatry 46:236.

Guralnick, M. J., and Paul-Brown, D. (1976) The nature of verbal interactions among handicapped and nonhandicapped preschool children. Paper presented at the 100th Annual Meeting of the American Association on Mental Deficiency, Chicago, Illinois.

Hartup, W. (1970) Peer interaction and social organization. In Carmichael's Manual of Child Psychology, Vol. II (Ed. Mussen, P.). New York: John Wiley.

Kazdin, A. E. (1973) The effect of vicarious reinforcement on attentive behavior in the classroom. J. Appl. Behav. Anal. 6:71.

Parten, M. (1932) Social participation among preschool children. J. Abnorm. Psychol. 27:243.

Ray, J. S. (1974) Ethological studies of behavior in delayed and nondelayed toddlers. Paper presented at the 98th Annual Meeting of the American Association on Mental Deficiency, Toronto, Canada.

Rondal, J. A. (1976) Maternal speech to normal and Down's syndrome children matched for mean length of utterance. Research, Development and Demonstration Center in Education of Handicapped Children, Research Report No. 98. Minneapolis, Minnesota.

Snow, C. E. (1972) Mothers' speech to children learning language. Child Dev. 43:549.

Wahler, R. (1967) Child-child interactions in free-field settings: Some experimental analyses. J. Exp. Child Psychol. 5:278.

Wolfensberger, W. (1972) The Principle of Normalization in Human Services. Toronto: National Institute on Mental Retardation.

RESEARCH TO PRACTICE IN MENTAL RETARDATION
Care and Intervention, Volume I
Edited by Peter Mittler
Copyright 1977 I.A.S.S.M.D.

PLANNING INTERVENTION FOR INFANTS AT HIGH RISK IDENTIFIED BY DEVELOPMENTAL EVALUATION

A. H. Parmelee, Jr.
Department of Pediatrics, School of Medicine and
Mental Retardation Center, Neuropsychiatric Institute, University
of California at Los Angeles, Los Angeles, California 90024, United States

This paper focuses on infants who do not have at birth stigmata of genetic or congenital defects, but are considered at risk for developmental disability in later life because they have suffered adverse prenatal, intrapartum, or neonatal biological events. As indicated in the reviews by Parmelee and Haber (1973), Sameroff and Chandler (1975), Broman, Nichols, and Kennedy (1975), and Hunt (1976), the degree of risk or the severity of the possible developmental disability for these infants cannot be readily predicted by the occurrence of any single hazardous prenatal, intrapartum, or neonatal biological event. Nor have neurophysiological or behavioral measures confined to the neonatal period improved the accuracy of the prediction greatly. It appears that some of these infants suffer only transient neonatal brain insult and recover completely, and others with brain injury manifest minimal neonatal behavioral changes. Even infants with brain injury identified in the neonatal period may compensate for this deficit so completely that no significant developmental disability is detectable in later life. In addition, prospective studies of infants considered at risk at birth have demonstrated that environmental variables such as mothers' education, fathers' occupation, or ethnic group have had a greater effect on the outcome than the perinatal risk factors. This does not deny the significance of

This research is supported by National Institutes of Health Contract 1-HD-3-2776, "Diagnostic and Intervention Studies of High Risk Infants," and NICHD grant HD-04612, Mental Retardation Research Center, UCLA.

the perinatal factors but indicates that the effect, as stated by Sameroff and Chandler (1975), and Beckwith (1976), is an interactional one with the environment and can attenuate or amplify the disabling behavior.

ASSESSMENT

Recognizing that the degree of risk for any single infant cannot be defined in the neonatal period and that environmental factors can attenuate or amplify the resulting disability, how should one organize a diagnostic program? We (Parmelee et al., 1975, 1976 a,b) decided to devise a system that would assess prenatal, intrapartum, neonatal, adverse biological events and neurophysiological, behavioral, and cognitive development in the neonatal period and at four and nine months past term. With the assessments distributed over the first year in this way, it is possible to identify those infants who have many problems in the beginning but show steady improvement, suggesting a good prognosis, and those infants with few problems initially but with continuing or increasing developmental difficulties, suggesting a poor prognosis. Not all the assessment procedures in our study are solely to document the infants' neurophysiological, behavioral, and cognitive development. Some are included in an attempt to determine the processes involved in the improvement or decline in performance in the first year. These include measures of attention, visual discrimination, fine motor hand precision and schema, play exploration, and details of mother-infant interaction in the home. Fourteen of these assessments, listed in Table 1, are treated cumulatively to identify those infants at nine months of age most likely to have developmental disability later in childhood.

To test the validity of this system we are studying prospectively 135 preterm infants. We have obtained significant correlations between the cumulative risk score, composed of the fourteen assessments from birth to nine months and Gesell and Bayley developmental assessments, and the Casati-Lézine cognitive test at two years. Further follow-up studies at later ages are planned.

INTERVENTION

We then had to deal with the problem of when to initiate intervention and in what form. Since the special needs of a given infant could not be clearly defined in the neonatal period, we felt that initially a more global intervention for the family was appropriate. In any case, we wanted to regard the family, and particularly the mother, as the primary agent of change for the infant. We planned to work with the family and mother rather than directly with the infant in order to have an effect that would be more lasting. Thus we decided to provide a general form of intervention for all families initially, and more specific forms of intervention limited to those infants still considered at risk at nine months, as described by Littman and Wooldridge (1976), Kass et al. (1976), and Bromwich (1976).

Table 1. Infant assessment procedures for the nine-month cumulative risk score[a]

---

1. Obstetric complications scale.
2. Postnatal complications scale.
3. Newborn sleep polygraph for assessment of state organization.
4. Newborn neurological examination.
5. Newborn visual attention assessment.
    At one month, home observations are made of mother-infant interactions and transactions.
6. Three months sleep polygraph.
7. Four months Gesell test of infant development.
8. Four months visual attention assessment.
9. Four months pediatrics complications scale.
    At eight months, home observations are made of mother-infant interactions and transactions.
10. Eight months exploratory behavior assessment.
11. Eight months hand precision and sensory-motor schema assessment.
12. Nine months Gesell test of infant development.
13. Nine months Casati-Lézine assessment of sensory-motor cognitive development.
14. Nine months pediatrics complication scale.

---

[a]All newborn assessment are given at term, 40 weeks conceptional age, and subsequent tests at 3, 4, 8 and 9 months past term or 53, 57, 76, 80 weeks conceptual age. Conceptional age is calculated from the onset of the mother's last menstrual period.

The ultimate objective of our interventions at all ages is to maximize the quality and quantity of the infants' interactions with their families and environment. The importance of this for infant cognitive and motivational growth was well described by Yarrow, Rubenstein, and Pederson (1975). We believe, as proposed by Sameroff (1975), that *transactions* describes more fully than *interactions* the desired nature of the activities between the infant and its environment. In this context the word transactions is used to mean the carrying on of activities to a conclusion, settlement, or reorganization of behavior. Interactions are viewed as reciprocal actions that do not necessarily lead to conclusion, settlement, or reorganization of behavior. Transactions start as interactions that are converted into transactions through subtle pacing by cues given by all parties involved, leading to a mutually acceptable conclusion.

The neurophysiological, temperamental, and cognitive development of infants determines how easily they can be involved in transactions and at what level of complexity these transactions can be conducted. In our study we are particularly concerned with infants who do not seem able to initiate interactions with people or objects in their environment and whose cues are so diffuse or obscure that interactions are difficult to convert into successful transactions. For example, even mild motor or sensory handicap, developmental delay, apathy, or irritability may interfere with the conduct of transactions. In addition, we believe there are infants who have suffered lesser degrees of brain damage perinatally and have no manifest neurological signs but suffer cumulatively in their emotional and cognitive development by subtle disruptions in their ability to enter into successful transactions with their environment. In the case of these infants with mild or no manifest neurological signs, we believe that specific knowledge of the infants' sensory, motor, and attentional processes and rate of development can be helpful in intervention. Our assessments from birth to nine months are designed to help us specify these problems in the infants and whether or not their families are able to surmount the infants' difficulties in conducting successful transactions.

We must, however, recognize that the emotional attachment of mothers and families to their infants, the emotional relations between family members, family life stresses, and other social circumstances limit or expand the opportunities for the successful conduct of transactions with their infants. Priority given to survival needs and family crises can supersede the skill and desire of mothers to focus on transactions with their infants. We have therefore organized our interventions to be concerned first with the attachment of the family to their infant, then with family social problems, and with the details of the transaction processes of the infant with his environment.

Since the infants we are studying were all born preterm, essentially all of the mothers in our study suffered unusual pregnancies or deliveries, or had newborn infants who were ill and required special care. These circumstances militated against the normal processes of mother-infant attachment. We therefore decided that all our families needed some form of intervention to deal with this. Early parental contact with their infant in the special care nursery is encouraged. However, this is often not sufficient to achieve attachment in these circumstances and sometimes alienates the mother and father further from their infant because of their anxiety, guilt, and grief when faced with their ill infant. It is, nevertheless, an essential step to help them deal realistically with their infant's health problems. To assist them in this we assign a nurse and physician team to each family while the infant is in the hospital. They provide opportunities for the parents to discuss their feelings. Since this nurse and physician continue to provide medical care for the infant at least through the first two years of life, these discussions can be continued after the infant is discharged from the hospital. At the time of discharge most parents state they feel inadequate to provide proper care for their infant, whom they are likely to still perceive as fragile and sick. To help reduce their anxiety and inadequacy feelings concerning care of the infant at home, the nurse plans to phone the home within 48 hours after the infant is discharged from the hospital and make a home visit within a week. The infant is also brought to the clinic to see the doctor and nurse two weeks after discharge. Such frequent contacts at home or in the clinic are continued through the first four months. During this time, as described by Brown (1976), the parents' concerns focus mainly on the physical welfare of their infants and their ability to provide adequate care for survival and normal physical development. Questions about feeding, crying, soothing techniques, and sleep patterns predominate. Reassuring the parents by emphasizing the normal sequences of both physical and behavioral development reduces their inadequate feelings and fosters attachment to the infant.

Monthly clinic visits continue from four to nine months, with phone contacts and home visits between as needed. During these periods, as the immediate health concerns about the infant diminish, family social problems emerge. It is as if these realities in their lives have been deferred until the infant's survival and their ability to sustain this is assured. If attachment has not been firmly established by this time, the family and social problems may severely interfere or cause regression in this process. Social work help is very important at this stage, particularly in guiding the nurse and doctor in their counseling with the family.

In the later part of the first year parents seem to focus more on behavioral development, particularly when their infant is not progressing as rapidly as anticipated. By this time we have obtained our cumulative risk score and are in a position to offer educational intervention for infants considered at continuing risk. The educational intervention provided between nine months and two years, although still concerned with the more global social interferences with family transactions, focuses primarily on more specific aspects of the infants' transactions, as is described by Kass et al. (1976). Particular attention is given to the mother-infant transactions, since it is felt that if the mother can accept the importance of the frequency and quality of these and can maximize these skills, the intervention can have a continuing effect.

The quality of the mother's interactions and transactions with her infant is assessed on several criteria, as outlined by Bromwich (1976). We observe whether or not the mother evidences any pleasure in her activities with her infant. A significant factor in this is the mother's success in eliciting the desired response from the infant. Often, if the infant has some neurological or developmental delay, the mother's expectations are not compatible with the infant's capabilities. The mother is then disappointed and begins to perceive herself or her infant as inadequate. Recurring failures in attempted transaction can result in decreasing attempts, creating cumulative negative effects on the infant. To improve this situation we help the mother find and build on the infant's most competent behaviors in order to increase pleasure in their interactions with each other during both caregiving and play activities. Then we help the mother adjust her expectations in the areas where there may be a lag in the infant's development or where her own unfamiliarity with infants has led her to place her expectations too high. This also helps her learn to be a more accurate observer of her infant's behavioral development.

These interventions do not always increase the number of successful transactions because they are in some degree dependent on the ability of mother and infant to read each others' cues in order to pace interactions into successful transactions. We also attempt to teach mothers to read their infants' cues more accurately and to give their cues to their infants more clearly during such activities as mutual smiling, vocalizing, physical play, feeding, and bathing.

If the interventions discussed have been successful, we expect the mother and other members of the family to engage in frequent interactions with the infant, choosing materials and activities that are appropriate for the infant's level of development, and, by reading of the infant's cues, to pace these interactions into successful transactions. We believe that families will continue effective parenting without further intervention when they are able to generalize their transactions with their infants to new situations and to plan appropriately for the infants' future developmental needs.

SUMMARY

Infants are identified as at risk for developmental disability by fourteen assessments administered between birth and nine months. Individualized intervention programs using the mother or other primary caregiver as the agent of change are planned for each family. Our objective is to maximize the effectiveness of their transactions with the infant.

ACKNOWLEDGMENTS

This chapter presents a summary of the work of a large number of people. I would like to give recognition to those who are providing intervention. The nurses are Mary Margaret Brown, R.N., M.A., Carmen Gonzales, R.N., and Patricia Wooldridge, R.N., P.N.P.; the physicians are Harris Greenwald, M.D., Diane Henderson, M.D., Judy Howard, M.D., Bruce Littman, M.D., and Cathryn Trowbridge, M.D.; the educators are Eleanor Baxter, M.A., Rose Bromwich, Ed. D., Dorothea Burge, M.A., Ronald Fishbach, M.A., Sue Fust, B.A., Ethel Kass, M.A., Ellen Kokha, M.A., Armony Share, B.A., and Gloria Tishkoff, M.A.

REFERENCES

Beckwith, L. (1976) Caregiver-infant interaction as a focus for therapeutic intervention with human infants. In Environments as Therapy for Brain Dysfunction (Eds. Walsh, R. N., and Greenough, W. T.). New York: Plenum Press.

Broman, S. H., Nichols, P. L., and Kennedy, W. A. (1975) Preschool IQ: Prenatal and Early Development Correlates. New York: John Wiley.

Bromwich, R. M. (1976) Focus on maternal behavior in infant intervention. Amer. J. Orthopsychiatry 46:439.

Brown, M. M. (1976) What's being missed in parent-infant counseling. Paper presented at the 11th Annual Conference, Association for Care of Children in Hospitals, Denver, Colorado, March 24—27.

Hunt, J. V. (1976) Environmental risk in fetal and neonatal life and measured intelligence. In Infant Intelligence (Ed. Lewis, M.). New York: Plenum Press.

Kass, E. R., Sigman, M., Bromwich, R., and Parmelee, A. H. (1976) Educational intervention with high risk infants. *In* Intervention Strategies for High Risk Infants and Young Children (Ed. Tjossem, T.). Baltimore: University Park Press.

Littman, B., and Wooldridge, P. (1976) Caring for families of high-risk infants. West. J. Med. 124:429.

Parmelee, A. H., and Haber, A. (1973) Who is the "risk infant"? *In* Clinical Obstetrics and Gynecology, Vol. 16. (Ed. Osofsky, H. J.) Hagerstown: Harper and Row.

Parmelee, A. H., Kopp, C. B., and Sigman, M. (1976a) Selection of developmental assessment techniques for infants at risk. Merrill Palmer Quarterly 22:177.

Parmelee, A. H., Sigman, M., Kopp, C. B., and Haber, A. (1975) The concept of a cumulative risk score for infants. *In* Aberrant Development in Infancy Human and Animal Studies (Ed. Ellis, N. R.). Hillsdale: Lawrence Erlbaum Associates.

Parmelee, A. H., Sigman, M., Kopp, C. B., and Haber, A. (1976b) Diagnosis of the infant at high risk for mental, motor, or sensory handicap. *In* Intervention Strategies for High Risk Infants and Young Children (Ed. Tjossem, T.). Baltimore: University Park Press.

Sameroff, A. J. (1975) Early influences on development: fact or fancy? Merrill-Palmer Quarterly 21:267.

Sameroff, A. J., and Chandler, M. J. (1975) Reproductive risk and the continuum of caretaking casualty. *In* Review of Child Development Research, Vol. 4 (Ed. Horowitz, F. D.). Chicago: University of Chicago Press.

Yarrow, L. J., Rubenstein, J. L., and Pederson, F. A. (1975) Infant and Environment: Early Cognitive and Motivational Development. Washington, D.C.: Hemisphere Publishing Corporation.

RESEARCH TO PRACTICE IN MENTAL RETARDATION
Care and Intervention, Volume I
Edited by Peter Mittler
Copyright 1977 I.A.S.S.M.D.

DEVELOPMENTAL INFANT PROGRAM
A Computer-Generated Treatment-Progress Program

W. Gingold
Southeast Mental Health and Retardation Center,
700 First Avenue South, Fargo, North Dakota 58102, United States

Intervention services for preschool children and their families can be perceived as existing on a continuum. This continuum can be provided via a variety of specific intervention programs. The programs may vary from prenatal parenting training to parent education, to parent-family counseling, to in-home teaching, or to intensive day or twenty-four hour programming for the child with extensive support services to the parents.

In considering the continuum of early intervention programming, recent data support the underlying assumption that parents, if involved in the intervention process, can affect results in significant child progress, particularly in the cognitive sphere (Bronfenbrenner, 1975). Furthermore, initiation of appropriate intervention at earlier stages (ages) can be expected to yield accumulative gains, particularly if the child is high risk or developmentally delayed. These factors, compounded by the fact that the family still is the most effective and economical system for fostering and sustaining the development of the young child, led us to consider the systematic utilization of this unit to provide the necessary and appropriate instruction/treatment.

The Developmental Infant Program (DIP) (Gingold et al., 1975) offers a computer-generated treatment-progress program for parents and caregivers of preschool children in order to assist them in more efficient, effective, and low-cost intervention programming in the child's most natural environment.

The basic intent of the Developmental Infant Program is to provide an extensive, functional, curricula support system consisting of specific methods, techniques, and approaches that can be used to teach specific skills/behaviors that reflect developmental sequencing.

The viability of the total DIP program is based on three major components and their subsystems. The first major component of the program is the Develop-

Table 1. Sample page from the Developmental Prototypic Curricula and Assessment tool, used for assessing a skill—communication

[Skill] (1) COMMUNICATION

[Sub-skill] (1) RECEPTIVE LANGUAGE

DATE

	Mean age in month		Pretest	Posttest
1. [Sub-sub-skill]	(1)	Loud sound causes startle reaction—arms extend, body stiffens		
2.	(1)	Reacts to sound of normal intensity		
3.	(1)	Often quieted by familiar voice (40–50% of the time)		
4.	(1)	Soothed by soft intimate talking or singing		
5.	(2)	When spoken to, looks at person's face; expression is alert		
6.	(2)	Smiles in response to being talked to		
7.	(2)	Sometimes ceases all activity to stare when sharp sounds are made—ringing bell		
8.	(2)	Eyes follow a moving person		
9.	(3)	Adult face still holds interest longer than anything else		
10.	(3)	When lying on back, motion of arms and legs increase at sight of bright colored object		
11.	(4)	Searches for sound with eyes		

mental Prototypic Curricula and Assessment (DPCA) tool (Table 1). This tool has two major uses. First, it can be used as a developmental assessment instrument, if desired, and second, it is used as a behavior/skill menu from which desired target behaviors can be selected for program intervention. If the DPCA is used as an assessment instrument, it must be utilized by the standards and procedures reflected in its technical manual (Gingold and Gingold, 1976). It should be noted that the DPCA can also be used as an independent developmental assessment inventory where appropriate. Other assessment instruments can be used to assist the potential user to identify more specifically what behaviors/skills are to be considered for intervention. Once this targeting process is accomplished, the potential user of DIP selects from the DPCA list the behavior/skill for which intervention is desired. Once the behavior/skill selection is made, the next step is to identify more specifically the child and his environment.

By utilizing the Student Characteristics Coding, the opportunity is provided to the DIP user to profile the child on multivariables (Table 2). This profiling makes the DIP program child-specific rather than the converse. In order to profile the child systematically, the Student Data Form must be used (Table 3). This form allows the user the opportunity to define and code numerically the behavior/skill or its subskill(s) to be taught and the defined student-environment characteristics. Thus the appropriately coded Student Data Form becomes the profile input for computer matching and sorting.

The third major component of the DIP program is the data or prescription file. This file consists of functional methods, techniques, and approaches on *how* to teach a defined behavior/skill. These "prescriptions" have been written based on the following criteria:

1. *What* is to be taught for a specific behavior/skill.
2. *How* that behavior or skill should be taught.
3. *What* should be done if the child does not learn the task as outlined.
4. *What* specific reinforcement procedures should be used in the teaching-treatment procedure.

In addition to the above four major criteria, the "prescriptions" have to also meet the following conditions:

1. The instructions must be written at approximately a fifth-grade reading level.
2. Each "prescription" narrative written must not be more than one hundred and fifty (150) words.
3. The written "prescription" narrative must be deplete of unnecessary verbiage.
4. The written "prescriptions" should stand by themselves and be understood without "consultive" support.

Table 2. Sample student characteristics coding

Age Level	Communication Output
1. 0–6 months	1. Oral
2. 7–12 months	2. Motoric
•	3. Oral-Motoric
•	4. Other
•	
12. 15–18 years	Instructional Media
13. Adult	1. Concrete objects
	•
Grade Level	•
1. Home	•
2. Early childhood	2. Parent or teacher
•	3. Other
•	
•	Instructional Strategy
10. Adult Basic	1. Play-chance
11. Other	2. Test-response
	•
Difficulty Level	•
1. Easy	•
2. Average	18. Reverse Chaining
3. Difficult	19. Other
4. Ungradable	
	Instructional Grouping
Communication Input	1. Parent-teacher/Large group
1. Auditory	•
2. Visual	•
•	•
•	8. Individual self-instruction
•	9. Other
9. Gustatory	
10. Tactile	

5. Whenever possible the content of written "prescriptions" is to be noncost (i.e., not requiring the purchase of special equipment or materials in order to implement the procedures or activities).

Even though at the present time there are approximately 20,000 "prescriptions" in the data file cross-tabbed to approximately 140,000 student profiles, which are in turn targeted to approximately 2,000 behaviors/skills, all components of the program remain open-ended. This "open-endedness" consequently allows for updating and modifications where necessary and appropriate.

Through the integration of the major components, we have a viable and functional curricula support system that can be utilized by parents and other child caregivers to provide appropriate specific behavior/skill intervention.

The integration of the program as such occurs in the following way:

1. Selection of a specific behavior/skill to be taught from DPCA is made.
2. Student characteristics are defined and coded appropriately on the Student Data Form.
3. A computer sort is initiated to match defined profiles with stored profiles.
4. A "shift" in the computer is used to attain the best profile match. Shifting is allowed for specific predefined variables.
5. "Prescriptions" output provided, based on match cross-tab, is generated on standard 8½ X 11 inch paper.
6. A maximum of ten (10) printed prescriptions per request, with accompanying profile match analysis, are produced.
7. Field use of prescriptions printed with accompanying Validation Feedback Questionnaire is made.
8. Returned, completed Validation Feedback Questionnaires are stored in the computer.
9. An annotated student record based on Validation Feedback Questionnaires is established.
10. Utilizing a 90% effectiveness criteria from the Validation Feedback Questionnaire, necessary corrections/deletions are made.

It should be noted that items 9 and 10 above reflect subsystems, not major components, of the program. These two subsystems of the program provide the validation of prescriptions based on field testing and at the same time establish and maintain an annotated student record reflecting requests made, profiles outlined, the extent to which profiles were computer matched, which prescriptions were recommended, which prescriptions were successful, and the time devoted to implementation of prescriptions.

DIP is a dynamic functional curricula support system which, in its present experimental phase, seems to show great promise in being an effective, efficient, and low-cost data-based intervention system that can be readily used by parents and other child-care providers at any location that has telephone or postal service.

More extensive work needs to be done to determine the efficacy of this approach compared to other early childhood intervention programming. Furthermore, extensive reliability studies need to be made reflecting implementation procedures of prescriptions. Finally, control group studies need to be utilized to truly validate dependent and independent variables.

SUMMARY

The computer-generated teaching treatment support system is designed for parents and professionals. Its job is to suggest specific methods, techniques, and

Table 3. Student data form

Date _____ Name of Requester _____ Child's Name _____

(If for a specific child)

Assoc. Operator's Name and Address (Bill to): _____

File Number _____

Profile Characteristics	Behavior Request/Student Characteristics—Code							
* Skill								
* Sub-skill								
* Sub-sub-skill								
* Sub-sub-sub-skill								
* Age level (CA MA if available)								
Difficulty Level								

Grade Level									
* Communication input									
* Communication output									
Instructional media									
Instructional strategy									
Instructional grouping									
MA									
LEM Request									
Other:									

approaches (from a prescription data pool of 20,000+) for specifically unique children (140,000+ profiles) on a developmental basis. Validation based on student records is an integral part of the system.

REFERENCES

Bronfenbrenner, U. (1975) Is early intervention effective? *In* Handbook of Evaluation Research Vol. II (Ed. Guttentag, M.) London: Sage Publications, p. 519.

Gingold, W., Ashley, C., Scharff, A., and Gingold, P. (1975) Expeditor Manual for the Developmental Infant Program. SEMH/RC, Fargo, N.D.

Gingold, W. and Gingold, P. (1976) Developmental Prototypic Curricula and Assessment: Technical Manual. SEMH/RC, Fargo, N.D.

RESEARCH TO PRACTICE IN MENTAL RETARDATION
Care and Intervention, Volume I
Edited by Peter Mittler
Copyright 1977 I.A.S.S.M.D.

CONTINUUM OF SERVICE DELIVERY TO PRESCHOOL HANDICAPPED AND THEIR FAMILIES

M. M. Bristol
Southeast Mental Health and Retardation Center,
700 First Avenue South, Fargo, North Dakota 58102,
United States

There is a story that I should like to share with you:

> Once there was a group of men fishing in a stream. They were having a very pleasant time when suddenly they noticed out in the middle of the stream some children were being carried downstream. Of course, all the fisherman jumped in and tried to rescue them. They pulled some out but others disappeared downstream, so the fishermen dried themselves off and returned to their fishing. Soon another group of children went by. Again, the fishermen jumped in and rescued some but others continued downstream. After awhile they got discouraged about their fishing. One fellow threw his rod down and started walking. The other fisherman asked, "Where are you going?" "I am going upstream", he answered, "to find out who is throwing those kids in" (Bower, 1964).

That story perhaps typifies the approach we at Southeast Mental Health and Retardation Center in Fargo, North Dakota have tried to employ in delivering primary, secondary, and tertiary services to handicapped preschool children and their families. We were saddened by the number of school-age children whose development may have been irreparably impaired because they and their families had received no adequate help in the preschool years. We were also struck by the number of children and families experiencing emotional problems seemingly unrelated to the nature and severity of the child's original handicapping condition. Our goal was to develop a delivery system utilizing various levels of professional support services that would prevent needless or disproportionate handicaps, provide early identification and intervention to children and families already in mild to moderate distress, and provide intensive evaluation and treatment for the severely handicapped child and his family. Children would be eligible for services from birth to age eight.

The plan for service delivery would have to take into account a number of factors. First, the estimated 900 preschool children in our catchment area needing services in 1973 were spread out over a 6,800 square mile area, in a state that averages about one person per square mile outside the city. Financial and professional resources were limited, so the delivery system would have to be cost-effective and make use of paraprofessionals for much of the service delivery. Virtually all handicapping conditions, ranging in severity from mild to severe, would have to be served. Travel from outlying areas to the Center was restricted both because of limited parental finances and by a winter characterized by snow, howling winds, and a temperature that dips below freezing half of the year, sometimes plummeting to thirty or even fifty degrees below zero. Another obstacle that had to be addressed was the fact that the majority of parents were sturdy, independent people used to harsh weather and the vicissitudes of life, people accustomed to "biting the bullet" and seldom allowing themselves the luxury of calling for help. In addition, community awareness and support of preschool services in general was very low. Indeed, kindergarten for five year olds was considered such a questionable venture that few towns offered kindergarten classes at all and most of those that did offered it for a total of six weeks. Outside of Fargo there were virtually no ongoing services available to preschool children and their families. Clearly the traditional "test, counsel, and refer" model was not a viable option. Under the direction of Dr. William Gingold, a service delivery system was developed that would take the resources and constraints of the area into consideration.

The constraints were at first more obvious than the resources. The school systems were all "downstream," frantically trying to provide legally mandated special services to school-age handicapped children. Preschool children enjoyed no such mandate. Professional services of any kind were severely limited in the outlying areas, and those that did exist were already overextended with crisis intervention problems. It was soon obvious that for many of these children their only real, ongoing resources were their parents. Compared to their parents, we professionals were only a fleeting moment in these children's lives. Parent training and support programs, then, had to be our first priority.

The initial service delivery model had three major program components (Figure 1) with supplementary programs (indicated by dashed boxes) added as the need arose. Supplementary programs are discussed later in this chapter.

First, "upstream" there is PACT—Parents and Children Together, community-based parent education clubs. STP, the Stimulating to Potential program, provides more intensive, home-based treatment for children with mild to moderate handicaps. Finally, TETC, the Therapeutic Evaluation and Treatment Center, provides in-depth evaluation and ongoing treatment in the Mental Health Center for the more severely handicapped and/or those children whose problems involve interacting with other children. Placement decisions for each component are made following the Flow Chart for Decision Making (Figure 2). Children may move from one program to another as their needs change.

In each major component, parents sign contracts with Center staff, a sample of which is given at the end of this chapter (p. 193). This clarifies role

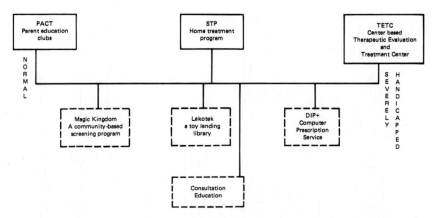

Figure 1. Continuum of service delivery to preschool handicapped and their families.

expectations and ensures public commitment by both parties to program goals.

The design of the PACT, parent education clubs, was influenced by our previous attempts to instruct parents and professionals. We had tried the lecture/ workshop approach and found that we were reasonably successful in changing people's vocabularies. We were less successful in getting them to change what they actually did with children. In addition, the audiences were almost exclusively made up of upper-middle-class parents who were generally articulate and comfortable in large, unfamiliar group settings. Somehow the parents we were most anxious to reach never seemed to be in the audience or had only sporadic attendance. The first order of business, then, was to get the parents to come regularly to the parent education clubs and to focus on activities rather than semantics. We reasoned that not only did children need trained parents, but parents desperately needed the shared knowledge and emotional support of other parents, particularly in remote, rural areas where contact may be limited. Because of the distances involved and limited professional time, the groups had to be reasonably self-sustaining and parent-directed.

Our PACT groups function as follows: Our community dynamics specialist goes out into a community either on request or as the Center perceives a need. With the help of the resource persons in the community, school and social service personnel, clergymen, and civic organizations, she identifies a parent initiator who will assume responsibility for the local group in exchange for reimbursement of expenses. The parent initiator is trained briefly in group dynamics and procedures for establishing and maintaining a PACT group. The initiator invites about fifteen to twenty of her friends and neighbors to attend ten meetings in her home at biweekly intervals. For attending meetings, getting spouses to attend meetings, and carrying out suggested activities with their children in their homes, parents receive PACT dollars, which they exchange for age-appropriate educational toys chosen from a Learn and Earn catalog. The

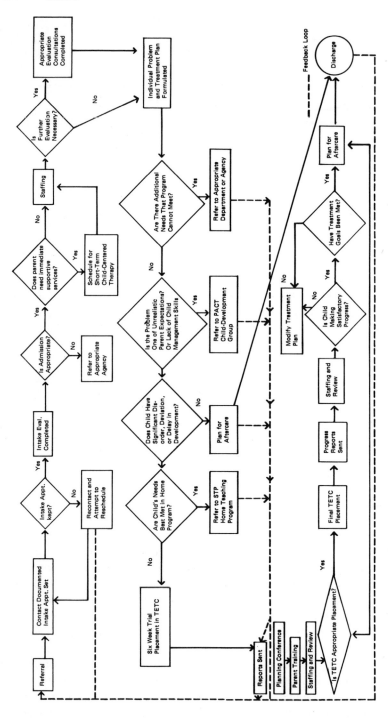

Figure 2. South East Mental Health and Retardation Center preschool programs flow chart for decision-making.

Center assists in providing meeting agenda, audio-visual materials, speakers on request, and take-home learning packets for each of the sessions. Existing materials were found to be either too expensive or too lengthy, so project staff wrote up brief (usually 10–15 pages) summaries of each of the content areas.

Four packets on child management skills, and one each on prenatal and sensory motor development, language development, intellectual development, and social-emotional development form the core instructional materials. Optional "alumni" packets on topics such as creativity in young children, sex education, and coping with stress are available after the initial ten sessions are completed. Each packet contains an overview of the area, with specific age-labeled activities recommended for stimulating the child's development in that area. The groups have been enthusiastically received, serving to instruct parents and to help build a natural network of parent support. They have also greatly increased community awareness of preschool children's needs and available Center services. In addition, parents complete a developmental profile for each of their preschool children. Children falling below norms are referred for more intensive evaluation and programming.

Children manifesting a twenty-five percent delay in one or more developmental areas or having significant behavioral or emotional problems may be served regularly in the STP or Stimulating to Potential Program. A Center therapist, in conjunction with the parents, formulates learning objectives for the child after an evaluation has been completed and programming suggestions made. The therapist visits the home weekly to demonstrate to the parent how to carry out the learning "prescription" and to record the child's weekly progress. The parent is the child's primary therapist, with the Center staff member providing written or tape-recorded prescriptions and weekly pre- and post-checks of child progress.

The most intensive programming is available to children seen in the Therapeutic Evaluation and Treatment Center. Children are evaluated over periods ranging from one-half a day to six weeks. Those enrolled in the regular program generally come four days a week for sessions that last two and a half hours. For each four sessions that the children come, the parents contract to come one. Parent training begins with a formal training program involving a minimum of lecture and a maximum of observation and demonstration facilitated by observation rooms with one-way mirrors and headsets. After the initial eight-week training program, parents assist in their child's group room one day per week. In addition, at least every other week, parents receive an individual coached session. The parent, child, and therapist conduct a session jointly. Gradually, the therapist is faded from the room and coaches the parent from behind the one-way mirror using a wireless transmitter. (Adult problems such as serious emotional disturbance, alcoholism, and marital conflict are referred to other Center departments or dealt with cooperatively.)

Referral to the program can be made by any concerned person. In a typical year, twenty-six percent of the referrals were from physicians, twenty-one percent from parents, thirty-seven percent from other agencies not including schools, ten percent from schools, five percent were referrals from other services in the Mental Health Center, and one percent were from miscellaneous other sources as diverse as the Welcome Wagon hostess. Unfortunately, initially virtually all referrals were from within the Fargo area itself. A mechanism was needed to identify children in the outlying area in need of services or, at least, in need of further evaluation. To meet this need, "The Magic Kingdom: A Preschool Screening Program" was implemented. This community-based screening program uses trained parents and community volunteers to screen approximately twenty children in up to forty skill areas in less than two hours. This procedure not only meets our objective of early and inexpensive identification, but the extensive involvement by parents, school, and civic organizations heightens community awareness of the need for early intervention.

The Developmental Infant Program (DIP), a computer prescription service, was added to provide an efficient way of generating prescriptions for use by parents. Learning prescriptions are written at a fourth- or fifth-grade reading level and make use of materials found in most homes. This eliminates the need for extensive professional "translation" of the prescriptions and high cost of commercial materials.

A toy lending library (Lekotek) is also operated to heighten community awareness of early stimulation needs. Manned by volunteers from the Fargo-Moorhead Junior League in space provided by the Moorhead Public Library, the Lekotek circulated 540 toys in its first month of operation. The Center provides preservice and in-service education to volunteers and parents.

During the past year, approximately 220 professionals from throughout the United States utilized the preschool Consultation and Education services that have been an outgrowth of the original program.

In a one-year period the project has served a total of 984 children directly and trained approximately 560 parents in the various program components and supplementary training programs.

The Gingold continuum of services model has proven to be a cost-effective means of providing a range of services to handicapped preschool children and their families in our catchment area. It has been replicated in whole or in part in various parts of the United States and appears to be a viable, alternative service delivery model that minimizes the use of professional time while maximizing the impact of trained parents and other support personnel.

SUMMARY

Procedures for the design, implementation, and evaluation of a community-based continuum of assessment, treatment, and training services for preschool handicapped and their families is discussed. Community-based screening, parent education clubs, home teaching, intensive in-Center evaluation and treatment, a toy lending library, a computer prescription service, and extensive parent involvement components are highlighted.

Sample TETC Parent Contract

Parent and therapist involvement is the most crucial factor in a child's progress in learning. Entrance into the TETC Program is contingent upon both parties' willingness to work together to help the child grow and develop.

The parent will:

1. Participate in the program one session for every four sessions the child participates in the program. Participation may include the following activities:
   a. Work with the child on assigned activities agreed upon by parent and therapist.
   b. Keep records of the child's progress as agreed upon by parent and therapist.
   c. Assist therapist with other children participating in the program.
2. Participate in the TETC parent training program. This will meet some of the requirement to participate in the program one time for every four times the child participates.
3. Notify the therapist in advance if it is not possible to keep appointments.
4. Make weekly written comments regarding the child, the program, or the therapist. The written comment sheets are to be returned to the Center on the child's last therapy session each week.

The therapist will:

1. Keep all appointments made with the parent, or will notify the parent in advance if unable to keep any appointments.
2. Assign activities each week that are appropriate to the child's needs and abilities.
3. Supply the parent with whatever materials would be needed to successfully carry out the prescribed activities.
4. Keep all records up to date. Inform parents of all assessment devices and results used with the child. Provide weekly feedback to parents on parent comment sheets.

Acceptance into the TETC program will be on a six-week trial basis. After this period, status will be determined by a mutual decision of parent, therapist, and other involved staff.

DATE_____

| Parent | Therapist |

RESEARCH TO PRACTICE IN MENTAL RETARDATION
Care and Intervention, Volume I
Edited by Peter Mittler
Copyright 1977   I.A.S.S.M.D.

EARLY PSYCHOSOCIAL STIMULATION PROGRAM FOR INFANTS (FROM BIRTH TO 24 MONTHS) OF LOW SOCIOECONOMIC CLASS

H. Montenegro, M. I. Lira, and S. Rodríguez
Sección Salud Mental, Monjitas 665, Of. 57
Servicio Nacional de Salud, Santiago, Chile

This is a preliminary report that includes results for infants up to 21 months of age.

GENERAL OUTLINE

There is sufficient scientific evidence available regarding the decisive influence of environment on psychosocial development. In the absence of certain stimulation conditions, retardation is produced that, according to some authors, is detectable as early as 18 months of age. There are several studies that allow us to affirm that it is possible to intervene in order to change the environment, and that when this occurs, significant improvement in the psychosocial development of children can be achieved.

Many factors permit us to affirm that in Chile as well as in other countries, children of a low socioeconomic level grow up in an unfavorable environment that hampers their psychosocial development from a very early age. In Chile, the National Health Department provides free services to 70% of the population. However, there are no services or systems that allow for the prevention, early detection, and treatment of this type of retardation.

Based on these considerations, the idea of planning a program for early stimulation that would reach large sections of the infant population of the lower socioeconomic level has been developed.

The concept of early stimulation has so far been linked to children of "high risk" of biological origin. The program that is presented here is based on the fact

195

that almost all children who live in a socioculturally deprived environment ought to be considered at "high risk."

With the possible extension of the program in mind, the Pediatric Clinics of the National Health Department were considered the most adequate structure, for both stability and scope, to carry out this pilot program.

HYPOTHESIS

In infants of low socioeconomic level it is possible to increase psychosocial development through a program of stimulation. Mothers from low socioeconomic level can be effective agents of psychosocial stimulation of their children. Nurses and nurses' aides, having been previously trained, can incorporate into the context of the Well Baby Clinics of the National Health Department (at present restricted to physical development) elements that contribute to the normal psychic development of the child.

OBJECTIVES

The objectives of this program are:

1. To prepare, to put into practice, and to evaluate a procedure of stimulation that significantly augments the psychosocial development of the infants participating in the program.
2. To prepare, to put into practice, and to evaluate a procedure for stimulation in the home that is practicable by the family, especially by the low socioeconomic level mothers.
3. To prepare and to test a procedure that permits the nurses and nurses' aides of the Pediatric Clinics of the National Health Department to evaluate the psychosocial development of the infants, and to help the mothers become agents of stimulation.

METHOD

For this program, to be conducted between March, 1974 and September, 1976, four clinics located in the lower income neighborhoods of Santiago were chosen.

In order to carry out the program, 24 Manuals were prepared, one for each month of age. These booklets (4–5 pages each) are directed mainly to the mother, and the contents derive, to a certain extent, from the theory of Piaget on the development of intelligence.

The criteria used in the preparation of manuals were:

1. To include for each month of age a varied number of situations that stimulate development in coordination, motor, language, and social areas.

2. To include general guidelines on the norms of child care, exposed in three items per folder (active reading).
3. To avoid, whenever possible, stimulation situations that are foreign to the environment, but being careful to take advantage of favorable situations present in it in a natural way. To give special attention to the fact that mothers from the low-socioeconomic level suffer from exhaustion caused by overwork, and have neither the time nor the energy for extra activities.
4. To consider that the material required for stimulation should, whenever possible, consist of objects that are readily available in the home or are very inexpensive, or are easily made from odds and ends.
5. To describe the exercises and activities in simple language and if possible with illustrations.

Sample

Two hundred mothers were chosen at random from the women who visited the clinics for prenatal check-ups, and whose expected term dates were between April and July, 1974. Neither premature infants nor children who suffered diseases during pregnancy or delivery were excluded. These conditions exist very frequently in the Chilean low socioeconomic level; their elimination would have signified working with an unrepresentive group. Nevertheless, the pre- and postnatal histories of each child were controlled in order to evaluate their influence at the end of the program.

Experimental Groups

The children chosen were divided at random as follows:

Experimental Group 1 (Stimulation Group), which consisted of children who were submitted to the stimulation program ($N = 41$).

Experimental Group 2 (Evaluation Group), which consisted of children who received no stimulation but whose psychomotor development was controlled monthly. This group was established in order to measure the effects of the evaluation itself ($N = 40$).

Experimental Group 3 (Home Visit Group), which consisted of children who received the same attention from the nursing staff as Experimental Group 1. The contents of this attention are strictly limited to the physical development of the child. This group was established in order to determine the effects of the home visits ($N = 43$).

Control Group 1, which consisted of children who receive no special treatment whatsoever, apart from a quarterly evaluation of psychomotor development ($N = 43$).

Control Group 2, which consisted of a group of 300 children of high middle socioeconomic level whose records were available from a previous study (Rodríguez et al., 1974).

Work Team and Functions

In order to carry out the program, the tasks were distributed as follows, based on a system of delegation of duties for each level:

Child psychiatrist: Promoter and Director of the Program (Chief of Mental Health Section).

Psychologists: Two psychologists charged with and responsible for development of the program (plan and content), training of the nursing personnel, supervision of the work in the four clinics, total evaluation of the information gathered, and promotion activities (information about the program to other groups).

Nurses (four people): One nurse in charge of and responsible for the development of the program in each of the four clinics: individual psychomotor assessment of the whole sample, supervision of the nurses' aides in her charge, counselling them in their work, supplying materials and collecting the information required for the evaluation of the program.

Nurses' aides (nine people): In charge of home visits, recording observations about the field work, setting appointments for evaluations, and taking the history of each child.

Evaluation Criteria

The progress of the children was measured by means of the Psychomotor Development Evaluation Scale (Rodríguez et al., 1974). This test was based on the French scale of Lézine (1965) and the American scales of Bayley (1969), Gesell (1941), and the Denver test (Frankenburg et al., 1970). It was standardized in Santiago, Chile, with a sample of 600 children. Basically, it measures the development of four areas: motor, language, social, and coordination.

Procedure

The program began with an intensive one-week theory-practice course for the nurses and nurses' aides from the participating clinics. Prior to the birth of the children, a meeting was held for the expectant mothers of Experimental Group 1 and their husbands to inform them about the program and to ask for their collaboration. All the mothers of the sample group were visited in order to obtain family and personal histories. Then, the program was carried out in the following way:

Experimental Group 1 (EG 1) Before the birth of the child, the mother was visited at home. During this visit she was given Manual 1, which contains the stimulation tasks corresponding to the first month of life. From the birth of the child, the nurses' aide made home visits of about 30 minutes duration for the purpose of *motivating* the mother in her role as stimulator of the psychosocial development of her child, *demonstrating* to her the exercises in the manual, and *rewarding* her participation. During the first three months the visits were weekly, then biweekly. (Between the infants' seventh and twelfth months, the visits were monthly because of the limitation of time on the part of the nursing staff.)

At the age of one month the child was taken to the Clinic, where the nurse evaluated his psychomotor development. If in the course of the evaluation the nurse found the progress to be insufficient in one or several areas of development, she underlined the exercises related to that area in the manual. This task was facilitated by putting in the manual beside each activity, a capital letter that indicated the area to which the exercise particularly refers. At the same time the mother received Manual 2, corresponding to the second month of age, and so on.

Experimental Group 2 (EG 2)   The only task performed with these children was the monthly check-up of the psychomotor development. This group as such was maintained for only three months, after which, for practical reasons, part of it was combined with EG 1.

Experimental Group 3 (EG 3)   These children had the same number of visits as EG 1. The only difference was that the content of the visits was limited to the physical development of the child (nourishment and hygiene) and that the evaluation of the psychomotor development was quarterly instead of monthly. From their 15th month this group was incorporated into EG 1.

RESULTS

Children

The progress of the children participating in the program has been analyzed on a quarterly basis in the following way:

1. Comparing the Developmental Quotients (D.Q.) of the experimental groups with those of Control Group 1.
2. Comparing the D.Q. of the children of Experimental Group 1 with Control Group 2 (middle high socioeconomic level).
3. Comparing the achievements of the experimental groups and Control Group 1 in the specific areas measured by the scale used.
4. Comparing the results of Experimental Group 1 with those of Control Group 2 (middle socioeconomic level), in the areas measured by the scale.

Once the program is finished, we hope that we can enrich the analysis of the information by studying the influence of personal as well as family variables registered on the achievements of the children.

Because of limited space, only the results of points 1 and 2 (above) are presented here.

1. Between the ages of six months and twenty-one months, significant differences have been noted between Experimental Group 1 and the Control

Group 1 ($p \leqslant 0.05$), with the exception of the twelfth month (in which $p \leqslant 0.06$, Figure 1).

2. Experimental Group 1 does not differ significantly from Control Group 2 (middle high socioeconomic level) in any of the evaluations calculated to date, with the exception of the sixth and twelfth months, during which the achievement of Experimental Group 1 was significantly superior ($p \leqslant 0.05$).

Mothers

To evaluate the results obtained in relation to the mothers, it would be necessary to determine whether or not they had learned the stimulation exercises, if they performed them, and if their attitudes had developed favorably.

It has not been an easy task to motivate the mothers, to maintain their interest, and to obtain their participation in the program.

When the program ends, we hope to be able to provide some indicators and qualitative appreciation of the achievements attained. For the moment it is reasonable to assume, given the differences observed between the children who participated in the program and those of the control groups, that the mothers have been effective stimulation agents for their children, performing the tasks with them month to month.

Nursing Staff

With respect to the task assigned to the nurses, the response has been generally positive. As for the nurses' aides, the main difficulty in achieving the hoped-for objective has been their limited level of theoretical-practical training.

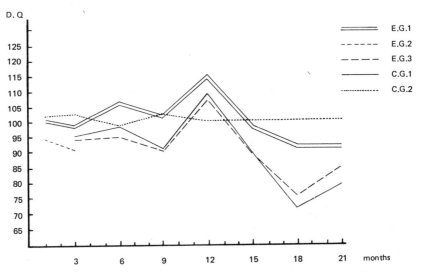

Figure 1. Averages of the developmental quotients by groups and by ages.

Because this is the first program of its kind in our field, carried out in spite of the most diverse difficulties, the results are both satisfying and promising.

SUMMARY

Prevention of cognitive retardation, following a Piagetarian framework, was performed at well baby clinics of the National Health Service. In a scheme of delegation of functions, nurses previously trained teach the mothers how to stimulate their offspring at home. Monthly evaluations were conducted. Significant statistical differences favor the experimental group.

REFERENCES

Bayley, N. (1969) Manual for the Bayley Scales of Infant Development. New York: Psychological Corporation.

Frankenburg, W., Dodds, J., and Fandal, A. (1970) Denver Developmental Screening Test. University of Colorado: Medical Center.

Gesell, A., and Amatruda, C. (1941) Developmental Diagnosis. New York: Harper.

Lézine, I., and Brunet, O. (1965) Le Dévelopement Psychologique de la Première Enfance. Paris: Presses Universitaires.

Montenegro, H., Lira, M. I., and Rodríguez, S. (1974) Estimulación Precoz: Diseño, Realización y Evaluación de un Programa Para Niños de Nivel Socioeconómico Bajo entre O y 2 Años. Santiago de Chile: Servicio Nacional de salud, mimeograph.

Rodriguez, S., Arancibia, V., and Undurraga, C. (1974) Escala de Evaluación del Desarrollo Psicomotor: 0 a 24 Meses. Santiago de Chile: Servicio Nacional de Salud, mimeograph.

WORKING WITH FAMILIES

RESEARCH TO PRACTICE IN MENTAL RETARDATION
Care and Intervention, Volume I
Edited by Peter Mittler
Copyright 1977 I.A.S.S.M.D.

PROFESSIONAL PRECIOUSNESS AND THE EVOLUTION OF PARENT TRAINING STRATEGIES

L. J. Heifetz
Department of Psychology, Yale University,
New Haven, Connecticut 06520, United States

In dealing with parents of retarded children, the typical response of the mental health professions has been some form of therapy or counseling, often with a psychodynamic orientation (Hersh, 1961; Wolfensberger, 1967). A major focus of therapy has been the exploration of parents' emotional reactions, variously characterized as guilt, shame, chronic sorrow, rejection, and denial (Baum, 1962; Olshansky, 1962; Schild, 1971). While acknowledging the effectiveness of this approach in many cases, an increasing number of professionals have begun to question the universal appropriateness of this 'neurotic' formulation, which implicitly ignores the reality-based nature of many parental needs (Baker, Heifetz, and Brightman, 1973) and can thereby do more harm than good (Kysar, 1968). Many parents are not emotionally overwhelmed and are primarily in need of honest information about their child, implications for his future, and concrete strategies for coping with his special needs as "essentially mature and rational people" (Matheny and Vernick, 1968, p. 953). It has been suggested that the emphasis on parental feelings is often a consequence of professional inability to manage practical problems (Menolascino, 1968). Professional ignorance all too quickly reifies the child's "untreatability," increases parental frustration and sense of helplessness, and ultimately legitimizes the need for psychotherapy: one small step for professional preciousness (Sarason, 1974) . . . one giant leap backward from solving the manpower shortage (Albee, 1961; Hobbs, 1964).

Recently, under the dual impetus of the behavior modification and paraprofessional movements, behavior-oriented training has begun to offer new, more collaborative roles for parents and professionals (Heifetz and Baker, 1975). Early reports in the literature usually involved one highly motivated parent, a specific child behavior, and considerable professional involvement in treatment, which was often restricted to clinic or hospital settings (Berkowitz and Graziano, 1972). More recently, there have been several trends toward higher cost-effectiveness: complex behaviors are being targeted; parents are being prepared for greater responsibility in all aspects of programming; there has been greater attention to training in, and for, the natural environment; and group training formats, offering added efficiency, are becoming more common (Benassi and Benassi, 1973; Hirsch and Walder, 1969).

However, these exciting demonstrations of parents' potential as teachers must be tempered by two observations. First, most training programs have emphasized short-term management of maladaptive, surplus behaviors (O'Dell, 1974), and less attention has been paid to children's skill deficits, which will require years of persistent and carefully structured teaching (Bricker, 1970; Kazdin, 1973). Second, as parent training adopts these more ambitious goals, group training formats become unwieldy, and the demands on scarce professional resources will increase. One possibility is to reduce the amount of direct professional training by providing parents with instructional materials that enable them to shape and manage their children's behavior. A few studies have used such materials, but always with professional instruction (Pascal, 1973; Salzinger, Feldman, and Portnoy, 1970). The utility of self-supporting instructional materials—drastically reducing the need for professional involvement—has yet to be explored.

The READ Project Series

Under a grant from the National Institute of Child Health and Human Development, a series of instructional manuals was written for use by parents in teaching self-help, language, and play skills, and managing behavior problems (Baker, Brightman, Heifetz, and Murphy, 1973, 1976). Each manual was designed to be self-contained and includes sections on: choosing a target skill, setting the stage for teaching sessions, principles of task analysis and reinforcement, record-keeping procedures, and responses to questions most frequently raised by parents. Each manual also contains: fictionalized mini-case studies that highlight central points in setting up and carrying out a teaching program, many explanatory illustrations, and a large number of step-by-step program outlines. A comprehensive evaluation of the manuals was conducted with 160 families.

Subjects

Families with a retarded child 3—14 years old and living at home were recruited through agencies and the media. These families were widely distributed across the five social classes defined by the Hollingshead (1957) two-factor index (Class I, 15.7%; Class II, 20.9%; Class III, 21.6%; Class IV, 34.0%; Class V, 7.8%). Family income ranged from under $5,000 to over $50,000. Average age was 39.1 years for mothers, 41.7 years for fathers; average education was 13.4 years for mothers, 14.3 years for fathers. As might be expected of a volunteer sample, these families had a history of active involvement in organizations for parents of retarded children. Thirty-nine percent had some awareness of behavior modification, but only 4% had actually used it before the study. Most children would be classified as organically retarded, with levels ranging from mild to severe; none met the usual criteria of cultural-familial retardation (Heber, 1961). Ninety-six percent were receiving some form of ongoing schooling.

Procedure

The manuals were evaluated as a self-contained resource and as part of three other training programs involving different amounts of professional supplementation. Families were randomly assigned to one of five experimental groups: group C (Control group which began training at the end of the study); group MO (Manuals Only with no other training inputs); group MP (Manuals plus biweekly phone consultations from a trainer); group MG (Manuals plus biweekly training group, meeting with seven other families and two trainers); group MGV (Manuals plus training group plus in-home visits from a trainer). The twenty-week treatment period emphasized the programming of self-help skills, with secondary attention to behavior problems and language skills. During this time, other ongoing services to the children and parents proceeded as usual. Comprehensive behavioral measures of child functioning were taken from parents before and after the training period. Measures were also taken of parental knowledge of behavior modification principles, participation in training, and attitudes related to retardation.

Trainers

Supplementary assistance to parents in groups MP, MG, and MGV was provided by trainers from the fields of clinical psychology, special education, and nursing. All trainers were familiar with the theory and practice of behavior modification and had previously worked with retarded children and their families. Half of the trainers were male and half female; each training group was co-led by a male-female pair.

Results

Overall, the data clearly showed the effectiveness of training formats based on instructional manuals, particularly in terms of mothers acquiring behavioral expertise and children improving in self-help skills. The startling result was that the MO group was equal or superior to the more expensive training formats in these two areas.

Parental Expertise

At the beginning and end of training, parents in each condition were given the Behavioral Vignettes Test (Heifetz, 1972)—a multiple-choice test of behavior modification as applied in home settings. Table 1 shows the mean gain in BVT

Table 1. Mean improvement on Behavioral Vignettes Test by mothers and fathers in each group

Group	N^a	Improvement	Pre-post t	Second-order t^b
Mothers				
Control	27 (28)	1.70	2.43^c	
Trained	93 (100)	3.85	10.53^d	2.76^e
MO	20 (25)	4.70	5.55^d	2.75^e
MP	23 (23)	2.30	3.44^e	.61
MG	23 (24)	3.74	5.77^d	2.10^c
MGV	27 (28)	4.63	6.57^d	2.94^e
Fathers				
Control	17 (28)	1.71	3.24^e	
Trained	60 (100)	2.83	5.91^d	1.19
MO	13 (25)	1.31	1.26	−.37
MP	11 (23)	2.46	2.40^c	.72
MG	16 (24)	3.19	3.12^e	1.31
MGV	20 (28)	3.75	4.80^d	2.09^c

[a]Numbers denote parents who took both pre- and post-BVTs. Numbers in parentheses denote parents who completed pre- and post-BAMs (Behavioral Assessment Measures).

[b]Comparisons were made against the mean improvement of the controls.

[c]$p < .05$.

[d]$p < .001$.

[e]$p < .01$.

scores by mothers and fathers in each group. In comparison with the controls, significantly more improvement was shown by mothers in groups MO, MG, and MGV, but not MP. Among fathers, BVT improvement increased with the amount of professional contact. The only significant improvement relative to controls was in group MGV, with a trend for MG.

Child Change, Self-Help Skills (Table 2)

Parents took pre- and posttreatment measures of 43 self-help skills, using scales that assessed the child's ability to perform the component parts of each skill. To gauge the accuracy of the parents' assessments, trained observers conducted independent ratings of a subsample of children; coefficients of agreement were quite high ($r = 0.87$–0.93). As a group, trained children gained 1.78 more self-help skills than controls during the twenty-week treatment period, a highly significant difference, t (126) = 3.35, $p < 0.001$. The difference was also significant for each training condition individually, all $ps \leqslant 0.01$, with no significant differences across the four training conditions.

The average trained parent programmed 4.2 self-help skills, or about 10% of the 43 skills measured. For each training condition, the total gain in *programmed* self-help skills was equal to or greater than the gain in *all* self-help skills

Table 2. Mean improvement in self-help skills: overall, programmed, and un-programmed

		Treatment				
			Trained			
Measure	C	Pooled[a]	MO	MP	MG	MGV
Aggregate improvement, all self-help skills[b]	1.28	3.06	3.54	2.72	3.30	2.68
Aggregate improvement, programmed self-help skills[c]		1.43	1.28	1.57	1.59	1.29
Mean improvement, unprogrammed self-help skills[d]	.08	.11	.16	.09	.11	.09

[a]Mean of children in groups MO, MP, MG, MGV.

[b]Sum of improvements in the 43 self-help skills in the BAM.

[c]Sum of improvements in self-help skills programmed by trained parents.

[d]Applies to self-help skills that were not programmed and that were not already mastered at the time of the pretreatment BAM and that therefore had room for improvement. Since control children had no skills programmed, it was more appropriate to use mean improvement than aggregate improvement.

by the controls. The evidence strongly supports the direct effects of parental programming efforts on therapeutic gains in their children, with no significant differences across training conditions.

A related issue is generalization—the extent to which children showed changes in skills that were not specifically programmed by the parents. Each of the trained groups showed a greater rate of gain on unprogrammed skills than shown by the controls, although the difference was significant only for the MO group, t (51) = 2.96, p = 0.002. The importance of these data for all training groups is that the gains in *programmed* self-help skills were not achieved at the expense of other, *unprogrammed* skills.

Confidence as Teachers

Although the primary focus of the study was on self-help skills, parents in the latter stages of training had a chance to work in the areas of behavior problems, toilet training, and language skills. On the average, MG and MGV parents extended their programming into twice as many additional areas as MO and MP parents; this difference was greatest for behavior problems, χ^2 (1) = 24.89, $p <$ 0.001. On a posttraining attitude questionnaire, MO parents expressed significantly *less* confidence in their teaching ability than parents in the other three training groups. Yet MO children showed the greatest self-help gains, and MO mothers improved the most on the BVT. These paradoxical results may be interpreted in terms of some social psychological features of the training conditions.

The MP group, unlike MG and MGV, could not easily be used for formal presentations of general principles; the natural tendency was to focus on current problems. To many MP parents it probably seemed easier to seek solutions from the consultant rather than deduce them from the manuals. Thus, from the outset, the MP format tended to foster dependence. MG and MGV parents, by being in a group with seven other families, participated in a variety of ongoing programs and saw a wide range of parental accomplishment, both of which may have elevated their standards of achievement. In contrast, MP parents had no peer reference points; and the MP consultants—consistent with good clinical and didactic procedure—reinforced whatever progress had been made by the parents. Consequently, MP mothers felt quite confident in their teaching ability, even though they were the only group who did not significantly outperform control mothers on the BVT.

MO parents—by completing the pre-assessment and then receiving a self-help manual that matched their child's functioning level—got an initial confirmation of their capacity for independent teaching and sufficient confidence to begin self-help programming. However, with no consultants to provide concrete suggestions, MO parents had to learn general principles from the manuals and tailor them to their own situations. This generalized level of learning produced the greatest BVT gains for MO mothers and the greatest improvement on unprogrammed self-help skills for MO children. Nevertheless, they were teaching without external feedback. While this may have driven them to more conscientious teaching, it was not conducive to building confidence. This was shown by their lower ratings of their teaching ability as well as by their reluctance to venture beyond the familiar bounds of the self-help skills teaching area.

These results suggest that future formats should combine the independence-fostering features of MO with the confidence-building elements of MG and MGV. One such format could provide group meetings, but only at transitional points in the careers of parents as teachers, and would include feedback on previous stages and an orientation to the next stage. Future formats might also involve the coordination of school and home programming. During the present study, most children were in school placements costing $750–$1,500; the high marginal utility of parent training would be further enhanced by such coordination.

Parents who were less highly motivated than the present sample could profit from preparatory formats, the initial emphasis of which would be more heavily clinical than didactic. Other investigations should address ways of getting fathers more actively involved in teaching. Various training methods should be studied not only for their initial impact, but also for their long-term effects; there is a real dearth of follow-up studies in the literature on parent training. Finally, as a body of large-scale and methodologically rigorous studies accumulates, it should be possible to analyze family background variables in order to pinpoint correlates of success under different training formats, with a view toward more precisely custom-tailoring treatment programs.

Parents have demonstrated a remarkable ability to redefine their roles in relation to their children and the service delivery system. It is incumbent upon professionals in the field to be flexible enough in their own roles to enable parents to fully realize their new found potential as teachers of their retarded children. The decline of professional preciousness can only mean an increase in professional effectiveness.

SUMMARY

Instructional manuals were written to assist parents of retarded children in teaching self-care skills, promoting language development, and managing behavior problems. Families in four experimental conditions used the manuals with different amounts of professional training and support. Effectiveness of the training was assessed on several dimensions after five months.

REFERENCES

Albee, G. W. (1961) Mental Health Manpower Trends. New York: Basic Books.

Baker, B. L., Heifetz, L. J., and Brightman, A. J. (1973) Parents as Teachers. Cambridge, Massachusetts: Behavioral Education Projects, Inc.

Baker, B. L., Brightman, A. J., Heifetz, L. J., and Murphy, D. M. (1973) The READ Project Series. Cambridge, Mass.: Behavioral Education Projects, Inc.

Baker, B. L., Brightman, A. J., Heifetz, L. J., and Murphy, D. M. (1976) Steps to Independence: A Skills Training Series for Children with Special Needs. Champaign, Illinois: Research Press.

Baum, M. H. (1962) Some dynamic factors affecting family adjustment to the handicapped child. Exceptional Children 28:387.

Benassi, V. A., and Benassi, B. (1973) An approach to teaching behavior modification principles to parents. Rehab. Lit. 34:134.

Berkowitz, B. P., and Graziano, A. M. (1972) Training parents as behavior therapists: a review. Behav. Res. Ther. 10:297.

Bricker, W. A. (1970) Identifying and modifying behavioral deficits. Amer. J. Ment. Defic. 75:16.

Heber, R. (1961) A manual on terminology and classification in mental deficiency. Amer. J. Ment. Defic. Mongr. Suppl. 2.

Heifetz, L. J. (1972) Behavioral Vignettes Test: instrument for measuring parental knowledge of behavior modification. Unpublished manuscript. Available from the author.

Heifetz, L. J., and Baker, B. L. (1975) Manpower and methodology in behavior modification: instructional manuals for the paraprofessional parent. In Manpower and methodology in behavior modification. (Chair: Heifetz, L. J.) Symposium presented at the Ninth Annual Convention of the Association for Advancement of Behavior Therapy, San Francisco.

Hersh, A. (1961) Casework with parents of retarded children. Social Work 6:61.

Hirsch, I., and Walder, L. (1969) Training mothers in groups as reinforcement therapists for their own children. Proceedings of the 77th Annual Convention of the American Psychological Association 4:561.

Hobbs, N. H. (1964) Mental health's third revolution. Amer. J. Orthopsychiat. 5:822.

Kazdin, A. E. (1973) Issues in behavior modification with mentally retarded persons. Amer. J. Ment. Defic. 78:134.

Kysar, J. (1968) The two camps in child psychiatry: a report from a psychiatrist-father of an autistic and retarded child. Amer. J. Psychiat. 125:103.

Hollingshead, A. B. (1957) Two-factor index of social position. Unpublished manuscript. Available from August B. Hollingshead, Department of Sociology, Yale University, New Haven, Connecticut 06520, U.S.A.

Matheny, A.P., and Vernick, J. (1968) Parents of the mentally retarded child: emotionally overwhelmed or informationally deprived? J. Pediat. 74:953.

Menolascino, F. J. (1968) Parents of the mentally retarded: an operational approach to diagnosis and management. J. Amer. Acad. Child Psychiat. 7:589.

O'Dell, S. (1974) Training parents in behavior modification: A review. Psychol. Bull. 81:418.

Olshansky, S. (1962) Chronic sorrow: A response to having a mentally defective child. Social Casework 43:191.

Pascal, C. E. (1973) Application of behavior modification by parents for treatment of a brain-damaged child. *In* Adaptive Learning: Behavior Modification with Children (Eds. Ashem, B.A., and Poser, E.G.) New York: Pergamon Press.

Salzinger, K., Feldman, R. S., and Portnoy, S. (1970) Training parents of brain-injured children in the use of operant conditioning procedures. Behav. Ther. 1:4.

Sarason, S. B. (1974) The Psychological Sense of Community: Prospects for a Community Psychology. San Francisco: Jossey-Bass.

Schild, S. (1971) The family of the retarded child. *In* The Mentally Retarded Child and His Family: A Multidisciplinary Handbook (Eds. Koch, R. and Dobson, J.) New York: Brunner/Mazel.

Wolfensberger, W. (1967) Counseling parents of the retarded. *In* Mental Retardation: Appraisal, Education, and Rehabilitation (Ed. Baumeister, A. A.) Chicago: Aldine.

RESEARCH TO PRACTICE IN MENTAL RETARDATION
Care and Intervention, Volume I
Edited by Peter Mittler
Copyright 1977 I.A.S.S.M.D.

SUPPORT SYSTEMS FOR THE PARENT AS THERAPIST

B. L. Baker
Department of Psychology, University of California,
405 Hilgard Avenue, Los Angeles, California 90024, United States

In contrast to the many reports of effective parent teaching *during* training, there have been very few considerations of whether changes in either child or parent behavior persist *after* training has ended. This kind of follow-up information is essential for a realistic assessment of program benefits relative to costs.

Our knowledge of long-term effects is limited to selected single cases and to a few larger series of cases. Generally, follow-ups are conducted shortly after training and are informal, relying more often on a telephone call than on the more extensive measures originally used during training. When follow-up is carried out, the focus tends to be narrow—exclusively on the maintenance of change in a specific child behavior, usually a behavior problem. If there are unintended negative effects or generalized positive effects of training, they are apt to remain unseen. This narrow focus may be reasonable for a child with only one isolated troublesome behavior that prompted parents to seek help. However, the aim of intervention and follow-up assessment must be different with retarded children. Here the aim is not to eliminate one isolated behavior problem but to decrease a number of such behaviors, while continuing to improve skills as well. The maintenance of original child gains is, of course, important, but the prime consideration is whether the family has become better able to cope with new problems and to teach new skills as the need arises.

The issues, then, for persons interested in cost-effective parent training are:

1. to assess accurately long-term parent programming efforts
2. to determine ways to enhance those efforts, both by inputs in the original training program and by continued inputs after formal training ends.

This paper is based on research supported by a contract between NICHHD (NO-1-HD-42848) and Behavioral Education Projects, Cambridge, Mass. The research was conducted collaboratively with Dr. Louis J. Heifetz, Dr. Alan J. Brightman, and Ms. Diane Murphy, R.N.

Unfortunately, the READ Project (Heifetz, this volume) offered families no continued contact with project staff posttraining. Hence our findings of necessity are limited to an assessment of continued programming in the absence of continued consultation. They can serve, however, as one form of baseline against which the effects of future follow-through programs will be measured.

The follow-up study was carried out fourteen months after the end of the READ Project training program. Of the 100 families completing the initial training and measures, 95 participated in the follow-up. Information was gathered through structured interviews in the home, usually with the mother only; this was coded on sixteen predetermined subscales, summing to a follow-through score. These scales were devised so that as parents reported increasingly more programming they were required to show concrete evidence (e.g., written programs, data), therefore tempering somewhat the self-report nature of these data. During the visit mothers also completed checklists about obstacles to programming and effects of training. The Behavioral Vignettes Test and Behavioral Assessment Manual, which we employed to measure gains in parent knowledge and child skills in the original READ Project, were readministered at follow-up.

Since we are interested here in how well families programmed during follow-through, we will just mention briefly the maintenance of original training gains. On the Behavioral Vignettes Test, mothers had essentially maintained their knowledge of behavioral teaching principles during the year following training, though they showed no further gains. Similarly, on the Behavioral Assessment Manual, children maintained their gains in self-help skills programmed during training, except that for condition MP (Parents trained by Manuals plus phone consultation) there was a slight loss.

Initially unmastered self-help skills that were not programmed during training represented a pool of skills from which parents could select target behaviors for new teaching during the follow-through period. All conditions showed some continued gains, except for condition MP, which again showed a slight decrease (an analysis of variance found this change over time by condition to differ significantly, $p = 0.05$). Overall, however, continued self-help improvement was slight—at a much lower rate than during training—and interpretation of even this progress must be guarded because there was no continuing control group of untrained families. We have no way of knowing how much development might have resulted from maturation, schooling, and/or other factors independent of parent teaching. Our main concern, then, was with a direct examination of parent follow-through teaching.

To What Extent did Parents Continue Programs They Began During Training?

In the home interviews, lasting for a median of two hours, mothers were asked about their continuation of the programming they had begun during training, their initiation of new programs, and their teaching strategies. The emphasis of the manuals and of training had been on formal teaching—setting aside a period of time for planned, regular teaching sessions, at least several times a week. It was therefore somewhat discouraging to find that only half (51%) of the families who were teaching skills at the end of training had continued a useful degree of regular teaching for these skills to the criterion of formal sessions of three or more per week, for longer than one month, or regular incidental teaching, continued as necessary. Of the 35 families programming at least one behavior problem at the end of training, 69% had made some effort to continue but only 29% had continued to carry through the program to satisfactory completion. Overall, then, the number of families continuing programs that were under way when training ended was lower than we had hoped for; there were no significant differences among training conditions in the continuation of programs.

To What Extent did Parents Begin
New Teaching, and What Forms did this Teaching Take?

Only 16% of families began new *formal* programs and carried out at least 26 regular planned sessions during the follow-through period. Yet fully 76% reported some new *incidental* teaching for one or more skills. By incidental teaching we mean incorporating behavioral principles into teaching that takes place in the normal daily routine; incidental teaching does not have regular sessions for repeated practice of a skill, but it must be consistently carried out in the daily routine and must appear to be in accord with behavioral teaching principles to be scorable. While the READ Project had encouraged formal teaching, incidental teaching in fact was more common.

Overall, 86% of families reported some scorable teaching efforts during the follow-through period. Only a small number of parents (14%) did no scorable teaching, formal or incidental, new or continued, during the follow-through period.

A total follow-through score, shown in Figure 1, was derived from interview items that asked about continued and new programming, teaching technique, and involvement of others in programming. Although the conditions did not differ overall by an Analysis of Variance, MO (Manual Only group) did score significantly lower than the other three training conditions combined ($t = 1.96$, $p = 0.05$).

What did Parents Perceive as Obstacles to Follow-through?

In the interview, mothers were asked to talk about what they perceived to be the major obstacles to carrying on with programming at home. They were also given a list of 24 statements mentioned by other parents as obstacles to in-home programming, items such as: limited time to teach, lack of support from my husband, lack of professional consultation, and finding teaching not interesting to me. Mothers rated each "not an obstacle," "somewhat an obstacle," or "very much an obstacle." The total obstacle score did not differ among the training

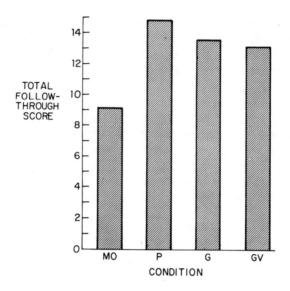

Figure 1. Total follow-through score, by training condition.

conditions, except that MP mothers tended to report more obstacles than those in other conditions. The Obstacle Checklist was divided for further analysis into six subscales, related to the following types of obstacles: limits in time, child limitations, limits in abilities and outside support, rejection of teaching, rejection of behavior modification, and limited resources. The training conditions did not differ significantly on any subscale. The extent to which each subscale was perceived as an obstacle is shown in Figure 2.

The main perceived obstacle to greater programming was *limited time,* or frequent and unanticipated interruptions. In some cases, the child's availability was limited; with school, afternoon naps, outside programs and the like, there seemed little time for regular formal teaching sessions. In other cases, the time limitations were the mother's, because of her work, the other children, frequent interruptions, or countless other and often unspecified factors. Nevertheless, although finding time in a busy day for formal teaching is obviously difficult, "lack of time" is too often a ready excuse; it is really just another way of saying that teaching was not a high priority.

The next highest ranked obstacles related to the *child,* to his behavior problems, lack of skills, and general lack of progress. In some cases, mention was made of the child's low functioning and slow learning per se, and, not unexpectedly, these were mentioned more by parents whose children had more limited self-help skills (r, post–self-help versus child as obstacle, $r = -0.31, p <$ 0.01). The child's lack of skills will to some extent be a persistent obstacle, though perhaps a more tolerable one if other obstacles can be overcome.

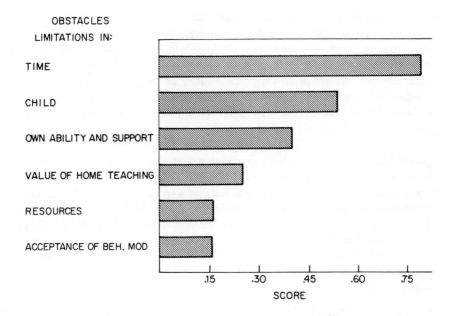

Figure 2. Mean scores for subscales of Obstacle Checklist.

However, limits in the child's motivation for learning or behaviors that interfered with teaching are obstacles that could conceivably be overcome partially by further enhancing parents' behavior management skills.

The next highest ranked obstacles related to parents' *perceived inability and their need for outside support.* Mothers frequently mentioned in the interview their lack of confidence in teaching their child; on the checklist, lack of outside support was frequently acknowledged to be an obstacle. This, and to some extent the previously named obstacles, is consistent with our clinical observations that, however skilled as teachers parents might become, they are still likely to maintain doubts about their expertise and sometimes even about the appropriateness of this role.

For example, the next most frequently cited obstacles were items related to parents' interest in and perceived value of teaching. These items relating to a *rejection of teaching* included feeling that teaching is the school's responsibility and/or that the child receives enough teaching at school, that teaching at home neglects the other children, or simply that it is uninteresting or of dubious value. On the checklist, one mother in five admitted to finding teaching uninteresting or being unsure of its value. It seems likely that some of these "rejection of teaching" items might have been checked even more if "limited time" had not been available as a more acceptable alternative.

It is interesting that parents generally did not attribute their lack of follow-through to a *rejection of behavior modification* per se. One mother in five felt the structure of behavior modification "doesn't fit my personality," but this was as likely to be seen as a personal shortcoming as it was to be seen as a problem with behavior modification. Only one mother in ten reported that she didn't "believe this approach is best for us." Those parents most inclined to reject the behavioral model altogether may have been among those who self-selected out before the end of training.

In sum, then, at follow-up more than a year after training we found that parent knowledge of behavior modification and child original skill gains were essentially maintained. Furthermore, most parents carried out some further teaching and about half (44%) of the families were scored as having undertaken substantial new teaching with good technique during the follow-through period. This teaching tended to be incidental rather than formal and tended to be less in MO families than in others. Overall, the cost effectiveness of MO would still be highest, but these findings and the obstacles perceived by parents suggest a number of modifications in training that might help parents to be more persistent teachers.

Modification in Training

Incidental Teaching Training might still encourage formal teaching at first as a vehicle for learning principles, but it might also acknowledge the value of incidental teaching. The training program could include inputs on analyzing and modifying the usual daily routine at home to make incidental teaching more likely.

Media Training might combine reliance on media, such as manuals and video tape, as the main source of information about teaching principles, along with group meetings to provide a forum for accountability, feedback on past teaching, and planning of future efforts. Increased use of visual media might be especially helpful in that parents seeing other parents carrying out programs may not only learn the techniques better but also come to value the enterprise more.

Follow-through Plan Training might terminate with a structured teaching plan for the first several months of the follow-through period; parents could select several target behaviors for future teaching and decide how they would assess progress in each.

Ongoing Meetings Periodic meetings during the follow-through period might be useful for continued support as well as accountability.

Incentives Finally, we would do well to acknowledge that parents also need reinforcement for their efforts, and that child progress alone is often too slow and too variable to be the only incentive. Some programs have introduced incentives for parents, such as rewarding attendance and programming efforts by returning initial money deposits, and contingent professional consultation and the like. These incentives have been found to be effective adjuncts.

Even the most cost-effective parent training will prove of little value if agencies are unwilling and/or unable to incorporate it into their service offerings. It is indeed hypocritical, or even impossible, for an agency to train parents toward good behavioral programming that the agency itself is not doing.

SUMMARY

Parents trained as teachers of their retarded children were interviewed fourteen months after training to assess maintenance of child gains and, more importantly, continued parental programming efforts. Also examined were perceived obstacles to further teaching with emphasis on limitations within the family system and the training formats.

RESEARCH TO PRACTICE IN MENTAL RETARDATION
Care and Intervention, Volume I
Edited by Peter Mittler
Copyright 1977 I.A.S.S.M.D.

PREVENTION OF FAMILY MALADJUSTMENT THROUGH COUNSELING IN A SPECIAL EDUCATIONAL SETTING

M. E. Adams
*Walter E. Fernald State School, Waltham,
Massachusetts 02154, United States*

INTRODUCTION

Although special education is a basic remedial tool for handicapped children it is important to recognise that its very provision embodies several subtle sources of potential stress for their families. These are: the overt social declaration of the child's deficits and special needs that is inherent in its acceptance by parents; parents' high investment of hopes for improved functioning through professional intervention; and the corresponding disappointment when these are not realized. From the practical angle there is the burden of actively cooperating in a regimen of child management that is likely to be unfamiliar, absorb an undue amount of time and energy, require a revamping of family living style, and even run counter to the social, cultural, and psychological mores by which the nuclear family and its wider network operate. These potential social pressures make it essential for an ongoing counseling program to be available to families of all children receiving special education; this chapter offers a plea and rationale for this service to be carried out by the handicapped child's teachers, and outlines the sort of training preparation needed to equip this group of professionals for this unfamiliar task.

ADVANTAGES OF COUNSELING IN THE EDUCATIONAL SETTING

Parent-teacher interaction is an acknowledged and normative feature of modern education—as seen in PTA groups—that has a special relevance to families with a child who has unusual and significant anomalies in physical, intellectual, and academic behavior. As well as assisting the former to follow the objectives of training, it also makes available to the teachers the parents' own invaluable observations on the child's behavior and functioning in the different social setting of the home. This cooperative relationship between the concerned professional directly engaged in the remedial care of the child and the parents has an important therapeutic value in keeping them actively involved in the child's progress, which helps to mitigate the sense of inadequacy and impotence so many parents feel (Jeffree and McConkey, 1975; Mittler, 1975; Tymchuk, 1975; Cohen and Gloeckler, 1976). Furthermore, since education is part of any child's normal experience, counseling provided in this professional environment carries a reassuring aura of normalcy instead of the more commonly held implications of individual psychological inadequacy, social pathology, or emergent crisis that families often associate with one of the more traditional counseling professions, such as social work, psychology, psychiatry. The fact that counseling focuses on social as well as educational issues also subtly reinforces the concept that some degree of social stress and family adaptation to it are an intrinsic feature of having a significantly handicapped member in the family (Schild, 1971).

This point introduces the further important factor that the regular ongoing contact between teacher and family, resulting from the child's presence in school, gives the teacher a unique advantage for case-finding latent family problems; these can emerge either directly in the course of parent-teacher interaction or be indirectly inferred from observation of the index child if his or her behaviour in class suddenly assumes more aberrant characteristics. Teachers who are equipped to perceive incipient or overt signs of family stress are in a very strategic position for offering intervention in this secondary area of problems, either by direct counseling themselves or by judicious referral to another, more appropriate professional agency.

INITIAL PROFESSIONAL
STUMBLING-BLOCKS TO TEACHER COUNSELING

A necessary preliminary to helping teachers learn the elementary basics of counseling skills and the social frame of reference in which they are applied is to identify which elements in their own professional training, orientation, and skills are likely to impede or facilitate the assimilation of this new skill and accompanying role. The latter facet introduces an immediate difficulty, namely, role-confusion and conflict over where professional loyalties primarily lie. Like many comparable professionals, such as occupational, physical, and speech therapists, teachers initially focus on the child's disability and needs, and they must also serve as advocates for the successful implementation of necessary remedial help. This approach, although intrinsic to their professional mandate, can limit receptivity to family stresses, stifle insight into both their origin and effects, and blind teachers to the reality that, if they are not dealt with, the family's capacity for cooperating constructively with the educational program may be impeded and in the final analysis sabotaged.

An additional problem is that the goals, satisfactions, and values of education are more sharply delineated than those of social work, which is less concerned with the programmed achievement of *one* individual than with the constantly shifting ecological process of individual interaction with the environment and its positive or negative effects (Meyer et al., 1968). This 'unstable' flexibility can be very threatening to teachers when they first embark on counseling and find themselves unable to set or to elicit clearly visible, circumscribed objectives and are compelled to take both their pace and cues from their client-parent.

Teachers' normal mode of communication, which is basically didactic, directed to imparting documented knowledge to a receptive listener, may further hamper effective counseling, which demands a diametrically opposite exploratory approach, geared to probing the vital material that resides *outside* of the professional ken and *inside* the family's problems, conflicts, and incentives for confronting and dealing with them. The unfamiliarity of *not* knowing the answers ahead of time can evoke fear of losing control of the interaction and eliciting emotionally charged material that is felt to be beyond their skills to handle. This results in over-caution, exemplified by a frequently encountered reluctance to follow-up clients' cues, or even ask a direct question, either of which would seem, by social work criteria, to have harmless consequences as well as being invaluable in moving the discussion along in a positive direction that the client has indirectly pointed by his or her comments.

ASSETS AND APTITUDES OF TEACHERS FOR COUNSELING FAMILIES

In contrast to the potential disadvantages just cited teachers also have very many unique assets for family counseling. Their firsthand knowledge of the child— both his or her positive and negative features—is a very strong force in establishing the relationship of trust that is such an integral feature of successful counseling, and also endows it with the invaluable authority of realistic experience that, skillfully manipulated, can be converted into a very potent role model for managing the child (Lessin et al., 1969; Smith and Loeb, 1965). The fact that the teacher also works directly with the child's handicaps and is seen as the visible means of effecting whatever improvement he or she shows makes her a very important person for the family. Studies have shown that professionals who focus initially on the child's disability have far greater credence in parents' eyes and through this service have freer access to the less tangible, and often more reluctantly discussed, social and emotional issues (Ehlers, 1964).

TYPES OF PROBLEMS
MOST APPROPRIATE FOR TEACHER COUNSELING

Because school is a normal experience to which everyone is exposed at some point in his life, teacher counseling lends itself most readily to issues that involve all family members and their reciprocal interaction (Farber and Ryckman, 1965; McAllister et al., 1973). In addition, since child development is a basic feature of their professional stock in trade, teachers are especially well-equipped to understand and communicate with the normal children in the family about the problems they inevitably experience through having a handicapped sibling (Kew, 1975). These are very often overlooked or denied by parents in their distressed overconcern with the handicapped child, with adverse consequences (Adams, 1967). To counteract these, the simple expedient of introducing normal brothers and sisters to the classroom, explaining the program, and from this the basis of the disability and its conspicuous functional manifestation, is invaluable in clearing up a lot of potentially disturbing fantasies, or at least confused misconceptions, and implicitly emphasises the common normal social aspects of the child because of the siblings' identification with education, which they themselves share. Where it seems acceptable or feasible the teacher can also judiciously give the normal siblings some rehabilitative responsibility for the handicapped child by showing ways in which their involvement at home can extend or support the school's efforts (Weinrott, 1974). Here a word of caution is necessary against inadvertently playing upon the guilty reparative drives experienced by some children (Farber and Jenne, 1963), and the aim should be to relieve such painful and distorted emotions by offering an opportunity to give realistic help that is within their practical and psychological means. The following case history illustrates some of these points:

Ruth B. is an 11-year-old girl with Cornelia DeLange syndrome (Holmes et al., 1972) whose manipulative behaviour over eating and sleeping, and outbursts of destructive activity, created considerable disciplinary problems and family conflicts. A strict behaviour modification program managed to eliminate much of this acting-out in the classroom but lack of follow-through at home not only undermined the teachers' efforts but also led Ruth to think that behaving well was not consistently required or rewarded. To neutralize this confusing impasse the parents were offered counseling, giving them an opportunity to ventilate their deep-seated disappointment, confusion about earlier diagnoses and predictions, and their ambivalence towards the girl. As they felt able to confess their negative feelings and admit the difficulties she was creating the parents became more comfortable in imposing limits and demands upon her, family tensions decreased, and the three older siblings were gradually coopted into the home regime, providing invaluable support by ignoring "bad" and enthusiastically reinforcing "good" social behaviour.

Because both parents were in their fifties and Ruth's management was anticipated to become more difficult in adolescence, they decided to request long-term residential placement. From the start all the siblings were implicated in this decision on the grounds that their reaction to the plan would be a major factor in its success. For example, guilty or resentful feelings about this seeming rejection could prevent their cooperating in preparing Ruth for this dramatic change, evoking opposition in Ruth that would make her settling in more difficult for all sides. To forestall this, the teachers discussed Ruth's abilities with the siblings, explained the current range of educational options, and emphasized the benign intent behind placement. This was to provide her with the 24-hour regimen of care that she now needed in order to develop her maximum potential, and without which she ran a serious risk of lapsing into chronic antisocial behaviour patterns. This would impede her successful transition into adulthood and, at worst, might necessitate permanent institutionalization if she became too difficult for community living.

SUPERVISORY CONSULTATION

An effective counseling program by teachers involves capitalizing on the assets just described and neutralizing those elements that impede development of this skill. This has been attempted by two routes. The first was a formal course in family counseling given for academic credit to graduate students in special education, each of whom was assigned to individual counseling with one family of a child attending the diagnostic classrooms at the Eunice Kennedy Shriver Center. The second took the form of weekly group consultation between classroom teachers and a social worker on the management of cases that were presenting serious social issues of the type outlined above. This latter approach, which is discussed here, has proved a very effective training vehicle on several grounds. First, it gave the teachers responsibility for identifying and initiating discussion of social problems, thus fostering and testing out diagnostic insights. Second, the format itself has served as a model for exploratory discussion, and the consultant's method of extracting principles and didactic concepts from concrete case examples made the former seem more lively and relevant and projected the idea that vital material in counseling invariably emerges out of dialogue on quite "down-to-earth" topics.

This technique also built up the teachers' confidence for assuming this new and somewhat daunting task when the case material—the index child's relationship with the family—was not only comfortably familiar to them but also demonstrated their expertise in the educational aspects, which the social work consultant lacked. The reinforcing experience of being able to demonstrate superior skills while learning new, less easy ones generated the insight that parents could also be helped to feel more competent in dealing with their child and the attendant problems if due credit was given to *their* expertise in understanding their child in some ways that no professional outsider could. Given the fact that the teaching role is traditionally invested with a high degree of authority, and in the case of severely disabled children, with no small measure of magic, a relationship of parity between teacher and parent is a vital therapeutic tool (Adams, 1971; Miller et al., 1976).

The peer-group support that group consultation (Smith, 1972) affords the participating teachers fosters this sense of egalitarian sharing in the child's rehabilitation, and on occasions, when a teacher has demonstrated irrational or rigid attitudes in discussing family management, group dynamics have often moved another member to point up the resemblance between this professional's behavior and that shown by a parent or family over a different *issue* that involved the *same* underlying psychological forces. Some of the dynamics of role-conflict were also acted out in their relationship with the supervisor consultant, who in one respect embodied the superior guiding role of the teacher at the same time as she was helping them to discard this stance for the different counseling approach (Heap, 1975). An illustration of this is what occurred when one teacher dealing with several grossly defective young children expressed a great deal of angry disappointment about a mother who was not following through on a feeding program at home, thus failing to foster the child's potential capacities and frustrating the teacher's professional efforts. The consultant pointed out that she was adopting a far too narrow child-focussed view and overlooking the fact that the mother was eight months pregnant, extremely anxious, and not likely to have the actual or psychic energy to invest in the handicapped child. While this clarification brought the situation into perspective it did not speak to the teacher's feeling of being unsupported in a heavy professional task, and instead of shifting her position she became more stubbornly critical and the supervisor responded with criticism of her attitude. The following session was given over to analysing the feelings, attitudes, and responsive behavior of all group members in this stormy situation; by actually experiencing divergent, irrational, and angry feelings the teachers were able to recognize first how their preoccupation with the child's needs interfered with their appreciating wider family issues, and second how professional frustration, as represented by the mother-teacher and teacher-consultant interactions, can set up unconstructive emotional blockages that consolidate resistance to resolution of conflicts.

SUMMARY

This paper discusses the development of family counseling skills in teachers in special education programs. The rationale for this innovation is presented with examples of problems and situations amenable to this sort of intervention and guidelines for consultation required to help teachers assume and sustain this unfamiliar professional role.

ACKNOWLEDGMENT

The author wishes to acknowledge the stimulation of ideas contributed by students of Lesley College Graduate School of Education, Cambridge, teachers of the Diagnostic Classrooms of the Eunice Kennedy Shriver Center, and to Jeanne Kantianis for manuscript review.

REFERENCES

Adams, M. E. (1967) Siblings of the retarded: Their problems and treatment. Child Welfare 46:310.

Adams, M. E. (1971) Mental Retardation and its Social Dimensions. New York: Columbia University Press, p. 164.

Cohen, S., and Gloeckler, L. (1976) Working with parents of handicapped children: A statewide approach. Child. Today 5:10.

Ehlers, W. H. (1964) The moderately and severely retarded child: Maternal perceptions of retardation and subsequent seeking and using services rendered by a community agency. Amer. J. Ment. Defic. 68:660.

Farber, B., and Jenne, W. C. (1963) Interaction with retarded siblings and life goals of children. Marriage and Family Living 25:96.

Farber, B., and Ryckman, D. B. (1965) Effects of severely mentally retarded children on family relationships. Ment. Retard. Abstr. 2:1.

Heap, E. (1975) The supervisor as reflector. Social Work Today 5:677.

Holmes, L. B., Moser, H. W., Halldorsson, S., Mack, C., Pant, S. S., and Matzilevich, B. (1972) Mental Retardation: An Atlas of Diseases Associated with Physical Abnormalities. New York: Macmillan, p. 276.

Jeffree, D., and McConkey, R. (1975) The parental involvement project. Paper presented at the 6th Congress of ILSMH, Dublin.

Kew, S. (1975) Handicap and Family Crisis: A Study of the Siblings of Handicapped Children. London: Pitman.

Lessin, S., Finnila, M., and Gorelick, M. C. (1969) A marathon workshop: Help for the retarded child with management problems. Child Welfare 48:560.

McAllister, R. J., Butler, E. W., and Tzeun-Jen-Lei (1973) Patterns of social interaction among families of behaviorally retarded children. Journal of Marriage and the Family 35:93.

Meyer, H. J., Likwak, E., and Warren, D. (1968) Occupational and class differences in social values: A comparison of teachers and social workers. Sociol. Educ. 41:263.

Miller, M., Harrison, M., Smith, V., Smithson, D., and Turner, S. (1976) Childhood disability—group work with mothers. Social Work Today 7:15.

Mittler, P. (1975) A rationale for parental partnership. Paper presented at the 6th Congress of ILSMH, Dublin.

Schild, S. (1971) The family of the retarded child. In The Mentally Retarded Child and His Family. New York: Brunner/Mazel.

Smith, D. M. (1972) Group supervision: An experience. Social Work Today 3:13.

Smith, I. W. and Loeb, D. (1965) The stable extended family as a model in treatment of atypical children. Social Work 10:75.

Tymchuk, A. J. (1975) Training parent therapists. Ment. Retard. 13:19.

Weinrott, M. R. (1974) A training program in behaviour modification for siblings of the retarded. Amer. J. Orthopsychiatry 44:362.

RESEARCH TO PRACTICE IN MENTAL RETARDATION
Care and Intervention, Volume I
Edited by Peter Mittler
Copyright 1977 I.A.S.S.M.D.

A PARENTAL INVOLVEMENT PROJECT

D. M. Jeffree, R. McConkey, and S. Hewson
Hester Adrian Research Centre, The University,
Manchester M13 9PL, England

The Parental Involvement Project started in 1973 and is a four-year research project carried out at the Hester Adrian Research Centre in Manchester. It is jointly financed by the Department of Health and Social Security and the Department of Education and Science (Jeffree, McConkey, and Hewson, 1975; McConkey and Jeffree, 1975a; McConkey and Jeffree, 1975b; McConkey, 1976). This research project arose out of the experience of earlier workshops in which both project directors had participated.

At the request of parents, evening workshops were organised in 1971 and 1972 at the Hester Adrian Research Centre. Both the parents workshops were intended for parents of preschool mentally handicapped children. These young parents were very aware of the importance of the early years in a child's cognitive and social development but often lacked confidence in their own expertise and welcomed the opportunity of further guidance (Cunningham and Jeffree, 1971, 1975; Jeffree and Cunningham, 1975).

The present project was designed to investigate means of helping these parents at a time when they were needing the most help and often getting the least.

AIMS OF THE PROJECT

The aims of the Parental Involvement Project are as follows:

1. To investigate means by which parents can best be guided to become more effective in aiding their child's development.
2. To establish the effectiveness of specially designed teaching games suitable for use by parents in the home situation.
3. To disseminate information arising from the project to:
   A. parents of young mentally handicapped children
   B. relevant professional workers who come into contact with parents in the early years.

THE PARENTS AND THE CHILDREN

In order to gain information on the families we planned to help, an initial visit was made to parents in the Greater Manchester Area with children between the ages of two and five years who had been assessed as ESNS (educationally subnormal (severe)).

A specially designed developmental chart (Jeffree and McConkey, 1976a) was completed for each child, in order to get a comprehensive overview of the children's abilities. This material would also suggest the kind of help that the children might require. Additional information was also gathered on family characteristics; the parents were also asked to state their greatest areas of concern and the kind of help they would welcome (Table 1).

Further contact with parents and children was planned on two levels:

1. The random selection of twenty children with their parents for intensive work at the University. Each family attended twelve fortnightly sessions with their child during the day as well as attending six group sessions in the evening. A playroom and observation room were available at the University with a one-way screen and videotaping facilities.
2. Descriptions of teaching games with specific objectives were made available to all the parents who had already been visited in the Greater Manchester Area. Eventually, revised versions of these games will be published in book form for use by parents and professionals in the field. (Jeffree and McConkey, 1976c; Jeffree, McConkey, and Hewson, 1977).

THE INDIVIDUAL SESSIONS AND GROUP SESSIONS

Twenty families were selected at random to attend the University for a course of twelve individual sessions with their child as well as six evening group sessions at fortnightly intervals. The main theme of these sessions was to help the child's learning. The six group sessions were used to reinforce points made in the individual sessions, to demonstrate teaching techniques, and to discuss points common to the whole group.

THE CHOICE OF TEACHING OBJECTIVES

Choice of teaching objectives is no easy matter because they are a reflection of one's educational aims, and the aims of parents and professionals are not always identical. Yet it is the parents who are going to implement the objectives and they are unlikely to be wholehearted in their teaching unless they are convinced.

Differences can only be resolved if there is a degree of honesty on both sides so that frank discussion is possible. Objectives can then be chosen on the basis of areas of parental concern.

Table 1. Areas of parental concern

| | | Percent of parents | |
| | | 3 years and under | 4 years |
Area of concern	Specific example		
Physical skills	Walking	28	16
	Sitting		
Social skills	Toileting	25	25
	Feeding self		
Communication	Speech	44	47
	Language		
Management problems	Screaming	21	41
	Temper tantrums		
	Defiance		
	Aggression towards others		

Developmental Relevance

A developmental profile was made out for each child using the PIP developmental charts (Figure 1). By filling up these charts, parents were able to gain information on their child's present developmental level and his strengths and weaknesses. They could also see the sequence of development from one important milestone to another, which helped them to appreciate that the chosen

Section 2. Climbing

YES	(54)	Walks up and down stairs on his own, alternating feet (using one foot per step)	NO
	(42)	Jumps down from second step of stairs	YES NO
	(36)	Alternates feet going *upstairs*	YES NO
Go to Section 3 Coordination	(33)	Jumps from the bottom step of stairs, both feet together	YES NO
	(24)	Goes up and down stairs in an upright position	YES NO
	(21)	Goes upstairs in an upright position	YES NO
	(21)	Climbs on furniture to look out of window or to reach objects out of reach and gets down again	YES NO
	(19)	Gets up *and* down stairs but not upright	YES NO
	(15)	Climbs stairs on hands and knees	YES NO
	(13)	Climbs on to a low step	YES NO

Go to Section 3. Coordination

Figure 1. A section of the PIP developmental charts.

objectives were developmentally appropriate and to see them in a wider perspective. Their copies of the charts could be updated and kept for future reference. These would be an aid to the parents in planning future programmes after completion of the course.

Observed Behaviour

The Child   Additional baseline information that guided the choice of objectives was provided by observations and recordings of each child's behaviour in a play situation with preselected toys. This yielded information on the child's distractibility or perseveration and also gave an indication of his level of cognitive development from the Piagetian standpoint. In the assessment of play, the scales devised by Uzgiris (1967) proved informative. Methods of recording symbolic play were devised by the project directors (Jeffree and McConkey, 1976b).

The Family   Wherever possible, both parents were involved in implementing the programmes, and often other members of the family were drawn in. Observations were made of the parent/child interaction in play situations both at the University and through home recordings. In some cases priority had to be given to bringing about an alteration in the parent's characteristic behaviour before any alteration in the child's behaviour could be expected, e.g., one parent was so overanxious that she gave her child little opportunity to do anything on his own.

Readily Attainable Goals

If parents are to strive towards teaching objectives for their children, they themselves need some immediate reinforcement. Initially, then, teaching objectives have to be chosen that are realisable in a short time. Only when they have experienced some initial success are some parents ready to strive towards less readily obtainable goals. To ensure such success, goal setters need, ideally, to be able to predict what skills lie on the periphery of a child's present attainments. Previous experience, careful behavioural observations, and a sound theoretical background all inform such predictions. Yet, like all predictions, they may not be realised. Nevertheless, the professional needs to remain positive and confident when dealing with parents.

DESIGN AND EVALUATION OF TEACHING SCHEMES

Task Analysis

Once each child's developmental profile had been ascertained, and his baseline behaviour recorded playing with toys, it was then possible to assess priorities and to select an appropriate task. The task was then analysed into small graded steps and presented as a teaching game. The selected goals were largely in the context of language development, fine motor development, and the development of play.

Teaching Games

Teaching schemes were devised that were aimed at enhancing and not disrupting family life. They were presented as games that could be enjoyed by both parent and child. Expensive equipment was avoided wherever possible. The equipment was either readily available or else specially constructed with readily available material. A variety of games was designed for each child to keep up the child's interest and to show the parents that many different games and toys can be made to serve the same end. These games were designed by the project staff in consultation with the parents.

Demonstration to the Parents

Teaching games and techniques were demonstrated with the child in question while the parents watched without being seen. Initially, the project staff demonstrated the games and then the parents took over and the project staff were able to monitor their progress. All these sessions were recorded on video tape. The teaching programmes were then carried out by the parents at home. At least fifteen minutes a day was set aside for the programmes, and the parents recorded the home teaching either on tapes or with written records.

Teaching Techniques

Initially, extrinsic reinforcement, such as a light switch or ice cream, was often used to start the child interacting with the play material and to show him what he had to do. Later, this often proved unnecessary and the game itself with some social reinforcement provided sufficient incentive. Extensive use was made of modelling and prompting techniques. Further details about many of the teaching games, which are classified according to developmental status, are available in two books, *Let Me Speak* and *Let Me Play*.

Evaluation

The video and audio tapes that were made during the baseline and teaching sessions yielded a wealth of information and enabled fine-grained analyses to be made of each child's progress. Multiple baselines were established and each child acted as his own control. Progress was often confirmed by an accelerated learning curve. Figure 2 shows the results of one child's progress. In this case the programme consisted of games designed to increase the child's use of specific two-word utterances that were generalisable to other situations. Figure 3 shows an example of change in the child's behaviour as a result of change in the parent's behaviour. In this case the records show that the parents were bombarding their child with language to such an extent that she had little opportunity to speak, except in answer to questions. When this was pointed out to the parents

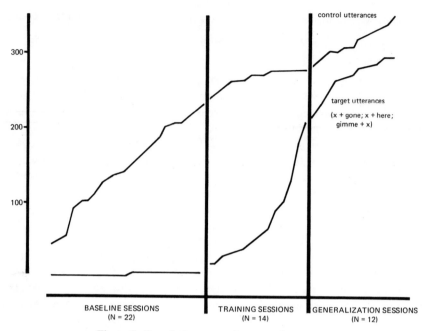

Figure 2. Cumulative count of two-word utterances.

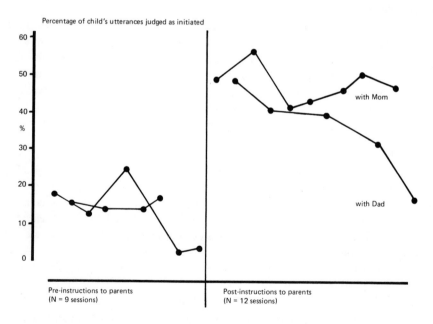

Figure 3. The effect of instructions to parents on child-initiated utterances.

they amended their behaviour at home, and in consequence, there was a dramatic increase in child-initiated utterances, and subsequent improvement in the child's expressive language.

DISSEMINATION

All the parents visited initially who expressed an interest in the project were put on our mailing list to be sent appropriate help. They were sent a free copy of one of the books of teaching games, either *Let Me Speak* or *Let Me Play*. As well as outlining a large number of teaching games, these books include developmental charts to be completed by the parents and indicate which games would be particularly suitable for their child's developmental level in each area. Experimental versions of both these books have also been distributed to a large number of parents and professionals who agreed to complete a questionnaire and comment on different aspects of the books. These comments have proved very helpful and have already enabled us to improve upon the experimental version of *Let Me Speak,* and the revised version of this book will be published at the end of 1976.

SUMMARY

This project is concerned with the active involvement of parents in the cognitive development of their preschool mentally handicapped children. Particular emphasis is laid upon the choice of learning objectives, the design and evaluation of teaching schemes, and the evaluation of the parents' progress in carrying out teaching games.

REFERENCES

Cunningham, C. C., and Jeffree, D. M. (1971) Working with Parents. Manchester: National Society for Mentally Handicapped Children.

Cunningham, C. C., and Jeffree, D. M. (1975) The organisation and structure of workshops for parents of mentally handicapped children. Bull. Brit. Psychol. 28:405.

Jeffree, D. M., and Cunningham, C. C. (1975) Workshops for parents of young mentally handicapped children. Proc. 3rd Congr. IASSMD. 1:336.

*Jeffree, D. M., and Cunningham, C. C. (1976) Barnaby Books. Wisbech: Learning Development Aids.

Jeffree, D. M., and McConkey, R. (1976a) P.I.P. Developmental Charts. London: Hodder and Stoughton.

Jeffree, D. M., and McConkey, R. (1976b) A description of a scheme for recording imaginative doll play. J. Child Psychol. Psychiatry 17:189.

*Jeffree, D. M., and McConkey, R. (1976c) Let Me Speak. London: Souvenir Press.

Jeffree, D. M., McConkey, R., and Hewson, S. (1975) Parental participation is essential. Apex. 3:3.

*Jeffree, D. M., McConkey, R., and Hewson, S. (1977) Let Me Play. London: Souvenir Press.

McConkey, R. (1976) Helping parents to help their child's development. *In* Early Management of Handicapping Disorders (Eds. Oppé, T. E., and Woodford, F. P.) Amsterdam: Associated Scientific Publishers.

McConkey, R., and Jeffree, D. M. (1975a) Pre-school mentally handicapped children. Brit. J. Educ. Psychol. 45:367.

McConkey, R., and Jeffree, D. M. (1975b) Partnership with parents. Special Education: Forward Trends 2(3):13.

Uzgiris, I. C. (1967) Ordinality in the development of schemes for relating objects. *In* Exceptional Infant, Vol. I. The Normal Infant. (Ed. Hellmuth, J.) New York: Brunner/Mazel.

*Books for parents.

RESEARCH TO PRACTICE IN MENTAL RETARDATION
Care and Intervention, Volume I
Edited by Peter Mittler
Copyright 1977 I.A.S.S.M.D.

TREATMENT OF AUTISTIC CHILDREN
Historical
Perspective

E. Schopler
*Department of Psychiatry, Memorial Hospital, University
of North Carolina, Chapel Hill, N.C. 27514, United States*

From the outset it should be acknowledged that autistic children are also frequently retarded and/or brain damaged (Hingtgen and Bryson, 1972; Rutter, 1968; Ornitz, 1973). Moreover, they have been treated with a wide range of techniques, including psychotherapy for the emotionally disturbed. Autistic children are unusual in the confusion they have generated among interested professionals, and their parents, too, of course. Although no two research groups characterize their autistic subjects in specifically the same way, most professionals will share some consensus in describing the disorder. That is, the children relate poorly. They have poor and peculiar use of language. The perceptual processes are abnormal, and they engage in peculiar body motions. Their mental functions are developmentally erratic and cover a wide range of impairment.

This chapter reviews what is known or inferred about these children and their treatment historically and before Kanner (1943) discovered them psychiatrically. It also reviews how they were understood and treated during the several decades following Kanner's discovery. Finally, it summarizes the most current approaches to these children, including the direct involvement of their parents in the treatment process.

HISTORICAL PERSPECTIVE

There is every indication that autistic children existed long before Kanner reported and named the syndrome in 1943, but the evidence is legendary and mysterious. Bettelheim (1959) was convinced that feral children, children raised by wolves and wild beasts, were really autistic. This raises the possibility that the earliest case of autism on record was Romulus and Remus. After a very precarious start they were credited with founding Rome.

Other such cases have been reported (Gesell, 1941). Their treatment ranged from death and neglect to the best of individualized treatment. The latter is illustrated at the turn of the 18th century in France by Itard's student, Victor. This boy spent his early years in the wilderness and was used as a savage in a carnival sideshow. Itard brought the boy into his own home and developed with him various special education techniques. These included sensory training, behavior modification, and special education techniques still in use today. Itard's intense efforts did not remove all of the boy's handicaps. However, the experience enabled him to develop the basis for special education techniques forwarded by Seguin and Montessori (Lane, 1976).

AUTISM AS EMOTIONAL DISTURBANCE—PSYCHIATRIC ERA OF KANNER

By the time the clear clinical description of Kanner's series was published, many overlapping diagnostic labels were also born. These included symbiotic psychosis, childhood schizophrenia, borderline psychosis, and atypical child, to name only the most popular ones. There was no agreement among professionals about how the children designated by these various labels differed from each other. However, most of these terms were explained within the framework of psychoanalytic theory. This meant that the causal emphasis for the child's autism was put on hostile or rejecting feelings in parents and other forms of parental psychopathology. Even though Kanner had referred to a constitutional predisposition in his paper, the children were widely believed to be the products of emotionally cold or compulsive parents, resulting in their social withdrawal from a hostile environment. Therapeutic treatment was centered on psychotherapy for resolving the emotional problem.

Research evidence for the social withdrawal formulation was not found. Psychotherapeutic treatment, as in play therapy, aimed at resolving the child's emotional blocks, proved ineffective and disappointing. This is not so surprising today when autism is recognized as a developmental disability. But in the two decades following Kanner's discovery of autism, the experience and knowledge available today, however limited, had not yet been developed.

The negative effect of treating autism as primarily an emotional disorder has been eloquently documented by Eberhardy (1967), Park (1967), Rimland (1964), and Schopler (1971). They included some of the following consequences:

Diagnostic Confusion

The diagnostic confusion resulting from attempts to designate various vague emotional processes has already been discussed. It resulted in too many autistic children falling between the cracks of existing services. Such a youngster, brought to a mental health clinic, could be refused services because he showed signs of mental retardation or brain damage. If he was brought to a center dealing with mental retardation he was refused because his psychotic behavior was interpreted as emotional disturbance, and so on.

Professional Specialization

The professional, whether psychiatrist, psychologist, teacher, or speech therapist, has certain professional sets and specialized skills that can lead to only a limited focus on the child's and family's adaptational problems. The specialized professional often responds to the child's difficulty in terms of his specialized knowledge rather than the child's special needs. This special professional investment is not surprising, considering that it takes from six to fifteen years to train a professional. However, it has led to a position where the social worker felt the need to protect the family against a child psychiatrist who was protecting the child; the educator advanced educational priorities against the psychotherapist's "emotional" concerns; and the psychologist was confined to "diagnostic assessments." This kind of specialized narrowness has led to the fragmentation of children and families into different problems, with no continuity of service. The conflicting opinions of professionals and the inconsistencies between their recommendations and actions were vividly documented by Kysar (1968).

Parental Confusion

During this period parental confusion was generated from diverse sources, including the widely disseminated idea by clinicians like Bettelheim (1967) that the autistic child deviated from the normal ranges mainly in response to environmental extremes or in response to improper conditioning procedures (Ferster, 1961). The parent then felt obliged to discover what sort of extreme he had supposedly inflicted on his child and whether the resulting stress was transmitted through faulty communication (Meyers and Goldfarb, 1961) or other personality pathology (Kanner, 1949). In addition to the confusing myths in the mass culture, shared by many parents and professionals, there was also lack of access to the results of diagnostic evaluations. The clinic records were often stamped "Confidential," which meant not for viewing by parents. Whether this kind of secrecy was caused by professional uncertainty over diagnosis, a concern about protecting parents from the anticipated shock of trying to explain soft neurological signs, or protecting parents from the highly negativistic attitudes toward them, often couched in psychoanalytic jargon, the results had the same effects. Parents' confusion reduced their ability to provide their autistic child with the needed special care.

Misleading Expectations

Parental confusion and perplexity in managing their autistic child was magnified by misleading or absent diagnostic information. This led to the related problem of increased uncertainty about the behavior that could reasonably be expected from their child. The prevalent assumption that the child had withdrawn from an unfavorable emotional climate led directly to the expectation that a normal child would emerge if the child were given free reign for expressing himself. This expectation prevented the development of the learning structures needed by autistic children (Schopler et al., 1971). Another source preventing the formulation of reasonable expectations was the use of psychological test results. Autistic children were generally regarded as "untestable." This result was often interpreted as indicative of emotional blocking, even for the most seriously impaired children, thus obscuring their actual needs for special education and management. Methods of overcoming untestability have been described elsewhere (Schopler and Reichler, 1971a), as has the evidence for the use of test scores as predictors for long range management.

These are some, but by no means all, of the factors limiting the development of effective services for autistic children during the two decades following World War II.

CURRENT CHANGES IN UNDERSTANDING AND TREATMENT

The era of causal emphasis on parental pathology terminated during the 1960s. That is not to say that the controversy does not continue today. However, certain milestones can be identified during the last two decades that have underscored the political and intellectual changes touching the treatment of autistic children. In 1964 Rimland published his book *Infantile Autism.* He conducted a scholarly review of the literature and found no empirical support for the psychogenic theory. He also participated in founding the first chapter of the National Society for Autistic Children. Where previously parents of autistic children were divided by the guilt experienced about their own childrearing failures, they now were able to unite, and to lobby for social help with education and research. Their efforts in part resulted in autism being officially designated as a developmental disability last year. Intellectually, there was an increased shift to accountability in treatment and empirical research evidence in place of theoretical formulations. Some of these studies were summarized by Rutter (1968).

In this context a greater emphasis on behavioral treatment evolved. Behavior modification was more widely accepted and used. Parents were more actively involved in the treatment process. I will describe this treatment shift from our own experience with parents of autistic children as cotherapists (Schopler and Reichler, 1971b). We saw that research data, our own and that of others, indicated that primary causal emphasis for the autistic condition should be on the early manifestation of some brain abnormalities in the afflicted child rather than on impaired management by a disturbed parent. It was also quite clear that peculiarities in parenting behavior were often a reaction to the effects of a confusingly handicapped child.

If these findings were true, then it followed that an educational approach could be taken with parents of autistic children. Since 1966 we have evolved a developmental assessment of the child's erratic learning style (Schopler and Reichler, 1976). From this assessment, individualized special education approaches and behavior modification techniques were developed, and were demonstrated to the parents as they observed through a one-way vision screen. A home program was written out for them which they used on a daily basis with the child at home. For behavioral changes not observable during visits to the Center, direct methods of behavior modification were worked out with parents.

This treatment structure was effective for both parents and children. We were able to develop the first state-wide program for young autistic and communications handicapped children (Reichler and Schopler, 1976). This program includes four centers in which individualized help is given to families and children. It also includes 18 classrooms located in the public schools throughout the state for the education of these children. With the involvement of parents an opportunity is offered for working out an educational approach integrated between school and home.

FUTURE TRENDS

I have given a brief summary of how autistic children appear to have been understood and treated historically. This included a review of the mythical assumptions and treatment procedures of the period marked by Kanner's identification of autism, followed by the last decade in which increased research knowledge and experience enabled us to overcome some of the shortcomings attending the psychodynamic orientation.

Although some noteworthy progress has been made, new issues are raised for the treatment of autistic children, including questions such as: What are the limitations of parent involvement in the autistic child's home treatment? Special needs in addition to what parents can offer become apparent with adolescents and adults who still have the need for special environments, such as sheltered workshops; special vocational opportunities; supervised living arrangements, as in group homes; and planned communities. These represent concerns that are shared by the autistic with those suffering other developmental disabilities. New treatment trends are emerging, but are not yet tested. Deinstitutionalization raises a question about the community's ability to meet the needs of those requiring a protective environment. Normalization raises a question about whether this principle will be interpreted to mean that all autistic individuals will be expected to cope with the same pressures as citizens without handicaps. There are other special treatment and educational techniques vying for institutionalization and categorical care. Will these pressures reduce the individualization so patently needed by the autistic? Our resolution of these issues will be important to the future of those members of our community suffering with the handicaps of autism. Equally important, our solutions will mirror the kind of communities we develop for all of us.

SUMMARY

The presentation includes a historical perspective on the understanding and treatment of autistic children. Three phases are identified, including 1) prepsychiatric, 2) Kanner's formulation, and 3) current modifications. The trend of treating autistic children at home is described, including a model for implementing home treatment. Limitations of this treatment modality are presented and future directions indicated.

REFERENCES

Bettelheim, B. (1959) Feral children and autistic children. Amer. J. Sociol. 64:455.

Bettelheim, B. (1967) The Empty Fortress. New York: The Macmillan Company.

Eberhardy, F. (1967) The view from the couch. J. Child Psychol. Psychiatry 8:257.

Ferster, C. B. (1961) Positive reinforcement and behavioral deficits of autistic children. Child Dev. 32:437.

Gesell, A. (1941) Wolf Child and Human Child. New York: Harper.

Hingtgen, J. N., and Bryson, C. Q. (1972) Recent developments in the study of early childhood psychosis: Infantile autism, childhood schizophrenia, and related disorders. Schizophr. Bull. 5:8.

Kanner, L. (1943) Autistic disturbances of affective contact. Nerv. Child 2:217.

Kanner, L. (1949) Problems of nosology and psychodynamics in early infantile autism. Amer. J. Orthopsychiatry 19:416.

Kysar, J. (1968) The two camps in child psychiatry: A report from a psychiatrist-father of an autistic and retarded child. Amer. J. Psychiatry 125:103.

Lane, H. (1976) The Wild Boy of Aveyron. Cambridge, Mass.: Harvard University Press.

Meyers, D. I., and Goldfarb, W. (1961) Studies of perplexity in mothers of schizophrenic children. Amer. J. Orthopsychiatry 31:551.

Ornitz, E. M. (1973) Childhood autism: A review of the clinical and experimental literature. Calif. Med. 118:29.

Park, C. (1967) The Siege. New York: Harcourt, Brace and World.

Reichler, R. J., and Schopler, E. (1976) Developmental therapy: A program model for providing individual services in the community. *In* Psychopathology and Child Development (Eds. Schopler, E., and Reichler, R. J.) New York: Plenum.

Rimland, B. (1964) Infantile Autism. New York: Appleton-Century-Crofts.

Rutter, M. (1968) Concepts of autism: A review of research. J. Child Psychol. Psychiatry 9:1.

Schopler, E. (1971) Parents of psychotic children as scapegoats. J. Contemp. Psychother. 4:17.

Schopler, E., Brehm, S., Kinsbourne, M., and Reichler, R. J. (1971) Effect of treatment structure on development in autistic children. Arch. Gen. Psychiatry 24:415.

Schopler, E., and Reichler, R. J. (1971a) Problems in the developmental assessment of psychotic children. Excerpta Medica International Congress Series, No. 274.

Schopler, E., and Reichler, R. J. (1971b) Parents as cotherapists in the treatment of psychotic children. J. Autism Child. Schizo. 1:87.

Schopler, E., and Reichler, R. J. (1976) Psychoeducational Profile. Chapel Hill, North Carolina: Child Development Products.

RESIDENTIAL
SERVICES

RESEARCH TO PRACTICE IN MENTAL RETARDATION
Care and Intervention, Volume I
Edited by Peter Mittler
Copyright 1977 I.A.S.S.M.D.

ALTERNATIVE PATTERNS OF CARE FOR THE MENTALLY RETARDED

D. Rosen
Macomb-Oakland Regional Center,
36358 Garfield Road,
Fraser, Michigan 48026, United States

The controversy that exists over "institutions versus community placements" is a pointless one. While it makes for interesting abstract debate, it serves little useful purpose other than as a gauge for measuring who has read the most idealistic literature. If either institutions or community placement programs adhere to accepted standards of quality, the argument neutralizes itself.

Any education, training, treatment, or residential facility, regardless of location, that is not attempting to achieve appropriate standards, or is not conducting internal evaluations of purpose and performance with normalization principles as the frame of reference, is to be admonished.

Institutions and community residential programs are equally responsible for eliminating their own "back wards."

What is critical to all residential programs, either community or institutionally based, is the adherence to stringent standards of care. The preparation of individual developmental plans with regular reviews, the frequent monitoring of progress, demands for service responsibility, and interagency accountability must be a part of every residential program. It goes without saying that the role of the advocate is clearly necessary in both, as is the scrutiny of parent-consumer associations.

The declaration of rights of the handicapped and the principles of normalization must be thematically observed, with respective standards of accreditation and evaluation.

If we adhere to this line of thought, we will not have to be concerned about whether or not institutions should continue to exist or debate whether institutional or community programs are best. Time and the continued sensitivity to these fundamentals will lead us to the path that will provide the best programs.

I have no doubt that such a course will lead to institutions changing for the better. Those beyond hope of conforming to standards will be razed. Populations will continue to be reduced. Short-term, time-limited, voluntary, or administrative admissions will increase. The admission of the mildly and moderately handicapped will virtually be eliminated. The number of acceptable placements directly from home to acceptable alternative living situations in the community for those who are severe and profound will grow. Services to parents for all the retarded in their homes and communities will expand and avoid for longer periods the need for alternative living situations.

What will the role of institutions be in the future? Will there be institutions in the future? Some professionals say that 50% can come out of the institutions today if we have appropriate living facilities in the community, some say 75%, others say 100%. We must stop talking and get to work. We need tens of thousands of appropriate placements for those who are ready to exit and for those who would not have had to enter if alternatives existed.

In this regard, we will eliminate the worn-out practice of keeping a person in an institution until he achieves his potential. He is enough like us that he will never reach his full potential, whether he be in the community or in the institution. He has the right to be placed in the least restrictive setting possible. The setting that may seem appropriate today may be too restrictive tomorrow. If we continue to establish permanent solutions for the retarded, we will be as wrong today as were our predecessors who stated that the only answer for the retarded was permanent institutionalization.

Until we develop an achievable, goal-oriented program within all our institutions, and community programs that ensure that each individual is given full opportunity for treatment, training, and therapy, or until we make sure that after the completion of a prescriptive program the individual is graduated to a less restrictive program and environment in the institution and the community, we are in fact still incarcerating the person. It is not normal to spend one's life in an institution. In very few cases should the retarded person, even the severely or profoundly handicapped, remain at an institution for a long period if properly developed alternatives existed or were developed. It is my belief that such alternatives can be generated. The responsibility is ours.

Developing a positive, cooperative relationship with the community at large is a vital prerequisite to community placement of the retarded. If we expect to have programs, facilities, and services to accomodate the life needs and desires of the mentally retarded, we must recognize the fact that there are strong concerns and objections felt and expressed.

RESEARCH TO PRACTICE IN MENTAL RETARDATION
Care and Intervention, Volume I
Edited by Peter Mittler
Copyright 1977 I.A.S.S.M.D.

EXTENDING THE ROLE OF THE INSTITUTION INTO THE COMMUNITY

H. A. Stevens
Harry A. Waisman Center on Mental Retardation and Human Development, University of Wisconsin, 2605 Marsh Lane, Madison, Wisconsin 53706, United States

A number of forces have brought about a reevaluation of the function(s) of institutions serving the mentally retarded. This has resulted in redefining the role of today's institution(s). One significant change has been in the relationship of the institution to the community.

A detailed examination of the many facets of this new role should help both the staff of the institution and the community agencies understand and respond to the challenge of this new responsibility.

INSTITUTIONS IN THE PAST

Institutions in Western countries have served the mentally retarded for more than 1,500 years. In the fourth century the Institutes of Justinian, as well as the Bishop of Myra, provided caretakers for "idiots" and the physically and mentally ill. The reformation period of the sixteenth century emphasized personal responsibility. Yet that society fostered harsh treatment of the handicapped— they required them to spend long periods in chains—and viewed them as being "possessed of the devil."

During the eighteenth century bits of knowledge concerning the "idiot" and the "imbecile" were acquired. A few concepts were formulated to provide a basis for their care, management, and education. The work of Itard in the late 1700s and of Seguin in the mid-1800s laid the basis for programs for the next 100 years.

At an 1876 meeting in London (England) the "experts" agreed that

1. a number of idiots and imbeciles could be made self-supporting,
2. segregation at an early age for training was desirable,
3. institutions' care for those who were profoundly or severely retarded was desirable, and

4. the condition of many mentally retarded in institutions could be improved by placing them in a home in the community.

By the early 1900s it was felt that large institutions would allow better classification for institutional management and facilitate educational training.

Institutions were unable, during the first half of the twentieth century, to fulfill the goals formulated in the late nineteenth century. Institutions became "custodial" in function. In general, the quality of services became substandard. The care and treatment of "patients" was described as "warehousing." Overcrowding, outmoded facilities, and shortage of staff resulted in "dehumanization" of the individual. *The institution was completely isolated from the community.*

By the early 1950s the public demanded reform. Governments and parent organizations set about to reorganize (public) services for the mentally retarded. The "rights of the retarded," "improved quality of life," and "normalization" became slogans that brought about radical changes in the care, treatment, and management of the mentally retarded.

A new foundation had been laid for the remainder of the twentieth century.

ROLE OF INSTITUTIONS TODAY

The primary function of an institution today is to provide an array of services in order to protect and nurture the physical, emotional, intellectual, and social growth and development of each individual requiring such services.

If one accepts this concept, then one is obligated to provide a range of services that will enable each retarded individual to

1. develop his physical, emotional, intellectual, and social capacities to the fullest extent possible,
2. develop the skills, habits, and attitudes essential to his return and successful adjustment to the community, and the institution must
3. organize activities that will enable him to live a personally satisfying life within the institution if he is in need of long-term care. (The President's Committee on Mental Retardation: "Residential Services for the Mentally Retarded: An Action Policy Proposal," Washington, D.C., 1970.)

EDUCATIONAL AND WELFARE SERVICES
WORKING WITH COMMUNITY AGENCIES

Residential institutions cannot exist today in isolation. They cannot function without continuously interacting with those established community agencies providing services to meet the needs of the general population and the needs of specialized population, such as the mentally retarded.

The staff of such agencies may be reluctant to work with the mentally retarded; the demands for services by the "normal" population may exceed the ability of the staff to devote the additional time required to serve the mentally retarded; there may not be sufficient services in a given community to provide the services required to meet the needs of the mentally retarded.

Community agencies have a responsibility to broaden their services and their staff capability to serve the mentally retarded and their families. The staff of an institution can help these agencies acquire the skills necessary to provide these services.

Community welfare and mental health centers should be helped to review their programs to determine how they can be changed appropriately to meet the needs of the mentally retarded and their families.

The institution should not undertake to develop community resources without first determining if the community agencies are willing to become involved and can assume a responsibility to do so.

It is essential that every effort be made to coordinate institutional programs with those community programs that can be used to meet the needs of the mentally retarded.

EXTENDING STAFF INFLUENCE INTO THE COMMUNITY

An institution that provides a variety of services for its residents usually has a number of well-qualified professional staff members. Only large metropolitan communities will have readily available such a diversity of qualified professional personnel. The knowledge and skills of these individuals should be shared with community agencies.

A program can be developed by the institution that allows selected staff members to assist community agencies in organizing their resources to provide appropriate services in the community to serve the mentally retarded individual and his family.

Making the staff available for work in communities requires that they be given sufficient time to carry out such activities. This requires careful scheduling; this is necessary in order not to reduce the staff effectiveness in carrying out their responsibilities to the residents. In some instances it may require the staff person to work far more efficiently than he previously had. In a few instances the staff may have to be retrained or be reoriented to working with community agencies.

Detailed planning must also be carried out with community leaders in order to develop and maintain effective working relationships.

SHARING USE OF INSTITUTIONAL FACILITIES

It costs a considerable amount of money to construct, maintain, and operate a facility to serve the mentally retarded. It is becoming increasingly difficult to obtain funds to serve an ever-increasing population of mentally retarded. Alternative methods must be found to meet the needs of the community adequately without significantly increasing the number of facilities.

An existing institution can make its staff and facilities available by a careful reorganization and rescheduling of their services and more efficient utilization of existing space.

INSTITUTIONAL SERVICES
THAT MAY BE EXTENDED INTO THE COMMUNITY

Institutions serving the mentally retarded have in recent years provided, through their staff, a variety of services directly to community agencies and to families having a mentally retarded child.

These services include:

1. diagnostic evaluation services,
2. home training services,
3. technical consultation services,
4. clinical services.

A brief description of these will illustrate the role of the institution.

Diagnostic and Evaluation Services

Diagnostic and evaluation services may be viewed in three different programs:

1. *Preliminary Evaluations* Preliminary evaluations permit the staff of the institution to travel into a community to examine selected individuals. This examination will determine 1) if the individuals require a more comprehensive clinical evaluation, 2) if they should be referred to a more appropriate diagnostic clinic, or 3) if the staff might recommend use of available community services.
2. *Clinical Evaluations* Clinical evaluations are conducted for both children and adults. The staff interprets its findings to the family and the referring community agency. It can also assist the referring agency in locating suitable community services.
3. *Pre-Vocational Evaluation* Pre-Vocational evaluation is provided for individuals over 18 years of age. In addition to the clinical evaluation, assessments are made through appropriate vocational and occupational testing procedures and on-the-job evaluations. The staff interprets its findings to the individual (when appropriate), to the family, and to the referring agency. Assistance is given in locating appropriate training, counseling, or employment for the individual in the community.

Home Training Service

Home training service is a relatively new service. The staff of the institution, working in close cooperation with a referring community agency, provides consultation to a family in the home. Assistance is given the family in 1) developing self-help skills, 2) managing behavior, 3) techniques for speech and language development, 4) information about leisure time activities, 5) sex education, and 6) how to use community resources. Assistance is also given to help community agencies to train their own staff to provide this type of service.

Technical Consultation

The institution staff can provide technical consultation to numerous community agencies that plan to serve the mentally retarded. These may include the generic health, education, and welfare agencies; day care services, mental health programs, public health agencies, public schools, rehabilitation agencies, etc.

Clinical Services

Several of the clinical services conducted by the institution may be reorganized to accommodate selected individuals from the community. Three of these programs will be briefly described.

Dental Services There is probably no aspect in the health care of the mentally retarded that has been more neglected than their dental care. New knowledge and new techniques are now available to ensure a quality dental care program for the mentally retarded. Adequate dental facilities should be provided and qualified personnel should be available.

The dental program of an institution can be reorganized to accommodate, on an outpatient basis, a significant number of individuals, thus facilitating their care at home.

This program should be carried out in close cooperation with the community dentist and the local Dental Society. Their cooperation will ensure the development of an effective community dental program.

Physical Restoration Programs Many mentally retarded individuals have physical defects that can be corrected or improved through a comprehensive physical restoration program. An institution having such a program will have appropriate facilities and the necessary professional and paraprofessional staff to conduct the programs.

A physical restoration program is aimed at improving the individual's level of mobility and self-help skills through the professional skills of a physical therapist, occupational therapist, and speech therapist. Severe orthopedic problems requiring corrective orthopedic procedures can be accomplished by an orthopedic surgeon and his supporting staff. Orthotic services are also available to ensure proper bracing and shoe adjustments. This specialized program must be carried out in close cooperation with the institution staff, who provide the necessary residential care, recreation, and educational services.

Genetic Counseling A number of residential institutions have established appropriate clinical programs required to support a genetic counseling service. This type of service enables the young family to consider the risk of having their next child born mentally retarded. It enables the siblings of the mentally retarded individual to determine the risk they may encounter in having a mentally retarded child.

Genetic counseling service is another service that can be appropriately and adequately extended to serve the community. It is one of the few services now available to an institution that can, in time, have a marked impact upon the reduction in the prevalence of mental retardation.

Short-Term or Respite Care

In recent years many institutions have developed a program that allows a mentally retarded individual to be admitted for a short period of time.

He is usually admitted for short-term care to the Institution when there is 1) a crisis situation in the family, or 2) the family and/or parents need a vacation, or 3) they need to be free of the burden of caring for the mentally retarded child.

A short-term care or respite program can be one way of delaying the admission of a child (or adult) for long-term care. It is a way to help the community to resolve many of its problems in providing long-term care for a retarded individual.

This type of service should not require additional staff. It can be accomplished by a reassignment of the activities and responsibilities of a few staff members.

Use of Community Resources by Residents

Many of the residents reach a point in their training and rehabilitation where they have exhausted the training resources of the institution, yet they are not completely ready for return to the community. Many could profit by additional training in a community program. The staff should seek out a variety of community resources that can be used to help the mentally retarded learn to adjust to community living.

Activities should be found that will enhance the individual's ability to participate in leisure time and recreational activities. Placements should be for on-the-job training in a variety of occupational settings within the community. When indicated, the educational and rehabilitation services of the community should be utilized for those who can profit from such organized programs.

Using community resources does, however, require considerable preparation of community personnel. Receptive employers must be assured that the mentally retarded individual is suitable for him to employ. He must be assured that the staff of the institution will be available to him to help train and supervise the individual. The community recreation people must be assured that their programs can be used by the mentally retarded. The special education teachers in the public schools need to be encouraged to accept these individuals. They, too, must be assured that the institutionalized mentally retarded individual does not present a threat or danger to others, that he can be easily managed, and that he has the potential for training.

If one is able to place the individual from the institution in a community program, opportunities will be available for staff to work more intensively with the more difficult institutional cases.

By doing this, one also develops the concept that the care, management, education, and rehabilitation of the mentally retarded is basically a community responsibility, and that the institution should only be used for those individuals who are not capable of, or have the potential for, community participation.

Satellite Community Residential Services

In recent years some programs serving the mentally retarded have been administratively reorganized to permit a "central" institution to operate several small residential facilities located in a community. These "satellite" institutions vary in size (from 8–12 to 3–50) depending upon the age of the individuals and their needs. In practice, children under 18 should be housed in small facilities while the adults can be cared for in a larger facility (30–50).

This type of program allows the "central" institution to develop highly specialized programs for the profoundly and severely mentally retarded, for those requiring extensive medical and nursing care, and for those requiring special behavioral management programs. It also allows an individual to be closer to his family and friends. It permits a freer movement of the individual between the variety of institutional services that he may require throughout his lifetime.

Satellite facilities should be made more homelike than can be obtained in the large, centralized institution.

While the small institution is desirable, it has its limitations. It may be difficult to locate a site to build such a facility because of "zoning" ordinances. It may also be difficult to use the limited community resources. It may be extremely difficult to find sufficient number of qualified staff to operate these facilities. The health of individuals may deteriorate because of the lack of adequate medical-nursing care. Small community institutions should, however, be encouraged, whether operated by a "central" institution or by a community agency or private corporation.

University Affiliations

Institutions that are able to establish and maintain effective and active relationships with institutions of higher education are very fortunate. Affiliation with such an institution is indicative of the high quality of the programs provided in the institution. University affiliations may be provided for in a number of areas.

Selected faculty members of a university should be invited to provide technical consultation to the staff of the institution, and to assist periodically in evaluating its programs. Members from the biomedical sciences and behavioral-social sciences should be encouraged to conduct research using institutional populations. This activity should be financially supported. This is another way to ensure quality programs within an institution.

There are many opportunities to provide field practicum experiences for students in training at a university. Some of these are: 1) social worker, 2) physician, 3) occupational therapist, 4) physical therapist, 5) professional nurse, 6) special education teacher, 7) speech therapist, 8) dentist, and 9) nutritionist.

These practicums usually require a survey and evaluation of the institutional programs by the sponsoring institution: 1) the quality of staff must be determined, 2) the availability of clinical material must be assured, and 3) the availability of staff to supervise these students and objective assessment of the student performance must also be available.

Field practicum programs are an excellent way for an institution to obtain qualified personnel, since many students will seek employment in the institution in which they had their field practicum. It will be evident to the professional community that the institution that is used for a field practicum by a university does have a well-qualified staff.

Provide Research Subjects and Cooperate in Conducting Research

Institutions serving the mentally retarded should organize themselves so that the residents can be made available to serve as research subjects and participants in demonstration programs.

"Research in mental retardation must conform to the scientific, legal and moral principles which justify all research and should emerge out of sound theoretical basis or follow previously accepted research design." ("Use of Human Subjects for Research." Policy statement of the American Association on Mental Deficiency, compiled by Planning Board, AAMD, May 13, 1969.)

An institution that has a research program of its own and cooperates in conducting research with qualified investigators and clinicians of universities will ensure itself of high visability in the academic and professional community.

Inservice Training and Staff Development

Selected faculty of a university can assist in developing and conducting inservice training and staff development programs.

Many of the nonprofessional staff members will receive their training in the care and management of the residents from the institutional staff. Inservice training staff are needed to carry out an effective program. The faculty of a university can assist the staff by:

1. providing the latest knowledge and information about mental retardation,
2. assisting in developing an appropriate training curriculum,
3. training the staff in effective teaching procedures and use of audio-visual aids, and
4. helping to evaluate the effectiveness of the program.

When necessary, additional personnel funds should be made available to enable the institution to provide for these services.

Institution Staff Assisting the University

Many institutions have well-qualified staff members who can assist a particular university program in its teaching of students. The staff has experience in dealing with the technical aspects of mental retardation. It has practical experience in the managing and treating of the mentally retarded. This is of considerable benefit to those faculty members who do not possess this knowledge and information or skill.

Where good institution programs exist, where there is a good working relationship with the university, qualified institutional staff will be invited to participate in the university teaching and research programs.

Many affiliation programs can be developed without encroaching upon the professional responsibilities of the institution staff. These activities should be compatible with their own duties and responsibilities within the institution.

The careful and thoughtful administrator encourages his staff to seek out these affiliations in order to raise the quality of the institutional programs and the effectiveness of his staff.

Social Action through the Legislative Process

Historically the professional staff of institutions have not been involved in or assumed the responsibility for effecting social change through legislative action. Additional staff and additional facilities can only be added through legislative action. Community and residential programs can only be expanded and improved by legislative action.

When appropriate, the staff must provide the legislative representative with the kind of information required to effect these changes. No longer can we negate our responsibility—we must, as responsible citizens, see to it that appropriate action is taken to bring about an improvement of services for the mentally retarded.

Changing Attitudes toward the Retarded

It has only been in recent years that the mentally retarded have been viewed by the general public as being in need of special services. In the past they have been poorly cared for, inadequately treated, and denied the dignity and respect due all members of a society.

In some societies, religious and social patterns and custom dictate how they should be cared for by that society. The social mores of the past (and present?) required families to keep the presence of a mentally retarded child a secret from relatives, neighbors, and friends. They were kept hidden in the home or secretly sent away to be cared for by a foster family, or placed in a private institution, or forgotten in a large public institution. Fortunately, these attitudes are slowly changing and being replaced with those that are not dehumanizing and that respect the dignity of the individual.

The staff of an institution—all of the staff—needs to be encouraged continuously to remind our colleagues of their professional responsibility toward handicapped members of our society, toward the disadvantaged, and particularly toward the mentally retarded.

The staff should recognize that they have an obligation to continuously remind the general public of the need to develop a more receptive attitude toward the mentally retarded. The staff has a responsibility to encourage their professional and nonprofessional colleagues to be more tolerant, more understanding, and willing to change.

BARRIERS TO EXTENDING SERVICES INTO THE COMMUNITY

Reluctance of Staff to Serve in the Community

It must be recognized that some individuals purposely seek employment in an institutional setting. Some individuals find the institutional environment very protecting and nonthreatening. Their duties and responsibilities are clearly defined; they are assured of a definite salary; they know exactly what they must do in order to advance in position; they know that it is more difficult to be discharged from employment in an institution than in a private employment program; they feel very secure in such a working environment. Thus, they may view participating in community activities as a threat to this security and may strongly oppose such action. Some, if they are directed to take on such responsibilities, will seek employment in a less threatening job situation.

The wise administrator will recognize this and carefully evaluate and orient each employee before moving him into the community. To do less is to invite trouble!

Shortage of Staff

To some degree an actual shortage of staff will prevent even the most enthusiastic administrator from using his staff to assist communities.

It would not be professionally or administratively sound to require an already overburdened staff to take on such time-consuming responsibilities. One must, unfortunately, wait until sufficient staff is available. Staff shortage should not be a crutch or an excuse to avoid moving in this direction.

Reluctance of Community to Accept the Staff

Unfortunately many institutions in the past have remained isolated from the community. Sometimes the community has not wanted to become involved in the activities of the institution; nor has the community encouraged the staff to become involved in community activities.

It becomes the responsibility of the institution staff to initiate a carefully planned program designed to improve relationships with community agencies and representatives. The alert staff will immediately recognize this responsibility and carefully plan to work with the appropriate community individuals. Through an effective program the community will benefit and the institution will have a better image in the community. *The real benefactor of such activities in the final analysis is the mentally retarded individual.*

Legal Authority to Work in the Community

It is not uncommon to find that some institutions do not have the legal authority to extend their services or activities into the community and that the staff is prohibited by law or administrative directive from practicing in the community or providing their services to individuals living in the community.

SUMMARY

The mentally retarded have progressed from total rejection by society, through imprisonment and grudging acceptance, through a century of devoted care by a handful of professionals and philanthropists, to emerge as a major health, education, and welfare problem today.

Today one sees increasing acceptance of the "rights" of the retarded person—the right of each to full realization of his potential, the right of affection and understanding from those charged with his care and guidance, the right to stimulation and guidance from a program of free education and training, and a recognition by society of the obligation of the retarded person, in return, to contribute to society to the fullest extent of his limited abilities.

The extension of an institution's services into the community and the reciprocal extension of the community into the institution is a significant step forward. Such activities will eventually result in improved services for the mentally retarded person and his family.

Above all, it will ensure future generations that society will provide a quality of life for its handicapped members equal to those available to all members of that society.

RESEARCH TO PRACTICE IN MENTAL RETARDATION
Care and Intervention, Volume I
Edited by Peter Mittler
Copyright 1977 I.A.S.S.M.D.

ASYLUM

D. A. Primrose
The Royal Scottish National Hospital, Larbert, Stirlingshire, Scotland

This paper is about the benefits of institutions that can arise, not from any of the many specific training programmes for individual members, but from the totality of the institution as a therapeutic community. When one speaks of an institution such as the armed forces there is a tendency to think of the people—soldiers, sailors, and airmen, and when one speaks of a school there is a tendency to think of the building, but of course most institutions comprise not only material facilities, but also the users—patients or clients, as well as the staff. More than these, there is in many institutions a continuum of a pattern of life that absorbs new entrants and tries to mould them into this pattern. This moulding is exercised not only by the staff but, albeit unconsciously, to a large extent by the existing members who have adopted the way of life as being acceptable to them—to that extent both staff and members are institution-alised—in the same way as the members of any club or organisation.

The institution where I work began in 1862 as the Training School for the Imbecile Youth of Scotland. A site was chosen beside the centre of communications for all Scotland—for Larbert, where it is, was then the main railway junction for East and West, North and South. Since then the motorcar has been invented and there are nearby motorways linking East and West, and North and South, for the Institution was never envisaged as an isolated backwater. The aim then was to train mentally defective children so that they could be returned to their parish as useful citizens—and many were. The period of residence was not normally expected to exceed five years, but there were some who could not return home, especially those with multiple handicap, and they continued to live as full a life as possible within the Institution. There was a continuous demand for the facilities and the numbers steadily increased until the original site, which had been planned for 200 children, was too small; in 1925 a nearby large estate was purchased to develop as a Colony, or Therapeutic Community for those adults who were not able to be discharged.

With the introduction of a training schools for idiots in the Bicêtre in Paris more than 140 years ago the model became medical and so in the U.K. with the introduction of the National Health Service in 1948 the large institutions were taken over as hospitals. From a small beginning with 30 children we now have about 1,240 patients, of whom 170, or 15%, are under the age of 17 years—and of these only three are less than 5 years old—this means that, like most of our institutions, which reflect the general population, the majority are adults.

Of the 1,240 patients there are some who were admitted as children many years ago, and who will remain here for the rest of their lives. In going consecutively through the case records I noted 32 patients who had in their files an IQ test form completed from 35 to 50 years ago. These forms were of the Binet-Simon test, mostly the Stanford-Revision, but some were Form L. The results obtained ranged from IQ 15 to 57. Clinically there was no specific medical diagnosis in the majority, but two had cerebral palsy, two were likely to have been caused by birth trauma, two had had postnatal brain infection, and one has an XXY chromosome constitution.

It should be realised that these patients are the residuum of those who came into the Institution, and were not able to leave again, and to that extent they represent the failures. Apart from any early schooling, they have, if possible, been occupied about the hospital and taken part in the usual social activities in their villas and the recreation halls. I thought it would be interesting to retest these patients. The first one tried was the XXY male, whose IQ on the Stanford Revision in 1926 when he was aged 14 years was 55. Forty-nine years later, using the Form L-M, I got a result of 57. The results of retesting 24 of these patients using the Stanford-Binet Form L-M are shown in Table 1, along with the original test scores and their ages at the time of testing. Because of their physical state it is not now possible to use this test on the other eight patients. The IQ results for adults have been those shown in the tables for chronological age 18 years.

These tests were performed after the patients had been admitted to hospital, and, except for a few of them, they show a surprising degree of stability over a period when they aged by 35 to 50 years. Indeed one would have expected a general reduction since the conversion from the mental age used here has been at the 18-year-old level, and that a reduction has not occurred is indeed remarkable.

Since 1948, when we were designated a hospital, our intake has been more selective. With the increasing provision in the community of special schools and training and occupation centres—for adults as well as for children—we seldom admit people who are suitable for these community facilities. Most mentally defective children and adults can remain at home and travel daily to their occupation like the other people in their neighbourhood, and for those with no suitable homes, small hostels are being provided. Now the hospital is expected to admit those who do not fit into this community pattern, and Table 2 is an analysis of long-stay admissions over a six-year period, showing the reasons for admission.

The first group are those with severe physical disability. These patients tend to be the severely mentally handicapped, and the request for admission is usually at an early age. The next, and largest group, is made up of those whose

Table 1. Results of IQ test scores—initial test and retest after 35 to 50 years in institution

A. Female

	First test (Form S-R or Form L*)		Second test (Form L-M)	
Year of birth	Age (years)	Result as IQ	Age (years)	Result as IQ
1931	7	35*	45	38
1931	10	38*	45	31
1929	11	44*	46	39
1919	11	42	56	41
1928	12	28*	48	30
1922	12	37	54	32
1920	14	31	56	<30
1914	16	32	62	31
1911	17	42	65	39
1906	22	27	70	32
1909	22	43*	65	33
1909	32	26*	66	<30
1909	32	56*	67	41

B. Male

	First test (Form S-R)		Second test (Form L-M)	
Year of birth	Age (years)	Result as IQ	Age (years)	Result as IQ
1924	9	44	52	42
1918	10	57	57	31
1921	12	47	54	50
1921	12	27	55	30
1920	13	39	55	43
1915	13	21	61	<30
1911	14	55	64	57
1913	15	49	63	44
1916	15	50	59	43
1914	17	46	62	42
1909	19	43	66	43

behaviour is such that the community cannot tolerate it. The third group that is shown are those in whom the precipitating factor is psychotic mental illness, mostly schizophrenia. They may also exhibit disordered behaviour. Those with behaviour disorders are more often physically normal, and less severely mentally handicapped, and they have usually had a lengthy trial of alternative community provisions before exclusion from their normal surroundings by admission to hospital is sought. In about one-third of those with behaviour disorder it is

Table 2. Analysis of long-stay admissions from 1st January, 1968, to 31st December, 1973

Reason for admission	N	Percent
Severe physical disability	136	22.4
Antisocial behaviour	361	59.5
Psychiatric disorder	58	9.6
Social	39	6.4
Inter-hospital transfer	11	1.8
Other	2	0.3
Total	607	100.0

mainly a frequent nuisance, and in the other two-thirds it would be criminal, if the patient were legally responsible for his actions—'his' because there are many more such men than women. The failure of these people to survive successfully in society is often a reflection of the demands that society imposes and of the lack of support that society gives them.

In 1952 the late Professor Ferguson of Glasgow showed that in city life most social breakdowns in adolescents were the result of several adverse factors, and that if in addition to mental deficiency there was poverty, or a broken home, then the mental defective was more likely to get into trouble. By moving such people into a more tolerant and stable environment such as the asylum provided by our institution one can expect an improvement in behaviour—but what of intelligence? If when a mental defective is admitted to an institution, or if after a period of time in the institution, there are changes in IQ test results, then these may be due to the effect of the Institution. For example, in 1953 Clarke and Clarke showed that the mean IQ of 59 hospitalised patients rose from 66.2 to 72.7 over a period of two years, an average increase of 6.5 points. In a series of 57 patients in our hospital, tested twice by the same member of our staff at different periods between 1968 and 1975, the mean IQ rose from 57.2 to 63.4, which is an average increase of 6.2 points, and is similar to the results obtained by Clarke and Clarke. The Clarkes went further and showed that the average increase of those who came from very bad homes was better than the rest. Within our group those who had been expelled from special schools because of their unacceptable behaviour improved not only in their behaviour but also in their IQ results, although with some the improvement was only back to the levels found before they got into trouble. For example, George D., whose IQ at age 14 years was 68, two years later at the time of his admission to hospital could only score 48. After two years in hospital the test results were up to 74. James B. is similar; he showed a drop from 74 to 59 at the time of admission, and then recovery after two years in hospital to 72. Thus, the mere change of environment from a bad one to one more suited to the requirements of the retarded person may result in higher IQ test scores.

The associated improvement in behaviour is exemplified by George S., who along with an IQ rise from 37 to 66 changed from being an aggressive, quarrelsome, difficult young man to a sensitive and likeable person. The change was not abrupt, such as might result from a response to medication in a psychotic person, but took place over a period of 15 years. In the hospital there is freedom within the large grounds, and asylum from an intolerant community whose patience is exhausted far sooner than that of our staff.

One advantage of a large institution is the ability to form peer groups for the patients, groups where they are no longer the least efficient member and where they are not ridiculed because of their inadequacy. There are many possible groupings—for occupation, for recreation, and in their residential quarters. If there is conflict within a group there is the possibility of movement to another group. Even within their peer groups some patients are quarrelsome but they may improve greatly when they are put in a group of much more handicapped patients, because then they realise their greater ability and by helping others they can be made to feel useful and responsible. Removing stresses allows patients to be more relaxed and happier.

I would like to mention a few other patients who showed particular improvement although they were not receiving any more training than the rest of the patients in their group, but before doing so it is only fair to point out that there are many patients who deteriorate while with us, and this applies particularly to those with progressive conditions. It may be that we prolong their life, but we do not stop the deterioration. For example, first there is Cathy, who is now 24 years old. Cathy has fucosidosis, and was still able to walk at the age of 12 years, but now is confined to a wheelchair, is doubly incontinent, and has to be fed. Also, there is Andrew, who was born in 1960. Andrew has gangliosidosis and is developing leg contractures and becoming progressively more paralysed. There is also deterioration in his mental state. Last, there is Stephen, who is aged five years; he has lipofuscinosis and, apart from being physically unable to do anything, is going blind and deaf.

To balance these three there is, first, Marlyn. Marlyn was born in 1952, and when a few months old she had meningitis and developed hydrocephalus. She was kept at home until she was 10 years old, and when admitted to hospital in 1963 she was doubly incontinent, could not feed herself, and frequently regurgitated. She could be lifted into a chair but could not sit up by herself or walk. When aged 17 years she was able to sit up, but because of frequent vomiting she was very thin. Two years later, although still fairly helpless, she was vomiting less and was putting on weight. After another four years, at the age of 23, she is able to walk with a little assistance.

Then there is Raymond, a Down's syndrome child who was born in 1959. When he was almost eight years old the doctor's letter asking us to admit him said "The boy is little more than a cabbage. He lies in blankets and is fed from a bottle." One year after admission he was able to sit up, but still would only feed from a baby's bottle. When he was 16 years old he was just learning to walk. Now he can sit at a table and is learning to feed himself.

Last, there is Andrew, who was born in 1960. He was 'a good baby' with the classical features of infantile autism, and when he was three years old a senior child psychiatrist wrote "there is little doubt that the clinical picture is that of infantile autism." He attended a clinic twice weekly for treatment but made little progress and, after two years of this, when he was five years old, we were asked to admit him. On admission his IQ was rated at 56 and he had just started to talk. Fourteen months after admission his mother said that he showed her some affection "for the first time ever." Two years after admission his IQ result was 73, and two years later it was 93. At that stage he was relating well and was discharged to his own home, to attend an ordinary school. He has continued to make good progress.

I should emphasise that, as with Marlyn and Raymond, Andrew had no particular individual therapy, but was treated in the same way as the rest of the children in his villa, and the progress of these three children is not easily explained in terms of any particular training or expertise. They were allowed to develop in a place where staff objectives are realistically modest, so that any little improvement, which might be regarded as insignificant by ordinary standards, is noticed and encouraged.

There is much talk of maximising the potential of the mental defective, and this is a good target, but very few of us operate at our maximum level, and if pushed too hard many of us would have a nervous breakdown. We live in a competitive society and those who cannot compete may make more progress when the tension is removed. If our institution can provide asylum in an alternative community whose ethos is social acceptability rather than financial gain, then we may bring happiness and a purpose in life to some who could not find it elsewhere.

REFERENCES

Clarke, A. D. B., and Clarke, A. M. (1953) How constant is the IQ? Lancet 2:877.

Ferguson, T. (1952) The Young Delinquent in his Social Setting. London: Oxford University Press, p. 86 et seq.

RESEARCH TO PRACTICE IN MENTAL RETARDATION
Care and Intervention, Volume I
Edited by Peter Mittler
Copyright 1977   I.A.S.S.M.D.

THE SOCIAL POLICY IMPLICATIONS OF A RESEARCH PROGRAM ON THE EFFECTS OF INSTITUTIONALIZATION ON RETARDED PERSONS

E. Zigler and D. Balla
Department of Psychology, Yale University, New Haven,
Connecticut 06520, United States

This chapter is about the impact of institutional experience on the behavior and development of retarded persons. Much less is known about the impact of institutions than would be expected, considering the importance of the issue. Reliable knowledge concerning the effects of institutions is important for several reasons. At a theoretical level, many investigations of the behavior of the retarded have involved comparisons of noninstitutionalized normal individuals and institutionalized retarded individuals. In this kind of study it is impossible to differentiate effects attributable to institutionalization from those that are attributable to mental retardation per se.

Second, increased knowledge about the effects of institutions would be extremely helpful to parents and professionals. The decision whether or not to institutionalize a retarded person is one of the most painful that parents can face. Many professionals hold strong views on this subject but they are often contradictory or too simplistic. If the effects of institutions were known, a great deal of conflict and pain on the part of the parents would be alleviated.

Perhaps of greatest importance, though, is that reliable knowledge concerning institutionalization effects would be extremely helpful in forming social policy in the field of mental retardation. We especially have in mind here the question of large central institutions versus community-based regional centers or group homes. For almost 15 years now, the predominant thrust of social policy in the mental retardation area has been a movement away from large central institutions to a community-based regionalization model in which the retarded are treated in the community in small residential settings. This social policy has evolved almost completely without an empirical base. If policy-makers cannot demonstrate that regional centers or group homes are cost-effective, it may well be that large central institutions will be rediscovered.

We have become convinced that any comprehensive understanding of the effects of institutionalization must require a consideration of three classes of variables. The first is the characteristics of the person. The effects of institutionalization have been found to be different as a function of such factors as the person's sex, his diagnosis, his developmental level, and his chronological age. Of particular importance is the preinstitutional life experience of the individual. We have found again and again that a retarded person's response to institutionalization is partially determined by the nature of his experiences before institutionalization.

The second important class of variables concerns the nature of the institution. Here we have found that it is crucial to go beyond the simple question of size. We must look at other demographic variables, such as cost, number of staff per resident, and employee turnover rate. We must go even further than this examination of multiple demographic variables and investigate the social-psychological characteristics of institutions, their administrative structure, employee attitudes, and the actual way in which the residents are cared for. We consider this class of variables to be especially important. The view that institutions with enlightened administrators, employees who have positive attitudes concerning the retarded, and with humane caregiving practices will promote more adequate adaptation and competence in the residents is certainly a plausible one. However, we feel that investigations concerned with the quality of life of the retarded are valuable in and of themselves. The retarded have a right to humane care and treatment whether or not such care ultimately results in greater behavioral growth—the final class of variables of importance is measuring the behavioral status and growth of retarded individuals, including both cognitive and motivational factors.

We consistently found that response to institutionalization was dependent on both the preinstitutional life experience of the individual and the characteristics of the particular institution in which he was placed. We became increasingly aware that institutions were not homogeneous entities but differ considerably in their social-psychological characteristics and in their impact upon their residents. It also became clear that the most adequate research design was a longitudinal one, with development of residents mapped over time.

Consequently, we decided to conduct a rather ambitious longitudinal cross-institutional study in collaboration with Earl Butterfield. We investigated four institutions in different parts of the country. In this study, we tried to take a much more fine-grained look at the nature of the institutions. We gathered data on size, number of residents per living unit, cost per resident per day, employee turnover rate, number of direct care personnel per resident, number of professional staff per resident, and number of volunteer hours per resident per year. We felt that an examination of these factors, in conjunction with our general impressions, would provide a reasonable framework from which to evaluate behavior change on the part of the residents. Indeed, the institutions varied in size from approximately 400 to approximately 2,000 residents. There was also considerable variation in cost, number of aides per resident, and employee turnover rate.

We examined residents in each of the institutions within six months of their admission date, and again after two and one-half years of institutional experience. In addition to the measure of responsiveness to social reinforcement that we had used in previous studies, we also obtained measures of mental age, IQ, verbal dependency, extent of imitation of adults, and variability in behavior. Contrary to our most pessimistic views concerning the effects of institutionalization, we found considerable evidence of psychological growth on the part of the residents. Over the course of two and one-half years in all of the institutions, the residents became less verbally dependent, less imitative, and more variable in their behavior. IQ level did not change and mental age level increased. To our surprise, very few of the findings were related to any characteristics of the institutions. Residents in the largest of the institutions were more responsive to social reinforcement than residents in the other three institutions. With this exception, none of the other demographic characteristics of the institutions was found to be related to the behavior or development of the residents. Our subjective impressions were equally inaccurate in relating to the behavior of the development of the residents. At this point, it seemed clear to us that an even more fine-grained measure of institutional characteristics was needed.

We were extremely fortunate in that King, Raynes, and Tizard, in England, had conducted extensive and sensitive cross-institutional studies of resident care practices in institutions for the retarded. These investigators developed a Resident Management Practices Inventory that we thought was an excellent measure of the social-psychological characteristics of the institutions. This inventory was conceptualized as tapping institution-oriented care practices at one extreme, versus resident-oriented practices at the other. Using this inventory, the English group investigated three types of facilities for the retarded: mental deficiency hospitals, ranging in size from 121 to 1,650 residents; voluntary homes, ranging in size from 50 to 93 residents; and local authority hostels, ranging in size from 12 to 41 residents.

The care practices were found to be more resident- as opposed to institution-oriented in the group homes and more institution-oriented in the mental deficiency hospitals. The voluntary homes fell between the hospitals and group homes. Of particular interest was the finding that, once type of institution was taken into account, there was no tendency for management practices to be associated with institution size. In other words, type of institution, rather than size of institution, was the important determinant of care practices. The importance of this point is underscored when you recall that the mental deficiency hospitals ranged in size from approximately 100 residents to approximately 1,600 residents, yet no differences in care practices were found within this type of institution. When type of institution was taken into account, no association was found between the number of residents in each living unit and the care practices observed. Neither was a relationship found between resident-to-staff ratios and care practices. Finally, the English group found that the level of retardation of residents in the individual living units was not an overriding determinant of care practices.

We felt that the investigations of the English group were important for several reasons. First, they studied different types of institutions at a time when far too little attention had been paid to the relative adequacy of central institutions, regional centers, and group homes. Second, they were directly concerned with the quality of life of the institutionalized retarded, a matter which has been grossly neglected in empirical research. Finally, these investigators underscored the importance of the living unit as a unit of analysis.

We decided that just such a study was needed for institutions in the United States. We were also quite fortunate in having the opportunity to study institutions in a Scandinavian country world-renowned for its humane care of the retarded. In collaboration with Mark McCormick, we studied the resident care practices in 166 living units from 19 institutions in the United States and 11 institutions in the Scandinavian country. We also examined a number of institutional demographic variables: institution type, i.e., large central regional center and group home; institution size; average number of residents per living unit; cost per resident per day; number of aides per resident; number of professional staff per resident; annual employee turnover rate; volunteer hours per resident per year; and mean institutional IQ. We also obtained additional information for each living unit studied: the level of retardation in each unit, i.e., mild, moderate, or severe-profound, and the age level of the residents in each unit, that is, child, adolescent, or adult.

We found that living units in the Scandinavian country were more resident-oriented than living units in the United States. In both countries, large central institutions were characterized by the most institution-oriented care practices and group homes by the most resident-oriented care practices, with regional centers falling between these extremes. This finding was consistent with that of the English group. Living units for more severely retarded residents were found to be more institution-oriented. We then went on to see if we could determine which of the demographic variables were most closely associated with care practices. Large living unit size and level of retardation were found to be predictive of institution-oriented care practices. Cost per resident per day, number of aides per resident, or number of professional staff per resident, *did not* predict care practices.

The lack of association of either financial (as measured by cost per resident per day) or human (as measured by number of aides and professional staff per resident) factors came as a considerable surprise to us. Apparently, simply increasing expenditures or personnel will not necessarily guarantee better care for the retarded. Rather, it is how these personnel are utilized in the settings in which they are found. The finding that living unit size was predictive of care practices is of special practical interest here. One way of creating more humane settings for the institutionalized retarded may well be to design living units small enough that each resident is, of necessity, seen as an individual. It is encouraging to note that it may be possible to pursue such a policy with existing resources. You will recall that the most resident-oriented care practices were found in group homes. The group homes were operated at less cost than either the regional centers or the large central institutions.

We did find one exception to the general lack of association of such "human variables" as number of aides per resident and aide turnover rate and care practices. In group homes in the United States, low aide turnover rate and a high ratio of professional staff per resident was found to be predictive of more resident-oriented care practices. It may well be that such human factors as continuity of staffing can only become operative in certain settings.

The results of this study, as well as the findings of the English investigators, convinced us that we had a sensitive method of characterizing the social-psychological milieu of residential settings for the retarded. What was lacking in both our work and in the work of the English group was a study in which both care practices and the actual behavior of the residents were investigated. In collaboration with Nancy Kossan, such a study was conducted. We examined a total of 114 retarded persons in 20 living units in seven institutions. Five of the facilities were regional centers and two were large central institutions. In each living unit, the Resident Management Practices Inventory of the English group was administered to the charge aide. We also obtained a measure of attitudes concerning the retarded from each aide in each living unit. We looked into such institutional demographic variables as cost per resident per day, aide turnover rate, and number of aides per resident. The association of preinstitutional life experience, chronological age, mental age, IQ, sex, and length of institutionalization with behavior was also examined. On the behavioral side, we obtained indices of responsiveness to social reinforcement or dependency, wariness of adults, and imitation. Our previous work has suggested that these three factors are particularly important in retarded individuals' daily competence.

We found no differences between persons residing in central institutions and persons residing in regional centers on any of our behavioral measures. These lack of findings were of some surprise in view of the fact that the average size of the large central institutions was 1,633, while the average size of the regional centers was 111. The central institutions also housed more residents per living unit and had a higher aide turnover rate. The cost per resident per day was twice as high in the regional centers as in the central institutions. The number of aides per resident was twice as high in the regional centers as it was in the central institutions. The proportion of professional staff per resident and the number of volunteer hours per resident per year was almost six times as great in the regional centers as in the central institutions. Such findings lend credence to the view that simply increasing cost and/or increasing staff will not, in and of itself, ensure greater behavioral competency on the part of residents in institutions. The findings also suggest that more intensive efforts need to be made to discover what particular experiences or programs enhance the behavioral competency of residents in institutions. The mere placement of a retarded person in a regional center did not seem to suffice as a means for increasing competency.

With one exception, no behavioral differences were found between persons residing in the two central institutions and persons in the five regional centers. There were also no behavioral differences between persons residing in the largest regional center, with a population of 290, and persons in the smallest regional center, with a population of 12. It seems most reasonable to conclude that the behavior of the residents in all of the institutions was similar.

We found that several of the characteristics of the institutions were associated with the behavior of the residents. The larger the size of the institution, the greater the motivation of the individuals to receive adult attention and support. In large institutions, individuals appear to be relatively deprived of this class of social reinforcer. It should be noted that this finding was the single instance in which institution size was predictive of the resident's behavior. To this point, we had been assuming that deprived socializing experiences lead retarded individuals to be excessively dependent upon adults when the adults are reinforcing their behavior by making supportive comments. However, there is a body of work in the tradition of Spitz and Bowlby that suggests that extreme forms of deprivation can result in apathy, withdrawal, and a lack of response to supportive adults. It seems that in order to develop attachments to adults and thus become responsive to their attention and support, the child must have some minimal number of positive encounters with them. Children extremely deprived of such encounters would be expected to show greatly attenuated responsivity to adult attention and support. On the other hand, if children experience some minimum of support and attention at the hands of adults within a general socializing history of deprivation, we would expect these children to show atypically high responsivity to attention and support. We found some support for this formulation in this study. Large professional staffs and active volunteer programs were found to be associated with higher responsiveness to social reinforcement.

We found considerable evidence that deprived socializing conditions produce wariness of adults. The larger the number of individuals in a living unit, the greater the wariness of the individuals who lived in the unit. Increased wariness was found in settings with high employee turnover rates and a high proportion of aides to residents. Thus, it would seem that the response to a large number of noncontinuous adult caregivers, and therefore nonpredictable adult caregiving, is the development of wariness. We also found that adverse attitudes concerning the retarded on the part of the aides was related to greater wariness on the part of the residents.

We found some evidence suggesting that some institutions socialize their residents in the direction of reduced behavioral spontaneity and/or conformity. We found high levels of imitation in individuals institutionalized a relatively long period of time and in individuals who were the recipients of institution-oriented, as opposed to resident-oriented, care practices. Thus, many of the institutionalized retarded appear to live in a highly predictable environment that emphasizes conformity. Such conformity may be a form of adjustment to the institution. The value of living in a well-organized and predictable environment can be seen in a finding that less wariness was displayed by residents receiving institution-oriented as opposed to resident-oriented caregiving practices. However, such conformity was probably purchased at too high a psychological cost. The conforming and imitative child distrusts spontaneous solutions to problems and may be ill-equipped to function in the much less organized and predictable environment outside the institution.

We have come to view either too little or too much imitation as negative psychological indicators, with some intermediate level of imitation being viewed as a positive developmental phenomenon reflecting both a person's healthy attachment to adults and a responsivity to cues that adults emit that can be used in problem-solving efforts. Consistent with this view was our finding that retarded individuals whose caregivers had negative attitudes toward them were less imitative. Persons consistently reacted to in a negative manner may respond by ignoring the cues provided by adults and thus become less imitative.

In addition to these effects of the institutions upon behavior, we found several characteristics of the persons to be predictive of their behavior. Consistent with earlier findings, residents of high mental age were found to be less motivated toward social attention and support than were residents of low mental age. Thus, retarded children, like their peers of average IQ, seemed to move from dependency to autonomy as their cognitive level became higher. Evidence was also found indicating that the higher the mental age level, the greater the wariness. This finding would appear to be consistent with the body of work that indicates that the higher the developmental level of the child, the greater his sensitivity to depriving events and his capacity to construct self-defeating mechanisms such as wariness and avoidance of adults. Consistent with earlier findings, mental age was found to be negatively related to imitation. This finding was in keeping with two facets of our outerdirectedness formulation. The higher the cognitive level of the child, the less the child employs imitation in his problem-solving efforts; the lower the IQ of the child, the more failure experiences the child has when employing his own cognitive resources and, thus, the greater his tendency for imitativeness.

Finally, we found that individuals who had experienced frequent changes of parenting figures before they were institutionalized were both more motivated to attain the attention and support of an adult and more wary of doing so. These findings provided additional evidence for the view that deprived retarded individuals have both atypically high positive and negative reaction tendencies. The subjects in this study had been institutionalized for an average of over eight years, and the fact that the effects of preinstitutional life experience were still in evidence after so long a time is consistent with our general position that social deprivation experienced relatively early in life can affect the behavior of the retarded when it is assessed many years later.

We are continuing our work on the effects of institutional living on the behavior and development of the retarded, paying especially close attention to the social policy implications of the work. We are also continuing investigations concerning the quality of life of the institutionalized retarded. We are conducting a five-year longitudinal study of the development of residents in central institutions, regional centers, and group homes. We are also conducting a study of discharge rates and success in community placement of residents in central institutions and group homes. We hope that the final result of this research program will be a determination of the optimal residential setting at the optimal cost.

RESEARCH TO PRACTICE IN MENTAL RETARDATION
Care and Intervention, Volume I
Edited by Peter Mittler
Copyright 1977 I.A.S.S.M.D.

VARIABLES RELATED TO OBTAINING NATURAL PARENTS' CONSENT FOR FAMILY CARE PLACEMENT

M. Sternlicht and J. Merritt
*Willowbrook Development Center, 2760 Victory Blvd.,
Staten Island, New York 10314, United States*

There are a variety of variables that relate to obtaining consent from natural parents in order to place their retarded child on community status, e.g., in family (foster) care. The most common and influential factor is the traditional cultural belief that family life is the most desirable milieu for the child. Foster care parents are perceived by natural parents as alternative "good parents" who are in competition for their child, more so than are the professional staff of an institution. The natural parents' perceptions of themselves as "bad" parents, unable to continue to provide care for their child, are magnified. Parental anxiety may be increased by fears that their children may change and turn against them, or that retribution in some way may follow this abdication of the parent role. The media may further intensify feelings of inadequacy, via coverage of foster parents compared to natural parents.

Lack of optimal placement and resources, and research findings about adverse development of placed children, additionally affect parental judgments. Further, questions are currently being raised about the societally supported view of the best milieu for child development.

VARIABLES RELATED TO PARENTAL CONSENT IN FOSTER CARE PLACEMENT DECISIONS

Little has been written on those characteristics that relate specifically to obtaining consent from natural parents to place their retarded child in foster care placement. However, a review of the literature reveals that variables related to the decisions by natural parents to institutionalize a child are the same or similar to those related to foster care placement.

FACTORS IN INSTITUTIONALIZATION

Hersh (1970) found that the five major variables that influenced the parental decision to institutionalize their children were: 1) the high regard they had for the school staff as experts and authorities; 2) the presence of a retarded child in the home was viewed as a disruption of some aspects of family life; 3) in instances where programs could not be worked out for the child at home, the child represented a threat to family solidarity; 4) whether or not parents have had experiences with residential schools; and 5) parents had become physically and emotionally weary.

Sternlicht (1967), in his study of the institutionalization of the retarded, discovered that young and elementary school-age children constituted the bulk of new admissions, and that the amount of care required for this age group often was too great for the parents to assume.

Saenger (1960) concluded that the significant factors in the institutionalization of a child were: 1) the greater the degree of mental retardation, the greater the probability of the child being institutionalized; 2) persons with secondary physical handicaps were institutionalized slightly more than others; 3) the majority of persons institutionalized come from low income families; and 4) among the severely retarded from middle-class families, the adjustment problems of the child in the home were a major factor in commitment to an institution.

Downey (1962) investigated the willingness of parents to institutionalize their retarded child and the effects of this decision upon them. His findings were that parents of high socioeconomic status institutionalized their child early and then afterwards forget about him, whereas parents of low socioeconomic status tried to delay placing their child. However, once the child is placed, this latter group continue contact with him.

Perhaps foster care placement is most likely to be considered by the parents after the child has been institutionalized if the parents are characterized as follows:

1. if parents have high regard for the institution;
2. if parents have had no previous experience with institutions except the one in which they are now involved;
3. if parents have become emotionally and physically exhausted from caring for their retarded child; and
4. if parents are in a middle or high socioeconomic class.

FACTORS IN THE GEOGRAPHICAL LOCATION OF THE INSTITUTION

A well-planned and well-staffed institution can meet immediate and long-range needs. However, as long as society removes the retarded as far as possible from the community these purposes are defeated. Institutions many miles removed from the community cannot aid their populations with integration in the community.

The institution that is within reach of towns and cities, medical facilities, public education, and the families of the mentally retarded will be able to: 1) offer well-rounded, effective services; 2) keep the retarded in touch with community and family ties; and 3) allow for exchange of services. Adequate social services are a must for any well-planned institution and may be more available if they can be shared with other agencies close by.

Parents are more likely to consent to foster care placement for their retarded child if they have been able to avail themselves of the casework services of the institution, especially where the institution is accessible.

FAMILY FACTORS

There is an accumulation of information that discloses that the presence of a handicapped child in the home creates many hardships for the nonhandicapped family members. For instance, Roe (1952) found problems in adaptation among families with a cerebral palsied child. In their Australian sample, Schonell and Watts (1965) uncovered many family upsets in families with a child with an IQ under 55. In London, Tizard and Grad (1961) found that 70% of retarded children below school age and an additional 25% of retarded children between ages 6 through 15 motivate severe management problems in the family.

Variations in parental regard for their children as deviant also affect interactions among family members. Elements in the definition of the child's deviancy include the etiology ascribed by parents, socioeconomic status, sex of parent and child, and religion. Korkes (1956) found that parents who accept personal responsibility for their child's illness also more often perceive the child as a human being with understandable behaviors, and that these parents tend to include the child in their future family plans. Thus, the definition of the child in terms of his being human might encourage parents to place their child in foster care, providing that the child can benefit from that foster care.

Another perspective on the relationship between the parental role and the definition of the child as deviant is in terms of kinds of crises related to socioeconomic status. Crises represent various ways in which parents perceive familial disruption. Farber (1960a, 1960b) presented two kinds of crises: the tragic crisis, and the role-organization crisis. The tragic crisis relates to families of relatively high socioeconomic status, who emphasize future aims and aspirations of their members. The child's handicap is thus regarded by these parents as an uncontrollable event that prevents fulfillment of their hopes and aspirations. In the family of high socioeconomic status, the parents' perception of the child's ability to fit into future family plans is a variable related to obtaining parental consent to place the child in foster care.

In role-organization crisis, the predicament facing the parents is one of coping with what appears to be an interminable care problem. The family is unable to organize a system of workable roles in order to control activities of individual members. According to a study by Kohn (1959), role-organization crises are pronounced in working class families, which would thus encourage taking the child out of the home.

The sex role of the parent and the child is another variable influencing the family's decision in relation to institutionalization, which can also be regarded as influencing foster care placement. In his study of 80 families with severely mentally retarded children in the San Francisco area, Tallman (1961) found that the mother's ability to cope with the child was associated with factors that were inherent in the parent-child relationship, while the father's ability to cope with the child was related to the child's sex and diagnostic classification. If the retarded child is male and if he lives with an "intact" family, then chances for institutionalization are narrowed, because the father of the child has a higher coping capacity for problems related to a mentally retarded male child than that required for a mentally retarded female child.

Farber, Jenné, and Toigo (1960) found that the initial impact of the diagnosis of severe mental retardation also may be somewhat sex linked. Mothers indicated a slightly greater impact if the retarded child was a female, and the father a markedly greater impact (regardless of socioeconomic status) if the retarded child was a male. A suggestion of the Farber, Jenné, and Toigo study is that if the child's family is a one-parent matriarchial one, a facilitating variable in securing consent from parents to place the child in foster care would be if the retarded child were male.

Institutionalization of the child also is influenced by the religious and moral principles of the parents. Zuk (1959) found that Catholic mothers were more accepting of institutionalization than non-Catholic mothers, and that mothers of younger retarded children institutionalized their children more readily than mothers of older retarded children, a finding also corroborated by Sternlicht (1966). Ray's study (1951) suggested that Catholic parents were helped in their denial of responsibility for the child's handicap. Ray indicated that the majority of the Catholic mothers felt that God had given them a handicapped child as a "cross to bear." Saenger (1960) found that Jewish parents were more overprotective and less likely to institutionalize their retarded child.

FACTORS IN CASEWORK WITH PARENTS

Parents have been considered of secondary importance as foster care services developed. They have been viewed as necessary evils obstructing care for the child and with varying degrees of resentment and distaste by child welfare workers and the community. A caseworker needs a keen, deliberate diagnostic understanding of what he is dealing with in terms of parents, especially knowledge about what parents can do for their children with the caseworkers' help. A facilitating variable for parental consent to place the child in foster care is a clear, concise collection of data on family integration and parent and child relationships, which enables a social worker to influence positively the parental decision-making process.

Goldstein's study (1970) of six parents tested on a "parenting scale" found that at the point of intake the scale determined the inadequacy or adequacy of the parental role. The study relates a worker's ability to obtain a continuum of consistent and vital points, particularly with regard to the dynamic gaps in parents' and children's functioning. Used on a continuum, the parenting scale would lead to a more appropriate decision-making process about parental consent to place a child in foster care. The scale eliminates a social worker's solitary decision about separation, which is often colored by many attitudes within the individual practitioner.

Kraus (1971) is consistent with Goldstein in that he found that social workers tend to select foster homes on the basis of their middle-class values and subjective judgments, rather than on the basis of a sound empirical approach. Because of this lack of empiricism, placements may break down and foster additional strain on foster care placement agencies, discouraging parents and foster parents from further involvement in foster care.

Therefore, a conclusion can be drawn that a continuum collection of data that encompasses essential factors in parenting is a facilitating variable in obtaining consent from parents for foster care placement of their child. Absence of empirical data, then, becomes a hindrance in securing parental consent.

CONCLUSIONS

Foster care has not been developed to any great extent in the United States because, among many other reasons, it is not easy to secure suitable family homes for the mentally retarded or to secure parental consent for such placements. Parents often are reluctant to accept foster care programs because of negative personal feelings and beliefs, as well as other factors. However, as placements increase parents might become more amenable. In summary, the following variables may be used as a guide to aid practitioners in securing parental consent to place their retarded children in foster care:

Facilitating Variables	Hindering Variables
—if the parents have high regard for the institution	—if the parents believe the negative propaganda, re: foster care
—if the parents' view of the retarded child is disruptive to family life	—if the child comes from a low income family

—if the child has a great degree of
mental retardation

—if the child comes from a middle
income family

—if the institution offers social
work applications to the family of
the retarded

—if the institution is located near
the community and local mass transit
system

—if the retarded child is a severe
management problem

—if parents perceive of the child as
not being able to fit into family plans

—if the child is viewed as an interminable care problem

—if the family of the retarded is one-
parent, matriarchial, and the sex of
the child is male

—if parents have low marital integration

—if the retarded child is the oldest or
the first-born child

—if there is adequate empirical data collection.

—if there is an absence of
social work applications
in the institution

—if the institution is removed
from the community and local
mass transit systems

—if the parents accept personal
blame for the child's handicap

—if the family of the retarded
child is intact, and if the
sex of the child is a boy

—if the retarded child is a
male, and is cared for by
the father

—if the parents are of the
Jewish religion

—if the retarded child is the
youngest and/or has older
siblings

—if there is an absence of
empirical data collection.

SUMMARY

This study highlights the various variables related to obtaining parental consent for foster care placement decisions, including: (a) factors in institutionalization per se; (b) factors in the geographical location of the institution; (c) family factors; and (d) factors in casework with parents. Developed conclusions are offered.

REFERENCES

Downey, K. (1962) Parental interest in the institutionalized mentally retarded child. Unpublished dissertation, University of Illinois.

Farber, B. (1960a) Family organization and crisis: Maintenance of integration in families with a severely mentally retarded child. Monogr. Soc. Res. Child Dev. Serial No. 75.

Farber, B. (1960b) Perception of crisis and related variables in the impact of a retarded child on the mother. J. Health Hum. Behav. 1:108.

Farber, B., Jenné, W. C., and Toigo, R. (1960) Family crisis and decision to institutionalize the retarded child. National Education Association Research Monograph Series No. 1.

Goldstein, H. (1970) A parenting scale and separation decisions. Child Welfare 16:271.

Hersh, A. (1970) Changes in family functioning following placement of a retarded child. Social Work 15:93.

Kohn, M. (1959) Social class and parental values. Amer. J. Sociol. 64:337.

Korkes, L. (1956) A study of the impact of mentally ill children upon their families. Trenton, New Jersey: Department of Institutions and Agencies (mimeo).

Kraus, J. (1971) Predicting success of foster placements. Social Work 16:63.

Ray, I. (1951) A study to develop a guide for the education of parents of cerebral-palsied children. Unpublished thesis, University of Iowa.

Roe, H. (1952) The psychological effects of having a cerebral palsied child in the family. Unpublished dissertation, Columbia University.

Saenger, G. (1960) Factors Influencing the Institutionalization of Mentally Retarded Individuals in New York City. Albany, N.Y.: State Interdepartmental Health Resources Board.

Schonell, F. J., and Watts, B. H. (1965) A first study of the effects of a subnormal child on the family unit. Amer. J. Ment. Defic. 70:210.

Sternlicht, M. (1966) A study of some religious factors, as they relate to the institutionalization of retardates. Psychology 3:2.

Sternlicht, M. (1967) The who, when and why of institutionalization of retardates. Psychology 4:6.

Tallman, I. (1961) A study of the effects of community and institutional school classes for trainable mentally retarded children. Washington, D.C.: U.S. Office of Education (mimeo).

Tizard, J., and Grad J. C. (1961) The Mentally Handicapped and their Families. New York: Oxford University Press.

Zuk, G. H. (1959) The religious factor and the role of guilt in parental acceptance of the retarded child. Amer. J. Ment. Defic. 64:139.

RESEARCH TO PRACTICE IN MENTAL RETARDATION
Care and Intervention, Volume I
Edited by Peter Mittler
Copyright 1977 I.A.S.S.M.D.

THE ROLE OF NURSING IN SERVICES FOR THE MENTALLY RETARDED

N. J. W. Hill
Department of Health & Social Security, Alexander Fleming House, Elephant & Castle, London, SE1 6BY, England

HISTORY

In order to understand the present practice of nursing in the services for the mentally retarded in England it is necessary to look at the historical background.

Prior to the 1913 Mental Deficiency Acts the care of the mentally retarded was regarded as part of overall mental nursing and not as a separate entity. With the massive development between 1845–1860 of local authority asylums providing residential places for both the mentally ill and mentally retarded, enlightened psychiatrists realised the need for well-trained attendants or nurses for the mentally disordered; and, with the increase in the number of both asylums and patients, this need became urgent. In 1885 a Committee of the Medical-Psychological Association (later the Royal Medico-Psychological Association—now the Royal College of Psychiatrists) printed a handbook, a manual of instruction for nursing and attendance on the insane, and five years later a two-year course of training, with central examinations and a certificate of proficiency was established. By 1899 over 100 asylums were participating in the scheme and 500–600 certificates were granted each year.

During the 1914–1918 war, following the development of local authority colonies for the mentally retarded, still the only residential accommodation for the mentally retarded, a special training programme and certificate for those experienced only in nursing mental retardates was established by the Royal Medico-Psychological Association. This historic period can be regarded as a creditable attempt as far as mental retardation nursing was concerned: the syllabus and the training were geared to the needs of those caring for the mentally retarded. In 1919 the first Nurses Registration Act received the Royal Assent. This Act set up the General Nursing Council and laid on it the duty of forming a Register of Nurses with five parts, of which part (c) was to be "a supplementary part containing the names of nurses trained in nursing and care of persons suffering from mental disease." However, it was agreed to go beyond the terms of the Act and include in this part of the Register for Mental Nurses a part for nurses trained in the care of mental retardates.

From 1925–1950 the General Nursing Council training and examinations and the Royal Medico-Psychological Association training and examinations continued side by side. The General Nursing Council refused to accept the Royal Medico-Psychological Association certificates after a short initial period of grace; the Royal Medico-Psychological Association refused to leave the field to the General Nursing Council. The Royal Medico-Psychological Association believed the General Nursing Council syllabus was inappropriate and the theoretical examination standard too rigorous; the General Nursing Council saw the nursing profession as an individual whole and were determined that the same standards should apply to nurse training schemes irrespective of specialty. Perhaps because of this conflict, recruitment to hospitals for the mentally retarded began to fall in the 1930s and early 1940s.

With the formation of the National Health Service in 1948, a new Nurses Act altering the constitution of the Council and widening its powers was passed. Under the new act a statutory Mental Nurses Committee was formed, with members both directly elected and appointed, as well as members of Council. It was agreed that no further candidates for the Royal Medico-Psychological Association (RMPA) examinations would be accepted after 1951. Existing holders of the RMPA certificates would be allowed to register with the General Nursing Council.

The first task of the new Mental Nurses Committee was to develop a syllabus more suited to those working in hospitals for the mentally retarded. The 1955/6 annual report of the General Nursing Council stated "General Nursing Council . . . has accepted the criticism . . . that the present training does not fit the mental nurse for the work she is subsequently required to carry out and the curriculum is unrealistic and biased in the wrong direction . . . it has been agreed that any attempt to relate (mental and mental retardation) training too closely to that for admission to the general part of the Register must be avoided."

In 1958 a new syllabus of training of the nurse for the mentally retarded was published with three broad fields of study:

1. a systematic study of the human individual (which began with a section on 'human development and human behaviour within the family and society')
2. the various skills required in dealing with mentally retarded individuals and in nursing bodily disorders associated with, or occurring in, the mentally retarded
3. concepts of mental retardation and the training and treatment of the mentally retarded including legal and administrative aspects.

During the period between 1951 and 1956, the number of student nurses training in hospitals providing residential accommodation for the mentally retarded dropped each year. In 1956 the trend reversed slowly, passed the 1951 mark in 1959, and has continued to rise steadily. The 'wastage' rate among those in training was high, and over half those in training left without completing the three-year course until well into the 1960s. Since 1966, the national minimum educational standard of entry for training has applied to student nurses wishing to train in the field of mental retardation. The result was an increase in those coming into training and for the first time there was an improvement in the 'wastage' rate amongst students.

In 1970 a new syllabus for student nurse training for the mental retardation part of the register was published and became compulsory for all those entering training after 1st September, 1972. This gave far more emphasis to community care, which became the fourth broad area of study. Compulsory practical experience during training included twelve weeks' experience in a school to observe teaching methods, and periods spent in occupational and/or industrial therapy departments as well as residential care experience. Wherever possible, student nurses spent 4-12 weeks in the community in mental health, education, and childrens' departments. Throughout the three-year training programme the student nurses' experience and progress is monitored by means of a "Record of Practical Instruction and Experience" in the practical situation by means of lectures, discussions, and written work in the Nurse Training School, and by written examination and assessments set by the General Nursing Council. The student nurse who successfully completes the three-year training course is registered by the General Nursing Council on the part of the register for nurses of the mentally retarded.

The object of nurse training in the field of mental retardation is well summarised by the General Nursing Council notes on the syllabus of training:

> In compiling this syllabus of training for student nurses in hospitals for the mentally retarded the Council has had in mind the need to provide a training which will give a comprehensive insight into, and an understanding of, the problems of the mentally retarded and to prepare the student for the duties which a nurse is called upon to perform in the care of the mentally retarded. Medical progress, social-economic advancement and greater integration of hospital and community services will engender changes in the patterns of care of the handicapped members of society. The syllabus seeks to ensure that the nurse is fully conversant with all aspects of the care, education and training of the mentally retarded both in hospital and the community. It is set out in broad terms to permit interpretation and adaptation necessary to meet changing needs.

In 1955 the Ministry of Health prepared a syllabus for training of nursing assistants in the field of mental retardation. This syllabus was successfully used by a number of hospitals for the mentally retarded in helping to train those who did not wish or were unable to take student nurse training.

In 1964 legislation was passed establishing pupil nurse training in the field of mental retardation. This training takes two years and is more practically based than the training for registration. Successful completion of the course admits the pupil nurse for admission to the Roll of Nurses. The General Nursing Council maintains the Roll and supervises national training. A syllabus for pupil nurse training was drawn up and published, and provision to allow experienced nursing assistants to enroll by virtue of experience was made (similar to the admission of those holding the RMPA certificate to the register in 1951). The object of this syllabus is to provide a realistic approach to the care and needs of patients who are mentally retarded and provide Enrolled Nurses who will take their place in the nursing team.

Recruitment continued to improve steadily until 1970, at which point the improvement became dramatic. Between 1971 and 1975, 5,430 students and 3,730 pupils entered training, an increase of nearly 200% over the previous five years. Wastage from mental retardation student training is now below 40%, and from pupil training it is 31%. The final examination pass rate for students is now 70%, and for pupils it is 90%. There are currently 21,084 nursing staff working in hospitals (55,000 residents) for the mentally retarded, of whom 5,261 are registered, 3,955 enrolled—a total of 9,216 trained. There are 2,329 students and 1,140 pupils in training, with 8,399 nursing assistants making up total nursing staff available.

There is a very real awareness at the present time of the need for better supportive services for the mentally retarded person and his family in the community. Support and encouragement of the family in caring for a handicapped child or adult can be undertaken by the hospital-based nurses, along with members of other professions. Mentally retarded people and their families need help from a wide variety of statutory and voluntary service agencies, and from the community at large. There is no doubt that all these agencies, though separately provided, should aim to deliver a service that is seen by the mentally retarded and their families as a unified one. The Government has recently given guidance on joint planning and joint financing which we believe will make a major contribution to a more co-ordinated and more effective service. During the last decade the nurses trained in the specialty of mental retardation have extended their rôle into the community. The nurse, as a member of a multidisciplinary team, can work effectively in order to give nursing care and therapeutic or rehabilitative support to the mentally retarded in the community taking fully into account his family and all relevant social contacts. The nurse can advise the family on the best approach in dealing with the problems presented by its handicapped member. These problems embrace the whole range of behaviour patterns including aggression, destructiveness, overactivity, withdrawal and isolation, faulty habits; in short the kind of problem which the nurse is daily confronted with in hospital, yet which taxes the resources of the most dedicated family. To meet the training needs of nurses selected to work in the community, the Joint Board of Clinical Nursing Studies has published an Outline Curriculum in "Community Psychiatric Nursing for Registered Nurses" (No.

800). The course is for registered nurses of the mentally subnormal and registered mental nurses and the period of training is 36-39 weeks exclusive of
holidays.

PRESENT-DAY SITUATION

The application of behaviour modification techniques to the mentally retarded
has shown substantial development over the last decade. One of the most
significant aspects of this development has been the demonstration that these
techniques can be taught to nurses, teachers, and parents of the mentally
retarded and used effectively by them in changing behaviour. The concept of the
nurse as a trainer or therapist for the mentally retarded is not a new one, and has
developed directly as a result of behaviour modification work. For some time
there has been an increasing emphasis on the inclusion of teaching in nurse
training programmes. The Joint Board of Clinical Nursing Studies has published
an Outline Curriculum in "Behaviour Modification in Mental Handicap" to help
registered nurses working in the field of mental handicap (No. 700). The aim of
these courses is "to develop general therapeutic skills in order to modify the
behaviour of the mentally handicapped to a socially acceptable level, and to
coordinate the activities of other nurses and personnel in the therapeutic team."
The period of training is 24 weeks, exclusive of any holidays. Nurses who have
successfully completed this course are now practising their skills in a number of
hospitals in England, designing programmes tailored to meet the individual needs
of their patients, and training other staff in the techniques involved.

The mentally retarded living at home rely on other components of the
nursing services for support in addition to the hospital-based nurse. The health
visitor is seen to have a key role, particularly in her concern with the family as a
whole. The health visitor's role is unique compared with the other disciplines, in
that other disciplines are sent for and visit at times of crisis, but the health
visitor will see the child in his own home as a routine. The early detection of
mental retardation is of utmost importance if the needs of a handicapped child
are to be met effectively. The "Guide to Syllabus of Training" for health visitors
states:

> Methods of diagnostic screening for specific conditions have increased, and
> as the health visitor is involved in the early detection of ill health, the
> student must learn that her main contribution lies in encouraging the public
> to take advantage of such schemes as are available, in allaying anxiety and in
> ensuring that any abnormality is followed up. (1970)

The work of the health visitor continues to expand and she now frequently
works within the setting of general medical practice, which, in addition to her
work with mothers and young children, provides further opportunities for
contact with vulnerable groups in the community and extends the scope of her
health teaching activities. Arrangements for liaison with hospital staff are also

increasingly opening the way for the health visitor to contribute more often to the after-care of hospital patients and to have the support of hospital-based staff when necessary.

It is possible by specific preventive measures to reduce the incidence of severe mental retardation. Vaccination against rubella, genetic counselling, family planning, skilled midwifery, and special care of the newborn are practical ways of achieving this end. In all these areas of prevention nurses have a key role to play. Paediatric nurses and nursery trained nurses have skills that should not be ignored by those providing services for the mentally retarded.

There is a growing awareness of the need for nursing to be a research-based profession. A research perspective is developing in clinical practice, teaching, and nursing management, and every nurse is affected by and involved in these changes. Only a few nurses will become full-time 'researchers,' but all will inevitably have an increasing part to play in relation to the research process. In consequence, nurses will need to have an understanding of research that may be going on around them. We should not make the mistake of giving research a 'mystique,' keeping it at a distance, or assuming it is too complicated to understand. Every nurse can learn some of the skills required and so make a positive contribution to the development of a research-based profession: how much a nurse will need to know will, of course, depend upon her own interests and responsibilities.

There are several research appreciation courses available that are designed to introduce nurses to research concepts and recent research reports. There are now about 15 research interest groups for nurses throughout Great Britain. These groups have developed to enable nurses who are actively involved in, or interested in, research to meet to discuss specific projects and problems, or just to learn more about research projects. Some nurses are needed to undertake research; this usually means that they should have a first degree. The Department of Health and Social Security awards a number of research fellowships by open competition each year, thus enabling a few suitably qualified nurses to carry out a research project. Nurses in the field of mental retardation have been attached to research units that have assisted in "Research to Practice." About one such research unit it has been said:

> It is one of the most important features of this Unit that the personnel work directly with the nurses and patients and are not producing designs, as many do, remote from the clinical environment. We educate engineers and designers by giving them close day to day contact, which, if real advances in caring for the multiply handicapped are to be made, is another reason why the Unit must develop.

The long-term aims of services for the mentally retarded in England are those proposed in the white paper "Better Services for the Mentally Handicapped," presented to Parliament in June, 1971, by the Secretary of State for Social Services. These aims can be summarised as:

... the provision of a satisfactory environment either at home or in residential accommodation; avoiding unnecessary segregation; developing ability through education and training, and support for families.

Full implementation of the white paper targets was envisaged as taking place over a twenty-year period. There are estimated to be about 110,000 severely mentally retarded people in England and more than 350,000 with mild retardation. In 1974, nearly 60,000 were in residential care, 9,000 in local authority homes, 50,000 in hospitals, and over 10,000 in lodgings, foster homes, etc.

Full achievement of the white paper proposals would mean a fall in the number of available hospital residential places from 60,000 in 1969 to about 30,000 in 1990, with a corresponding rise in residential accommodation management by local authorities. Any saving in hospital expenditure resulting from the reduced number of beds will be outweighed by an increase of perhaps more than 50% in expenditure per place over this period. This would reflect both an improvement in the quality of care and the greater dependency of those requiring hospital care as the more self-sufficient come increasingly to be cared for in the community. By 1985, for example, the national ratio of nurses to in-patients would be expected to fall to 1:1.6 from its present level of 1:2.4. Future hospital units are to be planned to provide a local service fully integrated with other services and serving a single district, in other words a population not exceeding 250,000. With the recommended ratio of 68 beds per 100,000 total population, future hospital residential places required in each district would not be more than 200 beds, and many of these beds would be in small units sited within the community.

Difficulties in achieving these and other goals described in "Better Services for the Mentally Handicapped" (London, H.M.S.O.) still remain, however, and will require additional resources. "The nurses, many working in overcrowded and understaffed hospital wards, are giving devoted personal service to their patients. We look to them with confidence to improve the quality of their patients daily life when the means of doing so are put into their hands."

SUMMARY

This chapter traces the development in England of a nursing service for the mentally retarded. Nurse training programmes are discussed, along with current trends and service roles. The nurse's role in the practice of research is explored.

REFERENCES

Anonymous (1976) Understanding research. An occasional paper. Nursing Times 72 (22):77.
Council for the Education and Training of Health Visitors (1970) Guide to Syllabus of Training. London: CETHV.
Department of Health and Social Security and Welsh Office (1971) Better Services for the Mentally Handicapped (Cmnd 4683). London: HMSO.

Department of Health and Social Security and Welsh Office (1974) The Facilities and Services of Mental Illness and Mental Handicap Hospitals in England and Wales 1972. Statistical and Research Report Series, No. 8. London: HMSO.

Department of Health and Social Security and Welsh Office (1976) The Facilities and Services of Mental Illness and Mental Handicap Hospitals in England and Wales 1973. Statistical and Research Report Series, No. 11. London: HMSO.

Department of Health and Social Security (1976) Priorities for Health and Personal Social Services in England: A Consultative Document. London: HMSO.

General Nursing Council for England and Wales (1964) Guide to the Syllabus of Training (Psychiatric) for Admission to the Roll of Nurses. London: General Nursing Council for England and Wales.

General Nursing Council for England and Wales (1970) Syllabus of Subjects for Examination for the Certificate of the Nursing of the Mentally Subnormal. London: General Nursing Council for England and Wales.

General Nursing Council for England and Wales (1976) Nurses Caring for the Mentally Handicapped. London: General Nursing Council for England and Wales.

Joint Board of Clinical Nursing Studies (1973) Outline Syllabus in Behaviour Modification in Mental Handicap for Registered Nurses, Course No. 700. London: JBCNS.

Joint Board of Clinical Nursing Studies (1974) Outline Curriculum in Community Psychiatric Nursing for Registered Nurses, Course No. 800. London: JBCNS.

Kiernan, C. (1973) Behaviour modification and the nurse. Nursing Times 69 (38):149.

RESEARCH TO PRACTICE IN MENTAL RETARDATION
Care and Intervention, Volume I
Edited by Peter Mittler
Copyright 1977 I.A.S.S.M.D.

A TRACKING SYSTEM FOR RESIDENTS' RECORDS TO MEET JCAH STANDARDS AND ICF-MR REGULATIONS

A. C. Repp
Unit A, Georgia Retardation Center, Atlanta, Georgia 30341, United States

There are many state and facility-specific regulations governing the operation of institutions for the mentally retarded that vary widely in their content and requirements. There are, however, two documents whose guidelines are consistently accepted throughout the United States. These are: 1) the regulations of the Department of Health, Education, and Welfare, commonly called the ICF-MR Regulations (45 CFR 249.13—Standards for Intermediate Care Facility Services in Institutions for the Mentally Retarded or Persons with Related Conditions; Department of Health, Education, and Welfare); and 2) the standards of the Joint Commission on Accreditation of Hospitals, alternately called either the JCAH or the AC/FMR Standards. (AC/FMR is derived from Accreditation Council for Facilities for the Mentally Retarded, JCAH from Joint Commission on Accreditation of Hospitals.)

While there are many sections to both these guidelines, much of the information is related to documentation of services provided directly or indirectly to residents of the facility. At first, documentation sufficient for both the Standards and the Regulations may appear to be inordinately complex. However, initial analysis of the contents of each indicates that there is considerable similarity between the two. Further analysis indicates that the content can be arranged in such a manner that a resident's continuing record can be tracked to determine whether or not the facility is in compliance with the Regulations and Standards. The following is a description of such an analysis that has resulted in an operable system for a unit at the Georgia Retardation Center.

In order to produce a tracking system, a matrix of event X time X responsibility can be determined that will allow a records manager to determine whether a resident's record is in compliance with the requirements of the Standards and the Regulations. Events associated with residents' records and described in these two texts can be grouped into eleven categories: 1) preadmission evaluation, 2) admission, 3) 30-day update, 4) management plan, 5) annual review, 6) resident living, 7) record keeping of the facility, 8) residents' records, 9) discharge summary, 10) transfer to another facility, and 11) discipline services, a category which is further divided into 13 discipline subcategories. These sections can then be abstracted with references to the Standards and Regulations to reduce the possibility of misinterpretation. An example of a portion of the tracking system, with sample abstractions and references, is presented in Figure 1.

Entries can then be further classified along a responsibility and a time dimension to provide a category X responsibility X time matrix. The three responsibility factors selected in the present analysis are: 1) medical (that to be entered by a medical doctor) or nonmedical (that to be entered by a nurse, psychologist, educator, etc.), 2) in residential unit's records (information to be recorded in the resident's record) or in residential unit but not in the resident's record (information or events that the administrator should ensure; e.g., Regulation bi iii and Standard 2.1.2.1 require that program plans for each resident be available to direct-care staff), and 3) the discipline responsible for making entries (e.g., social services). The first two responsibility factors can be entered into columns on the tracking system to begin the formation of a matrix while the third can be entered in rows under the eleventh category, discipline services, of the two documents. At the appropriate time-responsibility-requirement intersect, "Xs" can be entered to denote to the records manager what is due when. Requirements of when entries are to be made in the records are either time-based or event-based. Examples of event-based entries are *on admission* and *on occurrence,* with the latter being events that do not occur at stated intervals but rather occur as a result of a preceding event. For example, Standard 2.4.6 and Regulation b3 iii require that "orders prescribing bed rest or prohibiting residents from being taken out-of-doors shall be reviewed by a physician at least every three days," an entry into the resident's record that is made by a medical doctor not on a regular interval (e.g., monthly) but within a period after the occurrence of an event (the event being the implementation of the doctor's order).

Events that are time-based are those that, given the admission date, should occur at prestated times. These include: 1) one month after admission, 2) monthly, 3) quarterly, 4) semi-annually, and 5) annually. While not all sections of either the Regulations or the Standards define exactly when an event should occur (e.g., "frequently scheduled" is an often used phrase), events can be reasonably categorized into one of the five above time periods. When the entry into the record becomes due, the manager of the tracking system denotes the date on which the entry occurred and checks this against the date on which the event was due. For example, if a resident was discharged on 10/14/75, a discharge date would be entered on 10/14/75 and the manager would determine

Figure 1 — excerpt from the tracking system for residents' records.

Column headings (across top of chart):

DATE

- MEDICAL
- NON-MEDICAL
- ADMISSION — 6/1/75
- ONE MONTH AFTER ADMISSION — 7/1/75
- MONTHLY — 8/1/76
- 9/1/75
- 10/1/75
- 11/1/75
- 12/1/75
- 1/1/76
- 2/1/76
- 3/1/76
- 4/1/76
- 5/1/76
- 6/1/76
- 7/1/76
- QUARTERLY
- SEMI-ANNUALLY
- ANNUALLY — 6/1/76
- ON OCCURRENCE
- CONTINUOUS
- DISCHARGE
- RESPONSIBILITY
- IN UNITS NON RECORDS
- IN UNITS RECORDS

ICF-MR	(Page)	JCAH	MANAGEMENT PLAN
C3 ii	(024)	3.1.3.1	(1) individual programming based on reliable and valid evaluations
c3 ii	(024)	3.1.3.1	(2) activities designed to meet the individually designed objectives which are written in behavioral terms
c3 iii	(024)		(3) training plan available to staff
c3 iv	(025)	2.1.1.2.1	(4) programs supervised by QMRP
c3 v	(025)		(5) priorities for meeting the resident's training needs shall be stated in his program plan
		2.1.1.2.2	(6) each training program shall specify the behavioral objectives of the training, the methods to be used, the training schedule, the person(s) responsible for conducting the training, and the data that are to be collected in order to assess progress toward the objectives
		2.1.2.1.2.1.	(7) a monthly review and appraisal of the resident's progress toward achieving the objectives
		3.1.2.1.	(8) the management plan shall be provided and reviewed by an interdisciplinary team constituted of persons from disciplines relevant in each particular case, of persons who work most directly with the resident, and of the direct-care person responsible for the resident's program group
		2.1.3.1	(9) determine resident's responsibilities in the living units in order to develop skills of independent living
		2.1.3.2.5	(10) training, when possible, for self mobility for the multiply handicapped and nonambulatory residents
		2.1.8	(11) provision for prompt implementation of appropriate and effective programs to eliminate maladaptive behaviors defined as problems
		2.1.8.7.3	(12) specification of the reason for mechanical supports, the situations in which it is to be applied, and the length of time for which it is to be applied

Figure 1. An excerpt from the tracking system for residents' records. The section, described here in part, is the management plan, and indicates when entries in the record are due, given that the resident was admitted June 1, 1975.

whether or not the Discharge Summary was written and entered into the resident's record within seven days of discharge [Standard 4.2.4.2 and Regulation a2 viii (with the latter omitting the requirement of entry within seven days)].

A similar analysis can be applied to all sections of the tracking system such that a records manager can determine whether a facility is meeting the requirements of the JCAH Standards and the ICF-MR Requirements for the records of the facility's residents, and, if not, exactly where the deficiency lies. This information should allow an institution to minimize deficiences and to be prepared for inspections both by representatives of HEW and the JCAH.

SUMMARY

A system for monitoring the records of institutionalized residents, designed to meet JCAH Standards and ICF-MR Regulations, is explained. The texts of both these documents have been grouped into eleven categories, abstracted, and referenced to both the Standards and the Regulations. A matrix was then formed for each category by determining the date by which entries into the records are to be made and who is responsible for making the entry. These entries intersect in the matrix to form a tracking system whereby a records manager can determine whether or not the facility is in compliance with the resident-record portion of both these documents.

RESEARCH TO PRACTICE IN MENTAL RETARDATION
Care and Intervention, Volume I
Edited by Peter Mittler
Copyright 1977 I.A.S.S.M.D.

PATHWAYS TOWARD INDEPENDENCE FOR INSTITUTIONALIZED, MODERATELY RETARDED ADULTS

J. J. Parnicky
*Nisonger Center, Ohio State University, Columbus,
Ohio 43210, United States*

Just a few years ago Stanfield (1973) conducted a survey of 120 graduates of California public school programs for trainable (moderately retarded) students. When parents, or guardians, of these 19 to 21 year olds were asked what they wished their children were able to do that they could not do, the majority said they wished them to grow up, to be able to live on their own. The majority also believed that this is what their sons and daughters wanted: to be able to grow up and live as adults, to be *independent.*

Stanfield's findings about the degree of independence achieved after years of special education are not very promising, even if one makes allowances for the fact that the study data were compiled early in the post-school careers of his sample. With regard to employment, nearly half had no work history since graduation. Forty per cent were occupied in sheltered workshops, with weekly earnings generally under $10.00. But five individuals either had jobs in competitive employment, or in family business. The largest pay envelope contained $300 per month. Ninety percent were still living in their families' homes. Of the others, only one had set up an apartment of his own, four were in board and care homes; and two had been institutionalized. In the light of these results, Stanfield concludes, "the majority of the moderately retarded will always be

The Adult Training Project (ATP), to which reference is made in this article, was made possible by the joint planning and/or support of: Association for the Developmentally Disabled; Columbus State Institute; Franklin County Mental Health and Retardation Board; Franklin County Program for the Mentally Retarded: Ohio Department of Social Welfare; Ohio Division of Mental Retardation and Developmental Disabilities; Ohio Rehabilitation Services Commission; Ohio State University; and the United States Department of Health, Education and Welfare.

dependent upon some one to help them meet their human needs." (1973, p. 552)

These observations were, of course, based on young men and women who were living in the community. What about moderately retarded adults who reside in institutions, the population of concern to us in this chapter? Is the urge to grow up, to move into the community, to be independent present in individuals who have been confined on institutional grounds for years? What level of independent function can such individuals achieve in the community after spending a major part of their lives within institutions?

Aspects of these questions have been explored and the findings demonstrate that moderately retarded individuals do have the ability to function within communities after periods of institutionalization. The findings, however, also pose some serious issues (Windle et al., 1961). For example, Edgerton (1967), examining the quality of life led by persons discharged from Pacific State Hospital, reported that all too frequently they were leading impoverished, unsatisfying lives. It would appear that for some moving into the community has meant exchanging *back wards* for *back neighborhoods.*

Deinstitutionalization is by no means a simple task. Nor have we mastered accomplishing it satisfactorily. In approaching the problem from the perspective of a practitioner interested in enabling retarded individuals, I concur with the thesis presented by Gardner (1971), namely:

> ... that at least a significant degree of limitations of the retarded may well reside in an inappropriate or limited learning environment rather than being, as has been assumed too frequently, an unalterable manifestation of the individual's retardation. (p. 22)

I want to share with you an effort that was conducted at Ohio State University to provide institutional residents a more appropriate, an expanded learning environment—or to open new pathways toward community living, toward more independence. This was a cooperative endeavor involving the Nisonger Center, a university affiliated facility for developmental disabilities, and Columbus State Institute, along with a consortium of community agencies. The Adult Training Project, or ATP (Parnicky and Shea, 1972), was conducted over a three-year period, ending in 1975. During its operation, a total of 57 moderately retarded males between 18 and 30 years old were randomly selected from the institutional population. (Although the original proposal included both sexes, funding restrictions necessitated delimiting the sample.) Their degree of retardation was determined by intelligence and adaptive behavior measures (Grossman, 1973). In addition, the residents sampled had to be ambulatory and physically capable of work. Each person meeting these criteria had to give informed consent to entering a program designed to prepare individuals for community placement, with the understanding that, if enrolled, he could withdraw and return to the institution should he change his mind about moving into the community. The mean age of those sampled was 24 years; and the average number of years spent in institutions was 14—more than half their lifetimes. In the light of these facts, it is interesting that 96% gave their consent. They wanted to become more independent, to be out on their own in the community! However, there is no doubt that, despite careful explanations, some of the men had very limited or distorted ideas about what living off institutional grounds entailed. Residents giving consent were randomly assigned to the training and the contrast groups. Trainees (40) were enrolled in an intensive daily habilitation program in the center, as is described in the subsequent text; controls (15) continued to be programmed at the institution. Let me cite a second set of observations: Of the 40 who were enrolled in the training program, and therefore more adequately informed, only two asserted their right to return voluntarily to the institution. For those of us involved in the project, these results suggested that the desire for independence remains fairly high even after years of institutional conditioning.

Meeting the issue of what levels of independence institutional residents can achieve and maintain in a community, a training model was designed that incorporated several features. The curriculum was divided into three interrelated sequences: vocational skills, daily living skills, and social skills (Parnicky and Agin, 1975). Within each of these sequences several premises were consciously applied. The first was that classifying persons as moderately retarded does not eliminate individual differences in personality, interests, and capabilities. Secondly, such classification should not deny retarded persons the right to develop idiosyncratically.

For programatic purposes, the curriculum was divided into four levels: sheltered; semi-sheltered; semi-independent; and independent (Figure 1). The vocational skills training was primarily devoted to instilling motivation and appropriate attitudes for work and shaping critical behaviors for placements ranging from activities centers to competitive employment. The sessions in the daily living sequence prepared trainees to cope with living in the community in various settings, ranging from foster homes to one's own apartment. The social skills curriculum and training assisted the trainees in acquiring a positive adult self-concept through role playing, participation in group discussions, and engaging in social-recreational activities incrementally arranged. Individual counselling was provided on an as-needed basis.

Moreover, training was designed so that progress in one skill area did not necessarily determine progress in the other dimensions, and so that no trainee would have to relearn what he could already do. Each person should be able to progress at his own rate to the next programmed skill without having to wait for his peers, or they for him, and placements should not be exclusively for those who achieve full independent status across the entire set of sequences. Thus, when trainees entered the program their functional levels were observed and recorded for baseline purposes (Figure 2). Each was then programmed according to his demonstrated skills. For example, one trainee started in Level II in daily

TRAINING LEVELS

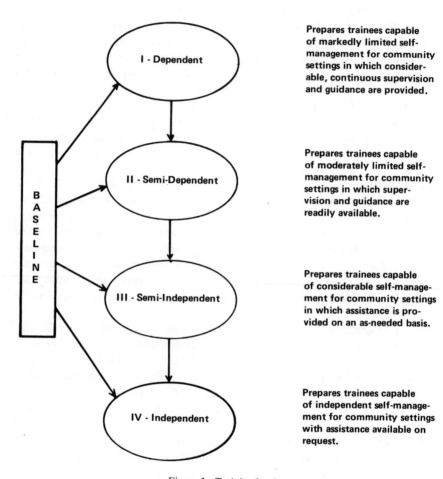

Figure 1. Training levels.

living skills, in Level I in social adjustment, and in Level III vocational training. Eleven months later he had plateaued at Level III in daily living and social adjustment skills, and at Level IV in vocational skills. Consistent with this profile, he was helped to find a room/board living arrangement and a competitive job.

One of the major problems in helping retarded individuals mature is counteracting the effects that the label of retardation has on them. Once applied, this label too often means that they are perceived and treated as children no matter what their age. What is even more damnable is that they then think of them-

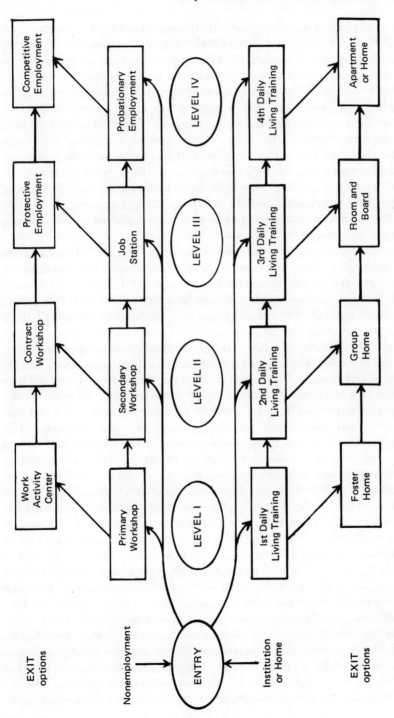

Figure 2. ATP training continuum and exit options.

selves as children. Transactional or PAC (Parent-Adult-Child) concepts, as developed by Berne (1964) and Harris (1967), suggest strategies for analyzing the individual life scripts of trainees. Measures can then be implemented so that the adult component is more strongly nurtured, and the role of the parent and child ego states readjusted. Transactional concepts provided guidelines not only for interacting with trainees but also for reviewing policies and procedures. The PAC formulations are unique in that they are so conceived and defined that the basic ideas are comprehendable by many retarded persons, even those moderately retarded. In fact, not only were the trainees attuned to the child, the parent, and the adult in themselves, but they also began to see those ego states in the staff and others with whom they interacted. Some became embarrassingly adept in applying PAC—embarrassing, that is, for the staff! When we imposed rules that made the trainees feel like children, there were trainees who were free—or should we say mature—enough to let us know.

Operant techniques for modifying behaviors (Skinner, 1953) have received much attention in recent years, and their utility in developing competencies of retarded persons is well demonstrated (Gardner, 1971; Lent and Childress, 1968). This was another training pathway incorporated into ATP. One goal of the project was to bring the behaviors of trainees under control of those reinforcers encountered in the community environment—as differentiated from the institution. For adults, reinforcers in large measure fall into two categories: social and monetary. While social approval/disapproval contingencies are familiar to institutional residents, all too frequently these have reinforced their childlike behaviors and highlighted their failures. On the other hand, for many institutionalized adults money is not a powerful reinforcer because of the fact that their needs have been mainly provided "in kind," and their experience with money had been restricted to occasional canteen purchases with coins. For such trainees conditioning procedures were applied to establish money as a reinforcer and work as a major means of obtaining money. The strategy used was one of multi-incentives tailored to the individual. All trainees were placed on the payroll from the first day of training, but only for participating in the vocational skill sequence. The wages, paid on weekly basis, were incrementally set, starting with a small hourly amount in Level I and reaching minimum wage rate in probationary job training (Level IV). In addition, a token economy was used in the first two levels. This was used for shaping specific target behaviors, with points being awarded promptly upon emission, and opportunity to exchange points for money and to make purchases scheduled several times a day. The time intervals were gradually increased as a trainee fulfilled incremental criteria.

Another concept applied in plotting the trainee's pathways toward independence was to teach skills wherever possible *in the environments* in which such would naturally occur. In the daily living sequence, trainees were provided opportunities for shopping in stores, riding in public buses, and using laundromats. In the vocational skills, training job stations and probationary employment were used as primary sites—off institutional grounds—for acquiring competencies for competitive employment in Levels III and IV. Trainees were likewise introduced to a range of recreational services within the community, to health and welfare agencies, and to educational and counseling services. Teaching in the natural settings has at least two advantages: it reduces the need for generalization training, as required when skills are taught in contrived settings, and it fosters the process of normalization by providing exposures to situations encountered in the real world.

Since the duration of ATP training was set at one year, two other guiding principles were applied. First, training would concentrate on those *skills critical to survival* in the community at each level, from dependent to independent. Second, when institutionalized trainees failed to achieve such, they were taught to use prosthetic techniques whenever possible to help them make it in the outside world. For example, a trainee who could not remember numbers or addresses was taught to carry identification cards in his wallet and trained in how and when to use them. The cards were color-coded so he knew which indicated his residence, which his clinic, and which his job. Digital timepieces were useful to some who found a conventional clock face confounding. One trainee, incapable of budgeting dependably, was helped to negotiate a bank account that would pay regular bills on a scheduled basis. Others were placed with landladies who were willing to assist with such matters. For a few, "buddy" placements were arranged, e.g., matching a trainee adept at keeping an apartment livable with a roommate who could handle money, but who was not interested in housework.

Given this network of training options, what were the results? Of the 55 institutionalized men who consented to being involved in the project, 40 were enrolled and 15 were designated as a control group, continuing to receive the institution's program. Looking first at residential placements in the community, the differences between the two groups are striking (Table 1). Of the trainees, less than one-third resided in the institution as of the end of the project. Two of the twelve were, as stated earlier, individuals who decided on their own to go

Table 1. Community residential placements

Levels	Trainees ($N = 40$)		Controls ($N = 15$)	
	f	%	f	%
Independent (apartment)	7	18%	0	0%
Semi-independent (room/board)	4	10%	1	7%
Semi-independent (group residence)	15	38%	1	7%
Dependent (foster care)	2	5%	2	13%
Institution	12	30%	11	73%

back, even though they were making progress within the training sequences. By contrast, more than twice as many controls (73%) were still in the institution on the same date. Whereas nearly one-fifth of the trainees had met criteria and moved into their own apartments, none of the controls was comparably placed. The rates of placement in a room/board arrangement were virtually equal (trainees, 10%; controls, 7%), but the proportion of trainees (38%) in group residences were five times greater than of controls (7%). Only at the dependent level, i.e., foster care, was the percent of controls (13%) higher than that of trainees (5%).

The data on community vocational placements were comparable (Table 2). None of the controls was employed in competitive or protective jobs, as compared with three-tenths of the ATP graduates holding such positions (competitive, 25%; protective, 5%). The largest proportion of trainees (32%) progressed sufficiently to be placed in sheltered workshops, with a modest number (8%) requiring placement in activities centers. Of the four controls in the community, one was in a training program and another in a workshop. The remaining two were unemployed, spending the entire day within their family homes.

Considering the vocational and residential placement data together, the project findings affirm that if learning opportunities and supportive services focused on community placement are made available to moderately retarded adults, even with histories of prolonged institutionalization, a substantial proportion—approximately one in four within the population sampled—can move into independent and semi-independent living and working settings. Without such assistance, the chances of institutional adults classified as moderately retarded moving into the community and functioning at similar levels of independence are much, much slimmer. Although comparisons with the data from California (Stanfield, 1973) noted at the beginning of this presentation can only be

Table 2. Community vocational placements

Levels	Trainees (N = 40)		Controls (N = 15)	
	f	%	f	%
Independent (competitive job)	10	25%	0	0%
Semi-independent (protective job)	2	5%	0	0%
Semi-dependent (workshop)	13	32%	1	7%
Dependent (activity center)	3	8%	0	0%
Training	0	0%	1	7%
Unemployed	0	0%	2	13%
Institution	12	30%	11	73%

Table 3. Follow-up status of trainees placed in the community ($N = 21$)

Levels	Residential		Vocational	
	f	%	f	%
Independent	8	38%	7	33%
Semi-independent	3	14%	2	10%
Semi-dependent	7	33%	8	38%
Dependent	3	14%	0	0%
Training			1	5%
Unemployed			1	5%
Institution			0	0%

tentatively made, the ATP results are somewhat more optimistic about the potential of the moderately retarded for achieving grown-up functioning.

Rather than trying to speculate about what may account for the similarities and differences in findings, let me address another question for which we do have project data. The question is: Are the trainee's achievements demonstrated on graduation sustained? To help get some measure of how well ATP graduates could maintain their levels of achievement, a follow-up of the 28 men who were placed in various communities in Ohio was undertaken. We were able to get data on 21 of them, or three-fourths of those who were placed. We made a rather extensive exploration, via a questionnaire, of the trainee's own impressions of how things were going for him, as well as of the impressions of one community person (e.g., case manager, group residence supervisor) who was acquainted with the trainee's adjustment. In no instance did any of the trainees indicate a desire to be reinstitutionalized, even those who were having some difficulty in making ends meet, or in finding a job, or in getting along with a roommate or a girl friend. Nor did any of the community resource persons contacted (with the trainee's assent, of course) believe that a single trainee should be returned to an institution. The individual status data regarding residential and vocational levels showed that in the interval since graduation—a minimum of one year and a maximum of just over two years—a few showed some slippage and others made gains. As a whole, the group (Table 3) was substantially maintaining the achievements demonstrated upon completion of training.

Besides the statistical evidence, there were many day-to-day interactions with the trainees that further substantiated that they can traverse new pathways of deinstitutionalization and move toward independence—providing the pathways are made available to them and assistance is available along the way. They also affirmed that the significance of their efforts may not lie just in the distance they actually cover or the speed with which they travel. Rather it can be more in the feeling of personal fulfillment they gain from the journey and the realization that they can have input into determining the direction in which they are going. For some, "moving into a foster home and spending workdays in an activities center may be as monumental accomplishments as living in an apartment and earning full maintenance" (Parnicky and Agin, 1975, p. 2) are for others. It is imperative that deinstitutionalization programs provide pathways toward independence that suit and stimulate moderately retarded adults across the continuum from dependence to independence, and provide community placement options across the spectrum of competencies that attain.

SUMMARY

This chapter is a report of progress made by 40 adult, moderately retarded males, with an average of 14 years of institutionalization, in an intensive, short-term program for developing competencies for living and working in the community. Initial and follow-up results suggest guidelines for programming exit options for retarded residents.

REFERENCES

Berne, E. (1964) Transactional Analysis in Psychotherapy. New York City: Grove Press.

Edgerton, R. B. (1967) The Cloak of Competence: Stigma in the Lives of the Mentally Retarded. Berkeley: University of California Press.

Gardner, W. I. (1971) Behavior Modification in Mental Retardation. Chicago: Aldine/Atherton.

Grossman, H. J. (Ed.) (1973) Manual on Terminology and Classification in Mental Retardation. Washington, D.C.: AAMD.

Harris, T. A. (1967) I'm O.K.–You're O.K. New York City: Harper & Row.

Lent, J. R., and Childress, D. (1968) A demonstration program for intensive training of institutionalized mentally retarded girls. (mimeo) Parsons, Kansas: Parsons State Hospital and Training School.

Parnicky, J. J., and Agin D. (1975) Pathways Toward Independence. Columbus, Ohio: Nisonger Center, Ohio State University.

Parnicky, J. J., and Shea, J. A. (1972) Adult training program for moderately retarded young men. Columbus, O.: Nisonger Center, Ohio State University (mimeo).

Skinner, B. F. (1953) Science and Human Behavior. New York City: Free Press.

Stanfield, J. S. (1973) Graduation: What happens to the retarded child when he grows up? Except. Child. 540.

Windle, C. D., Stenqart, E., and Brosn, S. (1961) Reasons for community failure of released patients. Amer. J. Ment. Defic. 66:213.

RESEARCH TO PRACTICE IN MENTAL RETARDATION
Care and Intervention, Volume I
Edited by Peter Mittler
Copyright 1977 I.A.S.S.M.D.

EFFECTS OF RESIDENTIAL SETTINGS ON DEVELOPMENT

R. K. Eyman, A. B. Silverstein, R. McLain, and C. Miller
University of California at Los Angeles
Neurosychiatric Institute,
Pacific State Hospital Research Group,
Pomona, California 91766, United States

Considerable debate has surrounded the effects of residential settings on the development and behavior of mentally retarded children (Edgerton et al., 1975; Balla et al., 1974). Wolfensberger (1971) has argued that "on programmatic, ideological, and fiscal grounds, the present institutional system is essentially unsalvageable. Indeed I believe that it is the duty of every institution's superintendent to do all he can to phase out his institution, and to encourage the new residential and service model." In contrast, other authors have emphasized the beneficial effects of institutions in terms of increases in IQ and autonomy in problem solving (Yando and Zigler, 1971; Clarke and Clarke, 1953; 1954; Clarke et al., 1958; Zigler et al., 1968).

Butterfield and Zigler (1965) appear to be the first to have maintained that institutions differ from one another in the effects they have on their retarded residents. More recently, McCormick et al. (1975) have argued that institutions for retarded persons are heterogeneous in their characteristics and have markedly different effects on their retarded residents (see also Zigler and Balla).

Studies by Balla et al. (1974) and Tizard (1970) found no systematic relationships between resident behavior and a number of physical characteristics of institutions, including size, staff-resident ratio, etc. It is generally believed that the identification and quantification of specific social-psychological characteristics of institutions will be necessary before further progress is made in the specification of variables that influence the development of their residents. Research attempting to operationalize these social-psychological characteristics has been undertaken by a number of investigators, e.g., Tizard and his associates (1960, 1961, 1964, 1967, 1970) in the United Kingdom; Klaber and his associates (1969, 1970) in the Northeastern United States; and Jackson (1964, 1969), in the Midwest, who attempted to objectify the theoretical concepts of Schwartz (1957) concerning the attributes of institutional treatment environments for mentally ill persons.

McLain, Silverstein, and their associates at Pacific State Hospital have used two instruments in studying residential settings for retarded persons—Characteristics of the Treatment Environment (CTE), both the original scale (Jackson, 1969) and a community version (McLain et al., in preparation); and the Residential Management Survey (RMS) (McLain et al., 1975), a questionnaire version of the Revised Child Management Scale (King et al., 1971). These researchers have demonstrated that the CTE and RMS differentiate not only among treatment programs with varying therapeutic goals, but also among living units within these programs and among various types of community facilities as well; that the responses of staff to the questionnaires are only minimally related to their demographic characteristics and employment history; and that CTE and RMS mean scores are relatively stable over time. McCormick et al., (1975) and McLain et al., (1975) have suggested that what is now required are longitudinal studies, in which an examination is made of the relationships between client management practices and the behavioral development of retarded individuals in various settings.

Some longitudinal research does exist on the acquisition of self-help skills among retarded clients admitted to Pacific State Hospital (Eyman et al., 1970, 1975). Little change was found over a three-year period unless special programming, such as sensory-motor training, was provided. Balla et al. (1974) also conducted a longitudinal study, over a two and one-half year period, of the effects of institutionalization on such measures as MA, IQ, verbal dependency, and imitativeness. Changes in development were noted, but these represented a complex function of preinstitutional experience, the particular institution to which the individual was admitted, and his demographic and behavioral characteristics.

The purpose of the present investigation was to examine the relationship between residential environments (McLain et al., 1975), special intensive programs, such as behavior shaping (Bijou, 1968; Gardner and Watson, 1969) and sensorimotor training (Kephart, 1960; Edgar et al., 1969), and changes in the adaptive behavior of mentally retarded individuals over a two- to three-year period. It was hypothesized that both residential environments and special programming would influence the development of adaptive behavior.

METHOD

The sample consisted of the residents of one state institution in California, another state institution in Colorado, and selected community facilities surrounding the California institution. Pacific State Hospital, the California institution, has an average daily population of about 1,800 residents. The residents range in age from less than one year to over 70, and they span all levels of retardation. The Colorado institution, which is similar to Pacific State Hospital in terms of the type of individuals served, has a resident population of about

1,100. The California community facilities sampled included convalescent hospitals, used primarily for older, profoundly retarded clients, as well as foster care homes and board and care homes in which the higher functioning children and adults tend to be placed (Bjannes and Butler, 1974).

Subjects remaining in the sample were followed for three years in California and two years in Colorado. Their residential placement, adaptive behavior, and mortality continue to be monitored. A version of the Adaptive Behavior Scale published by the American Association on Mental Deficiency (AAMD) (Nihira et al., 1974) has been administered once a year to all available residents in the sample. In addition, the two environmental measures employed by McLain et al. (1975, in preparation) were administered to selected staff once a year in all institutions and community facilities in the sample. Table 1 indicates the nature of the content of the environmental measures.

Since environmental scores are assigned to living units, it was necessary to identify each resident with a specific living unit. For residents who changed living units over the study period, composite scores were computed for the

Table 1. Description of environment measures: characteristics of the treatment environment (CTE) and residential management survey (RMS)

Example of items in the CTE Instrument:

I. Autonomy (36 items)

53. Patients are encouraged to start projects with other patients to improve the physical environment of the ward.
62. The staff encourages patients to take over management of their own affairs whenever possible.
49. Patients are not encouraged to take very much responsibility for maintaining their own quarters.

II. Activity (23 items)

24. Patients are kept busy on the ward by frequent social, intellectual, or recreational activities, conducted by members of the staff.
61. Patients have many opportunities to express themselves in music, painting, hobby-work, or other creative activities.
47. Members of the staff are constantly seeking ways of expanding patients' freedom of movement (about the hospital, grounds, and community).

Example of items in the RMS Instrument:

How many residents have been on outings in the last three months?
Does a caregiver eat with the residents?
How many residents have toys, games, or books of their own?
Does a caregiver sit and watch TV with the residents?

---

environmental measures, representing all of the residents' major living unit placements during that interval.

In addition to the environmental measures, information on specific programs was gathered. An attempt was made to determine which residents in the institutions participated in special programming using either sensori-motor training or behavior modification techniques. Both of these methods have been found effective treatment modalities at Pacific State Hospital (Eyman et al., 1970, 1975). In the community, a survey form was used to determine the extent to which various types of extramural services and community resources were used, e.g., public and private schools, day care and special training programs, or consultation with developmental specialists. A system of community program descriptions suggested by the work of Bjannes and Butler (1974) and O'Connor (1976) was adapted for use in the present study.

Changes in adaptive behavior were studied as a function of placement, environmental measures, and selected program designations. A recent factor analysis of the AAMD Adaptive Behavior Scale (Nihira, 1975) yielded three factors: 1) personal self-sufficiency, 2) community self-sufficiency, and 3) personal-social responsibility. These factors provided our units of measurement for development. Factor scores were obtained by simply summing the scores for the salient items on each factor.

RESULTS

Table 2 shows the changes observed over a two- to three-year period on each of the three factors of the modified Adaptive Behavior Scale by facility and group. It was considered necessary to partition the data in this manner because of gross differences among types of residents and types of facilities. More specifically, it was considered important to separate profoundly retarded individuals from those less retarded, because previous findings indicate the existence of substantial differences between these groups on mortality, acquisition of basic skills, service utilization patterns, and associated handicaps (Miller, 1975; MacAndrew and Edgerton, 1964; Eyman et al., 1970; Rowitz et al., 1975; O'Connor et al., 1970). Age was also found to affect these criteria, and so retarded individuals from 0 to 19 years of age were separated from those 20 or more years of age.

The results presented in Table 2 indicate limited mean change relative to the standard deviations. However, the foster care homes and board and care homes do evidence more positive change than do the other residential settings. These facilities house higher functioning persons, as is shown by the higher mean initial scores. The standard deviations associated with the mean changes suggest that most residents are undergoing substantial change in their adaptive behavior.

In order to relate changes on each of the three factors to environmental measures and treatment programs, a series of stepwise regression analyses were performed. As shown in Table 3, change scores were treated as the dependent or

Table 2. Changes observed on three factors[a] (AAMD Adaptive Behavior Scale) of mentally retarded individuals residing in selected community and institutional facilities in California and Colorado

Facility and group	N	Factor I			Factor II			Factor III		
		Mean change	S.D.[b]	Mean initial score	Mean change	S.D.	Mean score	Mean change	S.D.	Mean initial score
Pacific State Hosp., CA.										
Low age, low MR level	226	2.1	11.1	31.8	−.7	23.7	21.1	2.2	27.3	23.8
Low age, high MR level	215	6.9	13.2	48.9	4.7	22.1	42.5	1.9	26.3	45.2
High age, low MR level	253	−2.1	13.9	46.8	−2.6	24.5	37.6	.4	27.4	30.5
High age, high MR level	311	3.6	15.2	69.0	.6	17.3	70.9	−4.2	22.6	67.3
Convalescent Hosp., CA.										
Low age, low MR level	12	(Small N precluded calculation of mean and standard deviation)								
High age, low MR level	109	−6.8	19.0	32.4	3.2	25.5	22.8	1.6	30.9	22.0
Other Community, CA.										
Low age, high MR level	49	8.3	11.2	76.1	8.6	17.7	65.5	2.0	13.6	74.4
High age, high MR level	126	6.9	11.3	80.5	2.0	13.0	83.0	4.0	15.0	78.0
Colorado Institution										
Low age, low MR level	312	−2.1	9.6	24.4	−.2	13.4	16.0	−2.3	20.2	21.0
Low age, high MR level	139	−4.7	17.6	59.4	−1.1	11.3	57.1	.7	19.1	53.7
High age, low MR level	93	−1.3	8.6	28.8	−.1	12.2	20.2	.8	18.1	18.8
High age, high MR level	100	−6.9	18.8	68.8	−2.1	10.1	71.1	1.9	18.5	63.3

[a]Factor I = Personal self-sufficiency, e.g., toilet training, grooming, ambulation, etc. Factor II = Community self-sufficiency, e.g., communication skills, economic activity, etc. Factor III = Personal-social responsibility, e.g., initiative to engage in purposeful activities, etc.

[b]S.D. = Standard Deviations.

Table 3. Regression of three factors (AAMD Adaptive Behavior Scale) on environmental means (CTE-I, CTE-II, and RMS) and programs, controling for initial score on each factor[a]

Facility and group	Factor I		Factor II		Factor III	
	r^2	R^2	r^2	R^2	r^2	R^2
Pacific State Hosp., CA.						
Low age, low MR level	.02	.10 (.16)	.17	.31	.25	.32
Low age, high MR level	.00	.01	.06	.15 (.18)	.16	.23 (.28)
High age, low MR level	.00	.07	.16	.21	.27	.32
High age, high MR level	.00	.14	.09	.23 (.29)	.12	.27
Convalescent Hosp., CA.						
High age, low MR level	.24	.48	.29	.31	.27	.44
Other Community—CA.						
Low age, high MR level	.10	.34	.64	.79	.01	.09 (.21)*
High age, high MR level	.14	.20	.36	.42 (.46)	.33	.36
Colorado Institution						
Low age, low MR level	.15	.18	.18	.24	.31	.36 (.42)*
Low age, high MR level	.24	.24	.26	.34 (.37)	.34	.40
High age, low MR level	.11	.16 (.26)*	.17	.25	.32	.33
High age, high MR level	.14	.21	.20	.30	.30	.42

[a]r^2 is the proportion of the variance accounted for by initial score, R^2 the proportion accounted for by the addition of the environmental measures. The values in parentheses refer to variance added by programs and are listed only in those instances where the proportion of the variance accounted for was .03 or more in conjunction with environmental measures. The star values indicate those cases where the programs were selected before the environmental measures.

predicted variable, while environments and programs were treated as the independent or predictor variables. The initial scores on each factor were handled as covariates by forcing them into the regression equation before the independent variables. Although further analyses are required before firm conclusions can be reached, this procedure provides as a first step some indication of the amount of variance in change scores on the three factors that can be attributed to environmental and program variables.

In general, the environmental measures accounted for most of the variance of change in the three factors. However, there were three cases in which the programs were found to be more highly correlated with change than were the environmental measures. There were also instances in which the program information added to the predicted variance, although it remained as a secondary predictor.

For the most part, the relationships between environmental measures or programs and developmental change were higher in community facilities than in institutional settings. Environmental measures predicted 15% to 24% of the variance of change in the first two factors for the younger, higher functioning children in foster care and board and care homes. The relationships between environmental measures or programs and developmental change were much lower for the older residents in foster care and board and care homes. In contrast, environmental measures predicted 17% to 24% of the variance of change for the older, profoundly retarded residents in convalescent hospitals. It should be noted, however, that most of the change that occurred in convalescent hospitals represented regression, in contrast to the improvement noted in the higher functioning individuals residing in foster care and board and care homes.

The relationships between environmental measures and change on the three factors were moderately high for the older, higher functioning individuals in both the California and Colorado institutions. Beyond that, a consistent pattern in the correlations is not apparent. However, for the younger, profoundly retarded children at Pacific State Hospital, 14% of the variance of change in adaptive behavior Factors I and II could be accounted for by environments and programs, which also accounted for 11% of the variance of change in Factor II in the Colorado institution. The remainder of the relationships for the two institutions were generally lower, although still of interest.

The results presented in Table 3 also indicate some important differences between predicted change on the three factors. For example, the younger, higher functioning children in the foster care and board and care homes underwent changes in all three factors that were moderately related to environmental measures or programs. In contrast, similar children in the institutions evidenced lower relationships between change on the factors and environmental measures or programs, with the exception of Factor II. Relationships for the older, higher functioning individuals in board and care or foster homes were generally low compared to those for similar individuals in the institutions. These differences between the institutional and community settings are difficult to explain at this time.

DISCUSSION

The results demonstrated that differential change in the three adaptive behavior factors did occur over a two- to three-year period, and that they tended to be related to level of retardation, age, and facility. Generally, those higher functioning persons residing in foster care homes and board and care homes improved most across the three factors, although the younger, higher functioning children at Pacific State Hospital also showed improvement. The older, profoundly retarded individuals regressed for the most part.

Of primary interest in this study was whether or not any relationships could be found between development and residence in specific environmental settings or participation in special treatment programs. It was recognized at the outset that the environmental measures were better defined, and that the program data were based on more general information of unknown reliability. Hence, it was not surprising to find that the environmental measures were more highly related to behavioral change in most settings. However, the program information did contribute to the prediction of behavior change in several instances.

The relationships between change on the three adaptive behavior factors and environmental measures or programs were generally higher in the community facilities than in the institutions. However, environmental scores tended to be more variable for the lower age and level of retardation groups in the community than in the institution, which could partially account for this difference. The exception to this trend involved the older, higher functioning persons in community homes. The variability among their environmental scores was less than for their counterparts (who had lower initial adaptive behavior scores) in the institution. Given these circumstances, the higher relationships found in the institutional settings for this group appear plausible.

These preliminary findings tend to support the earlier work of Tizard as well as that of Balla, who would maintain that the social-psychological characteristics of a residence do in fact influence the behavior of retarded clients. Although the reported relationships between behavior change and environmental measures or programs may appear modest, it should be recognized that most of them were not only statistically significant, but more importantly, that they represent a promising amount of variance accounted for, given the anomalies of change scores, sample loss, limited length of follow-up, etc. The course to be followed is a continuing attempt to reduce the unexplained variance in behavior change.

Ultimately, it appears that it will be necessary to establish appropriate baseline data for behavior change. The effects of environmental factors or program intervention on behavior would best be evaluated in terms of change above and beyond that normally expected of a particular group of subjects.

SUMMARY

Three-year longitudinal data on development of mentally retarded individuals in a sample of community and institutional settings was correlated with ratings of residential environments and program participation. The findings revealed relatively high correlations between environmental ratings and changes in adaptive behavior for moderately retarded residents in the community.

REFERENCES

Balla, D. A., Butterfield, E. C., and Zigler, E. (1974) Effects of institutionalization on retarded children: A longitudinal cross-institutional investigation. Amer. J. Ment. Defic. 78:530.

Bijou, S. W. (1968) Behavior modification in the mentally retarded: Application of operant conditioning principles. Pediatr. Clin. North Amer. 15:969—987.

Bjannes, A. T., and Butler, E. W. (1974) Environmental variation in community care facilities for mentally retarded persons. Amer. J. Ment. Defic. 78:429.

Butterfield, E. C., and Zigler, E. (1965) The influence of differing institutional social climates on the effectiveness of social reinforcement in the mentally retarded. Amer. J. Ment. Defic. 70:48.

Clarke, A. D. B., and Clarke, A. M. (1953) How constant is the IQ? Lancet 2:877.

Clarke, A. D. B., and Clarke, A. M. (1954) Cognitive changes in the feeble-minded. Brit. J. Psychol. 45:173.

Clarke, A. D. B., Clarke, A. M., and Reiman, S. (1958) Cognitive and social changes in the feebleminded: Three further studies. Brit. J. Psychol. 49:144.

Edgar, C. L., Ball, T. S., McIntyre, R. B., and Shotwell, A. M. (1969) Effects of sensory-motor training on adaptive behavior. Amer. J. Ment. Defic. 73:713.

Edgerton, R. B., Eyman, R. K., and Silverstein, A. B. (1975) The mental retardation system: Institutional aspects. *Chapter in* Issues in the Classification of Children: A Handbook on Categories, Labels, and their Consequences. San Francisco: Jossey-Bass, Part II, No. 17.

Eyman, R. K., Tarjan, G., and Cassady, M. (1970) Natural history of acquisition of basic skills by hospitalized retarded patients. Amer. J. Ment. Defic. 75:120.

Eyman, R. K., Silverstein, A. B., and McLain, R. (1975) Effect of treatment programs on the acquisition of basic skills. Amer. J. Ment. Defic. 79:573.

Gardner, J. M., and Watson, L. A. (1969) Behavior modification of the mentally retarded: An annotated bibliography. Ment. Retard. Abstr. 6:181.

Jackson, J. (1964) Toward the comparative study of mental hospitals: Characteristics of the treatment environment. *In* A. F. Wessen (Ed.), The Psychiatric Hospital as a Social System. Springfield, Ill.: Charles C Thomas.

Jackson, J. (1969) Factors of the treatment environment. Arch. Gen. Psychiatry 21:39.

Kephart, N. C. (1960) The Slow Learner in the Classroom. Columbus, Ohio: Merrill.

King, R. D., Raynes, N. V., and Tizard, J. (1971) Patterns of Residential Care: Sociological Studies in Institutions for Handicapped Children. London: Routledge & Kegan Paul.

Klaber, M. M. (1969) A densely populated small state: Connecticut. *In* R. B. Kugel and W. Wolfensberger (Eds.), Changing Patterns in Residential Services for the Mentally Retarded. Washington, D. C.: U. S. Government Printing Office.

Klaber, M. M. (1970) Retardates in residence—A study of institutions. West Hartford, Conn.: University of Hartford.

MacAndrew, C., and Edgerton, R. (1964) The everyday life of institutionalized "idiots." Hum. Org. 23:312.

McCormick, M., Balla, D., and Zigler, E. (1975) Resident-care practices in institutions for retarded persons: A cross-institutional, cross-cultural study. Amer. J. Ment. Defic. 80:1.

McLain, R. E., Silverstein, A. B., Hubbell, M., and Brownlee, L. (1975) The characterization of residential environments within a hospital for the mentally retarded. Ment. Retard. 13:24.

McLain, R. E., Silverstein, A. B., Hubbell, M., and Brownlee, L. Comparison of the residential environment of a state hospital for retarded clients with those of various types of community facilities. (In preparation.)

Miller, C. R. (1975) Deinstitutionalization and mortality trends for the profoundly mentally retarded. *In* C. Cleland and L. Talkington (Eds.), Research with Profoundly Retarded. The Western Research Conference and the Brown Schools, 1—8.

Nihira, K., Foster, R., Shellhaas, M., and Leland, H. (1974) AAMD Adaptive Behavior Scale. Washington, D. C.: American Association on Mental Deficiency.

Nihira, K. (1975) The changing composition of "adaptive behavior:" A cross-sectional study. *In* C. Cleland and L. Talkington (Eds.), Research with Profoundly Retarded. The Western Research Conference and the Brown Schools, 21–36.

O'Connor, G. (1976) Home is a Good Place: A National Perspective of Community Residential Facilities for Developmentally Disabled Persons. Washington, D.C.: American Association of Mental Deficiency.

O'Connor, G., Justice, R. S., and Payne, D. (1970) Statistical expectations of physical handicaps in institutionalized retardates. Amer. J. Ment. Defic. 74:541.

Rowitz, L., O'Connor, G., and Borskin, A. (1975) Patterns of service use by severely and profoundly retarded individuals: A preliminary analysis. *In* C. Cleland and L. Talkington (Eds.), Research with Profoundly Retarded. The Western Research Conference and the Brown Schools, 9–20.

Schwartz, M. (1957) What is a therapeutic milieu? *In* M. Greenblatt, D. J. Levinson, and R. H. Williams (Eds.), The Patient and the Mental Hospital. Glencoe, Ill.: Free Press.

Tizard, J. (1960) Residential care of mentally handicapped children Brit. Med. J. 1:1041.

Tizard, J. (1964) Community Services for the Mentally Handicapped. New York: Oxford University Press.

Tizard, J. (1970) The role of social institutions in the causation, prevention, and alleviation of mental retardation. *In* H. C. Haywood (Ed.), Social-Cultural Aspects of Mental Retardation. New York: Appleton-Century Crofts.

Tizard, J. and Grad, J. (1961) The Mentally Handicapped and Their Families: A Social Survey. London: Oxford University Press.

Tizard, J., King, R. D., et al. (1967) The care and treatment of subnormal children in residential institutions. *In* What is Special Education? Proceedings of the First International Conference of the Association for Special Education, July 1966. Stanmore, England: Association for Special Education.

Wolfensberger, W. (1971) "Will there always be an institution? II: The impact of new service models." Ment. Retard. 9:31.

Yando, R., and Zigler, E. (1971) Outerdirectedness in the problem-solving of institutionalized and noninstitutionalized normal and retarded children. Dev. Psychol. 4:277.

Zigler, E., Balla, D., and Butterfield, E. C. (1968) A longitudinal investigation of the relationship between preinstitutional social deprivation and social motivation in institutionalized retardes. J. Pers. Soc. Psychol. 10:437.

RESEARCH TO PRACTICE IN MENTAL RETARDATION
Care and Intervention, Volume I
Edited by Peter Mittler
Copyright 1977 I.A.S.S.M.D.

COMMUNITY LIVING
Accommodations
and Vocations

M. M. Seltzer and G. B. Seltzer
Behavioral Education Projects, Inc., Nichols House,
Harvard University, Cambridge, Massachusetts 02138, United States

As the debilitating effects of total institutions became the object of study (Goffman, 1961; Klaber, 1969; Wolfensberger, 1969a, 1969b; King, Raines and Tizard, 1971; Rosenham, 1973), concepts and programs that were developed in Scandinavia (Grunewald, 1969; Nirje, 1969; Perske, 1969) began to penetrate the American service delivery system. Furthermore, as exposés condemned institutions (Blatt and Kaplan, 1966; Rivera, 1972) and class action suits bartered for the right to treatment (Wyatt V Stickney, 1971; Ricci V Greenblatt, 1972), the public consciousness was sufficiently aroused to effect legislative and program reform. The problem posed was: How should retarded people live? The solution put forth entailed integrating retarded people with the community at large.

The normalization principle attempted to ensure that retarded people would have available to them opportunities "as close as possible" to those typically available to members of society (Nirje, 1969). The vehicle chosen to implement this goal was the community residence, envisioned as a small home in the community, in which retarded people could integrate and acculturate with their neighbors. The technique of using housing as the means to integrate atypical persons with American society was not novel; it had previously been tried for the integration of racial minorities, ex-mental hospital patients, alcoholics, and juvenile delinquents, among others. Integration by means of housing is at best viewed ambivalently by many Americans, it being perceived on the one hand as consistent with the melting pot myth, and on the other as a threat to the sanctity of the community and to property value. Yet evidently the concept of the community residence was accepted, at least by planners of services; and as of 1973, 43 states had begun community residence programs (Baker, Seltzer, and Seltzer, in press).

This research was supported by a grant from the Massachusetts Developmental Disabilities Council.

The research presented here is intended to delineate the various types, or models, of community residential living that have developed in the United States. Our study of the community residence movement was undertaken as a quest for diversity. It seemed to us that in order to make available to retarded persons conditions "as close as possible" to mainstream society, it would be necessary to make available the considerable variability of that society, and still more. It would also be necessary to create special prosthetic settings with features designed to meet the special needs of retarded persons, and it would certainly be necessary to create training programs to help the retarded individual learn skills so that he or she could move still closer to that nebulous construct, 'mainstream society.' Furthermore, it should mean helping that society to move some itself, toward increased acceptance of differences. Hence, our descriptive study of existing programs was carried out in the spirit of examining what is, from the perspective of the comprehensive system that could be.

PROCEDURES

In the spirit of exploring as many viable residential models as possible, our definition of a community residence was broad, including only three criteria: 1) that it be an ongoing program, operating longer than six months; 2) that it accommodate no more than 80 retarded adults; 3) that it view itself as an alternative to the institution. From lists provided by state agencies and parent groups, 1,024 residences across the United States were located and sent questionnaires. Approximately 50% were returned completed, and of these, 381 were included as meeting these criteria in the final sample of residences primarily or partially geared to the retarded. The questionnaires were analyzed and divided into 12 program models, as follows:

First, the large pool of questionnaires from group homes was divided into four separate models on the basis of program size; these models ranged from small group homes (from 6 to 10 residents) to mini-institutions (from 40 to 80 residents). A fifth kind of group home was subsequently identified, namely group homes for mixed disability types, providing a home for retarded adults and most often, ex-mental hospital patients.

A second category of program included settings that had as a major goal the provision of a protected environment for residents. Among these were programs for elderly retarded people, foster homes for retarded adults, and sheltered villages that provided self-contained communities for residents and staff.

Training programs were included in the third group of models. Community preparation programs are sometimes located on the grounds of institutions and serve the function of equipping residents with skills needed in order for them to move to a more integrated community-based model. Another type of training program, workshop dormitories, provide short-term intensive vocational training.

A fourth type of community residence included all programs in which residents lived semi-independently, without 24-hour a day supervision by staff. The final group of facilities derived from the survey were comprehensive systems, defined as any program in which several different residential models were represented, all functioning within a single administrative and programmatic structure.

Although the survey data were invaluable in identifying these models, they provided little in the way of programmatic detail or information about the quality of life as experienced by residents. Consequently, a series of in-depth visits were made to 17 programs, representing nine of the 12 models. Some visits lasted for two days, while others extended to eight. Visiting teams sometimes lived at the residence, usually ate some meals there, and attended most ongoing meetings and residence activities. Staff were interviewed about program philosophy and goals, and about their attitudes to their work. Residents also participated in an interview, which focused on their experiences in the community residence and their satisfaction with their way of life. Structured observations and checklists measured program variables.

MODELS AND PROGRAM VARIABLES

The differences among models with respect to a variety of program variables were found to be statistically significant, and from the data there emerged a fairly clear understanding of the strengths and weaknesses of each model. A primary conclusion of this research was that no single model alone was successful in meeting the diverse needs of retarded adults. Rather, a continuum of services comprised of different models working cooperatively would best maximize the chance that a resident would be placed in the kind of program most appropriate for his or her needs. Such comprehensive systems of residential services are infrequently found, and only five programs in the sample met this criterion of encompassing several residential models.

Comprehensive systems are usually composed of a series of models graduated in the degree of independence given to the resident. Most have some sort of group home, as well as an intensive training stage, with the final model requiring semi-independent living on the part of residents. What follows is a summary of the dominant characteristics of models most likely to be included in comprehensive residential systems.

SMALL GROUP HOMES

The average small group home includes eight retarded adults. The program is likely to be run by four staff members, two of whom live in and fill the roles of housemanagers. Residents are relatively high functioning, with 35% being labelled as mildly retarded and 48% as moderately retarded. More so than in other models, these residents tended to come from institutions (57%).

Small group homes are likely to be situated in residential neighborhoods, in keeping with their general philosophy of integration with the community. Operationalization of the concept 'integration' varies from program to program, with some houses preparing residents for transition to independent living, while other houses characterize their program as providing a permanent home for residents. The turnover rate in small group homes was 62% per year, with well over half of the ex-residents moving to other community-based settings, such as independent apartments, other community residences, or to families. However, 19% of the ex-residents returned to institutions.

Relative to other models, residents in small group homes are likely to have a great deal of autonomy to set their own curfews and bedtimes, to invite opposite sex visitors and dinner guests to the house, and the like. Similarly, these residents are more likely to be expected to assume the responsibility for housekeeping and meal preparation than are residents in other models. Another characteristic feature of small group homes is the emphasis placed on the necessity of residents working during the day. Only 11% of residents in small group homes had no day placement. Indeed, 21% worked in competitive jobs and 50% either worked in sheltered workshops or attended educational programs.

The typical small group home program, then, appears to be quite normalized, with residents having high autonomy, extensive responsibilities, and work-oriented day activities. The small group home provides an effective vehicle for moving retarded adults from institutions and from families to community settings. The resident is resocialized as a result of participating in a program that models itself after family-style living.

A major problem with the small group home model is its staffing structure, with young, transient, and often poorly experienced staff predominating. This is a particular liability for the resident who poses problems requiring extended periods of specialized training in order to adjust to less highly structured settings. In order for such residents to be successful, they need a much more intensive skill building experience than the small group home can provide. Specialized work or community living skill training programs have been developed for this purpose.

WORKSHOP DORMITORIES

The workshop dormitory model is one type of specialized community residence, the goal of which is to provide intensive training in work skills to residents. This model was defined as including any program in which the residence and work components were coordinated administratively. Some professionals have raised objections about this model, speculating that the connection between work and home would make the program more institutional than if these two spheres of life were separated. In gathering the data about this model, then, we were interested to see if programs would be institutional in character or, conversely, if specialized work training would enhance the likelihood that residents would succeed in community living.

A striking characteristic of this model that emerged from the data is that workshop dormitories have *high* rates of resident turnover, with 71% moving out each year. Of these ex-residents, close to half move to other supervised settings in the community, which is consistent with the goal of the model to provide short-term specialized training and then to move residents to other programs for more general training in other skill areas. No more residents in this model move back to institutions than in any other model.

The programs found in workshop dormitories are highly structured, with almost all residents participating in workshops or other work training programs during the day. Relative to other models, residents in workshop dormitories rate second highest in the amount of responsibilities they assume for daily house maintenance, cleaning, and cooking. Interestingly, residents' autonomy to set their own curfews and bedtimes, to invite opposite sex guests to the house, and to plan other leisure time activities is more restricted than in several other models, yet this restriction is in many ways consistent with the training-oriented function of the program. In this model, residents typically spend more of their time in structured learning situations than residents in more casual models, such as small group homes.

Residents who have mastered most work and community living skills are often considered ready for semi-independent living, a sort of trial run during which the resident assumes primary responsibility for his or her daily living and decision making, relying on a minimal structure of staff for support.

SEMI-INDEPENDENT

Semi-independent programs can be characterized by two seemingly incompatible qualities: high autonomy for residents and high staff to resident ratio. There are as many staff in this model as, for example, in small group homes. In semi-independent settings, however, the staff are not full-time, and they play less of a supervisory role; instead they offer support to residents. Residents in this model are more likely to hold competitive jobs, to control their own money, to perform major household tasks, and to regulate independently their leisure time, than in any other model.

Although turnover rate is rapid in this model, with an average stay of 1 and one-half years, it is becoming increasingly more common for semi-independent programs to be less transitional for residents and instead provide them with a structured but highly independent home for an indefinite period of time. The option of being assured of minimal but reliable staff support is needed by many retarded adults in order for them to maintain their high level of performance. Totally independent living is not optimal for all, although it is a goal voiced frequently by staff. For some retarded adults, the prospect of living on marginal incomes, being forced to live in shabby roominghouses, and possibly encountering many social problems, is too overwhelming a risk and the semi-independent option might well be preferable.

CONCLUSIONS

The community residence movement has just begun. The hundreds of facilities surveyed are generally operating in some isolation from one another; many problems and solutions are discovered anew in each residence. Yet as one surveys these beginnings, there are exciting program models being developed and, in some, more comprehensive systems being combined. Hopefully, in the next few years community residential programs will expand, develop more in accord with careful needs assessments, continue to explore alternative models, and give more intentional consideration to the basic question of which residents are best served by which models.

SUMMARY

A project to investigate different models of community residential living began with a nation-wide questionnaire survey of 400 facilities, supplemented by 17 site visits. Ten distinct models of community residences were found and assessed in terms of: resident and staff roles; house programs and philosophies; and residential, vocational, and community adjustment.

ACKNOWLEDGMENTS

The authors would like to thank Bruce L. Baker for the central role he played throughout this research.

REFERENCES

Baker, B. L., Seltzer, G., and Seltzer, M. M. As Close as Possible: Community Residences for Retarded Adults. Boston: Little, Brown & Co., in press.

Blatt, B., and Kaplan, F. (1966) Christmas in Purgatory: A Photographic Essay in Mental Retardation. Boston: Allyn and Bacon.

Goffman, E. (1961) Asylums: Essays on the Social Situation of Mental Patients and Other Inmates. New York: Doubleday and Co.

Grunewald, K. (1969) A rural county in Sweden. In Changing Patterns in Residential Services for the Mentally Retarded (Eds. Kugel, R., and Wolfensberger, W.) Washington, D.C.: President's Committee on Mental Retardation.

King, R. D., Raynes, N. V., and Tizard, J. (1971) Patterns of Residential Care: Sociological Studies in Institutions for Handicapped Children. London: Routledge & Kegan Paul.

Klaber, M. (1969) The retarded and institutions for the retarded: a preliminary research report. *In* Psychological Problems in Mental Deficiency (Eds. Sarason, S., and Doris, J.) New York: Harper and Row.

Nirje, B. (1969) The normalization principle and its human management implications. *In* Changing Patterns in Residential Services for the Mentally Retarded (Eds. Kugel, R., and Wolfensberger, W.) Washington D.C.: President's Committee on Mental Retardation.

Perske, R. (1969) Diary of Travel to Scandinavia. Mimeograph.

Ricci V Greenblatt (1972) C.A. No. 72-469F (D. Mass Filed March 1972).

Rivera G. (1972) Willowbrook: A Report on How It Is and Why It Doesn't Have to Be That Way. New York: Vintage Books.

Rosenham, D. L. (1973) On being sane in insane places. Science 17:250.

Wyatt V. Stickney (1971) 325 F. Supp. 781 (M.D. ALA.) and 334 Supp. 1341 (M.D.ALA.), 1971

Wolfensberger, W. (1969a) The origins and nature of our institutional models. *In* Changing Patterns in Residential Services for the Mentally Retarded (Eds. Kugel, R., and Wolfensberger, W.) Washington D.C.: President's Committee on Mental Retardation.

Wolfensberger, W. (1969b) Twenty predictions about the future of residential services in mental retardation. Ment. Retard. 7:51.

RESEARCH TO PRACTICE IN MENTAL RETARDATION
Care and Intervention, Volume I
Edited by Peter Mittler
Copyright 1977   I.A.S.S.M.D.

COMPARISON OF LARGE AND SMALL LIVING UNITS FOR THE MENTALLY RETARDED

J. B. Tremonti and M. M. Reingruber
Kankakee Development Center,
1150 East Court Street, Kankakee, Illinois 60901, United States

The purpose of this chapter is to describe the programs offered, the various support services, and the cost of operating a large and small living unit structure, as well as to view realistically the effect this might have on the humanization, normalization, and development of the mentally retarded.

The facilities compared are in Illinois. The large living unit structure is Kankakee Developmental Center, located at Kankakee, Illinois, and it houses 800 residents. The small living unit structure is Ludeman Developmental Center, located in Park Forest, Illinois, and it houses 400 residents.

Kankakee has five units, each unit consisting of several large buildings. The older ward-like structures consist of an office area, large dayroom area, large dining hall, and one or two sleeping rooms with 15 to 30 beds in each room. Toilet and bath facilities have been remodeled to afford the resident some privacy. The newer structures still have the same large dayroom area and dining rooms, but the bedrooms have been designed to sleep two or four, and they have closet space and room for dressers. Every two rooms have a connecting room with a toilet and sink. Bath and shower rooms are in a separate area. This building is similar to a college dorm. Either type of unit may house from 25 to 50 residents.

Ludeman has five units, each unit consisting of ten homes, each home housing eight residents. These homes consist of living room, dining area, kitchen, playroom, four bedrooms, and two bathrooms. These are built so that they could be converted into typical suburban development homes with very little remodeling.

Both facilities are administered through the system called "unitization." This means that a larger whole is broken into units or smaller parts. In this instance the word refers to a facility for the retarded being built originally with units as part of its architectural design or an older centralized facility being broken into units so as to effect decentralization.

Wolfensberger, in his book *Normalization,* states that both the 5,000-bed institutions as well as the five-bed hostel are residential facilities, yet the first is apt to be labeled an institution and the smaller one something else. Thus it becomes necessary to distinguish the real factor that produces these various labels. He further states the deindividualization that permeates the atmosphere causes the label of institution.

In Illinois, all facilities, regardless of size, have been renamed Developmental Centers. The Mental Health Department has guidelines that require an individualized habilitation and/or treatment plan for every person who is a resident of a department facility.

The guidelines are as follows:

1. An initial habilitation/treatment plan must be prepared and entered into the resident's record within 24 hours of admission.
2. Within fourteen days, a detailed, revised habilitation plan based on observations and diagnosis of the person's behavior must be entered into the person's record. The plan shall be implemented immediately.
3. The individual's habilitation plan must be evaluated and updated monthly. Persons responsible for supervising and monitoring the plan must approve (in writing) the updated plan. Some of the items that must be entered into the resident's record are:
   A. a description of the review process and the names and titles of all persons participating in the review,
   B. any modification of the plan and the reasons therefore,
   C. a target date for the completion of each phase of the habilitation plan.

These guidelines assure that we have no institutions based on the factor of deindividualization as stated by Wolfensberger.

In light of the mandate to individualize programs, it was found that program initiation and development was identical; namely, after examination, testing, and assessment by professionals in the various disciplines, the findings were discussed using the interdisciplinary team approach.

The team is a group of professional, paraprofessional, and direct-care staff who, through the sharing of skills and expertise by the members, are responsible for all vital decisions affecting the resident's life. The team function is to design a program/treatment plan tailored to the individual needs of the resident, evaluating and re-evaluating progress or lack of it, and making recommendations for changes in the program plan in accordance with the ultimate goal of reintegration of the resident into his own home, or some other type of community setting.

The needs of the residents require a variety of services. For organization purposes the services found in both centers have been divided into eight program components (Figure 1).

The flow for delivery of programmatic services may be summarized as follows: The services begin with the individual resident assessment, followed by the development of an individualized program by the interdisciplinary team that may include a variety of the program components, depending on individual needs. The program components include: communication, personal management, environmental care skills, physical development, personal and social skills, basic knowledge, community living skills, and employment skills. These major areas are subdivided into various programs in which residents are to be trained according to needs.

Communication includes: compliance training, listening and watching skills, language stimulation, conversational skills, library, and alternate communications systems (such as Braille, sign language, etc.). Personal management comprises: toilet training, feeding skills, dressing and undressing skills, grooming skills, safety skills, dining programs, and advanced dressing and grooming skills. Environmental skills consist of: bed making, room cleaning, trash and garbage removal, care of clothing, table setting and clearing, washing and drying dishes, glass and utensil storage, sewing, and yard care. Physical development embraces all phases of: motor skill development, mat skills for the severely physically handicapped, physiotherapy, physical fitness, competitive sports, and olympic sports. Personal and social skills encompasses: training in social behavior, personality development, group participation, social amenities, and leisure time activities. Basic knowledge is training in: number, money, and time concepts, functional sign recognition, printing, basic arithmetic, and basic reading and writing. Community living includes: environmental awareness, planning and preparing meals, shopping skills, washing and ironing clothes, transportation, community facilities, and community safety. Employment skills includes: prevocational education, arts and crafts, Work Activity Center, and off-grounds workshops. The two facilities have the same programmatic scheme, with the exception of the Work Activity Center. Ludeman caters to children and makes use of community schools. The programs outlined are basic to both facilities and are not intended to be totally comprehensive.

The two facilities are similar in the programmatic areas. Each develops individualized programs and trains each resident in needed skills until he/she reaches maximum development. All training incorporates behavior modification techniques to achieve the goals in all programmatic areas. The state has funded a "Living Skills Program" that provides the funds for various types of rewards, which may include cards to be used at the facility commissary, or food, money, or other reinforcers as defined by the specific program outlined for the residents. Both facilities believe and use a positive approach in guiding the development of each resident. This program is documented and charted for follow through.

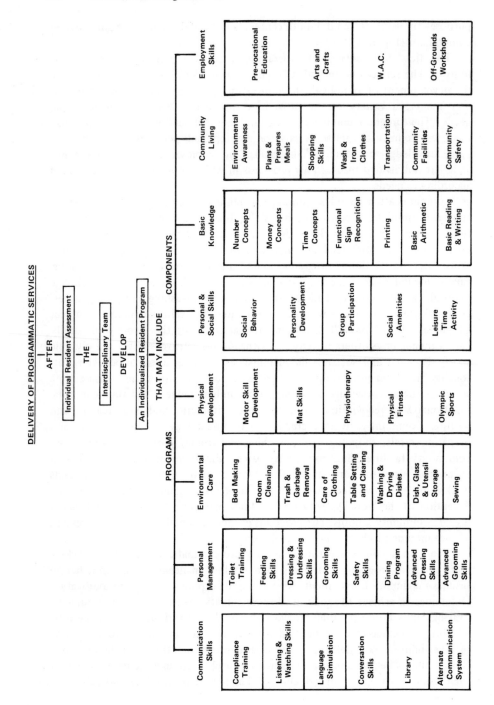

DELIVERY OF PROGRAMMATIC SERVICES

AFTER
Individual Resident Assessment

THE
Interdisciplinary Team

DEVELOP
An Individualized Resident Program

THAT MAY INCLUDE

PROGRAMS   COMPONENTS

Communication Skills	Personal Management	Environmental Care	Physical Development	Personal & Social Skills	Basic Knowledge	Community Living	Employment Skills
Compliance Training	Toilet Training	Bed Making	Motor Skill Development	Social Behavior	Number Concepts	Environmental Awareness	Pre-vocational Education
Listening & Watching Skills	Feeding Skills	Room Cleaning	Mat Skills	Personality Development	Money Concepts	Plans & Prepares Meals	
Language Stimulation	Dressing & Undressing Skills	Trash & Garbage Removal	Physiotherapy	Group Participation	Time Concepts	Shopping Skills	Arts and Crafts
Conversation Skills	Grooming Skills	Care of Clothing	Physical Fitness	Social Amenities	Functional Sign Recognition	Wash & Iron Clothes	
Library	Safety Skills	Table Setting and Clearing	Olympic Sports	Leisure Time Activity	Printing	Transportation	W.A.C.
Alternate Communication System	Dining Program	Washing & Drying Dishes			Basic Arithmetic	Community Facilities	
	Advanced Dressing Skills	Dish, Glass & Utensil Storage			Basic Reading & Writing	Community Safety	Off-Grounds Workshop
	Advanced Grooming Skills	Sewing					

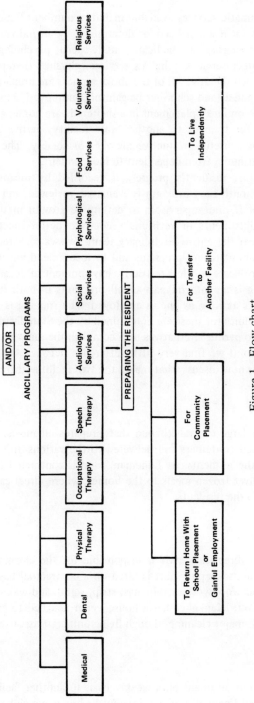

Figure 1. Flow chart.

The programmatic services available include a number of ancillary programs, again dependent on resident need, as determined by an individualized habilitation plan. These consist of: medical, dental, social, psychological, audiology, food, and volunteer services, religious services, physical therapy, occupational therapy, and speech therapy. All of the above services are preparing the resident: to return home and attend school or be gainfully employed, dependent upon his or her age, for community placement in a sheltered care home, a group home, or a foster home; for transfer to another state facility; or the ultimate, to live independently as a useful productive member of society. The entire program guide is on a continuum from dependent to independent.

Each individual resident's progress is recorded by means of charts and graphs. Once a month each program is evaluated, reviewed, and documented by unit or home staff and supervisors to determine growth in the various skills and/or make adjustments or revisions needed to better meet the individual needs. Once a year the entire disciplinary team reviews each record in order to make decisions about future programs and to recommend an ultimate, realistic goal and date for release to a less restrictive environment, if possible.

Staff training is an integral part of all programs in both facilities and this training continues as long as one in employed. The training is much the same, because the guidelines for these are determined by the State Department, but are flexible enough to permit alternatives to accomplish the same goals.

Up to this point we find very little difference between our large and small living unit. Let us now discuss what makes the two facilities different.

FOOD SERVICE

Kankakee has a large central kitchen that prepares all meals. These are then placed in insulated containers and delivered to the various units, where dietary personnel serve the residents. At Ludeman, food is contracted through catering services that deliver frozen meals to the homes, where direct-care staff prepare and serve them to the residents.

HOUSEKEEPING

At Ludeman the direct-care staff is responsible for the cleaning of the home. Every quarter a housekeeping staff is hired on a contractual basis and comes in to wash walls and woodwork, scrub rugs, strip, scrub, and wax floors, and wash windows in and out. Kankakee has a housekeeper assigned to each unit who is responsible for all major cleaning, though living unit staff assist somewhat.

LAUNDRY

Ludeman sends out all linens on a weekly basis to another facility. All clothes and any additional linens dirtied are done in the home, which has its own utility room with washer and dryer. Kankakee has a large laundry on grounds and they do most of the laundry. Washers and dryers are available in most units for training residents who are capable of doing their personal laundry.

Services such as security, maintenance, grounds-care, and pharmacy at Ludeman are on a contractual basis while Kankakee has its own staff to perform these services.

COSTS

The respective costs of running the two facilities are: Kankakee—$14.5 million, and Ludeman—$9.5 million. Pro-rating these figures with the number of residents served, the cost is 24% higher in the small unit structures. This can be further compared with cost per resident as reported from each facility. At Kankakee, the range is $35 to $55 per day, with an average cost of $40. Ludeman's cost is $60 to $65 per day.

Relating cost to number of positions, Kankakee Developmental Center has 1,031 and Ludeman has 635. This reveals that there are 19% more positions requested to man the smaller units.

The trend of utilizing the smaller residential units is becoming a pattern in Illinois for the new as well as the physical remodeling of the existing older facilities.

Much study and research still needs to be done in the area of living unit size in order to keep cost manageable and yet give each resident the best possible program to meet his or her needs.

From our experience and observations, we conclude that the paramount factor in achieving maximal humanization, normalization, and development of the mentally retarded is the programmatic design and staff size and commitment, not the structure of buildings.

SUMMARY

Does the type and size of a building and number of residents living together affect the humanization, normalization, and development of the mentally retarded? In reply to this question this paper discusses the programmatic areas, resident training techniques, resident grouping, food services, ancillary services, housekeeping needs, direct-care staff, and cost at two types of residential facilities in the state of Illinois.

REFERENCE

Wolfensberger, W. (1972) Normalization. National Institute on Mental Retardation. New York: York University Campus, p. 7.

RESEARCH TO PRACTICE IN MENTAL RETARDATION
Care and Intervention, Volume I
Edited by Peter Mittler
Copyright 1977 I.A.S.S.M.D.

ORGANIZATIONAL CHARACTERISTICS AND THEIR RELATIONSHIP TO THE QUALITY OF CARE

M. W. Pratt, N. V. Raynes,* and S. Roses
*Institute of Psychiatry, De Crespigny Park, Denmark Hill, London, SE5 8AF, England

Much has been written about the custodial and dehumanizing nature of large institutions for the mentally retarded. Whether we like it or not, however, large institutions will remain in use for some time to come, and a major priority must be to provide the most humane care possible within them. We have elsewhere presented evidence demonstrating that there is a great deal of variability in the care provided within the various living units that comprise such institutions. The focus of the present chapter is the relationship of this variability to the organizational climate of the living unit, as viewed by the staff of the unit themselves.

The impact of organizational factors on workers has, of course, a venerable history as a research topic. A number of studies have shown a relation between the decentralization of decision making and worker morale, for example. The relations between morale and actual behavior are likely to be complex, however (Vroom, 1964). In any investigations of organizational structure and behavior, therefore, both staff morale and caregiving practices should be examined. There have been few studies of residential facilities for the retarded that have investigated the relation of organizational factors to indices of the actual type of care provided in these settings (see King et al., 1971; Holland, 1973). In none of this research has the direct-care workers' view of organizational structure and climate been directly assessed. Instead, the reports of administrators in charge of the facilities have been used.

In the present chapter we describe the relations of several organizational features of the living units within the institutions to the care provided and the morale of staff in these living units. We assessed these organizational features both through questionnaire and direct observation, based on the personnel who staffed each of the residence halls.

METHOD

The setting of the research has already been described. The measures of care and of staff morale, as well as those on the organization of the living units, were obtained in all 21 of the residences studies, drawn from three different, unitized institutions for the retarded in the United States (Raynes et al., 1976).

Outcome Measures

We used two indices of the quality of care, the Revised Resident Management Practices Scale (R.R.M.P.) and the Index of Informative Speech. It will be recalled that lower scores on the R.R.M.P. indicate more resident-oriented, as opposed to institution-oriented, care practices (King and Raynes, 1968). The second measure, the Index of Informative Speech, i.e., the percentage of observations characterized as "informative" talk: speech that serves the function of informing either the residents or the staff, is being used as an index of the quality of care in the present study. Records of the performance of individual staff members were obtained, as well as an average measure characterizing the living unit as a whole.

These two indices of the quality of care have been found to assess independent dimensions of staff behaviour in residential settings (Pratt et al., 1976). Both indices were strongly associated with the level of resident handicap characterizing the living unit. More handicapped residents received less resident-oriented individualised treatment, and were less often addressed by their caregivers with informative talk. The R.R.M.P. was also associated with the size of the resident population. Consequently, in the analyses presented below, we have controlled statistically for the average degree of resident handicap and the size of the building population.

In addition to the two measures of care, we also obtained an index of worker morale from questionnaires given to all direct-care staff. We asked staff how helpful they judged other workers in their building to be in terms of carrying out their daily work responsibilities. Others have argued, too, that such ratings provide an index of one major component of worker satisfaction and morale (Aiken and Hage, 1966). As with care, averaged ratings for the staff of each building ranged widely on this index.

Organizational Measures

Two measures of organizational climate will be considered in detail in this paper. One is an index of perceived participation in decision making, derived from questionnaires given to all direct-care workers in each building. Slightly less than 65% of all staff returned the questionnaire, and the indices are based on a total sample of 125 staff members. Workers were asked to indicate which status groups participated in each of several types of decisions—such as when to take days off or vacations, or matters concerning routine domestic work. In general, direct-care staff in most buildings studied perceived themselves to be relatively uninvolved in most decisions, but there were exceptions.

A second organizational measure was derived from time-sampled observations of both subordinate and supervisory staff in each building. We developed from this a measure of the specialization of roles of the caregiving staff across status group lines. Staff activities were exhaustively classified into six types of behavior—three concerned with different kinds of resident care and three concerned with domestic or administrative activity. The reliability of these observations, totaling about five observational hours per building, was 0.85 overall. An index of the differences in percentage of time spent in each kind of activity by supervisors and their subordinates was calculated for each living unit. Scores on this index varied widely among buildings, and seemed especially related to the tendency of supervisory staff in some buildings to spend a great deal of time away from the residents, engaged in administrative paperwork.

RESULTS

The two dimensions of organizational structure we measured proved unrelated to one another in these 21 living units ($r = -.07$). To test the relationship between these organizational indices and the three outcome measures for each living unit, correlations of the organizational and outcome variables were computed. These correlations were statistically controlled for the level of resident handicap and size of the resident population in each building (see Table 1).

The most consistent relation to outcome is found for perceived decentralization of the decision-making process. The more workers feel themselves involved in decisions affecting their work, the better the quality of care provided for residents on both measures of care, and the higher the staff's morale. Further substantiating this result, we were able to show from our individual staff data on the informative speech index that staff within the same building who feel more involved in decisions do better on our speech index than those staff who feel less involved (Raynes et al., 1975). Feelings of control over one's own daily work role appear to have definite beneficial consequences for direct-care staff members' interaction with residents.

Table 1. Correlations between measures of organizational climate and three outcome indices for 21 Residences[a]

Organizational measure	R.R.M.P.	Language index	Staff morale
Participation in decision making	$-.51^b$	$.45^b$	$.50^b$
Building staff role specialization	$.12$	$.40^b$	$.49^b$

[a]Partial r's, controlling for size of building population and level of resident handicap.
[b]$p < 0.05$, one-tailed.

The measure of specialization is significantly correlated with the observed staff speech pattern to residents and with the staff morale index. This measure of specialization is not closely associated with the R.R.M.P., although we are unable to explain why this should be so. Greater specialization is found in residences with lower staff morale and with little staff-resident "informative" interaction. Jules Henry (1957) has pointed out that more individualized treatment can be provided where all aspects of the task of caring for residents are performed by each caregiver, and that specialization generates distancing between staff and clients. The present findings are consistent with his propositions regarding care. They also suggest that a substantial differentiation of activities along status group lines can engender low morale among subordinates. Specialization in the present instance almost always meant that the supervisory staff in the building delegated most resident care to their subordinates, while arrogating administrative duties to themselves. It seems quite likely that interaction with the residents is devalued under such circumstances.

DISCUSSION

Both the organizational climate and the care provided in residences within the same unitized institution appear to vary widely. Taking this variability as a departure point, we have considered some of the associations between measures of organization structure and the caregiving behavior and morale of staff within a living unit. We have shown that individualized, more stimulating care exists where direct-care staff perceive themselves as being more involved in decision making, and that under such circumstances, staff morale is higher. High levels of task specialization were found in settings with low amounts of informative talk by staff to residents, and with low staff morale.

But what do these findings have to say to those directly concerned with the difficult problem of improving the quality of care in residential facilities? We believe our evidence indicates the existence of a general organizational precondition to facilitate more individualized care and to improve staff morale. Feeling some control over one's work life is crucial, both for a worker's morale and for the level of stimulation he or she provides the residents. Administrative reform, such as unitization, which is aimed at decentralizing decision making, must therefore make certain that this process is carried to the level of the staff responsible for the day-to-day care of residents. Other findings from our study, not reported here, show that the participation of administrators in decisions has *less* relationship to care and to staff morale. This appears to confirm that it is direct-care workers' feelings of involvement in decisions that are crucial, if personalized, stimulating care is to be achieved.

The sentiments underlying many of these workers' feelings of powerlessness are best captured by the comment one made on our questionnaire: "Nobody listens to us." Obviously, feelings such as these are not going to be alleviated without some real commitment on the part of an administration to find ways of listening to, and sharing power with, direct-care workers in our residential institutions.

Just as subordinates need to be involved in the decision-making process, so superiors among the building staff should be involved in the day-to-day care of the residents. There are indications from our data that specializing the roles of caregiving staff in such facilities too highly can have a negative impact, both on the quality of care provided and on staff morale. One worker in a living unit where specialization was marked commented:

> There is too great a division between professional and administrative workers and the attendants. The communication level between upper and lower people is very low . . . An 'us' and 'they' type of situation results, a power struggle with both moving further apart . . .

Our results clearly support an "organic" model for the provision of care, in which both direct-care staff and their administrative superiors share in *all* the essential functions of the task of caring for residents, including both administrative decision making and the actual caregiving process. While it may be difficult to develop administrative structures characterized by low differentiation and high staff participation in large residential facilities, it is evidently not impossible. Several of the living units we studied demonstrated such patterns, and these were typically characterized by quite adequate care. Establishing such organizational conditions in our large institutions is no mean task. However, such positive examples ought to encourage us to try.

SUMMARY

The effects of decentralization and status differentiation on the quality of care provided in three large institutions for the retarded were studied. Staff members' sense of participation in decisions was closely related to their caregiving behavior; status differentiation had a smaller effect. Ways of increasing staff participation were discussed.

ACKNOWLEDGMENT

The work reported in this chapter was carried out from 1972–74 at the Eunice Kennedy Shriver Center, Waltham, Massachusetts, United States, with the support of NICHD grant No. HD 04147.

REFERENCES

Aiken, M., and Hage, J. (1966) Organizational alienation: A comparative analysis. Amer. Sociol. Rev. 31:497.

Henry, J. (1957) Types of institutional structure. *In* The Patient and the Mental Hospital (Ed. Greenblat, M.) Glencoe, Illinois: Free Press, p. 73.

Holland, T. (1973) Organizational structure and institutional care. J. Health Soc. Behav. 14:241.

King, R., and Raynes, N. (1968) An operational measure of inmate management in residential institutions. Soc. Sci. Med. 2:41.

King, R., Raynes, N., and Tizard, J. (1971) Patterns of Residential Care. London: Routledge and Kegan Paul.

Pratt, M., Bumstead, D., and Raynes, N. (1976) Attendant staff speech to the institutionalized retarded: Language use as a measure of care. J. Child Psychol. Psychiatry 17:133.

Raynes, N., Pratt, M., and Roses, S. (1975) Aides' involvement in decision-making and the quality of care in institutional settings. Paper presented at the American Association for Mental Deficiency Conference, Eastern Region, October.

Raynes, N. V., Pratt, M. W., and Roses, S. (1976) Variance in the quality of care in three unitized institutions. Paper presented at the 4th Congress of IASSMD, Washington, D.C.

Tizard, B., Cooperman, O., Joseph, A., and Tizard, J. (1972) Environmental effects on language development: A study of young children in long stay residential nurseries. Child Dev. 43:337.

Vroom, V. H. (1964) Working and Motivation. New York: Wiley.

RESEARCH TO PRACTICE IN MENTAL RETARDATION
Care and Intervention, Volume I
Edited by Peter Mittler
Copyright 1977 I.A.S.S.M.D.

A TYPOLOGY OF COMMUNITY CARE FACILITIES AND DIFFERENTIAL NORMALIZATION OUTCOMES

E. W. Butler and A. T. Bjaanes
*Center for the Study of Community Perspectives, and University
of California, Riverside, California, United States*

INTRODUCTION

There are essentially three basic assumptions underlying changes in policy related to the community care of the mentally retarded: 1) historic total institutions, i.e., large state hospitals, have failed to increase the competence of their residents, and may, in fact, have been detrimental to the development of social skills; 2) an environment providing "normal social contact" and the potential for "normal social interaction" has a positive "normalizing" effect on the mentally retarded; 3) community care facilities provide a relatively "normal environment," therefore, they have a "normalizing" effect on retardates, i.e., an increase in competence ensues.

A number of questions arise about the general validity of the assumptions outlined above. As indicated earlier, there is little doubt about the validity of the first assumption. There is considerable evidence indicating that total institutionalization tends to have a detrimental effect on motor skills, communication skills, learning skills, and social competence in general (Farber, 1968). There are, on the other hand, a limited number of studies supporting the second assump-

The observations and data used in this paper were made possible by NIMH grant MH 08667 and several Office of Developmental Disabilities Contracts from the State of California. This paper includes only a small portion of observations gathered to date. A revised version will include expanded analyses of observations in a stratified sample of *therapeutic, maintaining,* and *custodial* community care facilities.

tion. Several "special programs" have shown that *if the environment is significantly different* from that of the larger total institution, normalization can occur, and social and intellectual competence can be increased (Skeels and Dye, 1939; Kennedy, 1948; Baller, 1936; Edgerton, 1967; Mundy, 1957; McKay, 1946).

The last assumption is the most problematic. Are most current community care facilities significantly different from the total institution, and do they provide a relatively "normal" environment and thus have a "normalizing" effect on their residents? Obviously, the first problem is that this assumption takes for granted *uniformity* or *similarity* among various community care facilities. In fact, observations we have carried out in a large number of facilities indicate that there is a lack of uniformity and that a great deal of dissimilarity exists (Bjaanes and Butler, 1974; Butler and Bjaanes, in preparation; Butler et al., 1975, Moore et al., 1976; Butler, 1976). There is a range in size of community care facilities from 3–4 retardates up to 30 and more, and there are geographical differences, e.g., rural and urban, and differences in physical plants, to mention but a few of the facets in which considerable structural variation exists. Perhaps of more importance is the considerable variation in the "quality of life" support afforded individuals in different community care facilities. Furthermore, there is significant variability in the amount of social interaction, incentives for normalization, and caregiver knowledge, attitudes, behavior, and experience. Generally, variations range from small family care units to facilities that are replicas of larger total institutions, "mini-institutions." In view of the dissimilarities and lack of uniformity, it is clear that systematic investigation of type of community care facility and differential normalization outcomes is urgently needed.

An evaluation of the interrelationships between various factors in community care facilities affecting the success of placement is, by nature, a complex and difficult task (Butterfield (1967) summarizes major problems that must be taken into account). The ideal method of study would be experimental; the investigator should have both the ability and authority to control and manipulate significant variables such as caregiver characteristics, placement, and specific environment components. While this is not feasible, and perhaps not ethical, a similar in vivo experiment is taking place in the "social experiment" of placing retardates in community care facilities. Substantial numbers of retardates are currently being transferred from large state institutions to a variety of community care facilities. Thus, we have available different types of environments, and a substantial population entering different types of environments, making possible longitudinal studies starting with initial exposure to a changed environment.

Given a variety of community care alternatives, our hypothesis is that *different types of environments result in different kinds of normalization and social competence outcomes*. The speculative literature provides support for this hypothesis; however, to date, the effects of specific factors in the environment on social development have not been determined. Such information is essential to future planning, organization, and training required to optimize community care for the mentally retarded. Normalization outcomes of community care are related to the three major categories of variables of: 1) preplacement factors, 2) community care facility characteristics, and 3) type of care facility. A systematic assessment of *each* of these major groups is essential to determine the relationship among environments and social competence outcomes.

PREPLACEMENT FACTORS

Preplacement factors are those characteristics that the individual brings with him at the time of community care placement. Two categories of data are included under this heading, shown in Table 1. Individual characteristics include diagnosis, IQ, impairments, age, and family characteristics. Furthermore, preplacement information provides data on prior institutional and/or community care experience. In addition, level of social competence at *time of community care placement* provides baseline data against which competency levels over time can be examined by type of community care facility. Assessment needs to include information about the facility as well as the characteristics of the surrounding neighborhood and community.

At the individual level, the direction and magnitude of change in social competence relative to each individual's baseline social competency needs to be determined. At the care facility level, *mean* changes and directions of change can be computed, thus establishing patterns that may be different from individual change. If individual changes are regressive for some individuals and progressive for others within the same facilities, whatever changes take place are primarily due to individual factors. On the other hand, if a facility shows a specific uniform pattern of change among its residents, factors in the environment of the facility are associated with this pattern and specific factor(s) related to these changes must be determined. Mean changes and direction of change provide a basis for comparing various facilities in terms of their effect on residents.

TYPES OF COMMUNITY CARE FACILITIES

Preliminary observations indicate that community care facilities can be categorized into three types: 1) *custodial,* 2) *therapeutic,* and 3) *maintaining.* *Custodial* residences are those in which little or nothing is done to achieve normalization, and in which a lack of organized and structured activities may lead to retrogression by facility residents. *Therapeutic* facilities are those in which there is an active, ongoing attempt at enhancing the normalization process. There is a constant effort through organized activities to increase social competence and skills of residents. The third type is the *maintaining* type. Residents remain at more or less the same level of competence, i.e., little change takes place.

Table 1. A model for the evaluation of alternative community care facilities

Preplacement factors						
Personal	Prior placement(s)	Time of placement	Care facility characteristics	Type of care facility	Change	Differential outcomes
I. Individual's characteristic	I. Family of procreation	B A S E L I N E	I. Intra-facility characteristics	I. Therapeutic		
A. IQ	A. Time–in	S O C I A L	A. Population characteristics	A. Habilitative programs		Increased social competence
B. Education			B. Staff	B. Community contact		
C. Handicaps	II. Foster home		1) Number and ratio			Trend toward normalization
D. Physical handicaps	A. Location		2) Attitudes	C. Activities		
E. Physical health	B. Size		3) Training	D. Intensive caregiver involvement		
F. Mental health	C. Time–in		4) Experience	E. Other		
G. Sex	D. Programs (habilitation therapy)		C. Habilitative programs			
H. Age			1) Work training (vocational)	II. Maintaining		
I. Other	III. Home care facility		2) Physical therapy	A. Some habilitative programs		
			3) Educational			
			4) Other			
			D. Behavioral environment			
			E. Size of facility			

II. Family characteristic
   A. Size
   B. Marital history
   C. Marital status
   D. Occupational history
   E. Residential history
   F. Other

   A. Location
   B. Size
   C. Time—in
   D. Programs (habilitation therapy)

IV. Board and care facility
   A. Location
   B. Size
   C. Time—in
   D. Programs (habilitation therapy)

V. Institution
   A. Location
   B. Time
   C. Time—in
   D. Programs (habilitation)

COMPETENCE LEVEL

   F. Physical plant
   G. Other

II. Extra-facility characteristics
   A. Community-at-large
      1) Type of community
      2) Attitudes of population
      3) Recreational facilities
         a) Availability
         b) Use of
      4) Transportation
      5) Sheltered employment
   B. Immediate neighborhood
      1) Type
      2) Attitudes of population
      3) Recreational facility
         a) Availability
         b) Use of
      4) Sheltered employment
   C. Other

   B. Some community contact
   C. Some activities
   D. Some caregiver involvement
   E. Other

III. Custodial
   A. No habilitative programs
   B. No community contact
   C. No activities
   D. Little caregiver involvement
   E. Other

No change in social competence

Decrease in social competence (regression)

341

Preliminary determination of care facility type was made on the dimensions shown in Table 2. Criteria were developed during the early phases of the project; they are somewhat rudimentary and are subject to refinement and modification when more extensive systematic data analyses are completed. Care facilities identified as being custodial have the patterns shown, while therapeutic facilities are in direct contrast. Early findings suggest much closer analysis of factors that contribute to making a care facility either therapeutic, maintaining, or custodial is necessary, especially since they appear to be systematically related to the normalization process and development of social competence.

Clients living in a community care facility must utilize community opportunities to participate in outside normalizing activities. If not, the experience of the facility environment itself probably is not great enough to support the normalization process. Our data show that small facilities rarely utilize outside opportunities and that wide interaction with external settings is critically absent (Moore et al., 1976; Butler et al., 1975). Many small facilities are not providing the client those activities considered necessary for individual development, and in effect are *creating socially isolated total institutions within the community,* e.g., a custodial institution.

Caregiver interaction with clients *within* facilities varies with several important factors. Education of the caregiver influences both interaction and client opportunities more in a small facility than in a large facility. Caregiver experience and attitudes were critical across facility size. While experience has a negative effect on the amount of interaction, caregiver attitudes apparently create environmental support, nonsupport, or normalizing activities.

Caregiver attitudes were measured by a Therapeutic Orientation Scale measuring the caregiver's opinion of the capabilities of his/her particular clients and the developmentally disabled in general. Confidence in client abilities and accomplishments, accompanied by specific means of achieving development, placed the caregiver in a "high" category; those seeing little or no potential for their clients' improvement were ranked lower.

Table 2. Criterion measures used in establishing care facility types

Criterion measure	Care facility type		
	Therapeutic	Maintaining	Custodial
Habilitative programs	+	+−	−
Community interaction	+	+−	−
Recreational activities	+	+−	−
Sheltered workshop participation	+−	+−	−
Social activities participation	+	+−	−
Resident participation in chores	+	+−	−
Active caretaker involvement in care	+	+−	−
Daily activity routine	+	+−	−

Generally, a high therapeutic orientation is associated with both increased caregiver interaction and with more outside activities for clients. However, length of previous careprovider experience negatively influences interaction with clients. The amount of time spent in related work experiences (e.g., by nursing, technician, aide, etc.) and the length of time operating a facility has a dampening effect on interaction with clients.

Overall, the amount of *formal education* does not significantly affect the amount of caregiver interaction. This suggests that a therapeutic orientation and previous experience are more important than formal education. However, these factors may all be related to size of facility, which has been shown to have an important impact on creating normalizing opportunities. In smaller family care homes, where the caregiver's influence may not be mediated by additional staff, the relative importance of education may be more evident. Caregivers with more formal education tend to interact more with clients in small facilities. The effect of education is apparent in utilization of outside activities for clients.

FREQUENCY OF SPECIFIC TYPES OF BEHAVIOR

Perhaps of more interest is the extent to which specific types of behavior are participated in by clients within facilities. As shown in Table 3, active leisure activities are those that involve playing games, doing craftwork and dancing, and that are goal-oriented. For this type of activity to occur, there must be considerable involvement on the part of the caregiver in terms of planning and supervision (Bjaanes and Butler, 1974).

Passive leisure includes watching television, watching an activity take place, napping, and staring into space, and is not goal-oriented. This type of behavior requires little caregiver involvement. The observed frequencies for passive leisure behavior were greater in all cases than were frequencies for active behavior. In

Table 3. Frequences of observed acts falling in[a] each activity category by percentage

Activity category:	Board and care facility		Home care facility	
	I	II	I	II
Active leisure	5.5%	0.0%	3.5%	0.0%
Passive leisure	12.5	37.1	15.7	3.6
Work and chores	6.9	0.0	14.0	1.2
Personal activity	18.0	9.7	28.0	6.0
Interaction	56.9	53.0	38.5	89.1
	100.0%	100.0%	100.0%	100.0%
Total of acts observed (M)	71	113	57	83

[a]From Bjaanes and Butler, 1974.

contrast to the other care facilities, in one home care facility only 3.6% of all observed acts were of the passive leisure variety. Work and chores involve specific behaviors, such as cleaning, dusting, and cooking. This type of behavior was inconsistent between home care facilities and board and care facilities: in one board and care facility, 6.9% of all observed activities were work and chores, while in the other board and care facility no such behavior was observed.

Personal activities included grooming self, talking to self, talking to an inanimate object, and unintelligible mumbling. These activities were generally of an isolating type, not involving interaction with others. In terms of frequencies, there was a range from 6 to 28% in this kind of activity with no clear patterns of differences between the two types of community care facilities, although there was greater range within home care facilities. Interaction activities involved participation with others and included responses to suggestions, intelligible conversation, and physical show of affection. Of interest was the close similarity between the two board and care facilities, with a difference of only 4%, as compared to the 51% between the two home care facilities.

In summary, activities participated in by retarded persons vary within as well as between board and care facilities and home care facilities. The greatest variation in facilities was in the proportion of behavioral acts that were socially interactive in nature. Slightly over half of the behavioral acts of retarded persons in both board and care facilities were interactive. However, in one home care facility, interactive behavior accounted for only 38.5% of the observed behavior, while in the other it accounted for 89.1%.

PERCENTAGE OF TIME SPENT IN SPECIFIC TYPES OF BEHAVIOR

A different perspective on activities is shown in analyses that present amount of time spent in each type of behavior, as contrasted to frequency of occurrence. The main effect is to reduce the apparent extent of social interaction and to increase the importance of other activity categories.

Overall, only 3% of time was spent in active leisure behavior, with only one care facility having a significant amount of time spent in such activities. Twenty-two percent of time was spent in passive leisure behavior, although there was considerable variation. Both home care facilities were similar and both had a relatively high amount of time spent in this type of behavior. Board and care facilities showed a greater variation, with one having an amount twice as large as the mean time spent in passive leisure behavior. Also, this facility was the one in which no active leisure behavior was observed.

The mean time spent on work and household chores was 8.0%. Both home care facilities showed some time being spent on this type of behavior, with one of the facilities having 22% of the time being spent on work and chores. In board and care facilities, work and chores took place in only one facility; however, the amount of time involved there was slightly greater than in one of the home care facilities.

While there were significant differences between the four community care facilities in terms of the amount of time spent on personally oriented activities, there were no discernible patterns of difference between the board and care and the home care facilities, with variation within being as great as variation between. When passive leisure and personally oriented activity were combined, Board and Care Facility II and Home Care Facility I had a greater amount of time spent in behavior that tended to be isolated than did the other two care facilities. Social interactive behavior had a range of 55%, with the two board and care facilities being remarkably similar. There was, however, a significant difference between the two home care facilities. The amount of time spent on interactive behavior in one home care facility was almost twice the mean of 41%.

CONCLUSIONS

In order to provide a normalizing environment, community care facilities must provide an environment which is activity enriched both with internal programs and external contact and exchange. That is, the facility must be *therapeutic* as opposed to being a custodial or maintaining facility (Bjaanes and Butler, 1974). If normalization procedures are lacking, a deprived environment will tend to develop that will effectively hinder the normalization process. While this is obvious in large facilities, it is particularly critical in small care facilities, which, by virtue of size, must include activities and external interaction to approximate a normal environment. Isolation in small care facilities results in a social setting populated only by developmentally disabled persons, thus restricting activities, the number of role models, and experiences necessary for normalization to occur. Some learning theory suggests that a wide range of behaviors are learned through the process of imitation. Furthermore, enriched environments provide increased stimuli for learning. If there are no normalizing activities available, a deprived environment exists, the potential for normalization is negligible, and the facility is not fulfilling its intended function.

The results of this study, to date, clearly indicate several generalizations:

1. *There are substantial differences in the utilization of community agencies, services, and programs by community care facilities, as well as variation in normalizing activities within facilities.*

Generally, our data clearly indicate that in our sample interaction and exchange with the community is limited and intrafacility activities that could be considered normalizing are restricted in most facilities. The size of the sample and the wide geographical dispersion indicates that this may be, in fact, a general characteristic of small care facilities as they are presently staffed and operated.

2. *Variation in utilization of community agencies, services, and programs by community care facilities is associated with factors such as education and previous experience of the service providers, location of facility, size of*

facility, characteristics of the surrounding neighborhood, and extent of normalizing activities within facilities.

3. *Larger facilities, by and large, utilize agencies, services, and programs and have more internal normalizing activities; thus, they appear to be closer to the objective of normalization and developing social competence than smaller facilities.*

It has often been assumed, without carefully assessing the internal programs available and the extent of utilization of external community resources, that placing a developmentally disabled person in a community care facility is equivalent to providing a normalizing environment—*our data show otherwise.* This study, so far, shows quite clearly that if community care facilities are to provide normalizing environments, attention must be paid to the location and qualifications of service providers, the nature and extent of internal programs, and exchange with the community and utilization of community programs.

4. *It cannot and should not be assumed that a community care facility is a priori a normalizing environment. That assumption is much too likely to result in a shift from larger total institutions to smaller, dispersed community-based total institutions.*

A custodial or maintaining facility that has few or no internal and external programs to facilitate the normalization process can be considered just as much a total institution as a large state institution. It must be recognized that for a facility to be considered as therapeutic and enhancing normalization, internal and external programs must be *planned, implemented, and evaluated.*

SUMMARY

There is a wide range in community care environments, physical plants, types of supervision, and methods of care. A central question is which type of environment, or combination of various elements that comprise the total environment, is successful in the normalization process. This project empirically delineates optimum settings for enhancing the potential for normalization and increasing social competence.

REFERENCES

Baller, W. R. (1936) A study of the present social status of a group of adults who, when they were in elementary schools, were classified as mentally deficient. Genet. Psychol. Mongr. 18, June.

Bjaanes, A. T., and Butler, E. W. (1974) Environmental variation in community care facilities for the mentally retarded. Amer. J. Ment. Defic. 78:429.

Butler, E. W., and Bjaanes, A. T. A model for the evaluation of alternative community care facilities. In preparation.

Butler, E. W., Bjaanes, A. T., and Hofacre, S. (1975) The normalization process and the utilization of community agencies, services, and programs by community care facilities, June.

Butterfield, E. C. (1967) The role of environmental factors in the treatment of institutionalized mental retardates. *In* Mental Retardation: Appraisal, Education and Rehabilitation (Ed. Baumeister, A. A.) Chicago: Aldine.

Edgerton, R. B. (1967) The Cloak of Competence. University of California Press.

Farber, B. (1968) Mental Retardation, Its Social Context and Social Consequences. Boston: Houghton Mifflin.

Kennedy, R. J. R. (1948) The Social Adjustment of Morons in a Connecticut City, Hartford, Connecticut: Mansfield Southbury Training Schools, Social Service Department, State Office Building.

McKay, B. E. (1946) A study of IQ changes in a group of girls paroled from a State School for Mental Defectives. Amer. J. Ment. Defic. p. 496.

Moore, H., Butler, E. W., and Bjaanes, A. T. (1976) Careprovider characteristics and utilization of community opportunities for mentally retarded clients. Riverside: University of California.

Mundy, L. (1957) Environmental influence on intellectual function as measured by intelligence tests. Brit. J. Med. Psychol. 30:194.

Skeels, H. M., and Dye, H. A. (1939) A study of the effects of differential stimulation on mentally retarded children. Proc. AAMD. 44:114.

COMMUNITY
SERVICES

RESEARCH TO PRACTICE IN MENTAL RETARDATION
Care and Intervention, Volume I
Edited by Peter Mittler
Copyright 1977 I.A.S.S.M.D.

INTEGRATION OF THE MENTALLY RETARDED IN SOCIETY
Progress or Regress?

M. Egg-Benes
Voltastrasse 64, 8044 Zürich, Switzerland

The social integration of the retarded is in our days a major concern of all well-meaning people who are concerned with the problem of mental retardation. We all agree that the mentally handicapped have legal and human rights, the right to live, to be educated, to have work and leisure time. However, even at this point the basic disagreement starts.

Some of us claim for the retarded the same rights as other citizens have, pointing out that they are ordinary people and that they do not form a special group, so they should not be discriminated against as a group. Others, however, point out that the retarded are handicapped in different degrees and in different relations; hence they must be accepted *with* their handicaps, and society has a duty to offer them supporting services.

The question, then, is: Does every minority-group automatically create discrimination? I believe it does. For example, if a small group of highly qualified professors of medieval literature were placed on a farm, they would experience discrimination or even hostility. The same would happen if a small group of efficient and respected farmers were placed in the section for medieval literature of a college. With careful and intensive training some of them could probably adjust to the new surroundings, but, generally speaking, the farmers would not only be happier on the farm and the professors in the library, but they could only there develop to their fullest potential.

How does this example apply to the retarded? In earlier centuries, when we did not yet have residential institutions, they did live in their villages. Were they really integrated? They were caricatured as the "village idiot." At times they were worshipped as the personification of the "Holy Innocents," at other times they were banished because they were thought to be possessed by the devil. Hospitals were the only place of shelter for them. Has society changed so much that most of its members have already learned that the mentally retarded person is a person, nothing more, nothing less? If not, if there are still negative attitudes—which have to be broken down—then is it best to avoid segregation?

Even at the stage of child education there is disagreement about this question. Since the creation of public schools, every child has been expected to achieve the same educational goal. This is a wonderful idea, but it does not work. Therefore, special classes were opened for the retarded. Today some experts consider that the only sound formula is to integrate the retarded into ordinary classes. Others insist that retarded children could not withstand the stress of an ordinary school and therefore emphasize the value of placing them in special classes within the ordinary schools or even in special schools. Which of these ways offers education and training best adapted to the handicapped child's individual need?

Similar disagreement exists in the field of vocational problems. Much emphasis is laid on the provision of competitive jobs. Others recall that work in a sheltered environment often proves indispensable. The objective of rehabilitation is generally seen to be productive activity, but productivity is not an educational principle: it can serve the development of the handicapped person but it also can degrade him into a serving tool. History presents plenty of examples of this. Nowadays we seem to need to overcome the idea that if you are unable to engage in gainful employment, there is no purpose in living.

Today discussion centers on the question of where the adult retarded should live. We all agree that it is normal for adults to live apart from their family.

Some of the institutions for mentally retarded adults look back on a tradition of several centuries. They grew out of need. In most of them, handicapped persons can lead an existence filled with work and pleasure to the end of their lives, undisturbed by a hostile world, but others became too big and ceased to be homely places. So in some countries, especially in the United States, the movement of deinstitutionalization started, i.e., the transfer of retarded adults from large, state-run institutions to smaller community institutions or even into private foster homes.

It is still an open question whether or not the quality of a residential institution really depends mainly on its size. An institution of over a thousand residents can be an impersonal, overcrowded, inhuman place, but it can also be a happy community with the pulsing life of a prosperous village, where everybody can find what he needs. On the other hand, a small group home for six retarded persons can be a pleasant family-like place, but it can also be a ghetto, where handicapped persons live out their lives without the necessary special services and without the sympathy of their neighbours. Does the small size of an institution alone guarantee integration?

There are many more questions involved in integration. The mentally handicapped are a remarkably diverse group with a vast variety of impairments. What fits one does not fit others.

RESEARCH TO PRACTICE IN MENTAL RETARDATION
Care and Intervention, Volume I
Edited by Peter Mittler
Copyright 1977 I.A.S.S.M.D.

CULTURAL DIVERSITY, MENTAL RETARDATION, AND ASSESSMENT
The Case for Nonlabeling

J. R. Mercer
*Department of Sociology, University of California,
Riverside, California 92502, United States*

The identification of the mentally retarded through psychological assessment faces both conceptual and technical difficulties in culturally diverse societies. These difficulties are particularly acute in the assessment of organically intact persons who are not members of the dominant cultural group in the society. There are two basic conceptualizations of the society that can guide the assessment process: the conformity model of society and the pluralistic model of society. Figure 1 presents diagrams that depict these two concepts of society.

CONFORMITY MODEL OF SOCIETY

The conformity model visualizes the social order as consisting of one cultural tradition, that of the politically and economically most powerful group. The language, institutions, history, values, and life style of the dominant group are perpetuated through public education as a matter of public policy. Instruction is in the language of the most powerful group. The goal of public education is to acculturate the children of minority groups to the language and culture of the dominant cultural group and to wean them away from the language and culture of their parents. The implicit goal of public education is to produce monolingual, monocultural citizens acculturated to the dominant tradition. As is shown in Figure 1A, the conformity model assumes that nondominant cultural groups, shown as the broken circles *A, B,* and *C,* will acculturate and eventually disappear in the dominant culture.

The United States is an example of a culturally diverse society in which public policy has been based on a conformity model. The dominant group in the society for 300 years has been the English-speaking Caucasians, carriers of the

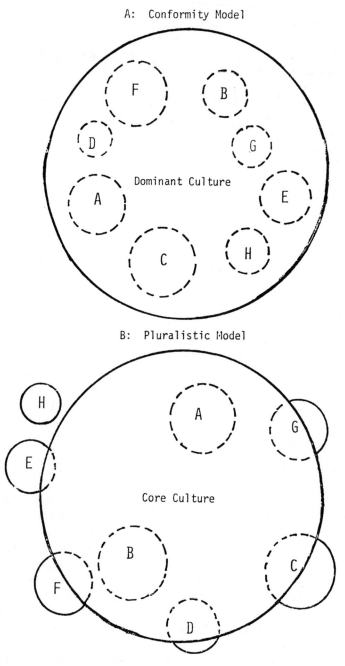

Figure 1. Two models of a culturally diverse society. *A*, conformity model; *B*, pluralistic model.

English cultural tradition. The dominant Anglo group has adopted a policy of anglicization in which public education has perpetuated the English language and the Anglo cultural traditions with the clear intent of "Americanizing" the children of migrant parents.

When the conformity model of society is the basis for public policy, assessment practices become part of the societal mechanism for enforcing and legitimizing cultural conformity. Standardized tests are designed to predict success in the monolingual and monocultural public schools. Tests are written in the language of the dominant culture, and test content is specific to that culture. A single normative framework is used to judge the quality of performance. Consequently, a child from the nondominant culture is compared with those of the dominant culture. Because he does not participate fully in the dominant culture, the average child from a minority group is likely to perform less well than a child being reared in the dominant culture. However, cultural conformists argue that the tests are "valid" because they predict accurately that children from minority backgrounds will perform more poorly in academic roles in school (Cleary et al., 1975). Historically, the monocultural framework has led to the belief that "achievement" tests and so-called "intelligence" tests tap psychologically distinct dimensions (Jensen, 1971; Eysenck, 1971), although this position recently has been abandoned by representatives of the American Psychological Association (Wesman, 1968; Cleary et al., 1975). The cultural conformity model also fosters the confusion of "prognosis" in psychological assessment with "diagnosis." Tests, designed as prognostic measures to predict future performance in the role of student, have been interpreted as if they yield diagnostic information on the etiology of the child's performance.

Testing based on a conformity model of society restricts the educational opportunities of minority children by assigning disproportionately large numbers to classes for the mentally retarded and disproportionately small numbers to classes for the gifted (Mercer, 1973). It results in greater stigmatization of minority children through placement in programs for subnormals. It has resulted in unidimensional assessment that has not credited the child with the ability to cope with complex social roles outside of school, e.g., in the family, community, and peer group. It devalues nondominant cultural traditions.

A PLURALISTIC MODEL OF SOCIETY

A pluralistic model visualizes the social order as being characterized by cultural and structural pluralism. Figure 1B pictures some of the complexities of the pluralistic model. It sees the culturally diverse society as organized around a core culture that consists of the common language(s) and the basic political and economic institutions that hold the society together. Various cultural groups have varying relations to the core culture. Some groups have been both culturally and structurally absorbed, such as the German Protestants, the Scotch-

Irish, and the Scandinavians in the United States. Other groups have been acculturated to the core culture but have maintained sufficient structural separatism through religious and communal organizations to remain identifiable. These groups are depicted by the dotted circles within the core culture. Irish Catholics and Jews would be examples of such groups in the United States. Still other groups span the boundaries of the core culture, as indicated by circles *C, D, E, F,* and *G.* Some members of these groups are acculturated to the core culture, while other members are varying socio-cultural distances from the core culture. Some members may be recent migrants who do not even speak the language of the core culture and share none of its values, beliefs, or behaviors. Examples of such heterogeneous groups in the United States would be Mexican-Americans, Puerto Ricans, Blacks, and Asians. Other groups, depicted by circle *H,* may still remain totally outside the core culture.

The ideology of cultural democracy (Ramírez and Castañeda, 1974) supports the maintenance of cultural pluralism. Unlike the ideology of conformity, cultural democracy regards all languages and cultures as having equivalent value. It supports the perpetuation of minority languages and cultures in the public schools as a matter of public policy, as well as the perpetuation of the core culture. It advocates educational alternatives within the public schools so that children have the option of participating in bilingual and multicultural educational programs. It sees the goal of public education as being the development of bilingual, bicultural, and bicognitive children who can operate effectively in the core culture *and* in one or more other linguistic and cultural systems.

When a pluralistic model of society forms the basis for developing an assessment system, conformity to the expectations of a monocultural school will not suffice as the basis for validating test instruments. Definitions of validity will need to be broadened to include performance in nonschool social roles. Test language and test content will be multilingual and multicultural. Multiple normative frameworks rather than a single norm will be needed so that a child's performance can be compared not only with that of the core culture but with that of other children from a sociocultural background similar to that of the child's. Multicultural tests would make it abundantly clear that all tests measure behavior learned in a sociocultural setting. Hence, all tests are achievement tests and no test is a direct measure of "innate ability." There would be a clear separation of prognostic information that predicts role performance in a particular social system and diagnostic information that seeks to explain the cause or etiology of a particular performance.

SYSTEM OF MULTICULTURAL PLURALISTIC ASSESSMENT (SOMPA)

The system of multicultural pluralistic assessment is designed for use in a culturally diverse society. It assumes a pluralistic model of society and seeks to implement the goals of cultural democracy. The system was developed on 700

English-speaking Caucasian children (hereafter called Anglos) from the Anglo core culture, 700 Black children, and 700 Latino children (90% were of Mexican-American heritage), 5 through 11 years of age. Each ethnic sample represents the population of children attending the public schools of California from that ethnic group in 1972.

SOMPA is based on three conceptual models: the medical model, the social system model, and the pluralistic model. Each model is based on a different definition of the nature of abnormality and a different set of assumptions.

Medical Model

The medical model was developed in medicine to understand biological malfunctioning and disease processes, such as measles, tuberculosis, or rheumatic fever. Although it is a powerful conceptual tool for explaining and controlling biologically based illnesses, attempts to use a medical model to explain nonmedical phenomena have been the source of much confusion in behavioral assessment.

The medical model identifies biological pathology through specifying symptoms. Because pathologies are defined by their symptoms, this model has also been called a deficit model. "Normal" remains a residual, undefined category consisting of those persons who do not have biological symptoms. This model assumes that pathological symptoms are caused by a biological condition. Because the biological organism of the human species is similar for all members of the species, sociocultural factors are not relevant to diagnosis when using a medical model. Tuberculosis can be diagnosed without knowing what language the patient speaks or the nature of his or her cultural heritage. Pathology is viewed as a characteristic of the organism of the person being diagnosed. When using a medical model, we say that a person "is" tubercular or "has" the measles. Cause-and-effect reasoning is appropriate in this model because the tendency is to seek biological causes for observed symptoms. Finally, a pathology can exist within a medical model, unrecognized and undiagnosed. For example, a person could have tuberculosis and not be aware that he or she was ill. Thus, within a medical model it makes sense to do epidemiologies in which the investigator seeks out hidden or undiagnosed illnesses by screening a sample population for tuberculosis, high blood pressure, cancer, or other biological conditions.

Since the medical model focuses on pathologies, measures operating from a medical model focus on deficits. Measures operating from this model tend to count or enumerate the pathological signs and to differentiate cases in the negative tail of the distribution. However, there is little differentiation among those diagnosed as "normal" because the normals consist of the large mass of persons who have no symptoms. The validity of measures operating from a medical model is determined by their correlation with other information about the biological organism. We would not expect to find high correlations with sociocultural characteristics, although there might be some elevation of the rate of pathology in those populations exposed to greater risk because of socioeconomic conditions or limited access to adequate health care facilities. Scores on tests for individual persons within a medical model can be interpreted without reference to their cultural background. They are not culture-bound.

Six measures in the SOMPA meet the assumptions of the medical model: the Physical Dexterity Tasks, the Bender-Gestalt Test, the Health History Inventory, visual acuity, auditory acuity, and the weight-by-height ratio. We do not list any "intelligence," "aptitude," or "achievement" tests as measures that meet the assumptions of a medical model. They *cannot* be interpreted from a strictly medical framework.

Social System Model

The social system model is derived from sociology rather than from medicine. Sometimes called the social deviance model, it defines abnormality as behavior that violates social system norms. Thus, there are multiple definitions of normal. Each role in each social system has its own set of expectations. For example, the behavior expected of a child who is playing first base on the softball team differs from that expected of the same child when playing the role of clarinetist in the band, which in turn differs from the behavior expected when playing the role of student in the sixth grade social studies class. To judge whether a particular set of behaviors is "normal" or "abnormal" requires four kinds of information. We must know the system in which the child is functioning, the role the child is playing in the system at the time the judgment is being made about his or her behavior, the expectations that others in the system have for behavior of persons playing that role, and information on the actual behavior of the child.

Norms for social systems are determined by political processes within the system. The dominant group in a system establishes the rules that govern behavior for various social roles. Present assessment tools are focused on a single role in a single social system: the role of student in the public schools. The norms that say that a successful student in the public school of the United States speaks standard English and has a knowledge of the Anglo core culture were established by the politically dominant group. Such expectations make "deviants" of those who do not belong to the dominant culture.

The social system model has seven characteristics: 1) it is a multidimensional model; 2) there are norms for each role in each social system, 3) it is an evaluative model—the values of the most powerful groups are enforced, 4) definitions of behavior are both role-bound and system-bound, 5) it is necessary to specify both the role and the system within which the assessment is being made, 6) it is both a deficit model and 7) an asset model because both the poor performers and the outstanding performers in various social roles can be identified. Consequently, test scores within a social deviance model form a normal distribution rather than truncated distributions such as are found in the medical model. Social deviance is a judgment about specific behavior. Hence, it is not appropriate to think in terms of deviance residing "in" the child nor to think of deviance as existing "undiagnosed." Since the political process defines what behavior is deviant, cause-and-effect reasoning is inappropriate when operating from a social system perspective.

Scores for social deviance measures form a normal distribution because there is a full range of differentiation. Measures assess competencies as well as deficits. Because scores should reflect social system norms, the validity of a measure within a social system model is determined by the extent to which scores on the measurement correlate with independent judgments of the person's behavior made by members of the system.

The Wechsler Intelligence Scale for Children—Revised (WISC-R), which is used in the SOMPA, is a social system measure. It identifies which children are likely to meet the expectations for the role of student. Hence, it is a measure of scholastic functioning level in the public schools as they are now constituted. The validity of the WISC-R and similar measures has been established by correlating scores on the test with teacher judgments, teacher grades, or some other measure of scholastic success. Scores on measures operating from a social system model relate to a specific role in a specific social system and should not be generalized beyond that role.

The Adaptive Behavior Inventory for Children (ABIC), which is also part of the SOMPA, is likewise a social system measure. It is designed to measure the child's role behavior in the family, community, peer group, nonacademic school roles, self-maintenance, and earner-consumer roles from the viewpoint of the family.

Pluralistic Model

The pluralistic model is a third model used in the SOMPA. It has a different definition of "normal" and a different set of assumptions from those of the medical or social system models. The initial idea for the pluralistic model developed during our earlier studies of the labeling of the mentally retarded in the community (Mercer, 1973). During that study, it was clear that psychologists believed that the scores on so-called measures of "intelligence" indicated something about the child's ability or aptitude in general. They were not limiting their interpretations entirely to predictions about scholastic performance. We theorized that it might be possible to make inferences about a child's learning potential *if* certain assumptions were rigorously observed: 1) that children whose performances are compared have had similar opportunities to learn the materials and acquire the skills covered in the test; 2) that the children have been similarly motivated by the significant other persons in their lives to learn this material and acquire these skills; 3) that they have had similar experience with taking tests; 4) that they have no emotional disturbances or anxieties interfering with test performance; and 5) that they have no sensori-motor disabilities interfering with prior learning or with their ability to respond in the test situation. When these factors are held constant, the pluralistic model assumes that the child who has learned the most probably has the most "learning potential" (Mercer, 1973, chapter 16). If a child's sociocultural background influences his/her opportunity to learn, motivation to learn, and test-taking experience, we reasoned that controlling for the child's sociocultural background would hold these three factors relatively constant. In a pluralistic model, "normal" is defined as performance near the average for children who are from similar sociocultural backgrounds.

We have used multiple regression equations to estimate the "average" performance for children from differing ethnic, sociocultural, and socioeconomic backgrounds. We have developed four sociocultural scales—Urban Acculturation, Socioeconomic Status, Family Structure, and Family Size—in order to measure background characteristics. Table 1 presents the nine sociocultural factors that make up the four sociocultural scales and the weight that is given each factor in calculating a child's raw score on each scale. These scales locate the child in the sociocultural space of American society, as depicted in Figure 1B. The four scores for the child's background are substituted into the multiple regression equations for his/her ethnic group, and the estimated average score for the group is calculated. The score for a particular child is then compared with the average for others from precisely the same sociocultural and socioeconomic background. The adjusted score is interpreted as the child's "Estimated Learning Potential."

A pluralistic model assumes that "subnormal" is a test score that is low when compared to the child's own sociocultural group. It assumes that all psychological tests measure learned behavior and that children from similar sociocultural settings are roughly similar in the opportunity to learn, the motivation to learn,

Table 1. The nine sociocultural factors that were combined to form the four sociocultural modalities: SOMPA

Sociocultural modality	Original factor	Weight	Raw score range
Urban acculturation	Anglicization	6	
	Sense of efficacy	2	0–88
	Community participation	2	
	Urbanization	1	
Socioeconomic status	Occupation of head of household	1	
	Source of Income	1	0–12
Family structure	Marital status	4	0–18
	Relationship of child to parents	3	
Family size	Family size	1	0–30[a]

[a]A high score on urban acculturation, socioeconomic status, and family structure characterizes families that are more like the dominant Anglo culture, while a high score on family size characterizes families that are less like the dominant Anglo culture.

Table 2. Percent distribution of Estimated Learning Potential (ELP) for WISC-R verbal, performance, and full scale scores for Black, Chicano/Latino, and Anglo children, 6 through 11 years old.

ELP	Verbal			Performance			Full scale		
	Black %	Chicano/Latino %	Anglo %	Black %	Chicano/Latino %	Anglo %	Black %	Chicano/Latino %	Anglo %
50–54			.16	.21	.37	.33		.19	.66
55–59		.19	.33	.21	.55	.50	.22		.50
60–64	.43	.76	.82			.33		.77	.50
65–69	1.52	1.14	.98	.87	1.47	.99	1.09	2.88	1.99
70–74	1.95	3.43	2.45	1.96	3.33	1.98	2.84	1.73	5.13
75–79	4.55	4.00	4.25	5.43	2.95	3.63	5.02	3.84	5.96
80–84	8.87	6.86	6.37	7.39	5.73	4.95	5.46	5.37	9.27
85–89	9.09	9.52	9.80	7.60	9.61	9.90	11.57	9.98	11.59
90–94	11.26	11.62	10.13	11.52	13.12	13.37	10.04	13.44	11.59
95–99	13.85	14.48	13.24	12.82	12.01	13.70	15.28	14.01	15.89
100–104	11.47	10.67	14.54	14.78	11.28	11.72	10.04	9.98	10.60
105–109	11.26	12.57	13.07	9.34	13.31	13.53	13.76	11.71	10.93
110–114	10.17	9.52	8.50	9.78	10.54	8.58	8.08	10.75	5.63
115–119	7.36	7.43	7.03	8.48	7.02	5.94	6.99	7.87	5.13
120–124	3.03	4.76	3.43	4.13	4.44	5.61	4.15	3.26	2.32
125–129	1.95	2.10	2.78	2.60	2.40	1.98	3.28	2.11	.66
130–134	1.08	.38	.65	1.96	1.29	1.49	1.09	1.34	.66
135–139	.87	.38	.65	.87	.55	.82	.22	.58	.66
140–144	1.30	.19	.49			.33	.66		.33
145–149			.16			.33	.22	.19	
150–154			.16						
Total N	462	525	612	460	541	606	458	521	604
Mean	99.54	98.99	99.60	100.22	99.65	100.19	99.77	99.21	100.05
S.D.	15.20	14.62	15.08	14.92	14.94	15.08	14.94	15.02	15.01

and test experience. Emotionally disturbed or physically disabled children are detected by other measures. The pluralistic model has as many distributions as there are possible combinations of the four sociocultural scales. It is evaluative. It assumes high potential is better than low potential. It is completely culture-bound. Scores reveal the child's relative rank among children from similar sociocultural backgrounds. It is primarily an "asset" model. In actual practice, scores of non-Anglo children are modified primarily in a positive direction.

The pluralistic model assumes that "learning potential" is an attribute of the child and that scholastic potential can exist, unrecognized, because the child's potential is masked by the cultural distance between the child and the culture of the school. Table 2 presents the distribution of Estimated Learning Potential for the children in our sample. The ELP is completely normalized for all groups.

The SOMPA is a system of assessment that triangulates the evaluation process. It looks at the child through a *medical model* and screens for possible biological anomalies indicated by the health history, performance on the physical dexterity battery, or tests of vision or hearing. Using a *social system model,* it looks at the child's performances in family roles, peer group roles, community roles, earner/consumer roles, self-maintenance roles, nonacademic school roles, and academic school roles. Using a *pluralistic model,* it evaluates the child's performance relative to others from the same socio-cultural background and makes inferences about the child's estimated learning potential. Through this process, we hope to identify the non-Anglo child whose potential may be masked by the distance between the child's location in sociocultural space and the culture of the school.

REFERENCES

Cleary, T., Humphreys, L. G., Kendrick, S. A., and Wesman, A. (1975) Educational uses of tests with disadvantaged students. Amer. Psychol. 30:15.

Eysenck, H. J. (1971) The IQ Argument: Race, Intelligence, and Education. New York: The Library Press.

Jensen, A. R. (1971) Do schools cheat minority children? Educ. Res. 14:3.

Mercer, J. R. (1973) Labeling the Mentally Retarded. Berkeley: University of California Press.

Ramírez, M., III, and Castañeda, A. (1974) Cultural Democracy, Bicognitive Development, and Education. New York: Academic Press.

Wesman, G. A. (1968) Intelligent testing. Amer. Psychol. 23:267.

RESEARCH TO PRACTICE IN MENTAL RETARDATION
Care and Intervention, Volume I
Edited by Peter Mittler
Copyright 1977 I.A.S.S.M.D.

MENTAL RETARDATION IN THE COMMUNITY
The Transition from Childhood to Adulthood

S. A. Richardson
Departments of Pediatrics and Community Health,
Albert Einstein College of Medicine,
Yeshiva University, 1300 Morris Park Avenue, Bronx, N.Y. 10461, United States

There have been no follow-up or longitudinal studies that deal with the total population of all subtypes of mentally retarded children in a community and follow the population through adolescence into adulthood. There are, however, studies that follow up particular subsets of people with mental subnormality. The earliest and most numerous studies deal with people who had been in residential institutions for the mentally subnormal and were released or had escaped from the institutions. The results showed that the subjects of the studies, in many cases, were able to function in the community, find and hold jobs, marry and raise families. They did not exhibit the social pathological behaviors expected of those who were retarded, and those who had children did not produce large numbers of severely retarded children (Tizard, 1965; Cobb, 1972; Goldstein, 1964). The studies were valuable in challenging the conventional wisdom of the early twentieth century that genetic factors were dominant in the etiology of mental retardation. It was a time of segregating the mentally retarded into large isolated institutions, a time when legislation was passed permitting sterilization of the retarded, and a time when there seemed little point in social habilitation.

Major difficulties in interpreting these studies are the absence of data on the level of functioning of the subjects when they were children, and the absence of knowledge concerning whether or not they were in any way representative of the populations in residential institutions. Placement in institutions occurred for many reasons other than clear evidence of severe mental retardation and included placement of people who were judged to be nuisances or trouble-makers by families, courts, or influential members of the community; many were orphans or persons for whom no other placement could be found. Although it might be expected that studies of residents and ex-residents of mental retardation institutions would focus on the severely retarded, for whom placement in residential facilities has some rationale, the focus has been largely on adults with mild degrees of mental retardation, for whom institutional care was inappropriate.

A second kind of study has been the follow-up into adulthood of young people who were placed in special classes for the mentally handicapped. These studies have shown that many of these young people were able, as young adults, to live in the community away from their parents' home, a proportion found employment, and some married, raised families, and were able to function in the adult society. Others experienced real problems in achieving satisfactory living conditions.

These studies have focused attention on neglected problems and have challenged dogmatic and limited conceptualizations of mental retardation. There are, however, a number of methodological and substantive limitations that make it difficult to generalize about the studies or apply them to some of the contemporary issues in the field of mental subnormality:

1. The studies are largely retrospective, with limited information on the adults when they were of school age.
2. The criterion for inclusion in the studies has predominantly been placement in special educational facilities for the mentally handicapped, and sometimes the availability of an IQ score.
3. Often the study population includes a heavy representation of individuals from minority groups or individuals who are recent immigrants.
4. The nature of the selection process for special educational placement is not known.
5. Few of the studies have any comparison group obtained from the same school or residential area, so it is not possible to interpret the extent to which their functioning in later life and place in society are consequences of intellectual impairment.
6. Because total populations of mentally subnormal young persons have not been followed up, it has not been possible to examine the subsequent life histories of young persons with different subtypes of mental subnormality living in the same community.
7. There have been no longitudinal studies of mental subnormality that examine the experiences of young people as they progress from childhood to adulthood and in which the emphasis is on the influences both of parents, relatives, neighbors, and friends who are significant to the young people, and of the various agencies of society, such as education, health, vocational, and residential services.

RESEARCH ISSUES

There are a number of critical issues related to mental retardation that deal with social policy, the planning and evaluation of services, and with the lives of young people who are mentally retarded and their families, and they cannot be properly examined without longitudinal research. The following are examples of these issues.

Young People Who Cease
to be Officially Considered Mentally Retarded After Leaving School

Many children who are administratively classified as mentally retarded when they are at school do not continue to be officially considered mentally retarded after they leave school. Gruenberg (1964) has pointed out that in a number of epidemiological studies, the prevalence of mental retardation after the age of 14 is only half as high as at the age of 14. These findings pose critical questions for understanding the nature of mental subnormality and for decision making in public policy. Gruenberg (1964) suggests for example:

> . . . For this drop in prevalence to occur, a large group of people regarded as retarded at fourteen must improve in their functioning to the point where people no longer regard them as retarded and [they] also must succeed in escaping their history of earlier unsatisfactory performance (p. 274).
> . . . Either these individuals are continuing to be extremely handicapped in later life and are unknown because the services they need are unavailable to them (in which case society is failing to do its duty toward them and ought to learn how to find and help them), or they have stopped being retarded in any real sense at all and do not need any special protection, help or services, in which case one had better change one's concept of what "real" retardation "really" is (p. 274).

The phenomenon "cries out for investigation."

To examine this issue requires identifying all children in a community who at any time during schooling have been administratively classified as mentally retarded and then following them into adulthood to determine who is, and who is not, receiving services related to mental retardation after leaving school. In addition to obvious questions such as whether or not they are employed, it will be necessary to examine the quality of their lives compared to peers who went to regular schools. Clearly a major research challenge is to work out objective indicators of what constitutes quality of life.

What New Perspectives Can be Gained from the Experiences
of Young People Who are Mentally Subnormal and Their Parents?

Assessment of Services   In the United States, the President's Panel on Mental Retardation emphasized the need for a "continuum of care" in developing a comprehensive program for the retarded. The continuum needs to be considered not only with reference to differing stages of individual development but also to the relationships among services at any particular stage of development. Assessment of services both during the school years and afterwards has been largely fragmentary, based on the view and experience of professionals in the field of mental retardation. The assessments have been of particular services, and the unit of study is generally the institution or organization and how it provides the service. Relatively little attention has been paid to the consumer's viewpoint and experiences and how the various forms of services affect a young person as he or she progresses from childhood to adulthood. Investigation of the consumer's viewpoint provides a method of studying directly how effectively a continuum of care is being provided and the interrelationships among various services. An important element in consumer research is determining whether there are unmet as well as met needs and whether there may be alternative forms of service consumers would prefer to those now given.

Learning from the Experiences of Parents in Bringing up Mentally Subnormal Children For most minority groups the experience of coping with their problems and disadvantages can be shared within and between families and passed on from one generation to the next. In this way a body of knowledge develops in the minority group that cumulates and can assimilate ingenious social inventions discovered by members of the group. Parents of children who are mentally subnormal are a minority group that do not have this advantage. They are generally unprepared for their role of rearing intellectually impaired children and have limited sources to turn to for help in socializing their child. A heavy emphasis in the literature on mental subnormality is the tragedy and problems associated with having, caring for, and rearing a child who is mentally subnormal. There is the widespread assumption that the experience of having a mentally subnormal child is negative and punitive. We need to learn from parents their positive as well as negative experiences with their children. There is need to cumulate the knowledge and experiences parents have gained and make it available to younger parents who are faced with the task of bringing up a child who is mentally retarded.

Encouraging Young People Who are Mentally Subnormal to Speak for Themselves It has not been customary to let people who are mentally subnormal speak for themselves about their experiences or to obtain from them an evaluation of their experiences. Spokesmen for the mentally subnormal have generally been professionals in the mental retardation services and sometimes parents of mentally handicapped people. Yet, we know from our experience and the reports of other investigations that, for all but the most profoundly retarded, it is possible with time, patience, and skill to obtain an account of their lives in considerable detail. Young people who are mentally subnormal can provide new insights and understanding into the day-to-day lives of people from whom we have much to learn.

Identification of Variables that may Predict the Level of
Adult Functioning for Children who are Mentally Subnormal

"What will my child be like when he is grown up?" is a question of profound concern to all parents of children who are mentally subnormal. At a more general level the same question is equally important to those responsible for the planning and operation of services for the mentally subnormal. In very broad terms some prediction can often be made for the profoundly retarded, especially when there are associated severe functional handicaps. But for most children with mild and moderate degrees of mental subnormality, as measured by intelligence tests, very little is known about what factors provide indicators for prediction. It is known that IQ, which was a measure developed and intended for the prediction of school performance only, is not necessarily a reliable predictor of future adult functioning. It will be necessary to obtain longitudinal data on biological and social experiental factors and the way these biosocial factors interact during the socialization of children who are mentally retarded.

Mental Subnormality and Stigma

Some studies suggest that young people who are mentally retarded are badly hurt by being the objects of stigma.

In a study of adults who had been in a residential institution and who were then released and living in the community, Edgerton (1967) was so impressed by the problems of stigma for the adults in his study that the concept is included in the title of his book, *The Cloak of Competence: Stigma in the Lives of the Mentally Retarded.* He found that those he studied went to great lengths to conceal the fact that they had been institutionalized and thus labeled as mentally retarded by the society. They also desperately tried to conceal their various forms of incompetence so as not to appear different from others.

It is important to find out whether these results from a very special subset of retarded persons will be found within various subtypes of mental retardation. It is necessary to examine what attributes or traits among mentally retarded of different subtypes form the stimulae for stigma reactions, e.g., if it is the knowledge that an individual has been classified as retarded or the cues of behavior, appearance, and movement that are used to infer that a person is slow, stupid, or whatever naive psychological categories are used by the perceiver, or if it is some combination of these factors.

School and Postschool
Careers of Young People who are Borderline Mentally Subnormal

The recent concern over the possible effects of labeling a child mentally subnormal has primarily focused on the stigmatizing aspects (e.g., Mercer, 1973. Evidence supporting the deleterious consequences has been derived from studies of children with IQs in the borderline and mild mental subnormality range who were placed in special classes). There has not been sufficient recognition that this evidence is one-sided, and children of comparable IQ who are not labeled and remain in regular classes have not been taken into account in research. It is true that they avoid the stigma attached to being labeled mentally subnormal. They are, however, deprived of the protection, special care, and concessions given to those in special education. Some educators believe that the borderline children in regular schools may experience severe difficulties in achieving any form of legitimate status and success at school and that their poor work performance is often interpreted as the result of inattention, laziness, or poor study habits. They can easily become the scapegoats of teachers and peers and develop resentment against authority figures. They may also seek to achieve some status among peers through delinquent and deviant behavior.

There are many formidable problems in the design and execution of studies to examine these issues. The problems include:

1. The initial identification of a total population of retarded children in a geographically defined community.
2. The selection of a comparison set of children who are not retarded but are otherwise comparable on matching factors such as age, sex, and socio-economic status of the family.
3. The identification of a total population of borderline retarded children who were not administratively defined as mentally retarded.
4. The tracing and follow-up of the three above sets of children into adulthood.
5. The design and use of standardized life history interviews covering the period from childhood to adulthood.

This author is currently attempting such a study and hopes to make some contribution to the understanding of these issues.

REFERENCES

Cobb, H. V. (1972) The Forecast of Fulfillment, A Review of Research on Predictive Assessment of the Adult Retarded for Social and Vocational Adjustment. New York: Teachers College Press.

Edgerton, R. B. (1967) The Cloak of Competence: Stigma in the Lives of the Mentally Retarded. Berkeley: University of California Press.

Goldstein, H. (1964) Social and occupational adjustment. In Mental Retardation. A Review of Research. (Eds. Stevens, H. A., and Heber, R.) Chicago: University of Chicago Press.

Gruenberg, E. M. (1964) Epidemiology. In Mental Retardation. A Review of Research (Eds. Stevens, H. A., and Heber, R.) Chicago: University of Chicago Press.

Mercer, J. R. (1973) Labeling the Mentally Retarded. Berkeley: University of California Press.

Tizard, J. (1965) Longitudinal and follow-up studies. *In* Mental Deficiency: The Changing Outlook (Eds. Clarke, A. M., and Clarke, A. D. B.) London: Methuen.

RESEARCH TO PRACTICE IN MENTAL RETARDATION
Care and Intervention, Volume I
Edited by Peter Mittler
Copyright 1977 I.A.S.S.M.D.

THE STUDY OF COMMUNITY ADAPTATION
Toward an Understanding of Lives in Process

R. B. Edgerton
The Neuropsychiatric Institute, University of California,
Los Angeles, California 90024, United States

It is, I believe, widely agreed that our current knowledge of the community adaptation of mentally retarded persons is inadequate in several important respects (Cobb, 1972; McCarver and Craig, 1974). First, we have yet to develop any prognostic variables that permit better than chance prediction of "vocational success" or "community adjustment." Second, and equally important, we have done little to develop a qualitative understanding of what it is like to be a mentally retarded person attempting to cope with the exigencies of community living. The first failing is scientific, the second is scientific *and* humanistic. Both kinds of failings need to be rectified if we are serious about our desire to comprehend and implement successful community adaptation.

It is widely recognized that most of the published research about the community adaptation of retarded persons has serious flaws. For one thing, this body of literature rests primarily on second-order data, not directly on observation of the lives of retarded persons. That is, what we know comes from official records, tests, demographic indices, and various kinds of interviews and self-reports from social caseworkers, parents, employees, and retarded persons themselves. What is more, most of this research is cross-sectional in design, but even the longitudinal research that examines adaptation over a period of several years relies on brief samples of data taken at various, usually widely separated, time intervals. This is true of even the best follow-up studies, such as those of Kennedy (1966) and Baller, Charles, and Miller (1966). To be sure, several

This research was supported by the National Institute of Child Health and Human Development, Public Health Service grant HDO4612, the Mental Retardation Research Center, UCLA, grant 05540-02, and U.S. Public Health Service grant HD-09474-01.

investigators have urged a more developmental perspective (e.g., Gunzburg, 1968), but even those who have most seriously attempted to collect data continuously rather than episodically have achieved only limited success (e.g., Deno, 1965; Shulman, 1967). There are very good reasons why this inadequacy should exist. Most basically, it is both very difficult and exceedingly expensive to collect data on a continuing basis over a period of years, especially when these data include such time-intensive techniques of data collection as direct observation, participant-observation, and life history interviewing.

A RESEARCH PROGRAM

In the hope of interesting other investigators in the same goal, I would like to describe a research program that is designed to produce a continuous record of community adaptation based on a variety of data sources. This research is both retrospective and prospective. It is retrospective in its use of life history reconstruction, and prospective in its effort to record the details of community adaptation on a daily basis over an extended period.

The use of a life history approach in the social sciences has long been attempted (Dollard, 1935; Allport, 1942), but as yet it has produced neither a standard methodology nor a solid corpus of data (Langness, 1965). Nevertheless, this approach continues to hold promise for improving our understanding of how retarded persons have lived their lives, as well as how they feel about themselves and their past (Bogdan and Taylor, 1975).

Life history approaches have only seldom been utilized in the study of mental retardation. It has been commonplace to publish vignettes about retarded persons (e.g., Earl, 1961; Sarason and Doris, 1969), and some of these vignettes are substantial, sensitive, and evocative (e.g., Blatt, 1970; 1973), but the usual result is a kind of case history—a brief synopsis of the salient points in a retarded person's past and present. Some of these case histories are longer than others (e.g., Lent et al., 1972), but even my own use of the technique has fallen far short of producing extended and detailed life histories or autobiographies (Edgerton, 1967).

Recently, some investigators have allowed mentally retarded persons to speak for themselves (e.g., Edgerton, 1967; Mattinson, 1970; Henschel, 1972; Bogdan and Taylor, 1975), but a full-scale life history is still a rarity. Oddly, the few that have been published either focus on Down's syndrome people or are the work of journalists or novelists. Thus, Seagoe (1964) provides a rich life-history of a Down's man, and another Down's man, Nigel Hunt (1967), has written his autobiography. The lives of mildly retarded persons have been more fully portrayed by popular writers such as Daniel Keyes in *Flowers for Algernon* (1966), more recently called *Charley,* or by journalists such as Danny Lyon, who helped to record the life of Billy McCune (1973). But an institutionalized, cerebral palsied man, called Joey, laboriously set down his own poignant life story in book form by devising a writing syndicate: his experienced friend interpreted his grimaces and gestures into words, one fellow spelled out the letters, the last man typed them out (Deacon, 1976). His life story and the making of the book were dramatized on television.

Life history recording is far more an art than a science, but our experience suggests that it is not a very much more difficult art with retarded persons than it is with so-called normal ones. In either event, a host of idiosyncratic factors must always be dealt with. What is important to note is that, in our experience at least, many mentally retarded persons of varied IQ levels, with varying degrees of articulateness, who live in various kinds of social circumstances are both willing and able to provide detailed and meaningful recollections of their lives. When their own recollections are supplemented by the recollections of various parents, siblings, friends, and employees, the result is a set of portraits of great complexity and potential value.

Because of the time involved in life history reconstruction, it can only be utilized with a small subsample of persons. We are working up life histories with approximately twelve persons from our larger sample of 100 men and women who are engaged in the process of adapting to some kind of community life. With the larger sample of 100 our basic approach is prospective; that is, we attempt to maintain a detailed record of each person's behavior on a daily basis. Although this is our ideal, in reality we can only approximate it. Again, time and money are the limiting factors. Our basic data collection strategy is participant-observation, and we attempt to have face to face interaction with each member of the sample on a weekly basis. These "visits" occur under varying circumstances (conversations in the person's residence, trips to an agency, recreational outings, etc.), and for periods of time ranging from one to six hours. These direct contacts provide a continuing source of first-hand knowledge of that person and his or her adaptive behavior in various community settings. In addition to these face to face procedures, we ask that each person in our sample maintain a daily diary of routine activities and noteworthy happenings, or, as we call them, "normalization incidents"—occurrences that have particular significance for the process of normalization. This they do, when literate, by actually keeping a diary; those who cannot maintain a written diary either use a tape-recorder provided for that purpose, or call us at an answering-recording telephone number and tell us about their day's activities.

We have found that most persons can maintain some form of record of their daily activities, including noteworthy occurrences either pleasant or upsetting. However, most of these daily records are typically quite brief. Therefore, we call or see each person each week to discuss with them their daily diaries in an effort to obtain a more detailed account of each day's activities. For this purpose, the daily record is used as a mnemonic and a means of focusing discussion. We have attempted this kind of daily activity recording with a small sample of persons in the past; recently we have extended it to a sample of 100. The research technology is not particularly difficult, but the research *is* time consuming, and despite our increasing use of student volunteers, shortage of research staff may eventually compel us to reduce our sample size.

We intend to continue this research for two years in an effort to record in as much detail as possible the processes by which various kinds of mentally retarded persons adapt to community living. The results of this two-year effort cannot now be anticipated in full, but our past several years of research using these methods with a small sample of persons suggest that useful findings will emerge. Space limitations do not permit any extended discussion of our present findings here, and since these findings are preliminary, extended discussion is not yet warranted. Briefly, however, our preliminary research with life history and daily activity recording suggests that these hypotheses will be confirmed:

PROVISIONAL HYPOTHESES

1. The most conspicuous feature of the lives of these people is change.
2. These changes sometimes occur continuously over the course of a life, so that a person who is now 50 years of age has a completely different set of adaptive behaviors and understandings than he did at age 20 or 30.
3. Other changes occur in the form of day to day fluctuations in adaptation after taking on crisis dimensions, which, in a significant number of cases, lead some normal person to intervene in the retarded person's life—with a resulting reduction in that person's opportunities for more normal adaptation (Edgerton, 1976).
4. Change away from middle-class standards toward "sub-standard" styles of adaptation are resisted by persons in service delivery systems (caseworkers, counselors, caregivers, parents), yet these "sub-standard" styles of dress, hygiene, diet, etc., may optimize community adaptation.
5. Positive change may be most likely to occur when assistance from the delivery system is minimal, not when it is maximal.

Whether or not any or all of these hypotheses is confirmed may prove to be less important for our understanding of community adaptation than one other outcome that we feel is assured—a detailed record of human lives in process. From this record should emerge a clear sense not only of variability and change, but also of continuity and development as well. If we examine these lives in process we may also come to respect both the capacity and the right of mentally retarded persons to live more nearly normal lives.

AN EXAMPLE

Perhaps an illustration would be helpful in indicating what such an examination can yield. Fred, a 48-year-old man, had an IQ of 52 when he was discharged from a large state institution in 1957. We have followed his life in the community on and off since 1960, and for the past several years we have employed the continuous data recording procedures described here. We have learned about his complex interpersonal relationships with family, friends, and employers before, during, and after his institutionalization. We have seen not only their roles in his life, but also his role in theirs. Each of these persons sees him somewhat differently, and in so doing adds new dimensions to our understanding. By the use of years of close participant-observation with him, we also know how he manages to support himself by working at four to six janitorial jobs at once (sometimes for more than 60 hours a week), how his adaptive skills vary from one situation to another (he is quite competent in some complex environments and not very competent at all in others), how he depends on a network of people for help and affection, and yet how many of these people depend on him in return. We have seen how his hopes and dreams, even his illusions, are not disembodied ideation, but are essential components of his adaptive armamentarium. And we see how his life changes from one week or month to the next. In recording this human odyssey, we have begun to understand how this mentally retarded man has not only managed to cope with life in an urban center, but more than this, how his life has enriched the lives of others around him. We do not fully understand him and we never will, but we do understand him much better and we fully respect him. When it is possible to write about his life in detail we are hopeful that others will be able to share this understanding and respect.

SUMMARY

The use of a life history approach, including the prospective recording of day to day behaviors over an extended period of time, is proposed as a useful means of better understanding the adaptive potential of mentally retarded persons as well as the applicability of normalization.

REFERENCES

Allport, G. (1942) The Use of Personal Documents in Psychological Science. New York: Social Science Research Council.

Baller, W., Charles, D., and Miller, E. (1966) Mid-Life Attainment of the Mentally Retarded, A Longitudinal Study. Lincoln: University of Nebraska Press.

Blatt, B. (1970) Exodus from Pandemonium. Boston, Mass.: Allyn and Bacon.

Blatt, B. (1973) Souls in Extremis. Boston, Mass.: Allyn and Bacon.

Bogdan, R. and Taylor, S. J. (1975) Introduction to Qualitative Research Methods. New York: Wiley.

Cobb, H. (1972) The Forecast of Fulfillment: A Review of Research on Predictive Assessment of the Adult Retarded for Social and Vocational Adjustment. New York: Teachers College Press.

Deacon, J. J. (1976) Joey. New York: Scribners.

Deno, E. (1965) Retarded Youth: Their School Rehabilitation Needs. Final Report of Project VRA-RD-681. Minneapolis: Minneapolis Public Schools.

Dollard, J. (1935) Criteria for the Life History. New Haven: Yale University Press.

Earl, C. J. C. (1961) Subnormal Personalities: Their Clinical Investigation and Assessment. London: Baillière, Tindall, and Cox.

Edgerton, R. (1967) The Cloak of Competence: Stigma in the Lives of the Mentally Retarded. Berkeley, Calif.: University of California Press.

Gunzburg, H. C. (1968) Social Competence and Mental Handicap. Baltimore: The Williams & Wilkins Company.

Henschel, A. M. (1972) The Forgotten Ones. Austin, Texas: University of Texas Press.

Hunt, N. (1967) The World of Nigel Hunt. Beaconsfield, England: Darwen Finlayson.

Kennedy, R. A. (1966) A Connecticut Community Revisited: A Study of the Social Adjustment of a Group of Mentally Deficient Adults in 1948 and 1960. Hartford: Connecticut State Department of Health, Office of Mental Retardation.

Keyes, D. (1966) Flowers for Algernon. New York: Harcourt, Brace and World.

Langness, L. L. (1965) The Life History in Anthropological Science. New York: Holt.

Lent, J. R., Dixon, M. H., Schiefelbusch, R. L., and McLean, B. M. (1972) The Hansens—Retarded Couple in the Community. In The Mentally Retarded—Case Studies (Eds. Hanck, B. B., and Frehill, M. F.) Dubuque, Iowa: Wm. C. Brown.

Mattinson, J. (1970) Marriage and Mental Handicap. London: Duckworth.

McCarver, R. and Craig, E. (1974) Placement of the Retarded in the Community: Prognosis and Outcome. In, International Review of Research in Mental Retardation (Vol. 7) (Ed. Ellis, N. R.) New York: Academic Press.

McCune, Billy (1973) The Autobiography of Billy McCune. With an Introduction by Danny Lyon. San Francisco: Straight Arrow Books.

Sarason, S. B. and Doris, J. (1969) Psychological Problems in Mental Deficiency. 4th Edition. New York: Harper and Row.

Seagoe, M. V. (1964) Yesterday was Tuesday, All Day and All Night. Boston: Little, Brown.

Shulman, L. S. (1967) The Vocational Development of Mentally Handicapped Adolescents: An Experimental and Logitudinal Study. East Lansing, Mich.: Michigan State University, Educational Publication Services.

RESEARCH TO PRACTICE IN MENTAL RETARDATION
Care and Intervention, Volume I
Edited by Peter Mittler
Copyright 1977 I.A.S.S.M.D.

A PROSPECTIVE STUDY OF CLIENT NEEDS RELATIVE TO COMMUNITY PLACEMENT

S. Landesman-Dwyer, J. J. Schuckit,
L. S. Keller, and T. R. Brown
CDMR, University of Washington, Seattle, Washington, United States

Historically, the planning, delivery, and evaluation of services for the mentally retarded have been far from scientific. At best, social policy decisions appeared to rely on the humanitarian beliefs of a few individuals, tempered by the realities of political, social, and economic forces. Currently, there is an increased awareness of the scientist's potential role as an adviser in the public process of making decisions (e.g., Arnhoff, 1975; Walsh, 1976). The impetus for the present investigation was the question: "Can the scientific study of mentally retarded individuals *directly* contribute to a changing service delivery system?"

This study was coordinated with state planners who received a legislative mandate to develop a ten-year master plan of services for the developmentally disabled in Washington State. The focus of this planning process was a) further deinstitutionalization and b) the development of new community alternatives for residential and training programs. Although Washington State has deinstitutionalized nearly 2,000 retarded persons in the past ten years (a 46% reduction in the institutional population), many parents and professionals have questioned the "success" in terms of normalizing and integrating the retarded into community life (Landesman-Dwyer and Schuckit, 1976; Landesman-Dwyer, Stein, and Sackett, 1976a, 1976b). Since no system of accountability—other than economic—was built into the state's deinstitutionalization program, no *facts* were available about where these 2,000 clients were placed, what programs were provided for them, and what their current service needs were. Similarly, there was no reliable information about clients remaining in state institutions or living with their families. Previous surveys of the institutional population were so poorly designed that the results were neither believable nor useful for making

---

This research was funded by the State of Washington, Department of Social and Health Services.

program decisions. Understandably, state planners were quite reluctant to trust researchers to provide answers to their questions, particularly within the brief period allotted by the legislature. Nonetheless, after extensive negotiations, and amidst ambitious promises, the research was funded.

The research strategy was influenced primarily by three assumptions. The first assumption was that *conventional methods for categorizing the retarded are not useful for program planning purposes.* The American Association on Mental Deficiency's classification of retarded persons into four levels (mild, moderate, severe, and profound) is too broad and, in practice, too inaccurate for valid assessment of either a) current behavior or b) service needs. Knowing a person's diagnosed level of retardation does not help in assigning that person to an appropriate residential, educational, or training program.

The second assumption was that *service needs can never be measured directly, but always represent inferences about what would be "good" for people.* Although these inferences seem necessary in the early stages of planning, the rationale underlying major decisions should be made explicit. For health services, the inferences frequently are clear. For instance, if a child has crooked teeth, the inference that he needs to have orthodontal work is fairly straightforward. However, concerning social services, the inferences often are more complex and less generally agreed upon. For example, if a child has a serious behavior problem, he may "need" a behavior modification program, a new place to live, psychological counseling, medical treatment, social stimulation, or some other programs. The full constellation of circumstances in individuals' lives is important for making judgmental inferences about service needs.

Finally, the third assumption was that *service systems must be evaluated scientifically if we intend to advance our understanding of the mentally retarded.* For such evaluations to be adequate, individuals representative of the target client populations must be studied over a period of time, in alternative programs and placements, by objective measures of their behavior and of the services provided. A prospective study, with adequate controls, would provide an opportunity to: 1) evaluate the validity of the inferences usually made about service needs; 2) assess the effectiveness of programs designed to meet these service needs; and 3) provide valuable longitudinal data about various types of mentally retarded persons within a complex service delivery system.

Originally, the major objective of this project was to provide needed and reliable data about the biobehavioral characteristics of the mentally retarded receiving services in Washington State. This involved studying approximately 10,000 clients in residential settings and in day training programs (excluding public education). An integral part of providing useful data was to develop a method for organizing and analyzing the 75-plus independent variables collected on each client. The method chosen was to subgroup clients based on current functional, behavioral, and medical profiles. Thus, a sequence of research and planning activities was evolved in order to maximize the possibility that the data collected would be used appropriately for critical decisions about policy and programs. Table 1 outlines this sequence.

The research activities constantly interfaced with planning efforts and with input from a Scientific Advisory Committee and a Special Task Force appointed by the governor. As a concrete example of how some of the data were collected and utilized directly for key decisions in the planning process, the survey of the institutional population is described.

METHODS

Data Collection

To eliminate possible errors from sampling such a heterogeneous group of individuals (Berkson, 1966), *all* 2,545 residents in Washington's state institutions were studied. Since state planners needed summary data within 28 days, both the quantity of data and methods for collection were limited. The variables collected related to a) demographic and diagnostic information, obtained from central medical records for individual residents; b) current functional and behavioral abilities, obtained from ratings by ward staff who cared for the residents on a daily basis; and c) medical and nursing needs, obtained from nursing staff on each ward. All data were collected and coded by ten research analysts familiar with standards for defining and classifying characteristics of the retarded (Grossman, 1973). Table 2 lists the items in the data set (see Landesman-Dwyer and Schuckit (1976) for definitions of levels or categories within each item). A reliability study was conducted in each institution, on a random 10% sample of residents by replicating the entire data set. In addition, ratings from ward staff who worked on three different shifts were obtained, in order to assess the consistency of staff perception about individual residents. Items that were in less than 80% agreement were not utilized for the planning process. Since nearly one-tenth of the current institutional population had been placed in the community at least once, and subsequently returned to the institution, a more detailed study of these returnees was conducted (Landesman-Dwyer, Schuckit, Curtis, Bunting, and Weatherlee, 1976).

Data Analysis

For each item, frequency and percentage distributions were computed (Landesman-Dwyer and Schuckit, 1976). In addition, a *descriptive profile* was generated by combining relevant items into three functional areas: 1) basic self-help skills, 2) basic social and communication skills, and 3) academic, vocational, and interpersonal skills. Two other areas, considered important for residential placement decisions, were a) behavioral problems and b) medical and nursing needs. Residents were scored in each area on a three-point scale, based on level of skills or severity of problems (see Landesman-Dwyer and Brown (1976) for a full

Table 1. Major research and planning activities in a state-wide survey of mentally retarded clients

Research activities	Planning activities
A. Establish scientific advisory board to:	A. Appoint special task force to:
1. Review sampling techniques	1. Identify major decisions that need to be made for the entire population
2. Consider data collection methods	2. Advise state planners about concerns of special interest groups, parents, clients, professionals, community representatives
3. Establish variables to be collected	3. Review all research findings and then potential use for planning
4. Ensure adequate reliability measures	4. Respond to early versions of plans for new residential and training facilities
5. Consider techniques for analyzing and presenting research findings	5. Make recommendations for changes in state's plans and/or priorities
6. Independently review the interpretation and use of findings by state planners	6. Assist in distributing information about the planning process and key decisions
B. Collect data on individual clients in:	B. Assess the current services available in:
1. Residential settings (institutions, nursing homes, congregate care facilities, boarding homes, group homes, foster care and family homes, and independent living)	1. Residential settings
2. Day training programs, (preschools, adult developmental centers, sheltered workshops, and other special services for the retarded)	2. Day training programs

C. Summarize and analyze findings in terms of:
1. Frequency distribution of all variables in each residential setting and day training program
2. Multiple characteristics of clients and relevant cross-tabulations or variables
3. Major sub-groups of clients within and across programs, based on natural clustering of client characteristics and decisions by state planners and Special Task Force

D. Prospectively study individuals from each of the major sub-groups, by collecting:
1. Baseline behavioral observations in current residential and training programs
2. Objective data describing the services
3. Continuous observations after changes in residential or training programs (including controls)
4. If possible, experimentally supplement programs that appear "unsuccessful" — by adding components that appear the most important in alternative programs

C. Develop a position paper to describe:
1. Goals of state planners in serving the mentally retarded
2. Current options (qualitative and quantitative) available for treatment
3. Subgroups of clients and what their inferred service needs are
4. "Gaps" in the service system, relative to the *type* and *extent* of services needed

D. Plan "Solutions" to meet the needs of clients who are not receiving adequate residential and training services. Design new residential and training centers in the community, remodel institutional facilities, and develop services in community and other residential settings.

Table 2. Data collection variables

I. Variables scored by research analysts from information
   obtained in institutional records

1. Institution of residence
2. Identification number
3. Ward on which resident lives
4. Birthdate (month and year)
5. Sex
6. Ethnic origin
7. County in which parent or legal guardian resides
8. Year in which the individual first entered an institution
9. Year in which the individual entered the present institution
10. Number of community placements
11. Major reason for return to the institution from
    community placement
12. Where individual was placed in the community
13. Length of stay in community
14. Employment history
15. Family involvement
16. Major reason for return to the institution from
    community placement

35. Functional hearing
36. Arm-hand use
37. Spasticity
38. Seizure frequency
39. Seizure severity
40. Current educational program
    that the resident attends
41. Other programs the resident
    regularly attends
42. Number of hours per day the
    resident spends in classes or programs
43. Reading skills
44. Writing skills
45. Number concepts
46. Toilet use skills
47. Eating skills
48. Dressing skills
49. Complexity of the resident's speech

17. Diagnosed level of retardation
18. Discrepant level of retardation in record
19. Infections and intoxications
20. Trauma or physical agent
21. Metabolism or nutrition
22. Gross brain disease (postnatal)
23. Unknown prenatal influence
24. Chromosomal abnormality
25. Gestational disorders
26. Genetic component
27. Secondary cranial anomaly
28. Impairment of special senses
29. Convulsive disorders
30. Psychiatric impairment
31. Motor dysfunction
32. Overall rating by research analyst of the quality of the record

II. Variables rated by staff who work directly with the residents

33. Ambulation skills
34. Functional vision

50. Understandability of the resident's speech
51. Resident's ability to understand others
52. Social interaction
53. Initiative in activities
54. Time concept
55. Money handling
56. Very aggressive towards others
57. Physical self-abuse or self-destructive behavior
58. Destroys property or objects
59. Severe hyperactivity
60. Withdrawn or apathetic
61. Repetitive abnormal or unusual behavior
62. Socially unacceptable behaviors
63. Sleep problems
64. Other emotional or behavioral problems
65. Overall need for medical and nursing care
66. Drugs
67. Special diet
68. Physical therapy
69. Major medical problems
70. Types of special intervention or treatment
71. Additional pertinent information

description of items and levels for each area). The first three functional areas were cross-tabulated and five major subgroups were defined. Table 3 identifies these subgroups. Subgroup *A* was comprised of residents who were the most capable in all three functional areas. Subgroup *E* was comprised of residents who had no skills or extremely limited skills in all three areas. Subgroups *B, C,* and *D* represented intermediate levels of functioning. The institutional population was distributed as follows: subgroup *A,* 6.3%; subgroup *B,* 29.2%; subgroup *C,* 23.9%; subgroup *D,* 22.6%; and subgroup *E,* 18.1%. Essentially, these subgroups

Table 3. Description and distribution of five subgroups (*A–E*) based on functional levels of: 1) basic self-help skills, 2) basic social and communication skills, and 3) academic, vocational, and interpersonal skills

Basic self-help skills	Basic social and communication skills			Academic, vocational and interpersonal skills
	High	Medium	Low	
High	A[a] 5.1%	A 0.8%	—	
Medium	A 0.2%	A 0.1%	—	High
Low	—	—	—	
	High	Medium	Low	
High	B 10.4%	B 16.1%	C 0.2%	
Medium	B 2.7%	C 19.7%	D 1.2%	Medium
Low	C 0.1%	D 0.7%	E 0.2%	
	High	Medium	Low	
High	C 0.3%	C 3.6%	D 0.4%	
Medium	—	D 20.2%	E 6.8%	Low
Low	—	E 3.7%	E 7.4%	

[a]Percentage of total institutional population.

portray different levels of adaptive daily functioning. The population distribution for the five subgroups is quite different from the diagnosed level of retardation according to AAMD standards. According to conventional categories, 2.2% were borderline retarded, 5.8% mildly retarded, 12.3% moderately retarded, 28.4% severely retarded, and 49.2% profoundly retarded. Moreover, an individual's diagnosed level of retardation was *not* necessarily a good predictor of his functional subgroup, particularly for the severely and profoundly retarded.

For planning purposes, the five subgroups were divided further, in order to identify the proportion of individuals who had extremely serious behavior problems (physically dangerous to others, self, or property), intensive medical and nursing needs, or both. Table 4 summarizes these findings. The majority of serious behavior problems were observed in subgroups *B* (8.5%), *C* (8.6%), and *D* (7.7%). The least functionally capable individuals, in subgroup *E,* had the greatest prevalence of serious medical problems (7.6%); in contrast to residents in subgroup *A,* who had the fewest medical problems (.3%). For each of the cells in Table 4, a detailed description of the individuals was provided, including demographic, life history, diagnostic, and behavioral information.

Data Utilization

Prior to this study, state planners had proposed another dramatic (50%) reduction in the institutional population, and the building of 80 new group homes. However, after carefully reviewing the descriptive profiles of the residents who remained in the institutions, this plan was modified. First, the state planners carefully considered the *unique* service needs of the different subgroups. Unfortunately, the literature was not very helpful in deciding which residents were most likely to "succeed" in community placement, or which individuals needed continued institutionalization (e.g., *Alternatives in the Community for the Developmentally Disabled: A Bibliographic Index on Community-based Alternatives to Institutionalization,* 1976; Baumeister and Butterfield, 1970; Butterfield, 1967). Therefore, state planners developed a position paper, outlining a continuum of services they sought to provide for various subgroups. The data provided projections for the number, ages, and characteristics of clients in these planning categories. For each category, a list of specific residential and training services considered desirable was generated, then compared to the services currently being provided.

From this evaluation, service "gaps" became obvious. For many residents with only minimal self-help and communication skills, and no serious behavioral and medical problems (subgroups *C* and *D*), community residential alternatives appeared feasible. Thus, a demonstration program for nine new community homes and three community training centers is being planned. The architects and program planners from the institution are using the data to consider the special needs of these severely and profoundly retarded adults who previously were not considered eligible for community placement. In addition, the two

Table 4. Distribution of subgroups[a] on medical and behavioral problems for Washington's state institutional population

| | Subgroups | | | | | | | | | |
| | A (Most capable) | | B | | C | | D | | E (Least capable) | |
Problems	Percent of Group A	Percent of Total	Percent of Group B	Percent of Total	Percent of Group C	Percent of Total	Percent of Group D	Percent of Total	Percent of Group E	Percent of Total
No serious behavioral or medical problems	57.9	3.7	48.4	14.1	36.7	8.8	29.5	6.6	19.2	3.5
Moderate behavioral problems	17.9	1.1	17.6	5.1	19.1	4.6	23.7	5.3	16.6	3.0
Serious behavioral problems	17.9	1.1	29.1	8.5	36.2	8.6	34.3	7.7	17.5	3.2
Serious medical problems	4.8	0.3	3.7	1.1	4.7	1.1	10.4	2.3	42.3	7.6
Serious medical and behavioral problems	1.4	0	1.2	0.3	3.3	0.8	4.0	0.9	4.3	0.8
Total	100	6.3	100	29.2	100	23.9	100	22.6	100	18.1

[a]Refer to Table 3 for description of subgroups based on 1) basic self-help skills, 2) social and communication skills, and 3) academic, vocational, and interpersonal skills. The subgroups represent a continuum from most capable (subgroup A) to least capable (subgroup E).

largest state institutions are being remodeled, with the concept of serving three target populations: those who need hospital-level care for medical problems; those who have no functional skills currently and need intensive care or training in basic areas; and those who need surveillance to protect themselves or society, but whose functional capabilities indicate that they may be placed in the community when these severe behavior problems are eliminated. Thus, the institutions are being designed for certain target groups and their multiple needs.

SUMMARY

There are no established empirical methods for planning services to meet the specific needs of target groups. Traditionally, programs were geared for clients with a common label, usually reflecting medical diagnoses, performance on standardized tests, or dire circumstances. Individuals are often multiply labeled. However, two children diagnosed as having cerebral palsy, being severely mentally retarded, and requiring residential care may be very different. One child may speak, dress, and feed himself with assistance, walk, and interact with others. The second child may have none of these skills. Moreover, the first child may have serious emotional and behavioral problems manifested by violent physical attacks on others. The second child may have uncontrolled seizures that disrupt program participation. Clearly, the IQ score of 35 and the diagnosis of cerebral palsy do not indicate *what* each child needs in terms of social, physical, or educational programs or *where* he should live.

Since planning is an integral part of our political and social system, certain guidelines and assumptions are unavoidable in estimating the *kind* and the *extent* of service needs. This report presented a method tried on an experimental basis, applied to a statewide plan to serve the developmentally disabled. The underlying assumption was that *programs should be designed to meet the current, multiple needs of individuals.* The translation of this principle into actual methods and prediction is complex and far from resolved. Ultimately, the merit and validity of such an empirical approach will be evaluated prospectively, by the degree to which the new service systems objectively achieve their goals.

ACKNOWLEDGMENTS

Without the cooperation of literally hundreds of people, the data presented in this chapter could not have been collected, analyzed, or utilized in the planning process. Special appreciation and thanks are extended to our research analysts (Idamay Bunting, Renee Coppel, Christine Curtis, Steven Drobinsky, Shelly Horst, Don Kay, Frederica MacLean, Maureen Miltenberger, and Mary Weatherley), our Scientific Advisory Committee (Irvin Emanuel, Richard Holm, Rosemarie McCartin, Gail O'Connor, Edgar Pye, Lou Rowitz, and Gene P. Sackett), and our state planners with whom we worked closely (Maurice Harmon, Ralph Littlestone, Lee Bomberger, Norm Davis, Leonard Long, John Stern, and Fred Thompson).

REFERENCES

Alternatives in the Community for the Developmentally Disabled: A Bibliographic Index on Community-based Alternatives to Institutionalization. (1976) Life Project, Harry A. Waisman Center on Mental Retardation and Human Development, University of Wisconsin.

Arnhoff, F. N. (1975) Social consequences of policy toward mental illness. Science 188:1277.

Baumeister, A. A., and Butterfield, E. C. (Eds.) (1970) Residential Facilities for the Mentally Retarded. Chicago: Aldine Publishing Company.

Berkson, G. (1966) When exceptions obscure the rules. Ment. Retard. 4:24.

Butterfield, E. C. (1967) The role of environmental factors in the treatment of institutionalized mental retardates. *In* Mental Retardation: Selected Problems in Appraisal and Treatment (Ed. Baumeister, A.) Chicago: Aldine Publishing Company.

Grossman, H. (1973) Manual on Terminology and Classification. AAMD, Spec. Publ. Ser. No. 2.

Landesman-Dwyer, S., and Brown, T. R. (1976) A method for sub-grouping the retarded based on functional abilities. State of Washington publication: Department of Social and Health Services.

Landesman-Dwyer, S., and Schuckit, J. J. (1976) Preliminary findings of the survey of state institutions for the mentally retarded. State of Washington publication: Department of Social and Health Services.

Landesman-Dwyer, S., Schuckit, J. J., Curtis, C., Bunting, I., and Weatherlee, M. (1976) A study of residents returned to institutions from community placements. State of Washington publication: Department of Social and Health Services.

Landesman-Dwyer, S., Stein, J. G., and Sackett, G. P. (1976a) Group homes for the developmentally disabled: A behavioral and ecological study. State of Washington publication: Department of Social and Health Services.

Landesman-Dwyer, S., Stein, J. G., and Sackett, G. P. (1976b) A behavioral and ecological study of group homes. *In* The Application of Observational/Ethological Methods to the Study of Mental Retardation, (Eds. Sackett, G. P., and Haywood, H. C.), in press.

Walsh, J. (1976) White House Science Office: House and Senate agree on bill. Science 192:445.

RESEARCH TO PRACTICE IN MENTAL RETARDATION
Care and Intervention, Volume I
Edited by Peter Mittler
Copyright 1977 I.A.S.S.M.D.

THREE-TRACK APPROACH TO PROGRAMMING IN A RURAL COMMUNITY-BASED MENTAL RETARDATION PROGRAM

R. L. Schalock and R. Harper
*Mid-Nebraska Mental Retardation Services, 518 Eastside
Blvd., Hastings, Nebraska 68901, United States*

The Nebraska approach to developing community-based mental retardation programs was set into action through the creation of six mental retardation regions. The regional concept was initiated in order to equalize the distribution of services to the population. Nebraska, like much of the mid-western United States, has a heavy concentration of its population in one part of the state. Our area (Region 3), for example, is composed of 22 counties, covering 15,000 square miles and containing 217,000 people. The task was to establish within this area a viable service delivery system based upon the principles of normalization and community integration.

The region is governed by elected representatives to a multi-county board, and is administered by a regional director and seven area directors, who are in charge of the seven area programs. The regional director provides general program direction and development, state-local relations, and state agency interactions, and relates officially to funding and legislative bodies. Each area director is responsible for his area program, including the identification of facilities, fiscal management, local public relations, staff hiring and firing, physical plant and program supervision.

Programmatically, rural community service systems face unique problems dealing with standardization, monitoring, availability of trained staff, financial resources, transportation, and limited professional generic staff. In light of these problems, and the fact that we were establishing programs where none before existed, we needed to develop a remediation program:

1. that was client-centered with lock-step progressions towards defined exits;
2. that provided the client and staff with one consistent message during the program day; and
3. that provided materials to and for the program staff that allowed them to

assess client strengths and weaknesses, to develop remediation strategies, and to evaluate systematically client attainments.

The lock-step progressions for each of the eventually developed program components are presented in Figure 1. These progressions reflect an attempt to organize our philosophy into definitions of program alternatives. The alternatives are arranged in a hierarchy, weighted to the degree of normalization.

Once the progressions were identified, the next step was to define and develop the procedures needed to move the clients to their highest level of functioning on the ladder, and, if possible, to total self-support. To do so in the adult component, we divested ourselves of both the sheltered workshop model and the large group home concepts. Programmatically, the adult component is divided into the "three-track system." The three tracks are operated in each of the seven communities throughout the region and include *basic skills, independent living,* and *competitive employment.* Each track has its own staff, program components (including screening test and remediation-teaching manual), location, and suggested exits. Programmatically, target behaviors are assessed by program staff when the client enters each respective track. Deficit target behaviors are then remediated through systematic prescriptive programming. Progress is monitored graphically through reassessment of the originally assessed target behaviors. Sequentially, adult clients move from:

Entry→Basic Skills→Independent Living→Competitive Employment→Exit

Basic skills focuses on remediating response deficits relative to sensori-motor functioning, auditory-visual processing, language, symbolic operations, and social-emotional development. *Independent living,* which is taught during the regular program day in the setting of the community residences, focuses on independent living skills including personal maintenance, clothing care and use, home maintenance, food preparation, time management, social behavior, community utilization, communication, and functional academics. *Competitive employment* training occurs either at a job training center or on the job and teaches job-related skills, responsibility towards work, work performance, behavior in the job situation, and personal appearance.

ADULT TRACK COMPONENTS

Each of the tracks has the following *program components:* target behaviors, assessment instruments, monitoring graphs, remediation-teaching manuals, and prescriptive programming.

Target Behaviors

Target behaviors are a prescribed set of sequenced behaviors on which clients are assessed both initially and periodically thereafter. Deficit target behaviors are remediated subsequently through systematic programming.

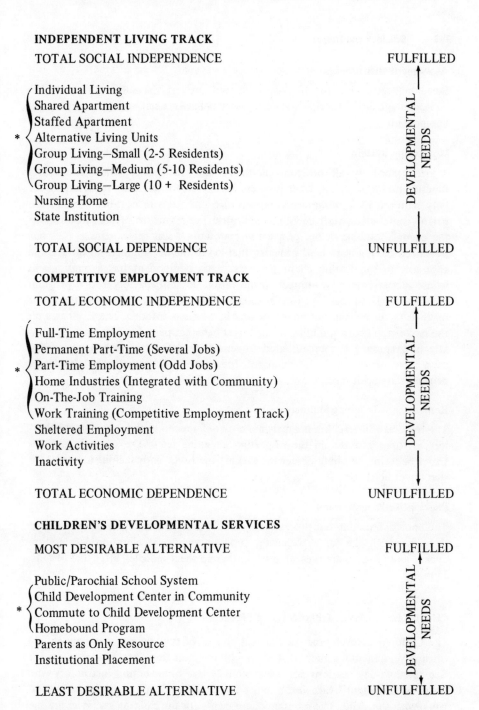

INDEPENDENT LIVING TRACK

TOTAL SOCIAL INDEPENDENCE   FULFILLED

* {
Individual Living
Shared Apartment
Staffed Apartment
Alternative Living Units
Group Living–Small (2-5 Residents)
Group Living–Medium (5-10 Residents)
Group Living–Large (10 + Residents)
}
Nursing Home
State Institution

DEVELOPMENTAL NEEDS

TOTAL SOCIAL DEPENDENCE   UNFULFILLED

COMPETITIVE EMPLOYMENT TRACK

TOTAL ECONOMIC INDEPENDENCE   FULFILLED

* {
Full-Time Employment
Permanent Part-Time (Several Jobs)
Part-Time Employment (Odd Jobs)
Home Industries (Integrated with Community)
On-The-Job Training
Work Training (Competitive Employment Track)
}
Sheltered Employment
Work Activities
Inactivity

DEVELOPMENTAL NEEDS

TOTAL ECONOMIC DEPENDENCE   UNFULFILLED

CHILDREN'S DEVELOPMENTAL SERVICES

MOST DESIRABLE ALTERNATIVE   FULFILLED

* {
Public/Parochial School System
Child Development Center in Community
Commute to Child Development Center
Homebound Program
}
Parents as Only Resource
Institutional Placement

DEVELOPMENTAL NEEDS

LEAST DESIRABLE ALTERNATIVE   UNFULFILLED

*Options currently provided by Mid-Nebraska Mental Retardation Services

Figure 1. Progressions toward exits from program components.

Assessment Instruments

Screening tests are also track-specific and present the suggested evaluation strategies and pass criterion for each target behavior dealt with in that program component.

Monitoring System

A need faced by all programs is to be able to specify where a client is functioning initially, and what progress occurs over time. Such reporting is not only required by funding agencies, but also essential for cost-benefit analysis, parent conferences, staff decisions, and most important, to present feedback to the client about his or her progress and growth. It was these reasons, plus our own need to monitor client progress, that led to the development of the graphic approach to monitoring client progress. Each component has a circle graph whose subparts refer by number to the various target behaviors of that program component. The procedure used throughout the region is to baseline the client on each target behavior of the track that he or she is entering. The small area on the circle graph corresponding to the target behavior passed is darkened. Systematic programming is then initiated to remediate deficit target behaviors, with subsequent dating and darkening of the circle graph area when the target behaviors are achieved.

Remediation-Teaching Manuals

The remediation-teaching manuals are cross-referenced to the same target behaviors as those assessed in the respective screening tests. The manuals give the target behavior, teaching object in teaching methods, and teaching materials for that target behavior.

Prescriptive Programming

The approach used in our programming is best described as prescriptive teaching, through which the target behavior, program events, acceleration/deceleration cycles, and progress are presented on a program sheet modeled after that of O.R. Lindsley.

CHILDREN'S DEVELOPMENTAL SERVICES

The Children's Developmental Services consist of two discrete components: 1) three developmental centers that work with children from 2 to 5 years of age for five one-half-day sessions per week; and 2) five home-bound instructors who travel to the client's (age 0–2) homes twice per week and train the parents to work with the child. The program components for the children's services are the same as for the adult services. Materials are generally those of the Portage Project (Portage, Wisconsin), with target behaviors assessed at entry and reassessed throughout the remediation period. Major assessment-remediation areas include cognition, self-help, motor skills, language, and socialization.

INSERVICE AND MONITORING

There is also a need to train new staff with program philosophy and implementation; to update staff in new techniques and methods; and to evaluate staff on how well they are implementing the region's philosophy and methods. Our inservice program is directed at the first two of these needs. Each new staff member spends two days in preservice orientation and training in which program philosophy and implementation techniques are presented via video tapes. Competencies that are taught and evaluated by our inservice coordinator include: Assessing target behaviors, writing specific programs, running programs, and recording-graphing behavioral results.

Updating staff is done via a number of techniques. One is by bringing experts in to present large workshops. A second, which is preferred by staff and administrators because of the distances involved, is to send "experts" to each area to do "over the shoulder teaching and training"; a third is a TV link between a psychiatric institute and the region. The TV link provides a two-way forum to present individual clients and ask specialists at the other end for their advice.

Monitoring staff is another need. Each program component has its local area coordinator who is responsible to the area director for implementing and directing the component. In addition, the regional director, regional social service director, and program consultant conduct a systems review twice per year for each program component in each area. Management by objectives (MBOs) are then presented to the respective staff to improve any deficiencies noted in the audit. The systems review not only provides ongoing program monitoring, standardization, and inservice across the region, but also has proven invaluable in our recent accreditation (Joint Commission) effort.

PROGRAM RESULTS

Program results are evaluated in two ways: first, in reference to client movement (i.e. placement); and second, in reference to the number of target behaviors acquired while in the training track.

Since the implementation three years ago of the above approach to our service delivery system, we have experienced significant client movement. The actual number of adult clients placed in various job areas during the last two years is as follows: kitchen helper, 34; assembler, 28; laborer, 38; maid, general, 16; clerk, general, 3; nurse's aide, 8; agriculture, 5.

Movement into independent living is measured in two ways: one is into staffed apartments; the second is into one's own apartment or house. One hundred and eighteen (118) of our clients have moved into their own apartments during the last two years.

Of the 133 children dealt with during the last two years, 47 were placed in regular school or EMR classrooms, 75 in TMR classrooms, and 11 either referred to other services or are being maintained in the program through special arrangements. Since the home-bound program has been operating for only one year, and typically deals with children from birth to two years of age, it is too early to evaluate its impact.

The second approach to program evaluation is client progress. Each client is evaluated on the respective screening test upon entrance, assigned to a track, and re-evaluated every six months thereafter. Client data, analyzed by track component and MA/CA categories, are available from the author.

Although standardization of programs, as described above, contains dangers related to potential stagnation and a pedantic approach, it has been our experience in dealing with the mentally retarded that mixed program messages are confusing to the client and require excessive program competencies of the staff. We therefore embrace a singularly simple approach to a very complex and difficult challenge.

SUMMARY

This chapter summarizes development, implementation, and results of a rural service delivery system. Each of seven geographical areas has its own adult and children's program in which target behaviors in the areas of basic skills, independent living, and competitive employment are assessed by program staff, with deficit target behaviors remediated through systematic prescriptive programming.

PSYCHIATRIC SERVICES

RESEARCH TO PRACTICE IN MENTAL RETARDATION
Care and Intervention, Volume I
Edited by Peter Mittler
Copyright 1977   I.A.S.S.M.D.

PSYCHIATRIC ASPECTS OF MENTAL RETARDATION

J. Jancar
Stoke Park Hospital, Stapleton, Bristol BS16 1QU, England

The theme of this section was set for us by a great pioneer, the late Professor Penrose, who concluded his Maudsley lecture in 1965 with the following words: "the various branches of psychiatry all have potential value for each other. Provided that we do not neglect or despise the data derived from one another's discipline, there are advances to be made in the diagnosis, prevention and treatment of apparently most intractable mental diseases." (Penrose, 1966.)

Historically, mentally ill and mentally retarded patients were treated together by various religious orders or in private institutions. During the last two centuries there was a gradual evolution of separate treatment and care of mentally retarded people, which was a step in the right direction because their long-term requirements are different from most of the mentally ill.

However, during the past two decades we have been constantly reminded, with the new discoveries of the causes of mental retardation, that the link between the mentally ill and the retarded is in many cases much closer than we were led to believe before. This sometimes causes problems with the right placement of the patients. What we see in the hospitals for the mentally retarded are often the end results of the most severe damage to the fetus during pregnancy by teratogenic agents, while less damaged patients are in mental hospitals or attending psychiatric or other out-patient clinics.

Two recent surveys in the United Kingdom—one in Scotland (Reid, 1972, 1976) and another in England (Heaton-Ward, 1976)—revealed a fairly high prevalence of psychoses in the hospital-based, mentally retarded patients. Both authors, while reviewing the available literature, noted that surprisingly little research has been done in the past into the causes of psychiatric disturbances in the mentally retarded.

In view of the recent discoveries and observations related to biochemistry, chromosomes, genetics, infectious diseases, drugs and other pathogens, one hopes that the diagnosis, treatment, and prevention of a number of psychiatric disorders, with or without mental retardation, will be more readily obtainable, particularly with new, improved techniques of amniocentesis and advances in the studies of amniotic fluid, maternal blood, and urine during pregnancy.

Since Garrod in 1908 introduced into medicine the term "inborn errors of metabolism," numerous metabolic disorders have been discovered and described in mentally retarded patients. A number of these conditions can already be diagnosed during pregnancy and a few are treatable with diet or drugs. In a number, superimposed psychotic episodes have been reported. Occasionally, psychoses can be induced in these conditions by drugs, e.g., by phenobarbitone or sulphonamides in porphyria.

Detection of chromosomal abnormalities has been made possible following the breakthrough in chromosomal studies in 1959 by Lejeune, Gautier, and Turpin. Psychotic disorders have been reported in a number of autosomal anomalies, particularly in Down's syndrome. Males with supernumary X chromosomes are more liable than others to mental retardation, mental disorder, epilepsy, and antisocial conduct. Females with more than XX can develop mental retardation and mental illness. Males with excess of Y chromosomes can suffer from mental illness and antisocial behavior (Forssman, 1970).

With greater life expectancy of the mentally retarded we are faced with the new problem of dementia in these patients, in particular senile, cerebral arteriosclerotic, and presenile dementia. Patients with Down's syndrome appear to be showing with an increased frequency signs and symptoms of a premature form of senile dementia. Because of the great importance of this topic and sparsity of the literature on the subject, I suggest to the organising committee of the next IASSMD Congress that they include in the programme a symposium on senescence and mental retardation.

This very brief review of the psychiatric aspects of mental retardation highlights the link and interaction between medicine and psychiatry and the frequent association between mental retardation and psychoses, so often overlooked in the past. It also focuses attention on the need for the well-trained physician-psychiatrist to lead a skillful and professional multi-disciplinary team in the search for the causes and prevention of mental disorders and to provide with his colleagues the best treatment and care available for the mentally diseased.

REFERENCES

Forssman, H. (1970) The mental implication of sex chromosome aberrations. Brit. J. Psychiatry 117:353.
Heaton-Ward, W. A. (1976) Psychosis in mental handicap. Brit. J. Psychiatry, in press.
Penrose, L. S. (1966) The contribution of mental deficiency research to psychiatry. Brit. J. Psychiatry 112:747.

Reid, A. H. (1972) Psychoses in adult mental defectives: I. Manic depressive psychosis. II. Schizophrenic and paranoid psychoses. Brit. J. Psychiatry 120:205.

Reid, A. H. (1976) Psychiatric disturbances in the mentally handicapped. Proc. Roy. Soc. Med. 69:13.

RESEARCH TO PRACTICE IN MENTAL RETARDATION
Care and Intervention, Volume I
Edited by Peter Mittler
Copyright 1977 I.A.S.S.M.D.

MENTAL RETARDATION AND CLINICAL PSYCHIATRY

G. Tarjan
UCLA School of Medicine and
The Neuropsychiatric Institute, 760 Westwood Plaza,
Los Angeles, California 90024, United States

Psychiatry played a historical role in mental retardation services in the United States for many decades. For example, 100 years ago all charter members of the American Association on Mental Deficiency were psychiatrists. This close relationship between psychiatry and mental retardation began to fade during the late 1950s, and by the mid-1960s mental retardation was described as the Cinderella of Psychiatry (Potter, 1965; Tarjan, 1966). As relatively fewer psychiatrists continued to have their primary interest in mental retardation, the quality and quantity of psychiatric care of mentally retarded individuals diminished. Although a host of other professional disciplines have picked up some of the slack, the mental health care of the mentally retarded population became an early casualty of the increasing separation between the mental retardation and the mental health movements. Through focusing on the clinical roles of psychiatry, this paper will attempt to emphasize the benefits that mentally retarded persons, their families, and professionals in both fields could derive from closer collaboration.

A few general observations will be followed by some comments on diagnosis, treatment, and consultation. Because of the author's interest, child, rather than adult, psychiatry will be emphasized.

There is no need to dwell on definition, symptomatology, etiology, or epidemiology, first because these subjects are well-known to this audience, and second because concise, recent reviews are available elsewhere (Richmond et al., 1974; Tarjan, 1974). Two comments, however, might be needed to place the syndrome of mental retardation into the context of United States clinical practice.

DEFINITIONS

Both commonly used definitions of mental retardation (American Psychiatric Association, 1968; Grossman, 1973) combine under one major diagnosis two substantially dissimilar groups. In the first and smaller one, composed of the "clinical types" of retardation, the behavioral aspects of the syndrome are accompanied by demonstrable somatic changes. A biomedical etiology is usually identified, the retardation is generally moderate to profound, is ascertained early, and remains relatively stable throughout life. These types of retardation occur in all social classes.

The second and larger group, currently classified under the term "mental retardation due to psycho-social disadvantage," on the other hand, is a class-dependent phenomenon observed almost exclusively in the educationally, economically, and socially underprivileged segments of the population. The clinical diagnosis is usually established after school entrance, and the overt symptoms disappear upon school exit. Current biomedical technology can neither ascertain concomitant organic signs nor demonstrate specific somatic etiological factors. Assumptions of causation range from genetic forces and nonheritable somatic agents to the impacts of early childhood experiences. The last set of factors is usually conceptualized in the context of quantitative or qualitative deprivations of growth-supporting stimuli (Tarjan, 1970a, 1970b). Although there is a tendency in clinical practice to extrapolate observations made in one group to the other, such generalizations are often unwarranted because of the substantial differences in symptomatology, etiology, and prognosis.

Another somewhat unique clinical problem in the United States pertains to the relationship between the early childhood psychoses and mental retardation (Tarjan and Eisenberg, 1972). Even relatively recently it was not uncommon for children to acquire, sequentially, the diagnoses of early infantile autism, childhood schizophrenia, and mental retardation, among others, often depending more upon the inclinations of the diagnosticians than upon the symptomatology of the child. Therapeutic interventions were then tailored more to the diagnosis than to the needs of the child. Fortunately, current classification schemes recommend the use of a combined diagnosis, i.e., "mental retardation following a psychiatric disorder," and a broader scope of therapies is being utilized.

A few additional, general comments are in order before turning to the specific clinical roles of psychiatry in mental retardation. Greater details on both sets of subjects are available in chapters of several books (Philips, 1966; Bernstein, 1970; Menolascino, 1970; Balthazar and Stevens, 1975; Robinson and Robinson, 1976), edited or authored in the United States.

Retarded individuals are highly vulnerable to emotional traumata (Philips and Williams, 1975). Stresses that result in no significant sequelae in an average child or adult can produce overt psychiatric manifestations in retarded persons. The symptomatology seen in retarded individuals often differs from that observed in intellectually better endowed persons, but the basic psychopathological processes are similar, and they require interventions modified only to accommodate to the cognitive impairment of the patient.

Mental retardation is a developmental disorder with an onset during the years of intellectual, emotional, and social growth. The cardinal deficits in intelligence and general adaptation that constitute the syndrome of mental retardation in themselves can significantly influence the rate of personality development. The repeated social failures often encountered by retarded individuals can also result in chronic stress, further modifying future behavior (Zigler, 1967). Psychiatric complications pose additional impediments to continued growth. The prevention and early treatment of such complications are therefore of major importance in support of development.

From the viewpoint of prevention, ideally each retarded child should be reared in an environment that provides the best opportunities for personality growth and the development of coping abilities. This goal can be best reached in an intact family in which the other individuals, particularly the parents, are unhampered by significant conflicts. Unfortunately, this is unlikely to be the case because the presence of retardation in itself often results in substantial intrafamilial stress (Group for the Advancement of Psychiatry, 1963). Difficult periods of adjustment follow, and these in turn reverberate in the child. Therapeutic support accorded to the parents can therefore become an important preventive activity with respect to the child.

The differences in the nature of the intrafamilial conflict in the two basic types of mental retardation should be noted at this point. Although the psychopathological processes that operate in families with mental retardation caused by psycho-social disadvantage are not as well explored as those observed in the clinical types, present evidence focuses on substantial differences (Group for the Advancement of Psychiatry, 1967). In the former group, the conflicts do not derive primarily from the presence of retardation in part because it often goes undetected by other family members. In fact, the diagnosis is frequently externally imposed by social agencies, primarily the schools. Parental reactions are often targeted not toward the identified retarded child, but rather toward the identifying social agency.

It is an accepted dictum in child psychiatry that meaningful treatment of a child must take into account the emotional adjustment of key individuals in the child's immediate environment. This principle derives from an understanding of all children's dependence on adults. Concurrent therapeutic work with parents therefore has become an integral part of psychotherapy of children. Mentally retarded individuals are more dependent than those better endowed, and such dependence often lasts through life. Hence, supportive work with parents is of even greater importance. The circle of critical individuals often reaches beyond the nuclear family, particularly in retardation. It can include the personnel of the agency that is involved in the comprehensive care of a retarded person. Such personnel, particularly when insufficiently acquainted with retardation, may respond emotionally rather than rationally. Guidance and support of the care-givers then become one anchor of the long-range management plan.

These general comments were selected to emphasize the need for mental health care for retarded individuals. They were not intended to imply that each retarded child and his family are in need of treatment or to single out psychiatry as the sole profession for delivering such services. Many retarded children and their families are quite well adjusted most of the time, and have higher priority needs than mental health care. Furthermore, many of the psychological needs of retarded individuals and their families can be met by several professions in addition to psychiatry.

SPECIFIC CLINICAL ROLES

Diagnosis

Comments on the specific clinical roles of psychiatry should start with remarks on the diagnostic process. This process involves several levels. The first focuses on the primary ascertainment of mental retardation and the establishment of a more specific, preferably etiologic, diagnosis; the second focuses on the identification of concomitant complications; the third on the "working through" of the impact of the diagnosis; and the fourth on the development of a comprehensive management plan. Psychiatry has different roles during each of these phases, and its contributions depend on factors such as the age of the patient, the nature and severity of the retardation, and the presence of emotional complications.

At the first level, psychiatry's main contribution may come from the differentiation between mild forms of retardation and other types of psychopathological processes that impair learning or general adaptation; at the second level psychiatry's concern is the ascertainment of emotional problems; at the third level it is the identification of the characteristics of the intrafamilial conflict; and at the fourth, on the potential contribution of psychiatry to the treatment and comprehensive management of the patient.

Treatment

Turning to treatment, it should be emphasized that a psychiatrist's involvement in any specific therapeutic approach will depend on his clinical experience and his personal inclinations. In regard to psychotherapy—the mainstay of psychiatric treatment—it is often assumed, because psychotherapy is based on verbal communications, and because retarded individuals cannot verbalize at a sophisticated level, that these individuals are unsuited for this therapeutic modality. This assumption has contributed much to the exclusion of mentally retarded individuals from treatment in traditional psychiatric settings. However, practitioners who have had sufficient, direct experiences with retarded patients have noted that even those with relatively low IQs can express their feelings and thereby benefit from psychotherapy. Difficulties arise more from the incongruence between the language of the therapist and the patient than from the patient's inability to communicate. When the therapist is able to gear his language to that level that makes it readily understandable to retarded persons, communication becomes effective. Under such circumstances dynamic, verbal psychotherapy has much to offer for selected individuals.

Nonverbal communications also have an important role, even when psychotherapy is primarily of the verbal type. Thoughts and emotions can also be communicated through the medium of play, particularly by children. In fact, play therapy has been a traditional technique in child psychiatry. Various forms of such therapies, which depend less on verbal communications, have been found appropriate and effective with mentally retarded patients. All the psychotherapeutic approaches discussed so far are useful, both when applied individually or in groups. Group therapy has some special benefits for mentally retarded individuals who have a substantial need for social interaction and are, therefore, particularly suited for group-based approaches.

Pharmacological agents of various types have become more popular in the management of mental retardation over the past decade. Some have even acquired fleeting reputations as being panaceas. Current experiences offer the following guidelines: There is no drug available at present that improves the cognitive abilities of mentally retarded individuals, and a good deal of skepticism is in order for the near future. There are numerous pharmaceutical agents that can effectively improve disordered thinking, mood, or behavior, independent of the cognitive functioning of the patient; they are, therefore, useful in the treatment of mentally retarded individuals when prescribed for specific indications. For example, when mental retardation is complicated by symptoms of psychosis, psychopharmacological drugs can effectively alter the psychotic process. Drugs that decrease hyperactivity in children with average or high intelligence can produce similar results in hyperactive mentally retarded children; the same holds true for anticonvulsants and other drugs used to control specific symptoms. In general, a conservative attitude is indicated because many of the patients are children, and definitive information on the long-range effects of most drugs, particularly the psychoactive agents, are not yet available.

Behavior modification is probably the therapeutic endeavor that has gained most in popularity in the last two decades. From careful research with single patients, it has reached large scale applications involving entire wards, classrooms, or other sizeable groups. The personnel applying this technique range from highly disciplined psychologists to a variety of technologists, and, by now, even include parents and other family members. There is no question that behavior modification adds bits of performance to the response repertoire of mentally retarded individuals and that it can also extinguish specific undesirable behaviors. However, at least two major questions remain unanswered: one concerns the generalizability of skills gained through behavior modification, and the other the justification of the use of negative reinforcers.

Prescribed or therapeutic education is an emerging technique in the United States. It is increasingly clearly distinguished from customary classroom education. The latter emphasizes the application of a predetermined curriculum to a group of children, whereas the former is based on specific educational interventions prescribed for a child after a defined diagnostic process. Therapeutic education is most useful in the prevention or amelioration of specific impairments, such as perceptual motor deficits, and it also holds promise in the prevention of sequelae of early nervous system damage in infants.

Several therapeutic interventions, particularly the group and individual psychotherapies, have much to offer in the support of troubled family members. They span from goal-oriented counseling applied in a group setting to intensive individual psychotherapy. Family therapy, i.e., the concurrent treatment of several family members at the same time by the same therapist, holds much promise, particularly in the management of crisis-related conflicts in mildly retarded adolescents.

With the increasing involvement of many disciplines in the therapeutic process, psychiatrists have a growing opportunity and responsibility in the area of clinical consultation. This process can range in focus from a single patient treated by a single professional to the personnel of an entire agency responsible for the long-term management of a large number of mentally retarded individuals.

In closing, one comment on the care system for mental retardation is offered. The mental health needs of these individuals might be best served if mental retardation and mental health programs were closely united. This solution offers simplicity and parsimony in the utilization of scarce manpower. It is doubtful, however, that, in light of prevailing parental attitudes, this concept could be implemented in the United States today. The disadvantages of excessive separation have been repeatedly emphasized (Tarjan and Keeran, 1970; Tarjan, 1976). The most practical solution is close collaboration between mental retardation and mental health programs. From the viewpoint of the retarded person and his family, of key importance in such an approach is the assurance of easy access to both systems and ready transfer between them with minimal loss of continuity. One guarantee for these conditions is the joint utilization of professional personnel. Implementation, however, also requires an accelerated education of psychiatrists in general, and child psychiatrists in particular, in the specific clinical problems of mental retardation.

SUMMARY

This chapter focuses on the role of the psychiatrist as a clinician and consultant. It emphasizes the psychiatrist's contributions to the treatment of mentally retarded patients and their families. Several therapeutic modalities, such as psychotherapy, pharmacotherapy, and behavior modification, are discussed.

REFERENCES

American Psychiatric Association (1968) Diagnostic and Statistical Manual of Mental Disorders, 2nd Edition. Washington, D.C.: American Psychiatric Association.

Balthazar, E. E., and Stevens, H. A. (1975) The Emotionally Disturbed, Mentally Retarded: A Historical and Contemporary Perspective. Englewood Cliffs, N.J.: Prentice-Hall.

Bernstein, N. R. (Ed.) (1970) Diminished People: Problems and Care of the Mentally Retarded. Boston: Little, Brown & Co.

Grossman, H. J. (Ed.) (1973) Manual on Terminology and Classification in Mental Retardation, Revised Edition. Washington, D.C.: American Association on Mental Deficiency.

Group for the Advancement of Psychiatry (1963) Report No. 56, Mental Retardation: A Family Crisis—The Therapeutic Role of the Physician. New York: Group for the Advancement of Psychiatry.

Group for the Advancement of Psychiatry (1967) Report No. 66, Mild Mental Retardation: A Growing Challenge to the Physician. New York: Group for the Advancement of Psychiatry.

Menolascino, F. J. (Ed.) (1970) Psychiatric Approaches to Mental Retardation. New York: Basic Books.

Philips, I. (Ed.) (1966) Prevention and Treatment of Mental Retardation. New York: Basic Books.

Philips, I., and Williams, N. (1975) Psychopathology and mental retardation: A study of 100 mentally retarded children: I. Psychopathology. Amer. J. Psychiatry 132:1265.

Potter, H. W. (1965) Mental retardation: The Cinderella of psychiatry. Psychiatr. Q. 39:537.

Richmond, J. B., Tarjan, G., and Mendelsohn, R. S. (Eds.) (1974) Mental Retardation: A Handbook for the Primary Physician, 2nd Edition. Chicago: American Medical Association.

Robinson, N. W., and Robinson, H. W. (1976) The Mentally Retarded Child, 2nd Edition. New York: McGraw-Hill.

Tarjan, G. (1966) Cinderella and the prince: Mental retardation and community psychiatry. Amer. J. Psychiatry 122:1057.

Tarjan, G. (1970a) Some Thoughts on Socio-Cultural Retardation. In Social-Cultural Aspects of Mental Retardation (Ed. Haywood, H. C.) New York: Appleton-Century-Crofts, p. 745.

Tarjan, G. (1970b) Sensory Deprivation and Mental Retardation. In Psychodynamic Implications of Physiological Studies on Sensory Deprivation (Eds. Madow, L., and Snow, L. H.) Springfield, Illinois: Charles C Thomas, p. 70.

Tarjan, G. (1974) Guest editor, special section on mental retardation. Psychiatr. Ann. 4:6.

Tarjan, G. (1976) Mental retardation and the organization of services. Psychiatr. Ann. 6:27.

Tarjan, G., and Eisenberg, L. (1972) Some thoughts on the classification of mental retardation in the United States of America. Amer. J. Psychiatry (Suppl.) 128:14.

Tarjan, G., and Keeran, C. V. (1970) The Mentally Retarded. In The Practice of Community Mental Health. (Ed. Grunebaum, H.) Boston: Little, Brown, p. 79.

Zigler, E. (1967) Familial mental retardation: A continuing dilema. Science 155:292.

RESEARCH TO PRACTICE IN MENTAL RETARDATION
Care and Intervention, Volume I
Edited by Peter Mittler
Copyright 1977 I.A.S.S.M.D.

THE ROLE OF PSYCHIATRY IN MENTAL RETARDATION SERVICES

J. Wortis
State University of New York at Stony Brook and
Maimonides Hospital, 4802 Tenth Avenue, Brooklyn,
New York 11219, United States

In the United States, psychiatry is now related to mental retardation services in two different ways: 1) by administrative fiat, and 2) through professional need or demand. In many states the state residential institutions for both the psychotic and for the retarded have long been under the jurisdiction of state psychiatric departments and the more recent extension of services into the community has followed that pattern. In addition, since mental retardation is sometimes associated with certain mental disturbances or disorders, the help of psychiatrists is often required. Both of these relationships—the administrative and the professional—have provoked difficulties and controversy and the entire role of psychiatry in this field is being questioned. As a psychiatrist working with the retarded, I think that psychiatry has an important contribution to make to the field but that it should not claim leadership or control.

The National Association for Retarded Citizens has always opposed psychiatric control for several reasons: 1) In recent decades American psychiatrists have shown little interest in mental retardation, 2) Parents resent the implication that their mentally retarded children are deranged, 3) On practical grounds, parents have found that when budgets and programs for psychiatry and mental retardation are merged, mental retardation fares poorly, and 4) Parents have generally felt that services to the retarded should be primarily educational rather than psychiatric.

In connection with this problem it should be emphasized that we have seen an enormous expansion of the area of responsibility assumed by psychiatry. At the beginning of this century psychiatry dealt mainly with major psychiatric disorders in residential institutions. Largely under the influence of psychoanalysis and the associated proliferation of private practice, psychiatry now regards itself as professionally responsible for the whole range of behavioral

409

problems, neuroses, conduct, and character disorders and their prevention, to say nothing of social problems like aggression, delinquency, sexual behavior, and morality. The late Professor Popov of Moscow once told me: "The difference between our psychiatry and yours is this: if a man does not get along with his wife we regard it as a misfortune, but you regard it as a disease."

With the assumption of this wide area of responsibility, it is not surprising that the American Psychiatric Association, starting in 1963, has issued a number of statements claiming leadership in the field of mental retardation. But in spite of their claims psychiatrists in recent years have been remarkably uninvolved. Half a century ago the American Psychiatric Association had a special section on Mental Deficiency, but it was abandoned in favor of a new section on Child Psychiatry. Mental retardation was scarcely mentioned in the report of the Joint Commission on Mental Illness (1960), papers on the subject are rarely published in the *American Journal of Psychiatry,* psychiatrists make up only 6% of the membership of the American Association on Mental Deficiency, and less than 1% of all board-certified psychiatrists can be found on the staffs of state institutions for the retarded. In fact, in spite of considerable psychiatric top-level control, less than half of our state institutions for the retarded are directed by psychiatrists. Of the hundreds of community clinics for the retarded in the United States, only a few are now under the direction of a psychiatrist: many more are under pediatricians.

The historic tradition of service to the retarded has not been psychiatric. Most of the great names singled out in Kanner's *History of the Care and Study of the Mentally Retarded* were not psychiatrists. Though Itard (1774–1830) was a physician, he specialized in otology, and his work with the wild boy of Aveyron was entirely educational. Guggenbühl (1816–1863) was another pioneering physician who realized very early that he needed training in education to work with cretins; he gave up his medical practice to join the staff of a pedagogic institution before establishing his own school, the famous Abendberg in Switzerland. Seguin (1812–1880) trained as a physician, too, and published studies of body temperature, but his mental retardation work was all educational, and his classic monograph was entitled *Theory and Practice of the Education of Idiots.* After he left France to reside in the United States, he was honored by his designation as United States Commissioner on Education to represent us in 1873 at the great Vienna Exposition. Howe (1801–1876) was also a physician who became an educator, and he founded the first American institution for the retarded, now known as the Fernald School.

None of these pioneering physicians was a psychiatrist. Indeed, the first attempts of psychiatrists, in the early nineteenth century, to work with the retarded in France at Bicêtre and at the Salpêtrière were failures, because only disgracefully neglected subsections for the retarded were provided in their large psychiatric institutions.

In the middle of the nineteenth century prevailing theory encouraged both a medical and nihilistic attitude toward mental defect. Virchow's theory of cellular pathology led to an emphasis on fixed cerebral defects that tended to discourage ameliorative efforts. Although most of the severe forms of retardation do indeed have a pathological basis, this emphasis obscured the fact that the defective child, like the normal child, can, within limits, be either helped or hindered in his development by vicissitudes of training and experience. The later psychodynamic reaction to these excesses of the pathologists on the other hand sometimes led to overoptimistic expectations for psychological intervention, and too often misdirected our interests into conventional psychotherapeutic approaches to patients and their parents. Finally, at the close of the century, the widespread and uncritical acceptance of the intelligence quotient as a substitute for differential diagnosis compounded all these errors by creating an illusion of homogeneity in the retarded population, and, obscuring the important distinction between psychosocial and biologic types, between ignorance and handicap.

Although, as we have seen, dedicated physicians inspired the first efforts at systematic treatment of the retarded, in the succeeding years in Europe it was usually clergymen, teachers, and other public-spirited individuals who took the initiative. Of the hundred or so special schools for the retarded that sprang up in Germany in the nineteenth century, for example, in only "a relatively small number did the impetus come from physicians" (Kanner, 1964, p. 55). In the United States, however, possibly because of the associated creation of state institutions for the insane, physicians continued to take the lead.

While administrative arrangements in the United States often place the retarded under the aegis of state psychiatric departments (in New York State for example under the State Department of Mental Hygiene), educational services for the retarded have always remained in the domain of state educational departments. Because at the present time the major service that can be rendered the retarded is educational, this has resulted in a great deal of administrative and clinical confusion, with the public schools on the one hand undertaking, most inadequately, diagnostic study of the retarded and neglecting the medical aspects of treatment, while on the other hand the clinics and residential institutions have been obliged to undertake major educational responsibilities with similar inadequacy.

To keep our judgment balanced it should be recognized that psychiatry is implicated in the treatment and management of retardates in several ways:

1) The cerebral defects and disorders that retard development also produce derangements of behavior. Hardly any retardate is the full equivalent of a normal younger person: there are nearly always some defects and distortions of behavioral development, too. Most of these are minor, serious distortions are infrequent, and the central problem is usually the intellectual backwardness.

2) The inadequate services and rejecting attitudes of family, age peers, and society create many psychological problems that need attention and help.
3) The retardate's own consciousness of his condition and plight creates reactions that need attention.
4) Retardates are subject, probably to an enhanced degree, to all the psychiatric diseases and disorders that can befall a normal population. In the careful study of the Isle of Wight school-age population, Rutter reports that by his criteria over a quarter of the retarded children showed significant psychiatric disorder, a rate over three times that of normal controls.

It is obvious that the skills of the psychiatrist are needed as part of a multidiscipline diagnostic and treatment team. What then is the proper role of psychiatry in this field? First it must be recognized that no psychiatrist should be denied the right to entry and even leadership here, provided that he has the motivation and acquires the experience he will need, and provided also that he is willing to expand his interests beyond the conventional role of psychiatry. The same applies to administrative arrangements: there is absolutely no reason why a state psychiatric department, or a university psychiatric department cannot, with adequate budget, staff, and policy, run good programs, but the past experience of consumer groups has made them skeptical and wary, and in New York State, to give only one example, the antipathy to psychiatric administration has reached the point of no return.

In summary one can say that although psychiatry has an important and indeed essential contribution to make to the field of mental retardation it cannot claim the right to control and leadership. The traditions of service in this area have not been psychiatric, the interest of psychiatrists in this field, certainly in the United States, has in recent decades largely disappeared, and the technical demands of the work do not call upon the special skills or training of the psychiatrist. Other medical specialists, i.e., pediatricians, neurologists, physical therapists, family physicians, have equal rights, and indeed any physician willing to commit his interest and learn the skills can assume leadership. Although many professions and disciplines are needed, the center of gravity of the mental retardation field should be in education, with all of the other disciplines in accessory relationship. Administrative policy based on recognition of this fact would promote clarity and enrich services in the field.

SUMMARY

Centuries ago when the humane protection of the handicapped began there was little distinction made between the retarded and the mentally ill, but as interest in treatment evolved, educational and rehabilitative interests dominated the retardation field, and tended to separate it from psychiatry. In recent decades the prominence of psychotherapeutic and psychopharmacologic treatment modalities in psychiatry have sharpened this separation. The parents movement in the United States has always opposed psychiatric dominance in this field. The present situation is analysed and reviewed in this historic context, and suggestions for the appropriate uses of psychiatry are developed.

REFERENCES

American Psychiatric Association (1966) Psychiatry and mental retardation. Amer. J. Psychiat. 122:1302.

Kanner, L. (1964) History of the Care and Study of the Mentally Retarded. Springfield, Ill.: Charles C Thomas.

Menolascino, F. J. (Ed.) (1970) Psychiatric Approaches to Mental Retardation. New York: Basic Books.

Rutter, M. L. (1971) Psychiatry. *In* Mental Retardation: An Annual Review, Vol. III, (Ed. Wortis, J.) New York: Grune and Stratton.

Wortis, J. (1958) Schizophrenic symptomatology in mentally retarded children. Amer. J. Psychiatry 115:425.

RESEARCH TO PRACTICE IN MENTAL RETARDATION
Care and Intervention, Volume I
Edited by Peter Mittler
Copyright 1977 I.A.S.S.M.D.

THE MENTALLY RETARDED OFFENDER

A. Shapiro
Harperbury Hospital, Harper Lane, Radlett, Hertfordshire, WD7 9HQ, England

Mental deficiency can be considered a primary social disability, and delinquency can be considered an inability to live in a community without offending the accepted code to the extent of coming into conflict with the recognised and accepted laws.

Such a breakdown is often attributable more to personality problems than to mere lack of intelligence, although inadequacy can play a determining role. Such a formulation would identify a group comparatively small in number, but of great significance if we consider the social disturbance, disruption, and family distress that they can cause.

In Britain, at least, it has fallen to the psychiatrists working in mental deficiency to take a disproportionate role in providing psychiatric care for these cases. This is partly because of the greater interest that we have in social adjustment and partly because many general psychiatrists tend to refuse difficult cases, especially those referred by the courts. Psychiatrists in mental deficiency thus come to deal with cases in which, for once, the level of intelligence is secondary to the personality disturbance, and affects therapy, management, and outlook relatively little.

Rules of thumb are useless, and a reasonable assessment and planning for action (remedial or containing) can only be reached by a full consideration of the constellation of all factors, including cultural and familial. Each case is unique and demands an individual and, therefore, clinical approach.

Probably the most important question to be answered is whether the delinquent should be considered as needing psychiatric services, or whether he should be dealt with by the legal correctional agencies. As with everything else related to mental handicap, it is impossible to draw sharp demarcation lines. The final decision whether or not the individual will be considered "bad" or "mad" will depend on a multiplicity of determinants, some of which may be quite fortuitous; e.g., whether or not the particular psychiatrist is interested in the problems of delinquency and even whether or not there is an available bed to admit the patient—if not, he may end up in prison (or Borstal).

Obviously even a penological approach is one which aims at modification of behavior—*correctional* results are the aim of all dealing with delinquency and crime. This is all the more so because many of these cases present in adolescence, a time when one always hopes to take advantage of more plastic personality and habits to effect beneficial changes. We become concerned not only with the individual's personality structure but also with the cultural factors that have moulded the personality and continue to exercise a formative influence.

In this connection we ought to step warily; applying therapeutic processes that deal with an individual's problems and inadequacies and allow him to function competently in society and to achieve a richer and more satisfactory pattern of living is a highly laudable aim against which no one would demur. However, we must be conscious of the fact that such an approach can also serve as camouflage for a ruthless and conscienceless misuse of psychiatry, and we must be aware of the fact that attempts at re-socialisation might lay us open to accusations of brain washing. Such political pressures might cause one to avoid the difficult area of rehabilitation of the delinquent individual.

There is at present a fair amount of forensic discussion about the best place in which to treat an individual who is delinquent, yet sufficiently disturbed to require a primarily psychiatric and therapeutic approach. A body of influential opinion would favour the provision of psychiatric treatment in prisons rather than in psychiatric hospitals, and this is in keeping with the present trends in general psychiatric hospitals. On the other hand, in Britain, following the Butler report, allocations of funds are being made by the Department of Health and Social Security for the building of so-called Medium Security Units, which would have the duty of containing all those psychiatric patients, including the mentally handicapped, who require treatment under secure conditions yet who are not so dangerous as to need the very high security of special hospitals.

Turning now to the clinical features, we find in our patients a number of distinct clinical groups. One group of offences is related to inadequacy. Many sex offenders fall within this category. They are usually younger persons, unsure and unable to compete with their peers. Under the pressure of sexuality emerging at puberty, they often turn to their much younger companions for the satisfaction of their instinctual drives. Patients committing this type of offence fall within a wide range of intelligence and age.

The lower grade lad tends to turn to children for company and sexual experience and the higher grade patient is more likely to attack older girls and young women. The older and high grade patient tends to compensate for his feeling of inadequacy by bluster and preoccupation with violence, and his offences can be characterised by considerable brutality; yet behind this facade of bluster and braggadocio it is easy to detect a frightened and insecure adolescent trying to come to grips with his sexuality.

Other disturbances of behaviour caused by inadequacy are generally associated with immature, childish patterns of reaction that are characterised by very low frustration tolerance leading to tantrums similar to those found in normal toddlers. These patients are particularly difficult to handle at home, where they frequently become violent, aggressive, and generally out of their parents' control, and frequently tend to wander away from home. Unless they commit petty larceny while away, or, what is much more serious, they take away cars to go for rides (when they become a serious danger to life and limb), they should be considered much more disturbed then delinquent, although occasionally legal procedures through the Courts must be used in order to allow them to be taken into care.

A second group is one in which behaviour disturbances are associated with, if not directly caused by, constitutional and organic factors. Aneuploidy of sex chromosomes and convulsive states are of relatively common occurrence. As far as is known, the majority of the individuals so affected do not exhibit either disturbances of behaviour or criminal tendencies—but the association between these findings and asocial behaviour is much too frequent not to have some validity. It is, of course, obvious that the hospital population is a very selected one on the basis of social breakdown.

Patients with chromosome disturbance tend to be more unstable, to be less responsible, and to be more prone to lapse into petty crime; their psychiatric hospitalisation rate is some three to four times the normal rate. These patients tend to exhibit personality disorders in a way reminiscent of the epileptic and characterised by much lower capacity for interpersonal relationship, egocentric irresponsibility of behaviour, and a tendency to give vent to their feelings by surreptitious and malicious damage of other peoples' property.

The epileptic patients become involved in patterns of delinquency either through a tendency to explosive behaviour reactions, during which they become episodically very aggressive and violent, or through a tendency to be self-centred, and, therefore, ignoring the rights and convenience of others, and at times leading to stealing. It is well known that temporal lobe epilepsy can be the cause of particularly violent behaviour; reactions to such behaviour are by no means limited to temporal lobe cases.

Many of these organic cases exhibit behaviour that is often ascribed to psychopathic personalities, and it is quite true that there is frequently little difference in behaviour between patients with demonstrable organic lesions and those in whom these lesions cannot be found. If cases with demonstrable organic or constitutional disturbance are found to be on one end of the continuum characterised by "asocial psychopathy," then cases of psychosis are found on the other.

Although the florid and hepephrenic types of schizophrenia may manifest themselves by delinquent behaviour, one group of patients who come in through the courts for petty offences are those who are suffering from schizophrenia simplex. These disturbances tend to be neglected both in psychiatric text books and in the literature, and nowadays when so much attention is paid to rigid diagnostic criteria, few of these patients are recognised as being schizophrenic at all. The typical cases become apparent in adolescence and in many ways appear to be a caricature of the least acceptable features of adolescence (especially to their families and people who have to live with them). They are characterised by: lack of any motivation; flattened emotional responses, except for expression of irritation when stressed, particularly by the family; an extremely poor capacity for interpersonal relations; a tendency to withdrawal and social isolation; a tendency to show resentment of slights, be they real or imagined; and excessive vindictiveness. Bomb hoaxes or activating fire alarms are common manifestations of the negative feelings of these patients.

These patients present a considerable management problem and require a comprehensive treatment programme, including manipulation of environment, sometimes medication, and, above all, time to effect improvements in their condition.

An interesting area that has also not been reported very frequently is the occurrence of acute psychiatric episodes (e.g., schizophrenic reactions or paranoid states). After these episodes have come to an end one generally finds that the patients involved are irresponsible, shallow individuals with little capacity for interpersonal relationships or social sense. They constitute an important proportion of patients admitted to units for young people with behaviour disorders, such as the one we have had at Harperbury Hospital for some 15 years now.

Most important of all are probably those cases in which no single factor is operating; we are dealing with personality disorder occasioned by disturbances of personality development due to adverse environmental factors and also possibly the presence of asocial cultural factors because of the subculture from which the individual comes.

It has been very difficult to correlate specific offences with specific mental conditions beyond the few that I have attempted in this paper. I feel strongly that there has been a dichotomy in approach, with workers either becoming interested in organic aetiology and constitutional factors, or approaching these cases from a purely dynamic point of view that ignores diagnoses and possible classification of types of behaviour and their correlation with organic aetiological factors.

The important components of the therapeutic process are:

1. dealing with the underlying cause, such as epilepsy or psychosis, by appropriate medication or use of psychotherapeutic techniques in those patients in whom the disturbance is a neurotic one; equally important is total social therapy by manipulation of the environment and utilising the living patterns within the unit
2. teaching the individual to lead a life in which he is obliged to make adjustments to others and to learn the skills of living in social groups.

RESEARCH TO PRACTICE IN MENTAL RETARDATION
Care and Intervention, Volume I
Edited by Peter Mittler
Copyright 1977 I.A.S.S.M.D.

OFFENDERS WITHIN ORDINARY SERVICES FOR THE MENTALLY RETARDED IN DENMARK

B. B. Svendsen and J. Werner
Unit of Forensic Psychiatry,
Ministry of Justice,
Nytorv 21, Copenhagen K, Denmark
DK-145o

HYPOTHESIS

For about 40 years Danish practice with respect to the mentally retarded offender with an IQ level of up to 75 has been that he is transferred to and taken care of by the ordinary services for the mentally retarded. He is redefined as a patient, and designated a patient-offender. The justification of this policy has been questioned during recent years.

The hypothesis to be tested here, if possible, is that there is no reason to change this policy, neither in the interest of the mentally retarded, nor in the interest of society.

DEVELOPMENT OF PRESENT DANISH PRACTICE

In Denmark separate services for the mentally retarded (with an IQ level of up to 75) were developed from the middle of the 19th century; they were run by medical men, pedagogues, and socially interested persons. In the beginning only those mentally retarded offenders who in principle were irresponsible, the imbeciles and the idiots, were transferred from the prisons.

In the 1920s, however, a Danish psychiatrist Schrøder (1917 and 1927) went through the Danish prison system and found that about 10% of the inmates were mentally retarded.

After a new penal law was introduced in 1930, practically all the mentally retarded were transferred to the ordinary services for the mentally retarded.

In 1959 a law changed the former paternalistic system for the mentally retarded into a system with *inter alia* open wards and normalization as guiding principles. The right of the patient or client to decide for himself as far as possible was underlined, and so was the right to normal living conditions and a normal sexual life. During this development the mentally retarded offender's "right to be sentenced" in the same way as normal offenders has been forwarded, by spokesmen and by mentally retarded offenders themselves, and a public debate has arisen.

Within the correctional services a related development, resulting in a majority of open prisons and an underlining of prisoners' rights, has taken place within recent years.

CENSUS STUDY

As a result of this public debate, a committee under the Ministry of Justice was set up, and as part of its work a census study was made.

Magnitude of Problems

It was found that on 15 January, 1973, valid penal court decisions on "detention" or "treatment" were in force for 290 patients. These patients were found among 22,000 patients taken care of by the services for the mentally retarded of Denmark (which has 5 million inhabitants)—for information about the epidemiology of, and the services for, the mentally retarded, see Dupont (1975) or Dupont and Berg (1975). This means that a little more than 1% of all the mentally retarded patients or clients are offender-patients. The magnitude of this problem should thus be believed to be of limited importance for the services of the mentally retarded.

Formal Status of Offender-Patients

What special conditions prevail for the offender-patients? For 10% a court decision for "detention" was in force, for 90% the court decision was for "care." The former means that restrictions stating that the patient has to stay in a center institution (which has 100-1,000 patients) are in force until the court changes the sanction to a "care" order; the patient can, however, be placed in locked or open wards in the center institution by the chief physician and be granted short excursions. The rest of the forensic patients with "care orders" can be placed where the responsible physician, in cooperation with the social worker, finds it appropriate: institution, boarding-house, family care, rented rooms, etc.

One-third of the patients (37%) were living in the center institutions on the census day and two-thirds were outside, this proportion being similar to that for all patients within the services for the mentally retarded. This means that *grosso modo* the status of the offender-patients is not very different from that of the non-offender-patients with whom they share facilities.

When estimating the findings of a census study, it should be borne in mind that a person who has been a patient within the services for 25 years has 25 as many chances to be represented in a census study than one who has been a patient for one year. Therefore, there is a gross overrepresentation of the chronic patients, compared with what would have been found in a cohort study or a study of retarded offenders admitted to these services during a certain period.

Crime

To characterize this group further, it can be mentioned that the dominant or sole offences concerned property in 60% of the cases, sexual transgressions of the law in 25%, and violence or arson in 15%.

Age and Sex

The dominant age group was 25–29 years of age, and the dominant age at the time of the offence 20–24 years of age. Ninety-four per cent of the offender-patients were males.

Duration of Stay

The duration of the current forensically determined stay in the services for the mentally retarded was most frequently between one and two years. In cumulative figures, approximately 10% had stayed less than one year after the crime causing the sanction, approximately 20% less than two years, approximately 40% less than five years, and approximately 75% less than ten years; or, the other way round, 25% had stayed more than 10 years after the crime causing the sanction, about 10% more than 15 years, and 2% more than 25 years.

Degree of Mental Retardation

The distribution of mental retardation, according to the WHO classification, among those studied in the census is given in Table 1. The table shows that less than 5% were moderately or severely retarded, one-third were mildly retarded, and one-half of the cases were "borderline."

ATTITUDES TOWARDS THE TURNING
OF OFFENDERS INTO OFFENDER-PATIENTS

The preceding information illustrates what the number and nature of offender-patients may be in a country where all mentally retarded offenders are transferred to and taken care of by the ordinary services for the mentally retarded, services of a certain standard as far as they fill a basic need, but that at the same time have a substantial proportion of outmoded wards and that are insufficient in several respects.

There are three main elements in the performance of these sanctions: the judicial system, the employees of the service system, and the offender-patients.

Table 1. Distribution of degree of mental retardation, according to WHO classification, among 290 patients in a 1973 Danish census of mentally retarded under penal "detention"

WHO	Classification	IQ	N	Percent of Total
310	Borderline	85–68	153	53
311	Mild retardation	67–52	108	37
312	Moderate retardation	51–36	23	8
313	Severe retardation	35–20	3	1
	Not given		3	1
Total			290	100

The functions of the judicial system express retaliation, general prevention, and individual prevention. The lawyers *also* aim at due process and recently heavy criticism has been forwarded against a too dominant and neglecting *parens patriae* policy. In this contribution neither juridical nor criminological viewpoints are forwarded, but we have tried to assess the attitudes of those employees who run the services, as well as the attitudes of the patient-offenders towards the measures taken. Our questions dealt with whether the measures taken were to be preferred to ordinary penal sanctions (generally a time-limited prison sentence).

We got four groups of answers, 1) both parties "accepted" the sanction, 2) one party, i.e., the patient, contested, the other party, i.e., the responsible physician, found the sanction "right," 3) vice versa, i.e., the patient accepted, while the physician found the sanction "wrong," and 4) both parties found the sanction wrong.

For the 290 cases we found that the responsible therapist (the physician for the central institutions, and the leading social worker for those in boarding houses, family care etc.) considered the placement appropriate in 68% and not appropriate in 17%, while 15% were unanswered. Seen from the viewpoints of the patients, 42% accepted the placement, 26% did not accept it, and 32% did not answer. In other words, the responsible employee finds at least three out of 20 patients wrongly placed, and out of 20 patient-offenders at least five would prefer an ordinary (prison) sentence. For two out of every 20, both parties agree that an ordinary sanction should have been performed.

It is not surprising that it is especially among the borderline cases that placements within the services for the mentally retarded are found inappropriate or unjustified.

We have no control figures; thus we do not know whether those running these services would find 15% of their nonforensic patients wrongly placed, or whether the percentage of nonaccepting (nonforensic) patients or clients is as high as 25%. It must, however, be considered thought-provoking that the placement of a substantial fraction of the offender-patients is considered problematic, and that ordinary sentences were considered preferable.

DISCUSSION

These findings do not justify major modifications of the Danish general policy with respect to mentally retarded offenders. Only on two points do we think that practice could be altered.

With respect to general policy, we still believe that mentally retarded offenders—as a universal policy—should be exempted from the general prison system. The main function of the prison system is to administer society's disapproval or revenge by locking up offenders for shorter or longer periods. The prison sentence has per se no primary content for the individual offender. This is not so with institutions for the mentally retarded. Today the goal of these services is to help the patients or clients to realize as many potentialities as possible for living the life they wish, to realize as many dreams of any child, any adolescent, any adult as possible, preferably outside or in half-way institutions, and only if necessary in ordinary institutions.

One condition is important if an offender is transferred to the services for the mentally retarded: as few special restrictions as possible should be made for the offender-patients; more particularly, there ought to be no opportunity for the judicial system to determine the duration of a patient's stay in a closed institution. With restrictions of this sort the institutions for the mentally retarded tend to be converted into branches of the prison system. On the other hand, those running the institutions for the mentally retarded should not ignore the probability of an offender's eventually committing new offences. This liability should be as realistically counteracted as any other symptom that complicates the prognosis for a patient. There should be no "overreaction" either; a relapse rate of offender-patients similar to "normal" offenders should be tolerated or aimed at.

CONCLUSION

The conclusions of the census-study are as follows:

1. that a policy of transferral of all mentally retarded offenders to the services for the mentally retarded is practicable, and that it is accepted in the majority of cases
2. that the transferred offender-patients represent only about 1% of all the patients or clients of these services
3. that the duration of the legal sanction is long in a substantial number of the cases

4. that in one-tenth to one-fourth of the cases considered an ordinary sentence was a preferable alternative to transfer.

Our hypotheses—that there is no reason to change the current policy—is not, according to our opinion, contradicted in the main. We do, however, consider it worthwhile to discuss the desirability of two modifications:

The first of the two points that appear objectionable to us in this study is the long duration of many of the sanctions. In our study 25% of the sample had had a stay of more than 10 years arising from the offence. As mentioned, such cases dominate in a census-study; it is, however, unreasonable that any offence of a retarded person should confer a sanction of such length. Maximum time limits (1–5 years) by which the legal sanctions become void should be introduced; after the lapse of these periods, the offender-patients should only be retained in accordance with the ordinary rules for the patients of these civil institutions.

The other point that impressed us was that 15% of the offender-patients, according to those running the services, and 25%, according to the patients or clients themselves, ought to have been sanctioned in the ordinary way, i.e., have had a prison sentence. We think serious consideration should be given to letting the debile and borderline-offenders themselves choose in court whether, this time, they would prefer an ordinary sentence or an offer to be taken care of by the services for the mentally retarded.

SUMMARY

Since the 1920s, practically all offenders estimated to be mentally retarded have been transferred to services for the mentally retarded. On 15 January, 1973, 290 persons were found for whom a valid court decision on "detention" or "treatment" existed. This corresponds to a little more than 1% of all those taken care of by the services for the mentally retarded. According to the authors, the findings do not indicate a change in the policy of transferring mentally retarded offenders to the ordinary services for the mentally retarded. It is, however, found desirable to discuss two modifications: 1) to fix a maximum duration of the penal sanction for the offender-patients, and 2) to let the debile or borderline offender choose in court between ordinary sentence and a special sanction in the form of a transferral to the services for the mentally retarded.

REFERENCES

Dupont, A. (1975) Mentally retarded in Denmark. Dan. Med. Bull. 22:243.
Dupont, A., and Berg, E. (1975) Some results of a national EDP-registration of 22,000 mentally retarded. Proc. 3rd Congr. IASSMD, p. 364.
Schrøder, G. E. (1917 and 1927) Psychiatric examination of male prisoners in the penal institutions of Denmark, Copenhagen (in Danish).

COSTS

RESEARCH TO PRACTICE IN MENTAL RETARDATION
Care and Intervention, Volume I
Edited by Peter Mittler
Copyright 1977 I.A.S.S.M.D.

THE USE OF COST EFFECTIVENESS ANALYSIS IN DECIDING ON ALTERNATIVE LIVING ENVIRONMENTS FOR THE RETARDED

A. M. Gross
Heller School, Brandeis University, Waltham, Massachusetts 02154, United States

Decision-makers in the field of social welfare have always been aware of the financial limitations that make their job a difficult one. Over the last few years, however, this difficulty seems to have been magnified not only by a world-wide recognition of the limitation and uneven distribution of financial resources but also by a realization of the high cost of the services needed to help people with special problems, e.g., the mentally retarded. Economists have long warned us that, where a great deal of money is needed and where there are limited resources, decisions about the use of these resources will be made much more difficult if the tools and procedures for making these decisions are not well developed.

Economists have worked diligently over the past twenty years to develop tools for decision-making in a rational manner. Realizing that the process we use to decide how to allocate our limited financial resources will never be an entirely rational process, it is important that we continue to strive towards the development of rational tools for decision-making that will maximize the possibility of making rational decisions.

Two tools that accomplish this aim are cost benefit analysis and cost-effectiveness analysis.

It is impossible within these space limitations to fully describe the theoretical basis for doing cost-benefit analysis because it is such a complex tool. The complex nature of cost-benefit analysis can be illustrated by attempting to define what we mean by "cost" in cost-benefit analysis.

It is generally agreed that in cost-benefit analysis both costs and benefits are measured in monetary terms, i.e., dollars, pounds, francs, marks, etc. In defining "cost" we of course begin with this basic monetary cost; however, there is also a social cost, and part of that cost is an opportunity cost. This means that the dollar we spend today is not just a simple dollar, but must also be looked at in terms of the foregone opportunity of spending the money in other ways. We arrive at this cost by hypothesizing that we have put the money in the bank and that it is receiving interest. We then compute the present value of this money. The value of the money we spend is also determined by how we got the money. If we are paying 12% interest on development bonds for that money, then its cost to us is at least one dollar plus 12%. There are also spillover costs to be determined. These are costs that are incurred to a population other than the one we wanted to charge. In determining cost, we should also calculate the amount of uncertainty involved in these costs (Conley, 1975).

In addition to the criticism that cost-benefit analysis is too complex a tool, others have argued that: a) not all benefits can be measured in monetary terms, b) costs and benefits of programs not as yet implemented fully are prone to a high degree of uncertainty, c) it is a weak tool for measuring more than two alternatives.

In attempting to counter the criticism of cost-benefit analysis that states that it only measures benefits in monetary terms and therefore was by and large not suitable for social welfare programs, economists turned to cost-effectiveness analysis.

When developing a more helpful methodology for doing cost-effectiveness analysis, four conditions must be met. First, the model must be as simple as possible. It must be understood that any kind of analysis is seen by service providers as a possible source of criticism. Second, we must develop a model that can be uniformly applied over a number of service providers. We cannot define costs in one way for a group home and another way for a developmental center. The data we collect must be comparable or we have no basis for ranking the results in any way. To assure that the model will be uniformly applied, a third condition is that our model be applied by a central organization that has complete information from all the service providers. The model is not meant to be applied by an internal evaluation unit in the organization that provides the service itself. Defining the elements of the cost-effectiveness model uniformly and then having the model applied in a variety of ways will not enhance our ability to compare the results. Last, the model must be developed keeping in mind that our purpose is to rank a number of alternative ways of reaching similar goals. A corollary of this last condition is that the goals of each alternative living environment are clearly defined, similar, and quantifiable.

One other step must be taken before we can begin to define what we mean by "costs" and "effectiveness" as applied to alternative living environments for the mentally retarded. We must decide what it is we want to accomplish by applying cost-effectiveness analysis. Among a number of alternative purposes, two have been chosen for this discussion. First we will want to use our results to provide better placement decisions for the mentally retarded. In effect we are seeking information to answer the question: "Which alternative living environment provides the highest probability for achieving the maximum results given the needs of the individual we are placing?" Second, we want to know what kind of resources must be allocated to assure that the individual we are placing will be given every opportunity to reach his maximum potential.

In the foregoing, we have defined the decision criteria for our cost-effectiveness analysis. In many cases the term "cost-effective" has been applied to those situations where the decision criterion was to minimize the cost for attaining a fixed level of effectiveness. It refers to choosing the cheapest way of reaching a goal. This is not the decision criterion chosen for the present cost effectiveness model. The decision criterion chosen for this model is to maximize effectiveness while, hopefully, keeping costs at a reasonable level. It should be noted that "reasonable costs" are usually not defined by the policy analyst, but are dependent on the political decision-making process through which it is decided whether a cost level is "worth it" or not.

The following list of alternative living environments has been categorized into two groups; one for children and one for young adults and adults. It has been compiled as a result of a cross-national study done by the author.

For children, the alternative living environments are: the natural home, an adoptive home, a foster home, a foster group home where a couple will care for a number of foster children, a developmental home where a child with severe problems will receive intensive therapeutic care from a couple, and developmental centers, which have been previously mentioned. For young adults and adults, the alternative living environments include: independent living, scattered apartment sites, apartment clusters, which are a group of apartments located close together, natural homes (for young adults), foster homes (for young adults), foster group homes (for young adults), hostels, group homes, developmental homes, developmental centers, and nursing homes for those with physical problems and for the elderly.

In determining the cost side of our cost-effectiveness model, there are a number of alternative methods that could be used. The procedure suggested for this model is to calculate the full 24-hour cost for life maintenance. The units of cost that comprise this calculation include housing, food, health, program, transportation, and administration.

Because providers of services such as nursing homes and developmental centers must give adequate financial reports to those who provide them with money, it is relatively easy to determine unit costs by first examining their yearly budgets, which are generally broken down into these categories, and then dividing this figure by the number of bed days. For living environments such as natural homes, independent living, etc., these costs are not as easily obtainable, but are available and can be determined without too much difficulty.

It should be mentioned that at this point one important cost is not included in our cost-effectiveness model, i.e., the capital cost of the building that houses the particular living environment. It does not seem fair to use the present replacement value for a residential center that was built fifty years ago and that we know will not be replaced for at least another fifty years. We cannot predict the cost of replacement fifty years from now, but it seems unreasonable as well to take the original cost of the building, which was a fraction of the cost today. Hopefully, in the near future, a way of computing these important costs will be developed so that they can be included in our analysis.

Program costs include all costs that are related to increasing the effectiveness measure. For instance, the costs of a day care center, sheltered workshop, speech therapist, physical therapist, and teacher are the kinds of costs that would fall under this heading.

If we were doing a cost-benefit analysis, we would now evaluate the output based on the monetary value derived. In a developmental center we would look for the amount of earnings for those who are "graduates" of that particular living environment. For those who would have to spend the rest of their lives in this environment we would examine the amount of money derived from their work in a sheltered workshop. Where the person made no money, the benefit would be zero.

When dealing with effectiveness, this is no longer our concern. We want to know what is accomplished in a particular environment with no connection to a money output. The results must, nonetheless, be quantifiable. It does us no good if we say that our goal is to make people feel better about themselves if we are not prepared to attack the difficult task of quantifying these feelings.

Although increased life-satisfaction and improvement of self-image has been mentioned in the literature as possible goals for working with the mentally retarded, these important items have not been chosen as effectiveness measures for this model. The reason is that we are usually dependent on a self-reporting instrument so that life satisfaction and self-image can be quantified. We want our model to apply for all levels of retardation, including those who may have difficulty verbalizing abstract feelings. In an effort not to eliminate these people from our study, another output measure has been chosen.

The effectiveness measure suggested here is based on the developmental model. This model "suggests that every person is capable of growth and change, that the rate varies with the individual and that the direction of change, whether good or ill, can be influenced by the environment" (Eleanor Roosevelt Developmental Services, 1973). At this point, it might be suggested that what we are really talking about is independence, and that we can just measure the level of the person's functioning in a variety of living environments and come up with our effectiveness measure. The reasons for not doing this are: 1) often we begin by talking about independence and then shift our attention to dependence by emphasizing what the person cannot do rather than what he can do, 2) independence is a very broad term and we sometimes forget that there are a number of specific developmental steps that all people go through in order to reach independence. The focus of our effectiveness measure is on evaluating each living environment, in particular an individual's movement from one developmental task to the next.

If we are only interested in the rate of learning these tasks, then, of course, the less handicapped person can move from developmental task to developmental task faster and is more likely to be in his natural home, and so the highest effectiveness measure will be in natural homes. The developmental model, however, causes us to concentrate on the needs of the individual and on providing the programs that will serve those needs. The effectiveness measure of a natural home with a teenager who can print his name but receives no stimulation to teach him to sign his name will be lower than that of a developmental center, which provides a program to teach a severely retarded person to eat with a fork rather than a spoon.

This approach to measuring effectiveness cannot be utilized unless we know what the needs of each individual person are. This process is usually called assessment. Actually, what we want is an accurate description, a snapshot, of a person at a particular point in time that tells us the level of his present development. Certain states, and, in some cases, the federal government in the United States, have made this assessment mandatory for all mentally retarded children.

Next, goals should be set. The only difficulty in setting goals is setting them low enough so that the person will reach the goal without undue frustration and high enough so that the person reaches his maximum potential.

After the goals are set, the key question becomes: "Does this living environment provide the kind of program environment that is most conducive to accomplishing that particular developmental task or set of developmental tasks?" The cost effectiveness question is: "What kind of inputs are needed to provide these kinds of outcomes?"

This kind of cost-effectiveness analysis has never been done, but in order to clarify the approach, let us hypothesize a case for illustrative purposes. Let us take a man, 24 years old, who has spent most of his life in a residential center for the retarded and has been labeled as moderately retarded. The developmental goal set with this person is to have him enter into a competitive work situation, and the immediate task is to place him in a sheltered workshop situation. In our hypothetical community there are only three alternative living environments to choose from, and, as a result of a study recently completed at Brandeis University, we have some preliminary figures for relative cost. The alternatives are: 1) a community residence (group home) that costs $24.00 a day, 2) a state-run institution that costs $28.30 a day, and 3) his natural home, which costs $10.06 a day (Jones and Jones, 1976).

An assessment has been done, and it is determined that the person has accomplished almost all the developmental tasks that would enable him to succeed in a sheltered workshop, but there is concern that he has some psychological problems stemming from his own feelings of inadequacy that have left him with paranoid tendencies and that cause him to be loud, argumentative, and unable to make friends.

We have also assessed the living environments in terms of their ability to meet the needs of this person. The group residence has eight tenants, two very sensitive staff people, and a psychologist available for staff consultation and direct counseling to the person. The parents in the natural home are very warm and honestly want their son to succeed. They have very little understanding of psychological problems and feel guilty about having placed their son in an institution. The institution is very supportive of the person, but, although it has a psychiatrist and psychologist on staff, they are both very busy because the institution is understaffed. The alternatives are discussed with our imaginary person but he feels positive about all the alternatives and has no preference.

A hypothetical rating scale from 1 to 5 has been developed (5 being the highest score) and a multi-disciplinary team has judged that for this kind of person, with these alternatives, the effectiveness ratings are: home—2, institution—3, and community residence—4. A cost-effectiveness ratio is developed by dividing the cost by the effectiveness rating. We then have a ratio of 24.00 divided by 4, which equals 6.0 (for the community residence), 28.30 divided by 3, which equals 9.43 (for the state-run institution), and a ratio for the natural home that is 10.06 divided by 2, which equals 5.03. The alternative with the best cost-efficiency ratio is the natural home. For the money spent it would seem to indicate that the best place for our resources and for the ultimate success of the person is the natural home.

After this computation was done, a member of our hypothetical team realized that another alternative was available. The family seemed so warm and interested in their son that they asked what would happen to the cost-effectiveness ratio if he were living at home and a psychologist met once a week with the parents and once a week with the son. The additional cost for the psychologist would be $40.00 a week. A reevaluation of the effectiveness rating is done for the natural home and with this added input the natural home is given a 3. Some members of the team are concerned that the person will be isolated when he comes home and will not be given the opportunity to accomplish the developmental task of establishing friendly relationships with others. The revised cost effectiveness ratio is a cost of $15.75 divided by 3, which equals 5.25. The natural home is still the best alternative living environment in terms of cost-effectiveness. The next best alternative would be the natural home with supplemental help.

SUMMARY

This chapter begins with a brief explanation of cost-benefit and cost-effectiveness analysis, with emphasis on the differences between the two. Using a cross-national study, alternative living environments for the retarded are discussed and a model using cost-effectiveness analysis will be presented for making decisions about the use of resources and placement for the individual.

REFERENCES

Conley, R. W. (1975) Issues in benefit-cost analysis of the vocational rehabilitation program. Amer. Rehab. Nov/Dec, p. 19.

Eleanor Roosevelt Developmental Services (1973) A plan of services for the five year period beginning April 1, 1974. Schenectady, New York: New York State Department of Mental Hygiene March 15, p. 2.

Jones, P. P., and Jones, K. J. (1976) The Measurement of Community Placement Success and its Associated Costs. Interim Report No. 2, January. Waltham, Massachusetts: Brandeis University, p. 86.

RESEARCH TO PRACTICE IN MENTAL RETARDATION
Care and Intervention, Volume I
Edited by Peter Mittler
Copyright 1977 I.A.S.S.M.D.

A COST-EFFECTIVENESS ANALYSIS OF A RESIDENTIAL TREATMENT PROGRAM FOR BEHAVIORALLY DISTURBED CHILDREN

B. T. Yates
*Department of Psychology, The American University,
Washington, DC. 20016, United States*

There is an obvious and profound need for accountability in the treatment and prevention of mental deficiency. We need to become more accountable for the effects our programs produce and for the money our programs consume. What we need is an accountability system that generates data for both interprogram evaluation and intraprogram improvement of costs and effectiveness. The best way to promote the dual accountability of costs and effectiveness may be to conduct cost-effectiveness analyses of our programs. This chapter provides examples of inter- and intraprogram cost-effectiveness analysis. These examples are simplified to get across the major message: cost-effectiveness analysis can be conducted so as to transform program evaluation into a stepping stone for program improvement.

Cost-effectiveness analysis can produce interprogram evaluations, based on macro analysis of the cost and effectiveness of different programs. Cost-effectiveness analysis can also produce intraprogram improvements, based on micro-analysis of the cost and effectiveness of different procedures used in a program. Both macro- and micro-cost-effectiveness analysis ask the same three questions: 1) How effective is the program?, 2) How much does it cost?, and 3) How cost-effective is it? By describing how I conducted macro- and micro-cost-effectiveness analyses of a residential program called Learning House, I will indicate several ways that each of the three questions can be answered.

MACRO-COST-EFFECTIVENESS ANALYSIS

Macro-cost-effectiveness analysis is conducted at a general level so that answers to the questions of effectiveness, cost, and cost-effectiveness will be in units that all programs can provide.

How Effective Is It?

Due to the diversity of effectiveness measures used in different programs, macro-answers to the question of effectiveness must use the "lowest common denominator" of the available measures. The "lowest common denominator" of effectiveness for residential programs is recidivism. Use of the recidivism measure causes the effectiveness question to become: "How many clients are still not in trouble several years after release?" Follow-up studies of the Learning House program show that the answer is nine, or about 70% of the 13 children who completed the program have stayed out of trouble.

How Much Does It Cost?

The next question in macro-cost-effectiveness analysis is "How much does it cost?" Data on the costs of operating programs are usually available from accounting records. The Learning House accounting records show that $978 is spent per child per month. However, costs can be measured from a variety of perspectives. The amount of actual money consumed by program operations provides only one costing perspective. It may be important to estimate the amount of money that would have to be paid for labor that is donated by students or volunteers to supplement the efforts of paid personnel. It may also be important to estimate the cost of donated facilities, equipment, and materials. Estimation of such "hidden" costs provides a social perspective on the resources consumed by programs. Social costs can be useful in interprogram evaluations. To evaluate the cost of programs independent of how attractive they are to volunteers or donation agencies, costs should be measured from the social perspective. To find out how proficient different programs are in obtaining donated resources, social costs should be measured for comparison with operations costs.

The social cost of the Learning House program is $1,915 per child per month—almost twice the operations cost. This means, for one thing, that Learning House receives much support from the local community. It can also be argued that the many educational and research benefits produced by the Learning House program should be subtracted from the social cost to arrive at a more accurate estimate of the net resources consumed by the program. However, because it is often difficult to accurately measure educational and research benefits, and to keep cost measurement simple and reliable, the operations cost will be used instead of the social cost to answer the third question of macro-cost-effectiveness analysis: "How cost-effective is it?"

How Cost-Effective Is It?

For interprogram comparisons of cost-effectiveness, one should calculate the amount of money that had to be put into each program to get a successfully treated—in this case, a nonreceded—client out of the program. This macro-cost-effectiveness index is computed by dividing the total cost of treating all clients by the number of nonreceded clients. Learning House consumed $18,557 on the average to produce a nonreceded child. By itself, this index provides a succinct argument for prevention.

Inter-program Comparisons

When compared with other macro-cost-effectiveness indices, the Learning House index would provide information on the relative cost-effectiveness of the program. Unfortunately, none of the other local programs contacted would provide recidivism data. Some of the programs could not provide recidivism data because they did not follow-up their clients. Other programs refused to disclose their recidivism.

So much for interprogram evaluation of macro-cost-effectiveness. The best that can be done at present is to point out to funding agencies that their programs need help in collecting data on effectiveness. It is important to provide this help in a manner that defuses the political pyrotechnics that can be ignited by the words "cost" and "effectiveness." Perhaps one way to defuse this situation is to show the programs that systematic collection of data on cost and effectiveness can actually help the program improve itself, via micro-cost-effectiveness analysis.

MICRO-COST-EFFECTIVENESS ANALYSIS

Although the same questions of effectiveness, cost, and cost-effectiveness are asked in both macro- and micro-cost-effectiveness analysis, micro-cost-effectiveness analysis asks the three questions in more detail. The quantitative picture of a program that is provided by micro-cost-effectiveness analysis must have enough detail to show which parts of the program are working well and which not so well.

How Effective Is It?

To find a micro-answer to the effectiveness question, the first step is to determine the exact goals of the program. The major goal of the Learning House program is to have children attain and maintain normative frequencies for a number of interpersonal behaviors. To obtain quantifiable measures of how closely the program approaches this goal, I met repeatedly with program staff in order to determine which interpersonal behaviors were most important and to define those behaviors operationally. It was decided that there should be an equal number of social desirable or *positive* behaviors and socially undesirable or *negative* behaviors. Labels for the ten positive and ten negative behaviors that we finally decided to monitor are listed in Table 1.

I designed and implemented an observation system to collect data on the frequency at which each Learning House child exhibited each of the twenty behaviors. During every two-hour observation session, two randomly selected and nonparticipant observers recorded the frequency of each behavior for a single, randomly selected child. Data were collected regularly in children's homes, schools, and at the program facility. To measure how closely the behavior frequencies of the Learning House children approached normal frequencies, data were also collected on normal children in the area. Observation data were collected over four consecutive quarters, with a mean reliability of .80. Because a number of changes were made in treatment procedures between the second and third quarters, the first two quarters are referred to as "treatment A" and the second two quarters are referred to as "treatment B."

The approximation of behavior frequencies of Learning House children to the behavior frequencies of the normal children was quantified by z scores. The z scores were calculated so that a positive z score meant the child was "better than normal." A negative z score meant the child was "worse than normal." Specifically, a positive z score for a behavior meant the child emitted a positive behavior at a higher frequency than normal, or emitted a negative behavior at a lower frequency than normal. A negative z score meant the child emitted a positive behavior at a lower frequency than normal, or emitted a negative behavior at a higher frequency than normal. To provide data on how effective the program was for positive versus negative behaviors, a mean z score was calculated for positive and for negative behaviors. The relative importance of each behavior was entered into these calculations as weightings of the z scores.

Figure 1 shows how the z scores of positive and negative behaviors change over quarters. The solid horizontal line indicates normality. The upper broken line indicates one standard deviation from normality on "the good side" of normality. The lower broken line indicates one standard deviation from normality on "the bad side" of normality. Figure 1 shows that during all four quarters children are "better than normal" in terms of the positive behaviors. Figure 1 also shows that the children are "worse than normal" in terms of the negative behaviors, especially during the fourth quarter. During the fourth quarter, the children emit negative behaviors at such a high frequency that they are more than four and one-half deviations from normality—on the wrong side! The Learning House staff is currently trying to find the procedural changes that produced this disturbing change from what had been fair effectiveness.

Table 1. Effectiveness variables of a residential treatment program for behaviorally disturbed preadolescents

Number	Negative variable	Positive variable
1	Lying/cheating/stealing	Honesty
2	Noncooperative verbal response to adult or peer request	Cooperative verbal response to adult or peer request
3	Noncooperative nonverbal response to adult or peer request	Cooperative nonverbal response to adult or peer request
4	Late/Off-task	On-time/On-task
5	Pestering following denial	Taking no for an answer
6	Complaining/crying to adults	Complimenting/thanking/smiling to adults
7	Negative verbal interaction with adults or peers	Positive verbal interaction with adults or peers
8	Negative nonverbal interaction with adults or peers	Positive nonverbal interaction with adults or peers
9	Playing alone	Playing with adults or peers
10	Improper manners	Proper manners

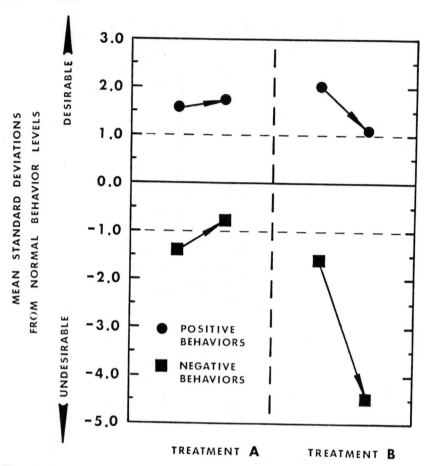

Figure 1. Program effectiveness as desirable and undesirable deviations from normality: *z* scores.

How Much Does It Cost?

As was the case in the measurement of effectiveness, costs are measured in more detail in micro-cost-effectiveness analysis than in macro-cost-effectiveness analysis. To provide more detail on the costs of different economic components of the program, both operations and social costs were calculated for the three basic components: 1) personnel, 2) facilities, and 3) equipment and materials. To compare costs over time, operations and social costs were adjusted for inflation. Figure 2 displays the cost of each component for treatment periods A and B from both the operations and social costing perspective. Figure 2 shows that costs of the components do not change radically between periods A and B, from either costing perspective. In addition, the extreme differences between the operations and social costs of personnel show that most of the "hidden" social

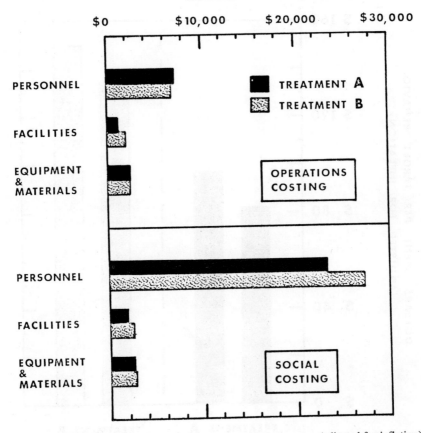

Figure 2. Bimonthly costs of economic components of the program (adjusted for inflation).

costs occur in personnel. This shows that Learning House uses a lot of volunteer labor. Finally, the difference between the cost of personnel and the costs of facilities and equipment and materials shows that personnel is the most costly component, from either costing perspective. This difference indicates that the program is quite labor-intensive.

The data in Figure 2 are still not sufficiently detailed for use in answering the third cost-effectiveness question. Because effectiveness data were calculated for each behavior of each child, cost data must be calculated for each behavior of each child. To this end, the operations cost data in Figure 2 were distributed over the different children according to the relative amount of time that therapists spent with the different children. The costs of other personnel and of facilities, equipment, and materials were distributed equally over children. The overall cost of treating a particular child was then divided among the different behaviors according to the importance of each behavior. The resulting cost estimates are shown in Figure 3.

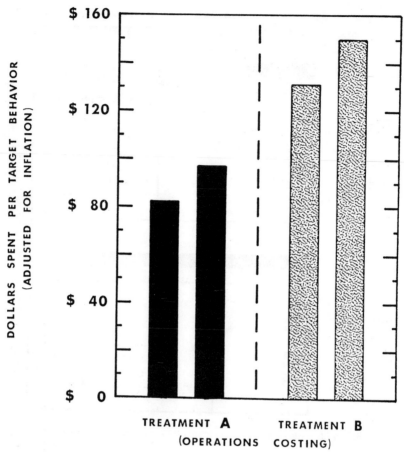

Figure 3. Mean bimonthly cost per behavior per child (adjusted for inflation).

Figure 3 shows that the average cost of treating one behavior for one child increases over quarters. This increase in the cost of treating a behavior is primarily due to a decrease in the number of children in the program. The high percentage of program costs that are "overhead" or fixed costs could not be reduced when less children were in the program, so the cost per behavior per child had to increase. It is interesting to see what these increasing costs, coupled with decreasing effectiveness for negative behaviors, do to program cost-effectiveness.

How Cost-Effective Is It?

Micro-cost-effectiveness was calculated by dividing the operations cost of treating a behavior of a child by the z score indices of effectiveness. The mean micro-cost-effectiveness of treating one positive behavior of a child is shown for each quarter in Figure 4. Before devoting much attention to Figure 4, please note that higher positive values of cost-effectiveness mean that more money was spent to produce a positive or "better than normal" deviation. This means that the more closely cost-effectiveness approaches zero from the positive direction, the better the program is in terms of cost-effectiveness. Figure 4 clearly shows that the cost-effectiveness of treating positive behaviors remains stable for the first three quarters but worsens during the final quarter. This is due to a slight decrease in effectiveness for positive behaviors and to an increase in the cost per behavior per child. Note how clearly these undesirable changes in effectiveness and cost are shown by the cost-effectiveness indices in Figure 4.

Before looking at cost-effectiveness indices for negative behaviors, it should be noted that negatively signed cost-effectiveness indices show the amount of money spent to produce undesirable deviations from normality. It would seem best to have minimal amounts of undesirable deviation per program dollar. Thus, if the program produces undesirable deviations from normality, it is better to

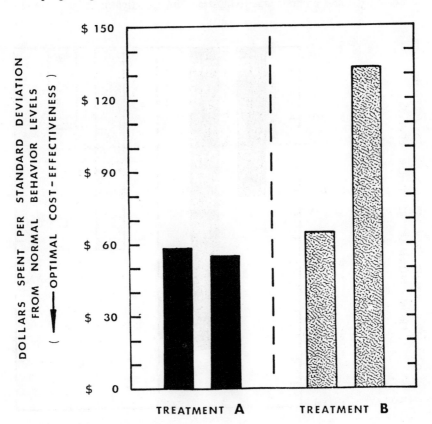

Figure 4. Mean cost-effectiveness for positive behaviors.

have a large ratio of dollars to undesirable deviations. In terms of negative cost-effectiveness indices, this means that the farther away from zero a negative cost-effectiveness index is, the better.

Figure 5 displays the mean micro-cost-effectiveness of treating one negative behavior of a child. Figure 5 shows that the cost-effectiveness of the program gets "less bad" for negative behaviors during the second quarter, but deteriorates thereafter. During the fourth quarter, the program is all too cost-effective in producing undesirable deviation from normality. Of course, this sort of cost-effectiveness was not intended. But it was produced. It is important that an accountability system be able to measure this sort of program performance as well as the more desirable sort.

DISCUSSION

The purpose of describing the macro- and micro-cost-effectiveness analyses of the Learning House program was to illustrate the operation of an accountability

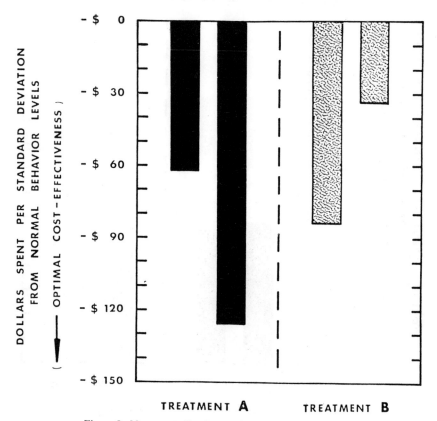

Figure 5. Mean cost-effectiveness for negative behaviors.

system that produces data for both interprogram evaluation and intraprogram improvement of both cost and effectiveness. The exemplary macro-analysis showed the need for standardization of costing procedures, for widespread use of some system of measuring macro-effectiveness, and for using care and tact when asking the effectiveness and cost questions in different programs. The examplary micro-analysis showed how a program can use cost-effectiveness analysis to find out where and when cost-effectiveness is good and not so good. This sort of information can help program staff improve the effectiveness, reduce the costs, and optimize the cost-effectiveness or their program. Taken together, the exemplary macro- and micro-cost-effectiveness analyses showed how cost-effectiveness analysis can help us meet demands for accountability while improving our programs. Certainly, there is a profound need for an accountability system that can both evaluate and improve the cost-effectiveness of programs in mental deficiency. The demand for cost-effectiveness accountability is here. A system for meeting this demand is here as well.

SUMMARY

A model for evaluating and improving the cost-effectiveness of social services is proposed. The applicability of the model is illustrated by data generated in macro- and micro-cost-effectiveness analyses of a residential treatment program for behaviorally disturbed children.

ACKNOWLEDGMENTS

William Haven, Stan Klein, Carl Thoresen, Curt Wilbur, and all the Learning House staff deserve credit for making possible these cost-effectiveness analyses.

LIST OF PAPERS GIVEN AT
CONGRESS SCIENTIFIC SESSIONS
THAT ARE NOT PUBLISHED
IN THESE PROCEEDINGS

The list below sets out the speakers whose papers have not been published in the three volumes of this set. The editor thanks all the Congress participants who forwarded copies of their papers for consideration and the excellent presentation of many of them was appreciated; he will gladly return any unused material upon application.

It is regretted that space could not be found for so many excellent papers. The editor considered every article forwarded to him, and for those papers in an area outside his competence he sought assistance from the editorial board and independent reviewers. In addition, the editor had access to the translators' copies, and some contributions were selected from this material.

Evaluation of High Risk Factors—Psychological Evaluation in Neonatal Period
  A. Abadi, Invedin Avenue, Los Mangos No. 10-09, Los Chorros, Caracas, Venezuela.
Sexuality in the Mentally Retarded
  T. Ackerman and J. Bassin, St. Louis ARC, 6372 Clayton Road, St. Louis, Missouri 63117, United States.
The Role of Maine Center for Development in Developing Services in Maine
  G. Ackroyd, Maine Center for Development, 103 Exchange Street, Portland, Maine 04111, United States.
Better Services for the Mentally Handicapped: How the Sociologist Can Help
  G. Adamson, 19 Chester Row, London, SW1W 9JF, England.
Problems of Mentally Retarded Children in Developing Countries
  H. Ahy, Amaniyeh Duma Building, Pahlaui Road, Tehran, Iran.
Epidemiologic Aspects of Mental Deficiency
  H. O. Åkesson, Psychiatric Department III, Lillhagen's Hospital, S-422 03 Hisings Backa 3, Sweden.
The Safety and Accuracy of Mid-Trimester Amniocentesis: The United States Amniocentesis Registry
  D. Alexander, NICHD, National Amniocentesis Registry, Westwood Bldg., Rm. 125, Bethesda, Maryland 20014, United States.
Prenatal Factors in Mental Retardation (Chairman's contribution)
  C. A. Alford, Department of Pediatrics, Medical College of Alabama, Birmingham, Alabama 35294, United States.
Psychological Variables Associated with Testing Spanish Speaking Mentally Retarded Children
  C. Alvarez, School of Education, Florida International University, Miami, Florida, United States.
Characteristics of Services to the Retarded in Brazil
  J. Amado, Centro de Habilitacao da APAE de S. Paulo 2249, Sao Paulo, Brazil.
Prevention and Treatment of Wilson's Disease
  M. Arima, Brain Research Institute, Tottori University School of Medicine, Yonago, Japan.
General Principles in Prevention of Developmental Disorders of CNS
  S. Autio, Children's Castle Hospital, Lastenlinnantie 2, 00250 Helsinki 25, Finland.
Application of Behavioral Modification Techniques for Mentally Retarded Children in Japan
  T. Azuma, Department of the Mentally Retarded, National Institute for Special Education, 2360 Nobi, Yokosuka, Japan 239.

Epidemiology of Mental Retardation in Portugal
J. Bairrao, Gabinete de Estudes e Planeamento do Ministerio dos Asountos Sociais, Ava Alvares Cabral 25, Lisbon 2, Portugal.

Effects of Comprehensive Treatment Program for Severely Retarded Children with Multiple Handicaps
S. N. Banik, Mental Helath Division of D.C., Glenn Dale Hospital, Glenn Dale, Maryland 20769, United States.

Development of Services for the Mentally Retarded in Greenland
N. E. Bank-Mikkelsen, National Board of Social Welfare, Kristineberg 6, 2100 Copenhagen Ø, Denmark.

Misconceptions of the Principle of Normalization
N. E. Bank-Mikkelsen, National Board of Social Welfare, Kristineberg 6, 2100 Copenhagen Ø, Denmark.

Modification of Curriculum and Materials for Use in the Resource Room Setting
E. Barnett, Richland School District, Columbia, South Carolina, United States.

Characteristics of Services to the Retarded in Brazil
H. Batista, Rua Jardim Votanico 660, Rio de Janeiro 20000, Brazil.

The Impact of Maternal Medication and Complications of Pregnancy
D. Beasley, 1 Bedlington Street, Whangerei, New Zealand.

Intervention During Adolescence with Disadvantaged, Functionally Retarded Children (Chairman's contribution)
M. J. Begab, NICHD/NIH, 7910 Woodmont Ave, Bethesda, Maryland 20014, United States.

Presentation of Findings to Date from a Three-Year Research Project on the Impact of Special Olympics
N. J. Bell, B. Morris, P. Baumgarner, and H. Orr, United States.

Regressive Techniques and Opening of Communication Channels in Mentally Retarded Children
R. Benenzon, Avda. Roque S. Pena 1110, 2° p. 1035, Buenos Aires, Argentina.

Genetic Considerations in Mental Retardation (Chairman's contribution)
J. M. Berg, Surrey Place Centre, 2 Surrey Place, Toronto, Ontario M5S 2C2, Canada.

Field Trips to Other Worlds: Brief Inspections of Homes for the Mentally Retarded—A Preliminary Analysis
B. Blatt, Syracuse University, New York, New York, United States.

Hepatitis and Mental Deficiency
K. Borglin, Vipeholms Hospital, Lund, Sweden.

The Family with A Mentally Retarded Child
A. Boric, University of Zagreb, Yugoslavia.

Extending Access to Computer-Assisted Learning Materials Through Specialized Hardware and Software
J. W. Brahan, W. C. Brown, and L. R. McNarry, National Research Council of Canada, Ottawa, Canada.

Mental Retardation in the Under-Developed Countries
L. Bravo-Valdivieso, Catholic University of Chile, Special Education Program, Santiago, Chile.

Maternal Medication, Neonatal Behavior and Mother-Infant Interaction
T. B. Brazelton, Child Development Unit, Boston Children's Hospital, 333 Longwood Avenue, Boston, Massachusetts 02115, United States.

A Constructive Interaction Adaptation Approach to Mental Retardation: Theory and Data
W. Bricker, Mailman Center for Child Development, P.O. Box 6, Biscayne Annex, Miami, Florida 33152, United States.

Implementing Planned Change in Institutional Settings
A. J. Brightman, Behavioral Education Projects Inc., Nichols House, Harvard University, Cambridge, Massachusetts 02138, United States.

Observation en Equipe Plurdiscipline sur Plateau T.V. d'un Enfant Place pour Psychose Infantile
J-P. Broche, Centre de Reeducation de Quidan, CE PO5 Av. Marlagne, Namur 5000, Belgium.

An Independence Training Program for Intellectually Handicapped Adults in Western Australia
B. Bubna-Litic and H. Macartney, Department of Psychology, University of Western Australia, Nedlands, W. Australia 6009.

Communication Assessment in the Mentally Retarded (Chairman's contribution)
E. Butterfield, Department of Pediatrics, University of Kansas Medical Center, 3933 Eaton Street, Kansas City, Kansas 66103, United States.

Perinatal Factors in Mental Deficiency
R. Caldeyro-Barcia, Latin American Center for Perinatology and Human Development, Casilla de Correo 627, Montevideo, Uruguay.

Non-speech Language Initiation: Status and Directions
J. Carrier, Parsons State Hospital and Training Center, Parsons, Kansas 67357, United States.

Optimizing Developmental Potential of Severely Handicapped at an Early Age
M. Chase, Nisonger Center, 1580 Cannon Drive, Ohio State University, Columbus, Ohio 43210, United States.

A Study of Cardiovascular Health of Institutionalized Retardates
T. Cho, M. Kitada, and I. Terada, Department of Public Health, Osaka University Medical School, 33 Joan-cho, Kita-ku, Osaka, Japan.

Systematic Approach to Training Severely Retarded Adults Basic Life Skills
S. Cibiri, Huronia Regional Center, Orillia, Ontario, Canada.

Detection in the Newborn of Atypical PKU
A. Ciortoloman and H. Docent *et al.*, Clinique D'Obstetrique et Ginecologie, 23 August, Bucharest, Rumania.

Follow-up Study of Clients in Vocational Workshop
F. G. Cipres, Rio Churubusco, Arboleda y Sur 81, Col. Ampliacion Sinatel, Mexico, D.F.

Comparison of Sleep in Normal and Down's Cases
J. Clausen, Department of Psychology, Institute for Basic Research in Mental Retardation, Forest Hill Road, Staten Island, New York 10314, United States.

An Environmental Stimulation Program for Children at "High Environmental Risk" in Bogota, Colombia: A Summary of the Children's First Year
R. B. Clement and A. Florez, I.C.B.F-Harvard-Giessen Research Project on Malnutrition, Bogota, Colombia.

Community Service Systems for the Mentally Retarded (Chairman's contribution)
J. Clements, Georgia Retardation Center, 4770 N. Peachtree Road, Atlanta, Georgia 30341, United States.

Historical Perspectives and Future Directions
H. V. Cobb, 1 Weiner Street, Chapel Hill, North Carolina 27514, United States.

Behavior Modification with the Multiply Handicapped
J. Cohen, Institute of Applied Human Dynamics, 2213 E. Tremont Avenue, Bronx, New York 10462, United States.

Language Development and Speech Dysfunction (Down's syndrome: a six year comprehensive study)
L. Cohen, Child Development Center, 593 Eddy Street, Providence, Rhode Island 02902, United States.

Forensic Aspects of Personality in the Maladjusted or Asocial Retarded Child
J. A. Connolly, Lissadell Mews, 9 Vesey Place, Monkstown, Co. Dublin, Ireland.

Educacion Habilitatoria a Nivel Vocacional, en un Centro Especial de Capacitacion de Mexico
G. H. Coronado, Av. Extremadura No. 28, Mexico 19, D.F.

Synaptic Reorganization Following Neuronal Death
C. Cotman, Psychobiology Department, University of California, Irvine, California, United States.

Proposed Australian Institute on Mental Retardation
D. Crawford, Minda Home, 76 Gladstone Road, Brighton, South Australia 5048.

Integrating Behavior Technology, Computer and Record Keeping Procedures: The Automated Management Information System
J. L. Crawford, Information Science Division, Rockland Research Institute, Orangeburg, New York 10962, United States.

Anthropometric Assessment: A Growth Study (Down's syndrome: a six year comprehensive study)
C. Cronk, Child Development Center, 593 Eddy Street, Providence, Rhode Island 02902, United States.

Chromosomal Studies in a Family with a Mentally Handicapped Child: The Outcome for Future Pregnancies
O-M. Crysotomidou, Department of Medical Genetics and Cytogenetics, Institute of Child Health, Athens, Greece 608.

Stimulation of Down's Children with Retarded Psychomotor Development
R. S. Cuevas Gajardo, Invedin Ave, Los Mangos No. 10-09, Los Chorros, Caracas,Venezuela.

State Education Agencies' Role and Responsibility for Mentally Retarded Children
W. Cullar, National Association of State Directors of Special Education, NEA Building, 1201 16th St. N.W., Washington, D.C., United States.

Toward Independent Feeding and Nutritional Assessment (Down's syndrome: a six year comprehensive study)
S. Cullen, Child Development Center, 593 Eddy Street, Providence, Rhode Island 02902, United States.
Training Monetary Skills in the Mentally Retarded
A. J. Cuvo, Southern Illinois University at Carbondale, Carbondale, Illinois 62901, United States.
Autism in Down's Syndrome
L. Cytryn, NIMH, Parklawn Building, Rockville, Maryland, United States.
Learning and Mental Retardation (Chairman's contribution)
J. P. Das, Centre for the Study of Mental Retardation, University of Alberta, Edmonton, Canada T6G 0Y1.
Training of Personnel in Brazil (Chairman's contribution)
O. da Silva Pereira, Servico Puglico Federal, Rue Gustavo Sampico, 29 Rio Leme, Brazil.
The Reaction of Indian Parents towards their Mentally Retarded Children
K. S. David, Child Guidance Clinic, City Hospital, M. G. Road, Colhin 682011, India.
Biochemical Disorders in Mental Retardation (Chairman's contribution)
G. Dawson, J. F. K. MR Research Center, University of Chicago, 5825 Maryland Avenue, Chicago, Illinois 60637, United States.
A Study of Psychotic Illness in the Mentally Handicapped—A Preliminary Report
K. A. Day, Northgate Hospital, Morpeth, Northumberland NE61 3BP, England.
Development and Treatment of Down's Syndrome Children (Chairman's contribution)
L. de Coriat, Neurological Center, Hospital de Ninos, Gallo 1330, Buenos Aires, Argentina.
Highlights of South American Programs on Early Stimulation (Chairman's contribution)
M. E. de Lorenzo, Mental Retardation Section, Inter-American Children's Institute (OEA), Montevideo, Uruguay.
Mental Subnormality under Supplemental Security Income
J. T. Diamond, Department of Sociology, Ohio State University, 112 Hagerty Hall, 1775 South College Road, Columbus, Ohio 43210, United States.
Prenatal Detection of Chromosomal and Metabolic Abnormalities in Mental Retardation
M. Diaz-Estrada, Central Georgia Development Center, Central State Hospital, Milledgeville, Georgia 31062, United States.
Early Intervention Programs for Potentially Retarded Children: Views of the Innovators
P. R. Dokecki, George Peabody College, Nashville, Tennessee, United States.
Guide for Determining the Developmental Age of Children
R. F. DuBose, Child Study Center, Box 158 Peabody College, Nashville, Tennessee 37203, United States.
Projects and Research in Mental Retardation in Developing Countries (Chairman's contribution)
A. Dupont, Demographic-Genetic Research Department, Aarhus Psychiatric Hospital, 8240 Risskov, Denmark.
Integration de Handicapes Mentaux et Evolution de l'Image Intercategorielle
J-J. Eisenring, B. Pasche, and A. Dupont, Centre Universitaire de Diagnostic et de Soins de la Deficience Mentale, Rue du 31 Decembre 6-8, 1207 Geneva, Switzerland.
Perception of Orientation by Autistic, Subnormal and Normal Children
R. Elliott, Lisnevin School, 22 Belfast Road, Co. Down, Ireland.
Epidemiological Studies in Mental Retardation (Chairman's contribution)
I. Emmanuel, Child Development and Mental Retardation Center, University of Washington, Seattle, Washington 98105, United States.
Obstetric Medication: How Safe is Safe?
A. J. Ericson, Department of Obstetrics, University of Kentucky College of Medicine, Lexington, Kentucky 40506, United States.
The Day Activity Centre as a Nucleus in Integrated Services
K. Ericsson, Psychiatric Research Center, University of Uppsala, Ulleraker Hospital, S-750 17 UPPSALA, Sweden.
Hearing and Speech Disorders
G. M. Faichini, Istituto de Psycologia de Universita di Bologna, Viale Berta Pichat 5, 40100 Bologna, Italy.
Public Education Services for the Severely and Profoundly Handicapped Child: A Review
K. Fatka and R. Schmid, University of Northern Iowa, 1429 Wildwood Drive NE, Cedar Rapids, Iowa 52402, United States.
Vocational Rehabilitation and Employment of the Mentally Retarded (Chairman's contribution)

J. Fenton, Social and Rehabilitation Service, HEW South Building, Room 3211, 330 C Street, S.W., Washington, D.C. 20201, United States.
Longitudinal Study of Meningitis in Children
T. A. Figari, Domicilio Particular, Virrey Arredondo 2.473, Departamento 3, Buenos Aires, Argentina.
Pragmatic Conditions in the Implementation of Resource Rooms for the Mildly Retarded 6–16 years
S. Finuf, Richland School District Special Services, Columbia, South Carolina, United States.
Massive Screening for Mentally Retarded: Its Application in U.S. and Abroad
W. Frankenburg, University of Colorado Medical Center, 4200 E. Ninth Avenue, Denver, Colorado 80220, United States.
The Program Approach for the Severely Handicapped in a Rural State
P. V. Freedlund, Bancroft North, Owls Head, Maine 04854, United States
An Alternative Pattern of Educational/Residential Care and Services for Mentally Retarded Children
M. A. Gage, H. D. Fredericks, V. Baldwin, W. Moore, and D. Grove, Teaching Research Infant and Child Center, Monmouth, Oregon 97361, United States.
Portrait of the Disabled in the Media
J. M. Gardner, University of Queensland, St. Lucia, Australia.
Programmers' Viewpoint with A-V Presentation of "Normalized" Programming
G. Garland, 114 N. Orchard Drive, Park Forest, Illinois, United States.
The Psychological Assessment of Behavior (Chairman's contribution)
M. Garrison, Temple University, Department of Special Education, Philadelphia, Pennsylvania 19122, United States.
Setting Realistic Expectations and Measuring Outcomes for the Mentally Retarded
G. Garwick, 529 Jackson Street, St. Paul, Minnesota 55101, United States.
Vitamin Dependency in Biochemical Disorders Associated with Mental Retardation
G. E. Gaull, New York State Institute for Basic Research in Mental Retardation, 1050 Forrest Hill Road, New York, New York 10314, United States.
Treatment of Self-injurious Down's Syndrome Adolescent with Omission Training, Overcorrection and Time Out Procedures
R. Gaylord-Ross, Ferkauf Graduate School, Yeshiva University, 55 Fifth Avenue, New York, New York 10003, United States.
The Usefulness of Acupuncture in the Management of the Brain Damaged and Emotionally Disturbed Child
T. Gencheff, Northside Acupuncture Clinic, 2718 Dryden Drive, Madison, Wisconsin 53704, United States.
The Role of Sex Chromosome Disorders in Mentally Retarded
P. Gerald, Boston Children's Hospital Medical Center, 300 Longwood Avenue, Boston, Massachusetts 02115, United States.
National Legislative Funding for Mental Retardation Programs in the United States
R. M. Gettings, NACSP, 2001 Jefferson Davis Highway, Arlington, Va. 22202, United States
National Legislative Funding for Mental Retardation Programs in the United States (Chairman's contribution)
M. J. Giannini, Mental Retardation Institute, New York Medical College, Valhalla, New York 10595, United States.
Facilitating Reading Acquisition in Mentally Retarded Children
A. Godwin, Department of Pediatrics, Medical College of Georgia, Augusta, Georgia 30902, United States.
Effects of Structured Learning on the Classroom Behavior of Minimally Brain Damaged Children
H. Goetze and H. Neukäter, Pädagogische Hochschule Ruhr, Kreuzstrasse 155, Postfach 380, 46 Dortmund 1, West Germany.
1. Recent Developments in Manual Skill Training of the Severely Handicapped
2. Communicating with People with Little or no Language
M. Gold, Children's Research Center, University of Illinois at Urbana, Champaign, Illinois 61820, United States.
Public Health Aspects of Mental Retardation in Latin America
R. Gonzales, Pan American Health Organization, 525 Twenty-Third Street, N.W., Washington, D.C. 20037, United States.
Parental Involvement in Early Education
L. Goodman and panelists: D. Kendrick, M. Hollier, and S. Searcy, Mental Health and

Mental Retardation Authority of Harris County, 2501 Dunstan, Houston, Texas 72005, United States.

GC-MS Techniques in Diagnosis of Inborn Errors
S. I. Goodman and D. O'Brien, The B. F. Stolinsky Laboratories, Department of Pediatrics, University of Colorado Medical Center, 4200 East Ninth Street, Denver, Colorado 89220, United States.

Care of the Retarded: A Philosopher's View
S. Gorovitz, United States.

Experience in Starting 200 Group Homes for Adults in Six Years
K. Grunewald, The National Board of Health and Welfare, Stockholm S-106 30, Sweden.

Another Aspect of Institutional Reform
D. Haar, Division of Research and Development DHEW, Washington, D.C., United States.

Munich Developmental Diagnosis Schedules
H. Haiboeck, School of Social Work, University of North Carolina, 223 Franklin Street, Chapel Hill, North Carolina 27514, United States.

The Prevention of Birth Trauma and Injury Through Education for Childbearing
D. Haire, American Foundation for Maternal and Child Health, Ind., 30 Beekman Place, New York, New York 10022, United States.

An Interdisciplinary Approach to Parent Education with Emphasis on Humanistic Principles
B. J. Hale, Crippled Children's Division, Child Development Center, University of Oregon Health Sciences Center, Portland, Oregon, United States.

Individual Analysis and Prescription Profiles for Deinstitutionalization
K. Hamel, Commonwealth of Virginia Department of Mental Health and Mental Retardation, 2100 Steppingstone Square, Chesapeake, Virginia 23320, United States.

The Role of Chromosome Rearrangements in the Etiology of Mental Retardation
J. Hamerton, Division of Genetics, Children's Centre, 685 Bannatyne Avenue, Winnipeg, Manitoba, Canada R3E 0W1.

Some Views on Cultural Factors Influencing the Mentally Retarded Child in Jakarta, Indonesia
B. Hardjawana, University of Indonesia Faculty of Medicine, Department of Psychiatry, Salemba 6, Djakarta, Indonesia.

Early Childhood Intervention: The Use of Non-Handicapped Peers as Educational and Therapeutic
R. J. Hartford, Letchworth Village, Thiells, New York 10984, United States.

Neurologic Substrates of Cognitive Process in the Mentally Retarded
L. Hartlage, Department of Neurology, Medical College of Georgia, Augusta, Georgia 30902, United States.

A New Short-Term Mode of Chelant Administration for Diagnostic and Therapeutic Lead Mobilization
H. Haust, Children's Psychiatric Laboratory, P.O. Box 2460, London, Ontario, Canada.

The First Three Years: A Challenge to Community Agencies
U. Haynes, United Cerebral Palsy Association, 66 E. 34th Street, New York, New York 10016, United States.

1. The Nature of Intelligence: Patterns of Cognitive Processing (Chairman's contribution)
2. A Theory of Cognitive Processes
H. C. Haywood, The John F. Kennedy Center for Research on Education and Human Development, George Peabody College for Teachers, Box 503, Nashville, Tennessee 37203, United States.

Early Intervention with Disadvantaged Children (Chairman's contribution)
F. R. Heber, Center for Research in Mental Retardation and Related Aspects of Human Development, University of Wisconsin, 750 University Avenue, Madison, Wisconsin 53706, United States.

The Merging of Community and Behavioral Approaches to Mental Retardation (Chairman's contribution)
L. J. Heifetz, Department of Psychology, Yale University, 2 Hillhouse Avenue, New Haven, Connecticut 06520, United States.

Resident-Environment Analysis by Levels: An Experimental Scale
R. W. Heiny, Institute for Development of Educational Alternatives, 3901 West 86th Street, Indianapolis, Indiana 46268, United States.

Early Infant Stimulation for Children with Down's Syndrome
W. Hellinckx, Schalbroekstrat 8, 3920 Lummen, Belgium.

A Block Program for Field Based Teacher Preparation in Special Education
E. Helsel, United Cerebral Palsy Assoc., Bellevue Hotel, 15 E. Street N.W., Washington, D.C. 20001

Prenatal and Postnatal Intervention in Malnourished Families
  G. Herrera, Department of Nutrition, Harvard School of Public Health, 665 Huntington
  Avenue, Boston, Massachusetts 02115, United States.
Musical Education of Children with Learning Disabilities
  M. E. Herrera, Giros Postales 1, Col. Postal, Mexico 13 D.F.
National Legislative Funding for Mental Retardation Programs in the United States
  N. J. W. Hill, Department of Health and Social Security, Alexander Fleming House,
  Elephant and Castle, London, S.E.1, England.
Child Care and Early Detection of Mental Retardation
  E. Hoejenbos, Institute Hendrik van Boeijen-Oord, Burg. Both. Lohmanweg 8, Assen, The
  Netherlands.
The Relationship of Perinatal Factors to Learning Impairment
  M. S. Hoffman, Dallas Academy, 3845 Oak Lawn, Dallas, Texas 75219, United States.
Instrumental Enrichment: A Program for the Cognitive Redevelopment of Retarded
  Performing Adolescents: Teaching Materials and Didactics
  M. Hoffman, Hadassah-Wizo-Canada Research Institute, 6 Karmon Street, Jerusalem,
  Israel.
Oligophrenia: Mental Retardation or Mental Deficiency?
  I. Z. Holowinsky, Department of Psychological Foundations, Rutgers, The State
  University of New Jersey, 10 Seminary Place, New Brunswick, New Jersey 08903, United
  States.
Exemplary Secondary Programs for Educable Mentally Retarded in Selected Southeastern
  States
  R. D. Howard, 3375 Maple Street, Winchester, Kentucky 40391, United States.
Benefits of Early vs Late Intervention and Cost Analysis
  S. B. Hussain, Woodward State School, Department of Social Services, Woodward, Iowa
  50276, United States.
Total Communication for the Hearing Impaired Mentally Retarded: A Comprehensive
  Program
  S. L. Hyde and D. Engle, D. C. Children's Center, Laurel, Maryland, United States.
Developing Instructional Decision Making Behaviors with Pre-Service Mentally Retarded and
  Physically Handicapped Teachers Utilizing an Interest Centered Approach: A Descriptive
  Study
  C. Iannaccone, Department of Mental Retardation and Physical Handicap, State University
  College at Buffalo, 1300 Elmwood Avenue, Buffalo, New York 14222,
  United States.
Vocational Education of Mentally Deficient Adolescents
  H. C. Inostroza, School No. 43, Valparaiso, Chile.
Social Rehabilitation of Different Groups of Mentally Defective Adolescents
  D. Isaev, Pediatric Medical Institute, 2 Litovstaya Street, Leningrad 197100, U.S.S.R.
Mental Retardation: A Social Psychological Analysis
  K. Ishtiaq, 600 4 Nishai Ganj, Lucknow, India.
Target Symptoms of MR-12 Years Experience of Drug Therapy in Outpatients
  G. M. Jacobides, Neuropsychiatry Department, Medical School, University of Athens,
  Greece.
1. Preventation: Minimum Occurrence of Mental Retardation
2. Community Utilization of Amniocentesis
  C. B. Jacobson, Reproductive Genetics Unit, Department of Obstetrics and Gynecology,
  George Washington University Medical Center, Washington, D.C. 20037, United States.
Cancer and Mental Retardation (A Forty Year Review)
  M. P. Jancar and J. Jancar, Stoke Park Hospital, Bristol BS16 1QU, England.
The Significance of Seasonality of Birth in Mental Deficiency
  P. H. Jongbloet, J. H. J. Zwets, and G. Holleman, "Maria Roepaan," Siebengewaldesweg
  15, Ottersum, The Netherlands.
Attitudinal Reflexes and Motor Abilities in Young Developmentally Retarded Children
  Z. Kalinowski, Neuropsychiatric Centre, Zagorze K Warsaw 05-462, Poland.
Alternative Residential Models for the Mentally Retarded: Current and Future Trends
  R. W. Kamphaus, 3243 Palmer Street, Springfield, Illinois 62703, United States.
Substitution Method for Linguistic Defects in the Mentally Retarded
  O. Kan, Y. Ogawa, and T. Honda, 1-7-2 Teraodai Tama-ku, Kawasaki-shi, Kanagawa-ken,
  Japan.
Full Citizenship: The Rights of Persons with Mental Retardation
  L. A. Kane, 2100 Fountain Sq. Pl., 511 Walnut St., Cincinnati, Ohio 45202,
  United States

Evaluation of Severely Retarded Clients
O. C. Karan, Educational-Rehabilitation Unit, Waisman Center on MR and Human Development, 2605 Marsh Lane, University of Wisconsin, Madison, Wisconsin 53706, United States.

The Impact of Early Education on the Slightly and Moderately Mentally Retarded
Y. Karoui, Tunis Union for Mentally Handicapped Children, 26 Rue Sidiali, Tunis, Tunisia.

The Right to Education: Due Process and the Inner City Child
L. J. Katz and R. J. Bonfield, University of Pittsburgh, Western Psychiatric Institute and Clinic, 3811 O'Hara Street, Pittsburgh, Pennsylvania 15261, United States.

Effects of Contact and Instruction on Regular Classroom Teacher Attitudes Toward Mental Retardation
D. J. Kauffman, 1650 S. Sycamore Street, Petersburg, Virginia 23803, United States.

The K.D.S. Developmental Approach: Empirical Findings and Theoretical Contemplations for Practical Usage in Programming and Accountability
H. Kaufman, Human Resources Division, Comprehensive Mental Health Center, Fond du Lac, Wisconsin 54935, United States.

Psychological Investigations into Mental Retardation: Relationship with Social Factors
L. Kebbon, Psychiatric Research Centre, Universitu of Uppsala, Ulleraker Hospital, S750-17 Uppsala, Sweden.

The Transdisciplinary Approach
M. Kennedy, Physically Handicapped Service, Faribault State Hospital, Faribault, Minnesota 55021, United States.

The Development of a Comprehensive Multidisciplinary Residential/Educational Training Center for the Severely/Profoundly Mentally Retarded and Physically Handicapped Children
W. J. Kirkpatrick, L. M. Bradtke, and L. Little, Pediatric Care Center, BKR Educational Projects Inc., 1790 SW 43rd Way, Fort Lauderdale, Florida 33317, United States.

Innovative Ideas in Teacher Training in Special Education
J. M. Kliebhan, Cardinal Stritch College, 6801 North Yates Road, Milwaukee, Wisconsin 53217, United States.

Deinstitutionalization: Training Toward Community Commitment
D. R. Knapczyk, Developmental Training Center, 2853 E. Tenth Street, Indiana University, Bloomington, Indiana 47401, United States.

Metabolic Errors Associated with Mental Retardation
R. Koch, Developmental Services, State Department of Health, Sacramento, California, United States.

Tactual Pattern Cognition in Down's Syndrome
M. Komiya, Department of Special Education, Kumamoto University, 2-40-1 Kurokami-cho, Kumamoto-shi 860, Japan.

Total Communication for the Severely Retarded: A 24 Hour a Day Approach
G. Kopchick, Speech and Hearing Department, Rosewood Hospital Center, Owings Mills, Maryland 21117, United States.

Prenatal Factors in Mental Retardation (Chairman's contribution)
N. Kretchmer, NICHD, Building 31, 9000 Rockville Pike, Bethesda, Maryland 20014, United States.

Analysis of Distractible Behaviors Exhibited by Retarded and Non-Retarded School Children
A. Krupski, M. Pullis, and N. Slaff, Graduate School of Education, UCLA Los Angeles, California 90024, United States.

Clinical Diagnosis and Teacher Identification of Retarded Children: Strategies and Problems in National Census in Taiwan, Republic of China
W. Kuo, Y. Chen, and N. Liang, Graduate Institute of Education, National Taiwan Normal University, 88 Sec. 5 Roosevelt Road, Taipei, Taiwan 117, Republic of China.

Plasma Norepinephrine and Dopamine-Beta-Hydroxylase in Trisomy 21
C. R. Lake, M. G. Ziegler, and M. Coleman, Laboratory of Clinical Science, Bldg. 10, Rm. 2D54, NIMH, 9000 Rockville Pike, Bethesda, Maryland 20014, United States.

Utilization of Private Residence for Retarded Citizens as a Pivot for Developing a Network of Satellite Groups
E. M. Langon, 406 N. Washington Avenue, Scranton, Pennsylvania, United States.

Prevalence, Treatment and Management of Down's Syndrome (Chairman's contribution)
G. D. Laveck, Clinical Training Unit, Child Development and Mental Retardation Center, University of Washington, Seattle, Washington 98105, United States

What is the Proportion of Cases of Severe Mental Handicap which can be Prevented by Prenatal Diagnosis?
R. Laxova, Waisman Center, 2605 Marsh Lane, University of Wisconsin, Madison, Wisconsin, United States.

Music and Rhythm Instruction for the Mentally Retarded
M-S. Lee, Taegu Bo-Myung School for Mentally Retarded, 2288 Nam-Gu, Taemyung-Dong, Taegu, Korea 630-10.

Teaching Exceptional Children and Adults to Dial the Telephone
R. B. Leff, 6589 N. Crestwood Drive, Glendale, Wisconsin 53209, United States.

Increasing Participation of Profoundly Retarded Students in a Group Activity via Token Reinforcement
J. Leon, D. Malloy, and B. Turpin, Psychology and Research O'Berry Center, Goldsboro, North Carolina 27530, United States.

Cognitive Processes Underlying Reading Deficit
C. K. Leong, Institute of Child Guidance and Development, University of Saskatchewan, Saskatoon, Canada.

Autism—Does It Exist?
L. Lipman, Hamlet School for Retarded Persons, 29 Congo Road, Emmarentia 2001, Johannesburg, South Africa.

Self-Concept and Self-Regulatory Processes in the Trainable Mentally Retarded: A Preliminary Report
A. J. Litrownik and L. R. Franzini, San Diego State University, San Diego, California, United States.

Language and Communication Training for the Mentally Retarded (Chairman's contribution)
L. L. Lloyd, Mental Retardation Program, NICH, 7910 Woodmont Avenue, Bethesda, Maryland 20014, United States.

Implementing Innovative Programs for the MR in a Local School: Wrestling with Survival while Attempting to Develop Programs
W. E. Loadman, Nisonger Center, Ohio State University, Columbus, Ohio, United States.

Creativity of the Developmentally Disabled
F. Ludins-Katz and E. Katz, Creative Growth, 2505 Broadway, Oakland, California 94612, United States.

Teaching Social and Vocational Skills to Developmentally Disabled Persons
K. P. Lynch, Institute for Study of MR, University of Michigan, 130 South 1st Street, Ann Arbor, Michigan 48108, United States.

"Steady Rate" Theory of Severe Subnormality
D. N. MacKay and G. McDonald, Muckamore Abbey Hospital, Co. Antrim, Northern Ireland.

Current Issues in Special Education in the U.S.
R. Mackie, 5111 Dalecarlia Drive, Washington, D.C. 20016, United States.

Community and Institutional Patterns of Care
P. Manson, United Rehabilitation Center, Detroit, Michigan, United States.

The Effects of Special Olympics Training and Athletic Participation on the Physical Performance of Mentally Retarded Children
A. S. Martin, B. Kozar, and J. L. Morris, Texas Tech University, Lubbock, Texas 79409, United States.

New Trends in the Education of the Mentally Retarded
S. Masovic, Faculty of Defectology, The University, Zagreb, Yugoslavia.

Generic Community Services for the Mentally Retarded
P. S. Massey, Holly Center, P.O. Box 2358, Snow Hill Road, Salisbury, Maryland 21801, United States.

Early Identification and Evaluation of the Developmentally Retarded
A. M. Matkin, Boys Town Evaluation Center, Omaha, Nebraska, United States.

The Treatment of Enuresis in Mentally Retarded Children
T. Matsubara, 3-3-5 Ishibiki, Kanagawa City, Japan 920.

The Treatment of Faecal Incontinence in Severely Defective Children
K. Matsushita, Orange-Gakuen Hospital, 771 Fukuyama-Cho, Aira-gun, Kogoshima Prefecture, Japan.

Individualized Cost Data in Institutions and Communities
T. Mayeda, 234 Armsley Square, Ontario, California 91762, United States.

Does Architectural Design Alone Make the Goal of Normalization Achievable
F. A. McCormack, Elisabeth Ludeman Center, Park Forest, Illinois 60466, United States.

Reversibility of Mental Retardation in Undernourished Preschool Aged Children
H. McKay, Human Ecology Research Station, Apartado Aereo 7308, Cali, Colombia.

Screening and Detection of Mental Retardation (Chairman's contribution)
    J. Meier, Office of Child Development, OND, DHEW, Washington, D.C., United States.
Social Aspects of Mental Retardation (Chairman's contribution)
    J. B. Meiresonne, Nationaal Orgaan Zwakzinnigenzorg, P.O. Box 415, Utrecht, The
    Netherlands.
Hand Puppets: Motivators and Innovators for the Mentally Deficient
    J. Meisner, Andrew McFarland Mental Health Center, Department of Mental Health and
    Developmental Disabilities, Springfield, Illinois, United States.
A Double Blind Study of 30 Spastic Children Treated with Acupuncture
    K. Metzgen, Rehabilitation Services, Central Wisconsin Colony, Madison, Wisconsin,
    United States.
Assessment of Behavior in the Mentally Retarded (Chairman's contribution)
    C. E. Meyers, Pacific State Hospital, 3530 Pomona Boulevard, Pomona, California 91768,
    United States.
Some Less Than Orthodox Views on Attitudes and Attitude Changes in Mental Retardation
    M. Miller, Yeshiva University, 55 Fifth Avenue, New York, New York 10003, United
    States.
Prenatal Diagnosis: Reality and Potential
    A. Milunsky, Eunice Kennedy Shriver Center, Fernald State School, Waltham,
    Massachusetts 02154, United States.
Chemotherapeutic Management of Enuresis in Adult Mentally Retarded
    M. Mirabi, Baylor College of Medicine, Department of Psychiatry, Texas Medical Center,
    1300 Moursund Avenue, Houston, Texas 77030, United States.
Learning and Cognition in the Mentally Retarded (Chairman's contribution)
    P. Mittler, Hester Adrian Research Centre, The University, Manchester M13 9PL, England.
Communication and the Developmentally Retarded Child (Chairman's contribution)
    J. S. Molloy, University of San Diego, Alcala Park, San Diego, California 922110, United
    States
Dysbalancing a New Approach to Profoundly Handicapped Children
    V. Molony, St. Ita's Hospital, Portrane, Donabate, Co. Dublin, Ireland.
**Medical Aspects and Gathering Accurate Information in Spanish of Spanish Speaking
Mentally Retarded Individuals**
    R. Montero, BISECT, P.O. Box 570504, Miami, Florida 33157, United States.
**Family Dynamics and Importance of Psychosocial Evaluation in Spanish for Families of
Spanish Speaking Mentally Retarded Individuals**
    P. Montiel, School of Medicine, University of Miami, Miami, Florida, United States.
Malnutrition and Mental Retardation
    J. O. Mora, Av. 68 Calle 64, Bogota, Colombia.
Static and Dynamic Balance of Mentally Retarded Children
    N. Moreno-Milne and G. Goodman, Department of Curriculum and Instruction, College of
    Education, University of Houston, Houston, Texas 77004, United States.
Treatment of Metabolic Errors (Chairman's contribution)
    H. Moser, Fernald State School, Waltham, Massachusetts 02178, United States.
Report on a National Census of the Mentally Handicapped in the Republic of Ireland
    M. Mulcahy, The Medico-Social Research Board, 73 Lower Baggot Street, Dublin, 2,
    Ireland.
Vigilance-Like Performance and SCR in Retardates and Normals
    R. F. Mulcahy, Centre for the Study of Mental Retardation, The University of Alberta,
    Edmonton, Canada T6G 2G5.
Investigation of Family Adjustment and Coping Mechanisms (Down's syndrome: a six-year
comprehensive study)
    A. Murphy, Child Development Center, 593 Eddy Street, Providence, Rhode Island
    02902, United States.
Psychiatric Needs of Children and Young People
    P. A. Murray, Our Lady of Good Counsel, Lota, Glanmire, Co. Cork, Ireland.
A Comprehensive Mental Handicap Service Designed to Meet Family Needs
    M. Myers, Beechcroft, Oakwood Hall, Rotherham S60 2UD, England.
**Mass Screening for Congenital or Juvenile Hypothyroidism with TSH Assay in a Dried Blood
Spot on Filter Paper**
    H. Naruse and M. Irie, National Institute of Mental Health, 1-7-3 Koonodai, Ichikawa
    City, Chiba-ken, Japan.
Early Stimulation of Down's Syndrome Infants
    J. Nascimento, Invedin Ave., Los Mangos No. 10-09, Los Chorros, Caracas, Venezuela.

Habilitation Programming of Spanish Speaking Mentally Retarded Individuals: A Multidisciplinary Approach
   D. E. Nathanson, Division of Psycho-Educational Services, Florida International University, Tamiami Trail, Miami, Florida 33144, United States.
The Secondary Cooperative Workstudy Programme: A Three Year Evaluation
   P. R. Nelson, Department CHM, Special Education, Will Rogers High School, Tulsa, Oklahoma, United States.
Dysgenesis of Myelin—An Autosomal Recessively Inherited Condition Causing Mental Retardation
   G. Neuhauser, E. G. Kaveggia, and J. M. Opitz, Kinderklinik und Poliklinik der Universität Erlangen-Nürnberg, 852 Erlangen, Loschgestrasse 15, West Germany.
Behavioral Assessment of Mental Retardation (Chairman's contribution)
   K. Nihira, UCLA, NPI Institute, 760 Westwood Boulevard, Los Angeles, California, United States.
Cost Effectiveness and Cost Benefit Analysis (Chairman's contribution)
   J. H. Noble, Social Sources/Human Development, HEW North Bldg., Rm 4544, Washington, D.C., United States.
Models for Training Group Home Parents
   B. Normark, Waisman Center, University of Wisconsin, Madison, Wisconsin 53706, United States.
Social Institutions for Moderate and Severe Mentally Retarded Children and Youth in Yugoslavia
   N. Novakovic, Federal Commission for Health and Social Welfare, Bulevar Aynoj-a 104, SIVII, 11070 Novi, Belgrade, Yugoslavia.
Olfactory Assessment Related to Diagnosis and Prognosis of Human Viability—Part II
   D. S. Nueva-Espana, Fairview State Hospital, Costa Mesa, California 92627, United States.
Disorders of Purine Metabolism
   W. Nyhan, Department of Pediatrics, University of California at La Jolla, La Jolla, California 92037, United States.
National Legislative Funding for Mental Retardation Programs in the United States
   D. O'Hare, Office of Maternal and Child Welfare, 5600 Fishers Parklawn Bldg. 1205, Rockville, Maryland 20852, United States.
The Nursing Process in Mental Retardation and Developmental Disabilities
   S. M. O'Neil, Child Development and MR Center, University of Washington, Seattle, Washington, 98195, United States.
Genetic Counseling in Mental Retardation
   C. Orlandi, Department of Obstetrics and Gynecology, University of Bologna, Via Masarenti 13, Bologna, Italy.
Effects of Simulator Training on Acquisition and Generalization of Pedestrian Skills in the Mentally Retarded
   T. J. Page, B. A. Iwata, and N. A. Neef, Department of Psychology, Western Michigan University, Kalamazoo, Michigan 49001, United States.
Comprehensive Rehabilitation Assessment Program
   D. Patten and R. R. van Deventer, Waisman Center, 2605 Marsh Lane, University of Wisconsin, Madison, Wisconsin 53706, United States.
Some Aspects of Immunology in Down's Syndrome
   D. Pitt, J. Kaldor, I. Gust, and S. Whittingham, Children's Cottages, P.O. Box 114, Kew, Victoria 3101, Australia.
Parents' Viewpoint with A-V "Away We Go"
   J. Powers, Elisabeth Ludeman Center, 114 N. Orchard Drive, Park Forest, Illinois 60466, United States.
Genetic Counseling in Mental Retardation (Chairman's contribution)
   D. A. Primrose, The Royal Scottish National Hospital, Larbert, Stirlingshire, Scotland FK5 4EJ.
Evaluation of Hydroxytryptophan and Pyridoxin Administration (Down's syndrome: a six year comprehensive study)
   S. M. Pueschel, Child Development Center, 593 Eddy Street, Providence, Rhode Island 02902, United States.
Toward a Neurobiology of Mental Deficiency
   D. Purpura, Albert Einstein College of Medicine, 1300 Morris Park Avenue, Bronx, New York 10461, United States.

Management of Atypical Epilepsy in Children
   B. N. Pyne and S. Chaudhury, The Institute of Child Health, 11 Dr. Biresh Guha Street,
   Calcutta 17, India.
National Legislative Funding for Mental Retardation Programs in the United States
   L. Randolph, 400 6th Street S.W., Washington, D.C., United States.
Basic Components of Motor Behavior of Educationally Handicapped Children
   G. L. Rarick, University of California, Berkeley, California, United States.
Variance in the Quality of Care in Three Unitized Institutions
   N. V. Raynes, M. W. Pratt, and S. Roses, Community Health Programme, Miner Hall,
   Room 01, Tufts University, Medford, Massachusetts, 02155, United States.
Nutrition and Brain Development
   O. Resnick, Worcester Foundation for Experimental Biology, 222 Maple Avenue,
   Shrewsbury, Massachusetts 01545, United States.
Malnutrition and Mental Retardation: Environmental Interactions (Chairman's contribu-
tion)
   H. Ricciutti, Department of Human Development, Cornell University, Ithaca, New York
   14850, United States.
Language Stories—Teaching Language to Developmentally Disabled Children
   M. Rieff, Julia S. Molloy Education Center, 8701 N. Menard, Morton Grove, Illinois
   60043, United States.
Teaching Research's Model of Integrating Handicapped Children into Structured Preschool
Day Care Center
   C. Riggs, Teaching Research Infant and Child Center, Monmouth, Oregon 97361, United
   States.
Determinants of Language Deficit among the Institutional Retarded
   P. B. Rosenberger, Harvard Medical School, Massachusetts General Hospital, Boston,
   Massachusetts 02114, United States.
The State of Maine's Utilization of Public and Private Agencies to Develop a Comprehensive
Network of Services
   J. Rosser, State of Maine, Department of Mental Health and Corrections, State Office
   Building, Augusta, Maine 04333, United States.
A Retrospective Study of Prior Service Use by Mental Retardation Clinic Users
   L. Rowitz, Illinois Institute for Developmental Disabilities, 1640 W. Roosevelt Road,
   Chicago, Illinois 60608, United States.
Behavior Modification in Profoundly Handicapped Children
   J. R. Sacristan, Isaac Peral 3, Seville, Spain.
Planning Services for Severely Retarded Children
   G. Saenger, Irene Straat 10, Cadier en Keer (L), The Netherlands.
Intercultural Implications
   R. Sajon, Instituto Interamericano del Nino, Av. 8 de Octubre 2904, Montevideo,
   Uruguay.
The Effect of Drug Addiction on Pregnancy Outcomes
   L. Salerno, New York Medical College, Department of Obstetrics and Gynecology, Flower
   and Fifth Avenue, New York, New York 10029, United States.
Education with Children
   R. Saquido, Philippine Association for the Retarded, Children's Medical Center, Banaue,
   Quezon City, Philippines.
1. Positive Values of Residential Services (Chairman's contribution)
2. Deinstitutionalization of the Mentally Retarded and Institutional Reform
   R. S. Scheerenberger, Central Wisconsin Colony, Madison, Wisconsin, United States.
Language and Communication Disorders of the Mentally Retarded
   R. L. Schiefelbusch, Bureau of Child Research, The University of Kansas, Lawrence,
   Kansas 66044, United States.
Parents as Primary Programmers
   M. Schilling, U.C.P., 66 E. 34th Street, New York, New York 10016, United States.
Cognitive and Behavioral Assessments (Down's syndrome: a six year comprehensive study)
   R. Schnell, Child Development Center, 593 Eddy Street, Providence, Rhode Island 02902,
   United States.
Deinstitutionalization of the Mentally Retarded (Chairman's contribution)
   H. Schroeder, Developmental Training Center, 2853 E. Tenth Street, Indiana University,
   Bloomington, Indiana 47401, United States.
Metrical Micro Manifestations in Parents of Children with Trisomy 21
   H. Seidler and A. Rett, Neurologisches Krankenhaus der Stadt Wien, Riedelgasse 5, 1130
   Wien, Austria.

Special Education for the Mentally Retarded (Chairman's contribution)
M. Semmel, Rural Rt. 3, Box 132, Inverness Woods Road, Bloomington, Indiana 47401, United States.
Role of Nutritional Status in Mental Retardation
B. B. Sethi, Department of Psychiatry, King Georges Medical College, Lucknow, India.
Perinatal Infections and Central Nervous System Damage
J. L. Sever, National Institute of Infectious Diseases, NIH, Bldg. 36, 9000 Rockville Pike, Bethesda, Maryland 20014, United States.
The Chromosomal Patterns of Down's Syndrome in Iraq
A. Shakir, Department of Pediatrics and Child Health, Baghdad University, Medical College, 19/5 Al-Yarmouk, Baghdad, Iraq.
A Critique of Normalization and Other Systems of Total Community Care
A. Shapiro, Harperbury Hospital, Harper Lane, Radlett, Hertfordshire WD7 9HQ, England.
Teaching Parents Early Intervention Techniques (Down's syndrome: a six year comprehensive study)
A. Shea, Child Development Center, 593 Eddy Street, Providence, Rhode Island 02902, United States.
The Beautification of Mentally Retarded People
R. D. Shushan, Exceptional Children's Foundation, 2225 West Adams Boulevard, Los Angeles, California 90018, United States.
Comprehensive Service for Infants—Insights on Service Delivery Systems
J. M. Siepp, United Cerebral Palsy Associations Inc., 66 E. 34th Street, New York, New York 10016, United States.
Interactive Home Television for Developmentally Handicapped Children
R. F. Simches and J. C. Marillo, 55 Elk Street, Room 215, Albany, New York, 12234, United States.
A Perspective Review on Viral Infections of the Fetus Associated with Congenital Defects and Mental Deficiencies
S. K. Sinha, Department of Virology, Central Wisconsin Colony and Training School, 317 Knutson Drive, Madison, Wisconsin 53704, United States.
Mild-Moderate Forms of Mental Retardation of Sociocultural Origin in Colombian Children and Levels of Reversibility
L. Sinisterra, Apartado Aereo 7308, Fundacion de Investigaciones de Ecologia Humana, Cali, Colombia.
Communication in the Developmentally Retarded: Early Identification and Evaluation of Hearing Loss
E. C. Skalka, Kendall Demonstration School for the Deaf, Washington, D.C., United States.
Definition and Measurement of Adaptive Behaviour in a Psycho-Educational Setting
M. Skuy, Centre for Clinical Studies, Education Department, University of Witwatersrand, Milner Park, Johannesburg, South Africa.
Training Lowest Functioning Children in Mentally Retarded Institutions for Better Communication
H. Sletved, Socialstyrelsen, Kristineberg 6, Postbox 2555, 2100 Copenhagen, Denmark.
Classroom Learning of the Mentally Retarded
I. L. Smith, Yeshiva University, 55 Fifth Avenue, New York, New York, 10003, United States.
Wessex Project—Evaluation
J. Smith and A. Kushlick, Health Care Evaluation Research Team, Dawn House, Sleepers Hill, Winchester SO22 4NG England.
Ethical Considerations in Conduct of Biomedical and Behavior Research (Chairman's contribution)
G. Soloyanis, American Association on Mental Deficiency, 5201 Connecticut Avenue, N.W., Washington, D.C. 20015, United States.
National Legislative Funding for Mental Retardation Programs in the United States
E. Sontag, BEH, 7th and D Streets, S.W., ROB 3, Washington, D.C. 20202, United States.
Investigation of the Scope of Special Education: Formation of Technical Equipment and Human Resources
M. Soriana, Oria 1, Madrid 2, Spain.
Promoting Piagetian Reasoning in Mentally Retarded Socially Maladjusted Pupils
R. Sower, 35 Highview Drive, Radnor, Pennsylvania 19087, United States.
Emotional and Mental Development through Environment Media Design (EMD)
R. Spiegel, 9204 Centerway Road, Gaithersburg, Maryland 20760, United States.

Behavior Modification in Retarded and Behavior Disordered Children (Chairman's contribution)
J. Spradlin, Bureau of Child Research, University of Kansas, Laurence, Kansas 66055, United States.

1. Analysis and Development of Reasoning in Emotionally Disturbed Mentally Retarded Children

2. Humane Services for Persons with Mental Retardation
B. Stephens, Program of Special Education, University of Texas at Dallas, Green Building, Room 4.106, Box 688, Richardson, Texas 75080, United States.

Helping Parents to Accept
B. M. Stokes, St. Michael's House, Goatstown, Dublin 14, Ireland.

Research in the Education of the Mentally Retarded (Chairman's contribution)
I. Stone, 29 Chicory Way, Irvine, California 92715, United States.

A Field Tested Program for Exploring Mental Potential and Educability
D. H. Stott, Center for Educational Disabilities, University of Guelph, 30 Colborn Street, Guelph, Ontario NIG 2M5, Canada.

Neuropathological Study of the Relationship Between Prematurity and Mental Retardation
S. M. Sumi and E. C. Alvord, Child Development and Mental Retardation Center, University of Washington, Seattle, Washington 98195, United States.

Sequelae of Low Birth Weight Infants
P. Sunshine, Department of Pediatrics, Stanford University, Palo Alto, California 92605, United States.

Community Care in Japan
A. Takahashi, 83-7 Kumegawa Kodan Jutaku, Higashimurayama, Tokyo 189, Japan.

The Autistic Child (Chairman's contribution)
G. Tarjan, Neuropsychiatric Institute, UCLA, 760 Westwood Plaza, Los Angeles, California 90024, United States.

A Parent's View: The Person and the Program
C. L. Taylor, The Bancroft School, Hopkins Lane, Haddonfield, New Jersey 08033, United States.

Project Face: Facilitating Adaptation to Community Environment
J. R. Taylor and H. Baker, Orange Grove Center for Mentally Retarded, 615 Derby Street, Chattanooga, Tennessee 37404, United States.

1. Highlights of South-American Early Stimulation Programme (Chairman's contribution)

2. Model for Research Utilization in the Caribbean
M. J. Thorburn, Caribbean Institute of Mental Retardation and Development Disorders, 2D Suthermere Road, Kingston 10, Jamaica.

Early Diagnosis and Intervention: A Comprehensive Approach (Chairman's contribution)
T. D. Tjossem, Mental Retardation Program, NICH, 7910 Woodmont Avenue, Room C-708, Bethesda, Maryland 20014, United States.

A Controlled Experiment in the Education of the Severely Subnormal
J. F. Toomey, Cork Polio and After Care Association, Bonnington Montenotte, Cork, Ireland.

The Pembridge Information Exchange: A Method for the Collection of Current Awareness Information
E. R. Tudor-Davies, National Society for Mentally Handicapped Children, Pembridge House, 17 Pembridge Square, London, W2 4EP, England.

The Bancroft Community Concept for the Adult who is Developmentally Disabled
J. R. Tullis, The Bancroft School, Hopkins Lane, Haddonfield, New Jersey 08033, United States.

Nursing Practice in Residential Facilities for the Mentally Retarded
N. Twardzicki, 26 Ray Road, Wrentham, Massachusetts 02093, United States.

Rationale for Selection of a Resource Room Model for Delivery of Services to Mildly Retarded in Public Schools
H. Tyler, Richlands II School District, 6831 Brookfield, Columbia, S. C. 29205, United States.

Parent and Family Therapy: Intervention with Families of the Developmentally Disabled
A. Tymchuk, Department of Psychology, UCLA, 760 Westwood Plaza, Los Angeles, California, United States.

National Legislative Funding for Mental Retardation Programs in the United States
W. M. Usdane, RSA-HEW 330 C Street, S.W., Washington, D.C. 20201, United States.

Neuroradiology and Mental Retardation
J. Valk, Valeriuskliniek, Valeriusplein 9, Amsterdam-Zuid, The Netherlands.

The Role of Sports in the Development of the Retarded
  A. J. C. Van Hal, Dutch Association for Sports for the Mentally Retarded, Koningennegracht 101, The Hague, The Netherlands.
New Approaches to the Solution of Communication Problems in the Multiply Handicapped
  J. M. A. van Mierlo and M. van Doremaele, Huize Zonhove, Nieuwstraat 70, Son, The Netherlands.
Some Basic Trends in Residential Care for the Mentally Handicapped in Belgium: An Orthopedagogical Challenge
  J. van Valckenborgh, Winkelstraat 2, 9030 Wondelgem, Belgium.
Origin of the Extra Chromosome No. 21 in Down's Syndrome
  P. Wagenbichler, W. Killian, A. Rett, and W. Schnedl, Neurologisches Krankenhaus der Stadt Wien, Riedelgasse 5, 1130 Wien, Austria.
Screening, Detection and Delineation of Inborn Errors of Metabolism (Chairman's contribution)
  I. Wald, Instytut Psychoneurologiczny, Al. Sobieskiego 1/9, 02-957 Warsaw, Poland.
Implementation of Community and Home re-entry
  G. F. Walsh, Mt. Olivet Rolling Acres, Route 1, Box 576, Excelsior, Minnesota 55331, United States.
Physical Therapy Intervention in Severely Physically Handicapped and Severely/Profoundly Retarded Persons
  R. Weidenbacker, 3610 Hamilton Street, Philadelphia, Pennsylvania 19104, United States.
Mild Variant Forms of Lipidoses
  D. A. Wenger, University of Colorado Medical Center, Department of Pediatrics, Denver, Colorado 80220, United States.
Ethical Considerations in the Care of the Mentally Retarded
  D. Wikler, Department of Philosophy, H White Building, University of Wisconsin, Madison, Wisconsin 53706, United States.
Behavior Modification in Retarded Preschool Children
  K. Yamaguchi, Research Institute for Education of Exceptional Children, Tokyo Gakugei University, 4-1-1 Nukui Hita-Machi, Koganei City, Tokyo 184, Japan.
The Influence of Aetiological Factors in the Formation of Structural Defect in Oligophrenia
  V. M. Yavkin, Flotskaya Street, House No. 7, Building 4, Flat 474, SSR 125499 Moscow A499, U.S.S.R.
Neurological Parameters and EEG Study (Down's syndrome: a six year comprehensive study)
  L. Yessayan, Child Development Center, 593 Eddy Street, Providence, Rhode Island 02902, United States.
Non-speech Communication in the Mentally Retarded (Chairman's contribution)
  D. E.Yoder, Communication Disorders Section, Center of Mental Retardation, University of Wisconsin, Madison, Wisconsin 53706, United States.
The Role of the Bancroft School in the Development of Services for the Severely Handicapped in the State of Maine
  C. N. York, United States.
The Bancroft Community: A System of Services for the Adult who is Developmentally Disabled
  C. N. York, J. R. Tullis, and C. Taylor, The Bancroft School, Hopkins Lane, Haddonfield, New Jersey, 08033, United States.
The Effect of Prenatal Factors on Subsequent Cognitive and Adaptive Behavior Development in Down's Syndrome
  A. Yusin, A. M. Vasquez, and K. Nihira, Eastern Los Angeles Regional Center, 801 South Garfield Avenue, Alhambra, California 91801, United States.
Transdisciplinary: A Team Approach to Services
  M. Zabel, Physically Handicapped Services, Faribault State Hospital, Faribault, Minnesota 55021, United States.
Some Work Done with a Group of Six Mentally Retarded Girls in a Self-contained Regular Classroom in Mexico City
  J. Zacarias, Universidad Iberoamericana, Centro de Orientacion Psicologia, Ave. Cerro de las Torres 395, Mexico 21, D.F.
Biochemical Disorders in Mental Retardation (Chairman's contribution)
  D. Zarfas, Children's Psychiatric Research Institute, London, Ontario, Canada.
Motor Function and Developmental Maturation (Down's syndrome: a six year comprehensive study)

E. Zausmer, Child Development Center, 593 Eddy Street, Providence, Rhode Island 02902, United States.

Development and Evaluation of the Essential Adult Sex Education (EASE) Curriculum for the Retarded

D. Zelman, Waisman Center, 2605 Marsh Lane, Madison, Wisconsin 53706, United States.

Scouting for the Mentally Retarded in Poland

A. Zychowski, Swierczewskiego 82/86, 00-145 Warsaw, Poland.

The editor regrets that the following papers, chosen for publication in full, were excluded only at the last minute because of space considerations.

An Animal Model for Evaluation of Early Postnatal Brain Damage

N. A. Buchwald, University of California, Neuropsychiatric Institute, 760 Westwood Plaza, Los Angeles, California 90024, United States.

A Follow Up Study of Mentally Retarded Rehabilitation Clients: Analysis of Research Data

S. B. Mitra, Department of Rehabilitation Counseling, Coppin State College, 2500 West North Avenue, Baltimore, Maryland 21216, United States.

Behavioral Changes in Rats Following Immunological Interference Prenatally

M. M. Rapport and S. E. Karpiak, Department of Mental Hygiene, New York State Psychiatric Institute, 722 West 168th Street, New York, 10032, United States.

Organizational and Sociodemographic Factors in the Quality of Care in Residential Institutions

S. Roses, N. V. Raynes, and M. W. Pratt, 1716 Cambridge Street, Cambridge, Massachusetts 02138, United States.

A System of Early Intervention Centers in Germany

O. Speak, Institute for Special Education, University of Munich, Pfarrer-Grimm Str. 42, Munich 50, Germany.

Results of a Year's Therapeutic Rehabilitation Programme in a Group of Young Retarded Children

D. Stomma and M. Gietko, Child Psychiatry Department, Psychoneurological Institute, Klinika Psychiatryezna, Al. Sobieskiego 1/9, 02-957 Warsaw, Poland.

AUTHOR INDEX

SUBJECT INDEX

g
i